"Up-to-date interpretations of the *Imago Dei* have long been needed. Richard Middleton has accomplished this considerable feat with great learning and sophistication, both by gathering the issues so clearly and accessibly and by providing an important advance in thinking about this theme. He has presented an expert historical and literary analysis, ranging widely across extrabiblical and biblical literature. Even more, Middleton has drawn out significant theological dimensions of the text and demonstrated the ethical implications of his analysis—with a lively engagement of contemporary concerns. Readers will encounter here fresh ways of considering both God and the human beings created in the image of that God."

—**Terry Fretheim,** Luther Seminary

"Middleton's study of the *Imago Dei* represents biblical scholarship at its best. Here is a book that displays careful and meticulous research, balanced judgment, and insightful application, all of which are clearly and logically presented in a most readable fashion. By engaging meaningfully with current ethical debates that utilize the concept of *Imago Dei*, Middleton highlights the importance of his conclusions for contemporary discussion. Readers will find their horizons broadened and their preconceived ideas challenged by a work that contributes very positively to a better understanding of what Genesis 1 means when it states that human beings were made in the image of God."

—**T. Desmond Alexander,** Union Theological College, Belfast

"J. Richard Middleton examines an exegetically worn phrase, 'the image of God,' and gives it a theological freshness. His careful attention to the Genesis context as the decisive factor for understanding this intriguing concept is a good example of exegetical method."

—**C. Hassell Bullock,** Wheaton College

The
Liberating
Image

THE *IMAGO DEI*

IN GENESIS 1

J. Richard Middleton

Brazos Press

Grand Rapids, Michigan

©2005 by J. Richard Middleton

Published by Brazos Press
a division of Baker Publishing Group
P.O. Box 6287, Grand Rapids, MI 49516-6287
www.brazospress.com

Printed in the United States of America

Library of Congress Cataloging-in-Publication Data
Middleton, J. Richard, 1955–
    The liberating image : the Imago Dei in Genesis 1 / J. Richard Middleton.
        p.   cm.
    Includes bibliographical references and index.
    ISBN 1-58743-110-6 (pbk.)
    1. Image of God—Biblical teaching. 2. Bible. O.T. Genesis I, 26–27—Criticism, interpretation, etc. I. Title.
    BS661.M49 2005
    233'.5—dc22   2004028522

Unless otherwise noted, all scripture quotations are the author's own translation.

Scripture quotations marked NRSV are from the New Revised Standard Version of the Bible, copyright 1989 by the Division of Christian Education of the National Council of the Churches of Christ in the USA. Used by permission.

Translations of ancient texts throughout this book reproduce the translators' typographic features (for example, question marks, brackets, parentheses, ellipses), which represent either (a) words missing from the original and supplied by the translator or (b) the translator's guess at the meaning of a difficult text. Foreign words in square brackets were inserted by the author.

Contents

Abbreviations

ANET   *Ancient Near Eastern Texts Relating to the Old Testament* (ed. James B. Pritchard; 3rd ed.; Princeton: Princeton University Press, 1969)

CAD   *The Assyrian Dictionary of the Oriental Institute of the University of Chicago* (Chicago: Oriental Institute, 1956–)

COS   *The Context of Scripture* (ed. William W. Hallo and K. Lawson Younger Jr.; 3 vols.; Leiden: Brill, 1997–2002)

MT   Masoretic Text

NRSV   New Revised Standard Version

Figures

Preface

This book is the fruit of years of academic reflection on the meaning of humanity as the image of God (*imago Dei*) in Genesis 1. I first began researching the subject during the nineteen eighties while I was a graduate student in biblical studies at Colgate Rochester Crozer Divinity School in Rochester, New York, and this research came to fruition in my interdisciplinary doctoral work at the Institute for Christian Studies in Toronto (in a joint degree program with the Vrije Universiteit in Amsterdam).

But the impetus behind this book is more than academic. Its origins are deeply rooted in my own life-long struggle with the question of identity. Intersecting vectors that have impacted this struggle—and the resulting book—include the extreme introversion and shyness I experienced as a child, which generated a sense of profound insecurity about the world, and the fact that I grew up white in predominantly black Jamaica and underwent the typical adolescent struggle with identity precisely at the time that the newly independent island was looking to Africa as a symbolic resource for defining a postcolonial cultural identity. On top of this, the sacred/secular, otherworldly dualism that pervaded my foundational church experience led to a personal crisis during my undergraduate theological studies (at Jamaica Theological Seminary) concerning the status and validity of my career choice of teaching and research (instead of pastoral ministry, which was the vocation of choice among nearly all my fellow students). This crisis led me to explore a biblical theology of creation and culture as the foundation for life in the so-called "secular" world. Finally, having immigrated from Jamaica to Canada as a newly-married young adult, and then moving from Canada to the United States a few years later, I came to know firsthand the dislocation and even alienation that being thrust into an alien culture often precipitates among immigrants and refugees (my wife and I finally settled on "Jamericadian" as an apt summary of our hybrid cultural identity). These varied experiences conspired to render the question of identity prominent in my consciousness over the years.

I don't remember when I first came across the notion of humanity as *imago Dei*, but this soon became the single most seminal theological concept for my own developing self-image and the one I have reflected the most intensely on. This book is an attempt to bring together the fruit of years of academic and existential reflection on the meaning and significance of the *imago Dei* in Genesis 1. My aim is to make Old Testament scholarship on the creation of humanity in God's image accessible as a resource for theological reflection on human identity and ethics in a world increasingly characterized by brutality and dehumanization. As such, this book is meant to facilitate an interdisciplinary conversation between theologians, ethicists, and biblical scholars on the *imago Dei*.

The book is structured as a complex argument that moves from an initial exploration of the meaning of the image (part 1) to consideration of the image in its ancient Near Eastern context (part 2) to interrogation of the image concerning its implications for ethics (part 3).

Part 1 lays the foundation of the later two parts by exploring the basic meaning of the image. Chapter 1 addresses the question of the interpretive stance we adopt toward the *imago Dei* in Genesis 1, highlighting the issue of hermeneutical subjectivity. How might we go about discovering or articulating the meaning of the image in a manner that does not simply impose ancient or contemporary theological categories on the text? Specifically, does the *imago Dei* in Genesis 1 refer, as Old Testament scholars have suggested, to God's delegation of power to humanity (a royal or functional interpretation)? This question is answered in chapter 2 by a close reading of Genesis 1:26–28, followed by attention to the literary patterns and broader symbolic world of Genesis 1:1–2:3.

Part 2 then addresses the question of the sociohistorical context that would have formed the background to the *imago Dei* in Genesis 1. Specifically, how plausible is the standard critical hypothesis of Babylonian exile as the context for Genesis 1? And how does the postulation of a particular social context contribute to the meaning of the *imago Dei* already explored in the previous section? These questions are addressed first by examining putative ancient Near Eastern parallels to the Genesis *imago Dei* notion, especially parallels with Mesopotamian royal theology (chapter 3), then by exploring in greater depth the broader Mesopotamian worldview (chapter 4), and finally by reading the *imago Dei* in the context of Genesis 1–11 is as a critical alternative to Mesopotamian ideology (chapter 5). The exploration of the social context of the image both supports the royal/functional interpretation proposed in part 1 and reveals the radical, subversive potential of the *imago Dei* to ground a vision of human life that is alternative to unjust systems of power in the world.

Part 3 focuses on the question of ethics, specifically the possibility that violence is implicated in the creative activity of the God in whose image humans are created. Does the *imago Dei* legitimate or contribute to a violent or oppressive use of human power, as some have claimed? Indeed, how should we understand the sort of power authorized by the *imago Dei*, both in its own day and in ours? These questions are addressed first by exploring the relationship of Genesis 1 to the motif of the "combat myth" (God's conquest of primordial powers) in the Old Testament (chapter 6) and then by carefully attending to the sort of power Genesis 1 portrays God as exercising, especially its foregrounding of God's primal generosity (chapter 7).

Various portions of this study have been presented as academic papers at the Canadian Society of Biblical Studies, the Canadian Theological Society, and the Society of Biblical Literature, and some of these papers have since been published.[1] I have also had the opportunity to teach the material for this book five times as a graduate seminar course (at the Institute for Christian Studies and Colgate Rochester Crozer Divinity School) and once as an upper-level undergraduate seminar course (at Roberts Wesleyan College). The feedback I've received from scholars and from my students has been invaluable to me in developing and clarifying the argument of this book.

More specifically, I want to offer my profound thanks to my doctoral mentor Jim Olthuis of the Institute for Christian Studies (Toronto) for his personal support and encouragement throughout the entire writing process. Not only did he graciously accept my initial proposal to write a book instead of a dissertation, his insightful interaction with the manuscript at every stage both nurtured my interdisciplinary vision for the project and encouraged my exploration of the relevant ethical questions.

---

1. "The Liberating Image? Interpreting the *Imago Dei* in Context," *Christian Scholar's Review* 24/1 (1994): 8–25; "Is Creation Theology Inherently Conservative? A Dialogue with Walter Brueggemann," *Harvard Theological Review* 87/3 (1994): 257–77; "Creation Founded in Love: Breaking Rhetorical Expectations in Genesis 1:1-2:3," in *Sacred Texts, Secular Times: The Hebrew Bible in the Modern World*, ed. Leonard Jay Greenspoon and Bryan F. LeBeau (Studies in Jewish Civilization 10; Creighton, NE: Creighton University Press, 2000), 47-85; "Created in the Image of a Violent God? The Ethical Problem of the Conquest of Chaos in Biblical Creation Texts," *Interpretation* 58/4 (2004): 341–55; "Identity and Subversion in Babylon: Strategies for 'Resisting Against the System' in the Music of Bob Marley and the Wailers," in *Religion, Culture and Tradition in the Caribbean*, ed. by Hemchand Gossai and N. Samuel Murrell (New York: St. Martin's Press, 2000), 181–204.

Henk Leene of the Vrije Universiteit (Amsterdam) persistently kept my feet to the fire by raising critical historical questions about Old Testament scholarship, which helped to hone my argument considerably. Richard Henshaw, emeritus professor of Bexley Hall (Rochester, NY), provided invaluable guidance on technicalities of the interpretation of ancient Near Eastern texts and culture, and Sylvia Keesmaat of the Institute for Christian Studies gave enthusiastic feedback to early chapters and wise advice on key interpretive matters. Terence Fretheim of Luther Theological Seminary (St. Paul, MN) and David Jobling, emeritus professor of St Andrews Theological College (Saskatoon, SK), both gave much-needed encouragement and helpful feedback on portions of the book presented as conference papers. David Basinger, chair of the Division of Religion and Humanities at Roberts Wesleyan College, was consistently gracious and supportive of the project even when it consumed much of the time that I might have otherwise contributed to the numerous committees that are a staple of faculty life on a college campus. Finally, I want to thank my wife Marcia, faithful friend and companion for almost thirty years, and my two sons, Andrew and Kevin (with such different personalities, but both a joy to their dad), for teaching me the nitty-gritty of embodied love in relationships and for keeping me constantly grounded in reality. To all these I am profoundly grateful.

J. Richard Middleton
August 6, 2004
Jamaican Independence Day

PART 1

The Meaning of the Image

1

The Challenge
of Interpreting
the *Imago Dei*

For nearly two thousand years the Christian tradition has singled out Genesis 1:26–27 for special attention. These biblical verses constitute the *locus classicus* of the doctrine of *imago Dei*, the notion that human beings are made in God's "image" and "likeness." The text (with 1:28, which is an essential part of its context) reads as follows:[1]

> Then God said, "Let us make humanity in our image, according to our likeness, and let them rule over the fish of the sea, and over the birds of the air, and over the livestock, and over all the earth, and over everything that moves upon the earth."

> So God created humanity in his image,
>   in the image of God he created him,
>   male and female he created them.

1. Although the Hebrew of Genesis 1 is largely prose, 1:27 is formatted here to indicate the presence of a three-line Hebrew poetic fragment. On the presence of poetic fragments embedded in the prose of Genesis, see Robert Alter, *Genesis: Translation and Commentary* (New York: Norton, 1996), xxxiv–xxxvi.

And God blessed them and said to them, "Be fruitful and increase, and fill the earth, and subdue it, and rule over the fish of the sea, and over the birds of the air, and over every living thing that moves upon the earth."

Although the Christian tradition has typically treated these verses as containing a central biblical affirmation with significant implications for human life, the entire Old Testament contains only three explicit references to the *imago Dei*: Genesis 1:26–27; 5:1; and 9:6.[2] Furthermore, these references are all found in that section of Genesis (chapters 1–11) known as the primeval history, in literary strands typically assigned by critical biblical scholars to the priestly writer(s).[3]

With the exception of a few apocryphal or deuterocanonical references (Wisdom of Solomon 2:23; Sirach 17:3; and 2 Esdras 8:44),[4] the idea that humans are made in God's image does not surface again until

2. Many biblical scholars also connect Psalm 8 with Genesis 1, since the texts share similar ideas. Although the psalm does not actually use the terms *image* or *likeness*, Psalm 8:5 (MT 8:6) explicitly compares humans to God, and 8:3–8 (MT 8:4–9) understands the role of humanity vis-à-vis the nonhuman creation in royal terminology reminiscent of Genesis 1. Henk Leene also notes an adumbrated *imago Dei* theme in Isaiah 44, where YHWH's glorification in his servant Israel (44:23) is contrasted with the prohibition of humanly constructed images (44:13); see "Summons to Be Human," *Journal for the Study of the Old Testament* 30 (1984): 111–21.

3. Since Julius Wellhausen's influential documentary hypothesis about the composition of the Pentateuch, argued in *Die Composition des Hexateuchs* (4th ed.; Berlin: de Gruyter, 1963 [1st ed. 1876–78]) and in *Prolegomena zur Geschichte Israels* (3rd ed.; Berlin: Reimer, 1899 [1st ed. 1878]), it is standard scholarly practice to attribute the final literary form of the book of Genesis (plus Genesis 1, 5, 17, 23, and strands of 6–9) to one or more authors or redactors thought to be of an exilic (or postexilic) priestly orientation (typically designated P). In the closing decades of the twentieth century, however, this scholarly consensus seriously eroded. For a convenient summary of the history and present state of pentateuchal criticism as it applies to Genesis, see Gordon J. Wenham, *Genesis 1–15* (Word Biblical Commentary 1; Waco: Word, 1987), xxv–xlv. For an incisive, extended evaluation of the past century of scholarship on Genesis, see Duane A. Garrett, *Rethinking Genesis: The Sources and Authorship of the First Book of the Pentateuch* (Grand Rapids: Baker, 1991). But see David M. Carr, *Reading the Fractures of Genesis: Historical and Literary Approaches* (Louisville: Westminster John Knox, 1996), for a comprehensive, recent attempt to argue for a version of source analysis for Genesis.

4. Wisdom of Solomon 2:23, under the influence of Platonism, identifies the image of God with immortality or incorruptibility, while Sirach 17:3 (in the context of 17:1–4) interprets it in terms of dominion or authority over creation, and 2 Esdras 8:44 uses the *imago Dei* as a basis for the valuation of humanity, specifically arguing that this is the reason that God should spare Israel, despite their sins. Both the Wisdom of Solomon and Sirach (also known as Ecclesiasticus or the Wisdom of Jesus Ben Sira) are found in the Septuagint, while the apocalypse known as 2 Esdras, although not in the Septuagint, is included as 3 Esdras in the Slavonic Bible (used by the Russian Orthodox Church), with 2 Esdras 3–14 (the main body of the work) included in the appendix to the Vulgate as 4 Esdras.

the New Testament. Even then, however, only two texts speak of human *creation* in God's image (1 Corinthians 11:7 and James 3:9).[5] The rest either exalt Christ as the paradigm (uncreated) image of God or address the salvific renewal of the image in the church.[6]

The Appeal to Extrabiblical Paradigms

The paucity of biblical references to the *imago Dei* contributes to a wide diversity of opinion over what it means to be made in God's image. The problem is exacerbated by interpreters treating the immediate context of Genesis 1:26–27 as unimportant for determining the meaning of those verses. It is not unusual for interpreters explicitly to affirm, contrary to standard hermeneutical practice, that here context does not clarify meaning. Thus G. C. Berkouwer states that Genesis 1 affirms a likeness between humans and God "with no explanation given as to exactly what this likeness consists of or implies."[7] In a similar vein, Carl F. H. Henry claims that "the Bible does not define for us the precise content of the original *imago*," and Charles Lee Feinberg asks: "After all, what is the image of God? The biblical data furnish no systematic theory of the subject, no clue as to what is implied."[8] As a result of this inattention to context, many interpreters turn to extrabiblical, usually philosophical, sources to interpret the image and end up reading contemporaneous conceptions of being human back into the Genesis text.

Paul Ricoeur could be taken as a charitable commentator on this state of affairs when he introduces his own essay on the *imago Dei* with the following words: "When the theologians of the sacerdotal [that is, priestly] school elaborated the doctrine of man that is summarized in the startling expression of the first chapter of Genesis—'Let us make

---

5. Pseudepigraphal writings (contemporaneous with or later than the New Testament) that refer to the creation of humans in God's image include 2 Enoch 44:1–3; 65:2; and Testament of Naphtali 2:5.

6. Christ is described as the image of God in 2 Corinthians 4:4; Colossians 1:15; Hebrews 1:3 (cf. John 1:18; 14:8–9), and the salvific renewal of the image of God in the church is mentioned in 2 Corinthians 3:18; Ephesians 4:22–23; Colossians 3:10. These two themes are intertwined in Romans 8:29; 1 Corinthians 15:49; Ephesians 5:1–2; and 1 John 3:2–3. These texts speak of the church's (ethical) imitation of or (eschatological) conformity to Christ.

7. G. C. Berkouwer, *Man: The Image of God* (trans. Dirk W. Jellema; Grand Rapids: Eerdmans, 1962), 69.

8. Carl F. H. Henry, *God, Revelation, and Authority*, vol. 2: *God Who Speaks and Shows: Fifteen Theses, Part One* (Waco: Word, 1976), 125; Charles Lee Feinberg, "The Image of God," *Bibliotheca Sacra* 129 (1972): 238. Such quotations could be multiplied at will.

man in our image and likeness'—they certainly did not master at once all its implicit wealth of meaning."[9] Ricoeur justifies his own attempt to explicate this "implicit wealth of meaning" by adding that "each century has the task of elaborating its thought ever anew on the basis of that indestructible symbol which henceforth belongs to the unchanging treasury of the Biblical canon."[10]

A different reading of the history of interpretation is given by theologian Hendrikus Berkhof. Berkhof replaces the explication of implicit meaning with another (less charitable) metaphor. "By studying how systematic theologies have *poured* meaning *into* Gen. 1:26," he notes, "one could write a piece of Europe's cultural history."[11] Berkhof's judgment is anticipated, in somewhat more colorful language, by Old Testament scholar Norman Snaith: "Many 'orthodox' theologians through the centuries have lifted the phrase 'the image of God' (*imago Dei*) right out of its context, and, like Humpty-Dumpty, they have made the word mean just what they choose it to mean."[12]

Although this may be something of an exaggeration, it is not much of one, for the vast majority of interpreters right up to recent times have understood the meaning of the image in terms of a metaphysical analogy or similarity between the human soul and the being of God, in categories not likely to have occurred to the author of Genesis (see fig. 1).[13] Most patristic, medieval, and modern interpreters typically asked not an exegetical, but a speculative, question: In what way are

9. Paul Ricoeur, "The Image of God and the Epic of Man," in his *History and Truth* (trans. Charles A. Kelbley; Evanston, IL: Northwestern University Press, 1965), 110.

10. Ibid. Ricoeur's comments are, of course, consistent with his own hermeneutical theory, which includes the notion that every interpretation of a text transforms the text and enlarges it. Although the resulting transformed or enlarged text usually refers to the *actualized* text (that is, the text *as read or interpreted*), Ricoeur's language here of the "implicit wealth of meaning" of Genesis 1 suggests a bolder position, namely, that all later meanings are already implicit in the original. For Ricoeur's own summary of his position, see "What Is a Text? Explanation and Understanding," in his *Hermeneutics and the Human Sciences* (ed. John B. Thompson; Cambridge: Cambridge University Press, 1981), 145–65. I sketch my own hermeneutical approach later in this chapter.

11. Hendrikus Berkhof, *Christian Faith: An Introduction to the Study of the Faith* (trans. Sierd Woodstra; Grand Rapids: Eerdmans, 1979), 179 (emphasis added).

12. Norman Snaith, "The Image of God," *Expository Times* 86 (1974–75): 24.

13. For an extended history of interpretation of the *imago Dei* in the Christian theological tradition, see David Cairns, *The Image of God in Man* (New York: Philosophical Library, 1953), chaps. 4–13. Useful historical summaries are found in Berkouwer, *Man*, chap. 2; Douglas John Hall, *Imaging God: Dominion as Stewardship* (Grand Rapids: Eerdmans, 1986), chap. 3; Emil Brunner, *Man in Revolt: A Christian Anthropology* (trans. Olive Wyon; London: Lutterworth, 1939), appendix 1; and Anthony A. Hoekema, *Created in God's Image* (Grand Rapids: Eerdmans, 1986), chap. 4. For an extended account of the *imago Dei* in Jewish thinking, see Marcel S. F. Kemp, *Het verscheurde beeld: De vraag naar lot, kwaad en lijden in de pastoraal-theologische theorievorming, benaderd vanuit het joodse*

The substantialistic interpretation of the *imago Dei*

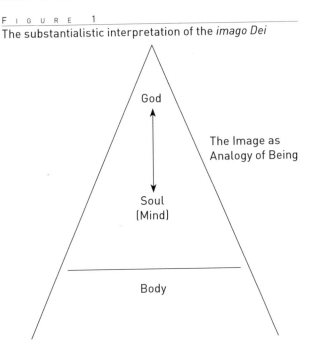

humans *like* God and *unlike* animals? Although various candidates were suggested for the content of the image, David Cairns can comment that, as a bare minimum, "in all the Christian writers up to Aquinas we find the image of God conceived as man's power of reason."[14] This notion of the rational, substantial soul mirroring its divine archetype—which is part of the pervasive influence of Platonism on Christian theology—is nuanced or supplemented in the Latin West by notions such as conscience, spirituality, immortality, freedom, and personhood and by Augustine's famous proposal of various intrapsychic trinitarian structures (particularly memory, intellect, and will), which correspond to the triune nature of God.[15] In the Greek East the substantialistic image was often understood dynamically, as the

denken over de mens als beeld Gods (The Hague: Boekencentrum, 2002), esp. 139–302 (English summary on 613–33).

    14. Cairns, *Image of God in Man*, 110.

    15. Augustine's most systematic treatment of the *imago Dei* is found in *De Trinitate*, especially books 7–15. For a comprehensive analysis of Augustine on the *imago Dei*, see John Edward Sullivan, *The Image of God: The Doctrine of St. Augustine and Its Influence* (Dubuque, IA: Priory, 1963). This Augustinian triad is the basis of the later popular tradition of defining the image as intellect, emotion, and will.

progressive conformity of the soul to God or a salvific partaking of the divine nature, a process typically called "divinization."[16]

Although certainly not all proponents of a substantialistic interpretation have been as aware as Augustine was of Middle Platonic and Neoplatonic speculation about the intricacies of *eidōla, phantasia*, and psychic self-reflexivity, their dependence on extrabiblical paradigms of philosophical and theological lineage is nevertheless patently obvious.[17] This dominant metaphysical stream of interpretation stretches from the ante-Nicene fathers through the high Middle Ages and until the middle of the twentieth century held sway even in the modern period.[18]

There was, however, a significant minority reading of the image, beginning in the Reformation, which attempted to supplement the emphasis on a metaphysical, substantialistic analogy with a dynamic, relational notion of the image as ethical conformity or obedient response to God.[19] This attempt begins with Martin Luther, who rejected the metaphysical interpretation and substituted instead a reading of the image as original righteousness, which Adam (and all humanity) lost through sin and which

16. See Cairns, *Image of God in Man*, chap. 7, on the divinization theme in Irenaeus, Clement of Alexandria, and Athanasius.

17. Throughout his analysis in *Image of God*, Sullivan makes clear the importance of Plotinian Neoplatonism for understanding Augustine's doctrine of the image. Even Aquinas's willingness to admit "vestiges" of God's glory (a sort of lower-grade *imago Dei*) in the human body and external nature is traceable (as is his emphasis on the importance of the resurrection body) to his more positive appraisal of physical reality, which is informed by Aristotelianism. Aquinas's views on the *imago Dei* are most clearly evident in *Summa Theologiae*, part 1, Q. 93 and in *De Veritate* Q. 10. On these two texts see Aelred Squire, "The Doctrine of the Image in the *De Veritate* of St Thomas," *Dominican Studies* 4 (1951): 164–77; and Jaroslav Pelikan, "*Imago Dei*: An Explication of *Summa Theologiae*, Part 1, Question 93," in *Calgary Aquinas Studies* (ed. Anthony Parel; Toronto: Pontifical Institute of Medieval Studies, 1978), chap. 2.

18. Rare recent proponents of a classic Platonic substantialistic interpretation of the image as reason include Henry (*God, Revelation, and Authority*, vol. 2, chap. 10) and Gordon Clark (*The Biblical Doctrine of Man* [Jefferson, MD: Trinity Foundation, 1984]; and "The Image of God," in *Baker's Dictionary of Christian Ethics* [ed. Carl F. H. Henry; Grand Rapids: Baker, 1973], 312–13). Both Gordon D. Kaufman ("The *Imago Dei* as Man's Historicity," *Journal of Religion* 36 [1956]: 157–68) and Ricoeur ("Image of God," 110–28) utilize Hegelian notions (among others) to propound a more dynamic metaphysical version of the image.

19. For the terminology of *substantialistic* and *relational* interpretations, I am indebted to Hall, *Imaging God*, 89, who modifies the categories of Paul Ramsey's *Basic Christian Ethics* (New York: Scribner, 1950). I omit from my account reference to minority interpretations that are proposed from time to time, such as the physical one (that the image refers to upright posture or some other dimension of the external human form), since such interpretations have found no significant hearing among Jewish or Christian faith communities.

is restored through Christ.[20] John Calvin's view is more complex in that he attempted to hold together a version of the substantialistic interpretation with a relational, ethical interpretation, leading to the classic distinction in Reformed theology between the broad and narrow senses of the image (*humanitas* and *conformitas*).[21] The Reformed view is thus similar to Irenaeus's proposal centuries earlier that "image" (*imago*) refers to that which is ontologically constitutive of humanness (for Irenaeus, rationality and freedom), while "likeness" (*similitudo*) designates the ethical similitude that had been lost by the fall and is restored through Christ. Calvin, however, rejected the linkage of this distinction to the terms *image* and *likeness*. While most Lutherans have followed Calvin rather than Luther in accepting a substantialistic image, Calvin's extra feature of an almost-physical dimension, whereby the created/renewed/eschatological glory of the full-bodied human person is seen to reflect God's uncreated glory, has been largely ignored (or is at least underdeveloped) by subsequent interpreters (whether Lutheran or Calvinist).[22]

Although this relational-ethical stream of interpretation does not do full justice to Genesis 1:26–27, it nevertheless draws on the New Testament's *imago Dei* texts and thus can claim some degree of exegetical support. It is, therefore, perhaps unfair when Karl Barth lumps the Reformers with the substantialistic stream of *imago* interpretation and claims "genuine astonishment at the diversity of man's inventive genius."[23] Anticipating the judgments of Berkhof and Snaith, Barth further comments:

20. For Luther's views, see his "Lectures on Genesis Chapters 1–5," in *Luther's Works* (ed. Jaroslav Pelikan; St. Louis: Concordia, 1958), esp. 1.55–65 on Genesis 1:26.

21. For Irenaeus's views, see his *Adversus Haereses*. For Calvin's views, see his commentary on 1:26–27 in *Genesis* (trans. and ed. John King; repr. Edinburgh: Banner of Truth, 1965), 91–97; and *Calvin: Institutes of the Christian Religion* (ed. John T. McNeill; trans. Ford Lewis Battles; Library of Christian Classics 20; Philadelphia: Westminster, 1960), §1.15. Whereas most Reformed theologians attempt to affirm both broad and narrow senses of the image, a prominent exception is Berkouwer, who is closer to Luther in affirming only the narrow (relational-ethical) sense. Berkouwer's clearest statement on the matter is found in *Man*, 58–62, although the entirety of this magisterial study is pervasively concerned with the juxtaposition of human sinfulness and God's grace (which already gives an indication of his perspective).

22. Although Calvin locates the image primarily in the soul, he claims that at creation "there was no part of man, not even the body itself, in which some sparks did not glow" (*Institutes* 1.15.3), and he anticipates that at the resurrection the image "will be restored to fullness, in our body as well as our soul" (commenting on 1 Corinthians 15:49 in *The First Epistle of Paul the Apostle to the Corinthians* [trans. John W. Fraser; Grand Rapids: Eerdmans/Carlisle: Paternoster, 1979], 341).

23. Karl Barth, *Church Dogmatics*, vol. 3: *The Doctrine of Creation*, part 1: *The Work of Creation* (trans. J. W. Edwards, O. Bussey, and Harold Knight; Edinburgh: Clark, 1958), 192.

We might easily discuss which of these and the many other similar explanations is the finest or deepest or most serious. What we cannot discuss
is which of them is the true explanation of Gen. 1. For it is obvious that
their authors merely found the concept in the text and then proceeded
to pure invention in accordance with the requirements of contemporary
anthropology.[24]

There is, however, some justification for Barth's critical remarks,
since, even granted the New Testament basis of the Reformers' interpretations, they are, like the substantialistic interpreters before them,
decisively conditioned by their own historical contexts and theological
concerns. Thus Luther's replacement of a substantialistic image with an
ethical one (now lost through sin) is clearly motivated by his opposition
to Roman Catholic natural theology and by his concomitant stress on
sola gratia and *sola fide*, while Calvin's more expansive interpretation,
which modified an ontological image with both ethical and bodily categories, testifies to the power of his comprehensive theological vision
of a sovereign God glorified throughout all creation.

In contrast to the main tradition of substantialistic interpretations,
as well as the more recent ethical-relational modifications to this tradition stemming from the Reformers, Barth attempts to root his own
relational reading of the *imago Dei* in exegesis of the Genesis text. To
that end he suggested that the key to the meaning of the image is the
reference to "male and female" in Genesis 1:27, along with the human-
divine, I-Thou encounter presupposed in the text.[25] Drawing explicitly
on Wilhelm Vischer's and Dietrich Bonhoeffer's interpretations of the
Genesis text and implicitly dependent on the relational or I-Thou anthropology found in the works of Emil Brunner and Martin Buber,
Barth proposed that the image of God refers to the God-given capacity of
human beings in their cohumanity (as male and female) to be addressed
by and to respond to God's word.[26] Specifically, Barth postulated two
sets of relationships, ontologically constitutive for humanness, both of
which image the intradivine I-Thou relationship of the triune God (see
fig. 2). He aptly summarizes his position as follows: "The relationship
between the summoning I in God's being and the summoned divine

24. Ibid., 193.
25. This is, of course, Barth's mature position. His early position, represented in his
debate with Emil Brunner in *Natural Theology* (trans. Peter Fraenkel; London: Bles, 1948),
is basically Lutheran (the image as *justitia originalis* that was lost through sin). Barth's
mature proposal of the meaning of the image, although likewise relational, is significantly
different from the ethical conformity discussed by the Reformers.
26. See *Church Dogmatics* 3.1.194–97, where Barth mentions Vischer and Bonhoeffer,
explaining that he has supplemented their views.

Thou is reflected both in the relationship of God to the man whom He has created, and also in the relationship between the I and the Thou between male and female, in human existence itself."[27]

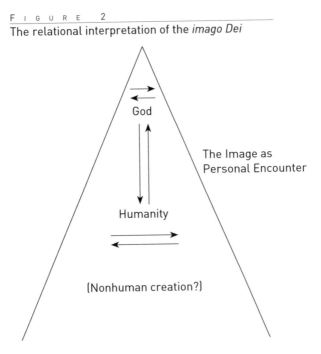

F I G U R E   2
The relational interpretation of the *imago Dei*

Although Barth certainly attempts to root his own interpretation of the *imago Dei* in biblical exegesis, it is not clear that he fares any better than the interpreters he critiques. Despite Barth's relational reading of the *imago Dei* having been widely received in the latter half of the twentieth century, effectively supplanting the Platonic, substantialistic interpretation in theological faculties and popular church circles in both North America and Europe,[28] his proposals are clearly conditioned, on the one

27. Ibid., 196.
28. The pervasiveness of a relational reading may be seen in the brochure of a 2001 interdisciplinary conference on the nature of human persons (entitled "Who Are We?" sponsored by the Trinity Institute, New York). The brochure proclaimed that beyond the traditional emphasis on rationality as definitive of humanness, "scientific inquiry is revealing another side to human nature that is surprisingly similar to the scriptural concept of *imago dei*," namely, that humans are "profoundly relational" beings. Among the many contemporary theologians who utilize a version of Barth's relational interpretation of the *imago Dei* are Paul K. Jewett, *Man as Male and Female: A Study in Sexual Relationships from a Theological Point of View* (Grand Rapids: Eerdmans, 1974); Ray S. Anderson, *On Being Human: Essays in Theological Anthropology* (Grand Rapids: Eerdmans, 1982);

hand, by Buberian "existential," I-Thou ontology, which predisposes him to read the image as (personal) relationship and, on the other, by his opposition to the appeal to nature in the German National Socialism of his day, leading to a resolute attempt to prevent any possible autonomous interpretation of the human condition (relationship is here opposed to autonomy).[29] Whatever his disclaimers, Barth thus shares with previous interpreters of the image an evident dependence on theological paradigms and agendas derived from outside the Genesis text.

Old Testament Scholarship on the *Imago Dei*

This is not, of course, intrinsically problematic, since all interpreters come to the text with their preunderstandings (acknowledged or not). What is problematic is that most contemporary proposals of either substantialistic or relational interpretations—which tend to be found in the writings of systematic theologians—simply ignore the massive literature in Old Testament scholarship on the *imago Dei* that developed in the past century.[30] This lack of theological engagement with Old Testament scholarship is regrettable, in my opinion, on two counts.

First of all, the interpretation of the *imago Dei* among systematic theologians almost universally excludes the *body* from the image (whether explicitly or by omission), thus entrenching a dualistic reading of the human condition. Although few contemporary interpreters come to the Genesis text with the ascetic predilections of Origen or Augustine, nevertheless the unwarranted limitation of the image (to either a set of properties of the soul or to the human-divine relation) continues to perpetuate an implicit devaluation of the concrete life of the body in relation to spirituality.[31]

Stanley J. Grenz, *The Social God and the Relational Self: A Trinitarian Theology of the Imago Dei* (Louisville: Westminster John Knox, 2001); and Colin E. Gunton (who was a featured speaker at the above conference), *The Triune Creator: A Historical and Systematic Study* (Edinburgh Studies in Constructive Theology; Grand Rapids: Eerdmans, 1998), chap. 9; and idem, *The Promise of Trinitarian Theology* (Edinburgh: Clark, 1997), chap. 6.

29. For the development of Barth's antithetical stance to Nazism, see H. Martin Rumscheidt, *Revelation and Theology: An Analysis of the Barth-Harnack Correspondence of 1923* (Cambridge: Cambridge University Press, 1972).

30. Note the observation by Terence E. Fretheim that, in the context of research on the doctrine of God, he was struck both by the frequent references to the Old Testament by systematic theologians and by their lack of engagement with the work of Old Testament scholars on the texts being cited; *The Suffering of God: An Old Testament Perspective* (Overtures to Biblical Theology; Philadelphia: Fortress, 1984), 17.

31. Despite many theological interpreters asserting in recent times, especially since Barth, that the whole person, and not just the soul or mind, is made in God's image, this assertion typically plays no further role in the majority of such interpretations.

What is regrettable about this is that any Old Testament scholar worth her salt will acknowledge that the semantic range of *ṣelem*—the Hebrew word for image in Genesis 1—includes idol. Although its semantic range is broader than this single meaning, we need to account for *ṣelem* in many contexts clearly referring to a cult image, which in the common theology of the ancient Near East is precisely a localized, visible, corporeal representation of the divine. A basic word study would thus lead to the preliminary observation that visibility and bodiliness may well be important for understanding the *imago Dei* and that this dimension of its meaning should not be summarily excluded from consideration.[32]

The lack of engagement of Old Testament scholarship by theologians is also regrettable for another reason. As Gunnlaugur Jónsson's 1988 Lund dissertation reveals, a virtual consensus has been building since the beginning of the twentieth century among Old Testament scholars concerning the meaning of the *imago Dei* in Genesis, and this view is quite distinct from the typical proposals found among systematic theologians.[33]

This virtual consensus is based on a combination of two factors. The first (less prominent) factor is exegesis of Genesis 1:1–2:3, the textual unit that forms the immediate literary context of 1:26–27.[34] Such

32. My point here is not that the image consists in a bodily resemblance between God and humanity, but that the invisible God is imaged by bodily humanity. See chapter 2 for an analysis of the semantic range of both *ṣelem* (image) and *dĕmût* (likeness).

33. See Gunnlaugur A. Jónsson, *The Image of God: Genesis 1:26–28 in a Century of Old Testament Research* (trans. Lorraine Svendsen; rev. Michael S. Cheney; Coniectanea biblica Old Testament Series 26; Stockholm: Almqvist & Wiksell, 1988), 219–25. Jónsson's survey of a century of research in English, West European, and Scandinavian languages shows that the degree of consensus among Old Testament scholars (which I call "virtual") is close to unanimity.

34. Substantive literary analyses of Genesis 1:1–2:3 are found in John H. Stek, "What Says the Scripture?" in *Portraits of Creation: Biblical and Scientific Perspectives on the World's Formation* (ed. Howard Van Till et al.; Grand Rapids: Eerdmans, 1990), 203–65; Bernhard W. Anderson, "A Stylistic Study of the Priestly Creation Story," in *Canon and Authority: Essays in Old Testament Religion and Theology* (ed. George W. Coats and Burke O. Long; Philadelphia: Fortress, 1977), 148–62, repr. in Anderson's *From Creation to New Creation: Old Testament Perspectives* (Overtures to Biblical Theology; Minneapolis: Fortress, 1994), 42–55; Walter Brueggemann, *Genesis* (Interpretation; Atlanta: John Knox, 1982), 22–39; Terence E. Fretheim, "The Book of Genesis: Introduction, Commentary, and Reflections," in *The New Interpreter's Bible* (ed. Leander E. Keck et al.; Nashville: Abingdon, 1994), esp. 1.340–47; William P. Brown, "Divine Act and the Art of Persuasion in Genesis 1," in *History and Interpretation: Essays in Honour of John H. Hayes* (ed. M. Patrick Graham, William P. Brown, and Jeffrey K. Kuan; Sheffield: JSOT Press, 1993), 19–32; and idem, "It Was Good, It Was Hallowed: Integrity and Differentiation in the Cosmic Sanctuary," in Brown's *Ethos of the Cosmos: The Genesis of Moral Imagination in the Bible* (Grand Rapids: Eerdmans, 1999), 35–132. Although it goes beyond literary analysis, an important study by a Jewish scholar is Jon D. Levenson, *Creation and the Persistence of*

exegesis notes the predominantly royal flavor of the text, beginning with the close linkage of image with the mandate to rule and subdue the earth and its creatures in 1:26 and 1:28 (typically royal functions). But beyond this royal mandate, the God in whose image and likeness humans are created is depicted as sovereign over the cosmos, ruling by royal decree ("let there be") and even addressing the divine council or heavenly court of angelic beings with "let us make humanity in our image," an address that parallels God's question to the seraphim at the call of Isaiah: "Whom shall I send? And who will go for us?" (Isaiah 6:8). Just as Isaiah saw YHWH "seated on a throne, high and exalted" (6:1), so the writer of Genesis 1 portrays God as king presiding over "heaven and earth," an ordered and harmonious realm in which each creature manifests the will of the creator and is thus declared "good." Humanity is created *like* this God, with the special role of representing or imaging God's rule in the world.[35]

The second (and more historically prominent) factor behind the virtual consensus in Old Testament scholarship is attention to the ancient Near Eastern background of the *imago Dei*. One possible line of evidence is that cited by Gerhard von Rad in his widely used Genesis commentary: "Just as powerful earthly kings, to indicate their claim to dominion, erect an image of themselves in the provinces of their empire where they do not personally appear, so man is placed upon earth in God's image as God's sovereign emblem."[36] Without disputing the importance of the royal metaphor for interpreting the image, I note that the particular ancient Near Eastern parallel that von Rad alludes to is by no means the most persuasive. On the contrary, we are on firmer ground with the wealth of comparative studies of Israel and the ancient Near East that cite the *Königsideologie* of Mesopotamia and Egypt, in which kings (and

---

Evil: The Jewish Drama of Divine Omnipotence (San Francisco: Harper & Row, 1988; rev. ed. Princeton: Princeton University Press, 1994), 53–127.

35. The significance of Isaiah 6 for interpreting Genesis 1 will be explored in chapter 2. For now we may note the following parallel: just as Isaiah's vision of YHWH issues in the commissioning of the prophet to speak God's word to Judah, so the depiction of God in Genesis 1 serves to introduce the creation and commissioning of humanity to represent the divine purposes on earth.

36. Gerhard von Rad, *Genesis: A Commentary* (trans. John H. Marks et al.; rev. ed.; Philadelphia: Westminster, 1972), 60. This particular passage from von Rad is by far the most cited source for the royal interpretation of the image in popular Christian writing on the *imago Dei* in the English-speaking world. Also significant in disseminating this interpretation were von Rad's contribution to the multiauthor article "εἰκών" in *Theological Dictionary of the New Testament* (ed. Gerhard Kittel; trans. Geoffrey W. Bromiley; Grand Rapids: Eerdmans, 1964), 2.392; and his *Old Testament Theology*, vol. 1: *The Theology of Israel's Historical Traditions* (trans. D. M. G. Stalker; New York: Harper & Row, 1962), 146.

sometimes priests) were designated the image or likeness of a particular god, whether Enlil, Shamash, Marduk, Amon-Re, or Horus, a designation that served to describe their function (analogous to that of a cult image) of representing the deity in question and of mediating divine blessing to the earthly realm. Indeed, in some of the Mesopotamian examples the word used for "image" is precisely the Akkadian cognate of Hebrew *ṣelem*.[37]

When the clues within the Genesis text are taken together with comparative studies of the ancient Near East, they lead to what we could call a functional—or even missional—interpretation of the image of God in Genesis 1:26–27 (in contradistinction to substantialistic or relational interpretations).[38] On this reading, the *imago Dei* designates the royal office or calling of human beings as God's representatives and agents in the world, granted authorized power to share in God's rule or administration of the earth's resources and creatures (see fig. 3).[39]

Since the main function of divinity in both Israel and the ancient Near East is precisely to rule (hence kings were often viewed as quasidivine), it is no wonder that Psalm 8 asserts that in putting all things under their

37. For references to ancient Near Eastern kings (and priests) as the image of a particular god, see Werner H. Schmidt, *Die Schöpfungsgeschichte der Priesterschrift* (Neukirchen-Vluyn: Neukirchener Verlag, 1964), esp. §3.B.9; Hans Wildberger, "Das Abbild Gottes: Gen. 1,26–30," *Theologische Zeitschrift* 21 (1965): 245–59, 481–501; D. J. A. Clines, "The Image of God in Man," *Tyndale Bulletin* 19 (1968): 53–103, repr. as "Humanity as Image of God" in Clines's *On the Way to the Postmodern: Old Testament Essays, 1967–1998* (Journal for the Study of the Old Testament Supplement 293; Sheffield: Sheffield Academic Press, 1998), 2.447–97; Phyllis A. Bird, "'Male and Female He Created Them': Gen 1:27b in the Context of the Priestly Account of Creation," *Harvard Theological Review* 74 (1981): 129–59; and Jeffrey H. Tigay, "The Image of God and the Flood: Some New Developments," in *Studies in Jewish Education and Judaica in Honor of Louis Newman* (ed. Alexander M. Shapiro and Burton I. Cohen; New York: Ktav, 1984), 169–82. For an extensive comparative study of the relevant data, see Edward Mason Curtis, *Man as the Image of God in Genesis in the Light of Ancient Near Eastern Parallels* (Ph.D. dissertation; University of Pennsylvania, 1984), the results of which are briefly summarized in idem, "Image of God (OT)," in *The Anchor Bible Dictionary* (ed. David Noel Freedman et al.; New York: Doubleday, 1992), 3.389–91.

38. In his commentary on Genesis 1:26–28, von Rad emphasizes the functional character of the image; *Genesis*, 60.

39. Both functional and (Barthian) relational interpretations of the image are, like substantialistic interpretations, strictly speaking metaphysical, in that they also make ontological assumptions about human nature. Whereas a Barthian interpretation is historically dependent on Martin Buber's relational ontology, a functional interpretation might be seen as consonant with some version of action theory. For an accessible introduction to action theory (as applied to moral education), see Nicholas Wolterstorff, *Educating for Responsible Action* (Grand Rapids: Eerdmans, 1980), 1–29. Wolterstorff's focus is on persons as agents who act responsibly (or irresponsibly). Action, on this model, includes all that an agent does, including thinking, as an integral unity.

The functional interpretation of the *imago Dei*

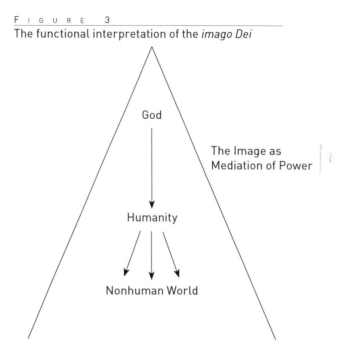

feet and giving them dominion over the works of God's hands, God has made humans "little less than *ʾĕlōhîm*" (8:5–6 [MT 8:6–7]). It does not matter whether *ʾĕlōhîm* is translated "God" or (with the Septuagint) "angels," the meaning is virtually unchanged. In the theology of both Psalm 8 and Genesis 1, humans (like the angelic heavenly court) have been given royal and thus godlike status in the world.[40]

While versions of a royal reading of the *imago Dei* may be found sporadically in the writings of the ante-Nicene fathers (especially in the Antiochine school), in the tenth-century commentary on Genesis by Jewish scholar Saadiah, and among sixteenth-century (heretical) Socinians (being explicitly formalized in the Socinian *Catechismus Racoviensis* of 1605),[41] the royal-functional interpretation of the image came to have a particu-

40. On kingship in the ancient Near East, the classic study is Henri Frankfort, *Kingship and the Gods: A Study of Ancient Near Eastern Religion as the Integration of Society and Nature* (Chicago: University of Chicago Press, 1948). Also useful are Gary V. Smith, "The Concept of God/the Gods as King in the Ancient Near East and the Bible," *Trinity Journal* 3.1 (Spring 1982): 18–38; and Ivan Engell, *Studies in Divine Kingship in the Ancient Near East* (2nd ed.; Oxford: Blackwell, 1967).

41. On the ante-Nicene fathers, see the references in Curtis, *Man as the Image of God*, 20, 21, 66, 71. On Saadiah, see Levenson, *Creation and the Persistence of Evil*, 112. On the Socinians, see Berkouwer, *Man*, 70.

larly significant role among Renaissance humanists in fifteenth-century Italy. Although often left out of historical accounts of *imago* interpretation because they were not members of the theological or clerical guild, thinkers such as Ficino, Morandi, and Pico della Mirandola developed an interpretation of the *imago Dei* as godlike power that humans exercised on earth.[42] Blending the volitional emphasis of Augustinian theology with the divinization notion of the Eastern fathers (mediated through the Hermetic literature), these Renaissance thinkers imagined a creative, transformative energy by which humans (in imitation of God's own creative activity) shaped earthly life through cultural-historical action, whether in city-building, alchemy, politics, scholarship, or the arts.

But the career of the royal-functional interpretation of the image in the field of modern Old Testament scholarship proper does not begin until the start of the twentieth century, with the work of H. Holzinger and Johannes Hehn.[43] And while there are at present a few important dissenters within Old Testament studies, such as Claus Westermann (who holds to a modified Barthian interpretation)[44] and James Barr (who claims that the Genesis text does not intend to specify the content of the image and neither should we),[45] the last thirty years of the twentieth century saw the royal interpretation of the *imago Dei* come virtually to monopolize the field.[46] Thus Barr himself acknowledges that, his own views notwithstanding, among Old Testament scholars the image as humanity's royal function is "the most influential opinion today."[47]

42. On the Renaissance humanists and the *imago Dei*, see the massive study by Charles Trinkaus, *In Our Image and Likeness: Humanity and Divinity in Italian Humanist Thought* (2 vols.; Chicago: University of Chicago Press, 1970); and Cameron Wybrow, *The Bible, Baconianism, and Mastery over Nature: The Old Testament and Its Modern Misreading* (New York: Peter Lang, 1991), 103–9.

43. See H. Holzinger, *Genesis erklärt* (Freiburg-im-Breisgau: Mohr, 1898), 12; and Johannes Hehn, "Zum Terminus 'Bild Gottes,'" in *Festschrift Eduard Sachau* (ed. Gotthold Weil; Berlin: Reimer, 1915), 36–52. For an account of the pioneering work of Holzinger and Hehn, see Jónsson, *Image of God*, 55–60.

44. Claus Westermann does not utilize Barth's notion of the male-female relation constituting the image, but argues that the image refers to the creation of humanity to be God's "counterpart" or relational partner. Westermann's extensive treatment of the *imago Dei* is found in his magisterial three-volume commentary on the book, *Genesis: A Commentary* (trans. John J. Scullion; Minneapolis: Augsburg, 1984), 1.142–61.

45. James Barr, "The Image of God in the Book of Genesis—A Study of Terminology," *Bulletin of the John Rylands Library* 51 (1968): 11–26.

46. Even Karl Barth's son Christoph Barth (an Old Testament scholar) argues against the relational reading (without naming his father) in favor of a royal-functional interpretation of the image; see *God with Us: A Theological Introduction to the Old Testament* (ed. Geoffrey W. Bromiley; Grand Rapids: Eerdmans, 1991), 27–28.

47. This acknowledgement comes in James Barr's 1991 Gifford Lectures, published as *Biblical Faith and Natural Theology* (Oxford: Clarendon, 1993), 158. See pp. 156–73 for

The Need for an Interdisciplinary Approach

Old Testament scholars, however, tend to be notorious in their hesitancy to make broad theological pronouncements based on their research, preferring instead to remain submerged in the textual and linguistic minutiae of their discipline.[48] It is not, therefore, simply the fault of theologians for ignoring biblical scholarship on the *imago Dei*. Old Testament scholars must shoulder their fair share of responsibility. As Brevard Childs comments: "The inability of most systematic theologians to make much sense of the Old Testament stems in part from the failure of the biblical specialists to render it in such a way which is not theologically mute"; hence he proposes that we attend to "the Old Testament within a theological discipline."[49] Werner Lemke likewise notes that

> the field of biblical studies has become so complex that few systematic theologians have either the interest or the energy to be fully conversant with developments in biblical exegesis. Here OT theologians can perform a valuable service for systematic theologians by presenting them with a theological synthesis of the results of biblical exegesis in a form which is more readily accessible and useful to the latter. In order to do this effectively, however, biblical scholars in turn must become more conversant with theological perspectives and be willing to move beyond merely antiquarian concerns.[50]

This is not to say that Old Testament scholars have totally refrained from disseminating a royal-functional interpretation of the *imago Dei* beyond the borders of their specialization. Many propound a royal interpretation of the image in popular biblical commentaries[51] and other

---

Barr's thoroughgoing critique of Barth's interpretation of the *imago Dei*, including his brief dismissal of Westermann's reading of the text (168).

48. Barr, himself a biblical scholar, speaks of a "lack of philosophical insight or ability" on the part of most biblical scholars that is the result of their "professional concentration" or "occupational unwillingness" to look beyond a narrow field of competence; *Biblical Faith and Natural Theology*, 119.

49. Brevard Childs, *Old Testament Theology in a Canonical Context* (Philadelphia: Fortress, 1986), 17.

50. Werner E. Lemke, "Theology (Old Testament)," in *The Anchor Bible Dictionary* (ed. David Noel Freedman et al.; New York: Doubleday, 1992), 6.455.

51. See, for example, Eugene H. Maly, "Genesis," in *The Jerome Biblical Commentary* (ed. Raymond E. Brown, Joseph A. Fitzmyer, and Roland E. Murphy; Englewood Cliffs, NJ: Prentice-Hall, 1968), 1.11; Meredith G. Kline, "Genesis," in *The New Bible Commentary* (ed. Donald Guthrie et al.; rev. ed.; London: InterVarsity/Grand Rapids: Eerdmans, 1970), 83; John C. L. Gibson, *Genesis* (Daily Study Bible; Philadelphia: Westminster, 1981), 1.77, 80–81; Eugene F. Roop, *Genesis* (Believers Church Bible Commentary; Scottdale, PA/

accessible studies—whether monographs or essays.[52] Yet, with a few notable exceptions, such discussions of the royal interpretation do not typically elaborate on the theological or ethical implications of this interpretation. The task has thus fallen to biblical or theological nonspecialists. As it turns out, the most widespread reception—and dissemination—of a royal reading of the image in our day, outside the confines of the biblical studies guild, occurs among Reformational or Calvinian Christians (especially those of a Kuyperian bent), who typically connect the image with the notion of the "cultural mandate" and use this notion to explore various aspects of a Christian worldview.[53] Influenced by the

---

Kitchner, ON: Herald, 1987), 322–23; Christiana de Groot, "Genesis," in *The IVP Women's Bible Commentary* (ed. Catherine Clark Kroeger and Mary J. Evans; Downers Grove, IL: InterVarsity, 2002), 2–4; Brueggemann, *Genesis*, 32; Fretheim, "Book of Genesis," 345–46.

52. See, for example, Odil Hannes Steck, *World and Environment* (Biblical Encounters; Nashville: Abingdon, 1980), 102–8; Bruce C. Birch, *Let Justice Roll Down: The Old Testament, Ethics, and Christian Life* (Louisville: Westminster/John Knox, 1991), 87–89; Barry L. Bandstra, *Reading the Old Testament: An Introduction to the Hebrew Bible* (2nd ed.; Belmont, CA: Wadsworth, 1999), 59–60; Levenson, *Creation and the Persistence of Evil*, 112–16; Hans Walter Wolff, "God's Image—The Steward of the World," in Wolff's *Anthropology of the Old Testament* (trans. Margaret Kohl; Philadelphia: Fortress, 1974), 159–65; Bernhard W. Anderson, "Human Dominion over Nature," in *Biblical Studies in Contemporary Thought* (ed. Miriam Ward; Burlington, VT: Trinity College Biblical Institute/Somerville, MA: Greeno, Hadden, 1975), 27–45, repr. in Anderson's *From Creation to New Creation*, 111–31; Waldemar Janzen, "Created in God's Image," in Janzen's *Still in the Image: Essays in Biblical Theology and Anthropology* (Newton, KS: Faith & Life Press/Winnipeg, MB: CMBC, 1982), 51–59; Bruce C. Birch, "In the Image of God: Humanity at the Dawn of Creation," *Sojourners* 13.1 (Jan. 1984): 14; Stek, "What Says the Scripture?" 250–52; Ian Hart, "Genesis 1:1–2:3 as Prologue to the Book of Genesis," *Tyndale Bulletin* 46 (1995): 317–18 (which attempts to address the implications of a royal-functional interpretation of the *imago Dei* in the context of Genesis 1 for a theology of work).

53. Writers in the Kuyperian tradition who interpret the cultural mandate (human rule of the earth) as the basic meaning of the image include Paul Schrotenboer, *Man in God's World: The Biblical Idea of Office* (Toronto: Wedge, 1972), esp. 8–9; Brian J. Walsh and J. Richard Middleton, *The Transforming Vision: Shaping a Christian World View* (Downers Grove, IL: InterVarsity, 1984), esp. 52–59; A. M. Wolters, "The Foundational Command: 'Subdue the Earth!'" in *Year of Jubilee; Cultural Mandate; Worldview* (Study Pamphlet 382; Potchefstrom: Institute for Reformational Studies, 1999), 27–32, esp. 29–30 (previously distributed as an unpublished paper by the Institute for Christian Studies, Toronto, 1973); Mary Stewart Van Leuween, *The Person in Psychology: A Contemporary Christian Appraisal* (Studies in a Christian World View 3; Grand Rapids: Eerdmans/Leicester: InterVarsity, 1985), esp. 48; Paul Marshall, *Thine Is the Kingdom: A Biblical Perspective on the Nature of Government and Politics Today* (London: Marshall, Morgan & Scott, 1984/Grand Rapids: Eerdmans, 1985), esp. 21–22; Paul Marshall and Lela Gilbert, *Heaven Is Not My Home: Learning to Live in God's Creation* (Nashville: Word, 1998), esp. 19; H. Henry Meeter, *The Basic Ideas of Calvinism* (rev. Paul A. Marshall; 6th ed.; Grand Rapids: Baker, 1990 [1st ed. 1939]), esp. 58; William D. Romanowski, *Eyes Wide Open: Looking for God in Popular Culture* (Grand Rapids: Brazos, 2001), esp. 36–37.

Neo-Calvinian vision of Dutch statesman and scholar Abraham Kuyper (1837–1920), Kuyperian Christians typically assert human responsibility for transforming culture to God's glory, and many ground this insight in a royal reading of the *imago Dei*.[54]

These popular references to the royal interpretation, however, whether among Kuyperian writers or in nontechnical works by Old Testament scholars, tend to be quite brief, often perfunctory. What is missing, and vitally needed, is an extended conversation between theologians and Old Testament scholars on the meaning of the image as rule.[55] This study thus proposes to take up the challenge of Childs and Lemke in an attempt to bridge the disciplinary gap between systematic theology and Old Testament studies, as it applies specifically to the *imago Dei*.

It is important to state, however, that concern for a theological reading of the *imago Dei* as rule does not justify imposing, in any heavy-handed fashion, categories or criteria from the Christian theological tradition (or even from the New Testament) on the Genesis *imago Dei* texts. Rather, my reading of the *imago Dei* is an attempt, in Rolf Rendtorff's words, "to make the findings of modern Old Testament research fruitful for a theological understanding of the Old Testament *on its own ground*."[56] As an Old Testament scholar engaged in Jewish-Christian dialogue, it is significant that Rendtorff refuses to allow *either* interpretive tradition (Jewish or Christian) to set the definitive theological agenda for reading their shared canonical text. "Theological interpretation of the Hebrew Bible," he argues, "is not dependent on the theological system of the religious tradition to which the particular interpreter belongs; the Hebrew Bible is a theological book in its own right, which can be, and must be, interpreted theologically from the inside."[57]

---

54. Not all Kuyperian Christians who appeal to the cultural mandate make an explicit connection to the *imago Dei*. Some older commentators even combine an emphasis on the cultural mandate with a substantialistic interpretation of the image.

55. Some theologians have begun to address the insights of Old Testament scholarship on the *imago Dei*. A prime example is Michael Welker, "Creation, the Image of God, and the Mandate of Dominion," in his *Creation and Reality* (trans. John F. Hoffmeyer; Minneapolis: Fortress, 1999), 60–73. A major theological study that draws on the royal-functional interpretation is Hall's *Imaging God*. Yet Hall does not explore the biblical roots of this interpretation in any depth, and he further (unhelpfully, in my opinion) treats the image as rule as an aspect of the relational interpretation. William A. Dyrness also utilizes a royal interpretation of the image for theological purposes in *Let the Earth Rejoice: A Biblical Theology of Holistic Mission* (Westchester, IL: Crossway, 1983), 33–34.

56. Rolf Rendtorff, *Canon and Theology: Overtures to an Old Testament Theology* (trans. and ed. Margaret Kohl; Overtures to Biblical Theology; Minneapolis: Fortress, 1993), 88 (emphasis original).

57. Ibid., 40.

Nevertheless, respect for the text's own theology does not mean we can arrive at this theology in any "objective" way. As Rendtorff himself admits, "the interpreter's theological approach will unavoidably be influenced by his or her own religious tradition."[58] Far from constituting some sort of (unavoidable) taint, sullying the purity of unbiased research into the Old Testament's own theology, Rendtorff acknowledges the positive value of blending Old Testament study with contemporary theological concerns. Not only is it the case, he notes, that many of our contemporary theological ideas have already been influenced by the Old Testament in its canonical function as Scripture, but Rendtorff suggests that "it would be an important experiment to put certain present-day theological questions to the Hebrew Bible, and to see whether they prove to be appropriate."[59]

The purpose of such theological interrogation of Scripture, however, is not simply academic, as if interdisciplinary conversation were an end in itself. On the contrary, this conversation is explicitly undertaken for the sake of the church's praxis. I am in agreement with R. W. L. Moberly's assessment that a theological reading of the Bible ought to illumine the contemporary Christian community of faith especially "in the area of spirituality, whereby contemporary patterns of living—ethics, values, assumptions about the nature and purpose of life—are informed by the biblical text."[60] Or, to cite a Jewish source, I intend to take seriously Abraham Heschel's critical comment addressed to Christian theologians: "It has seemed puzzling to me how greatly attached to the Bible you seem to be and yet how much like pagans you handle it. The great challenge to those of us who wish to take the Bible seriously is to let it teach us its own essential categories; and then for us to think *with* them, instead of just *about* them."[61]

Thinking *with* Scripture means—for the purposes of this book—that I intend to explore a reading of the *imago Dei* in Genesis 1 that is rooted in careful study of this canonical, paradigmatic text in such a manner that it might function normatively as a theological and ethical resource in the contemporary world. Specifically, reflection on

---

58. Ibid.

59. Ibid., 41.

60. R. W. L. Moberly, *The Old Testament of the Old Testament: Patriarchal Narratives and Mosaic Yahwism* (Overtures to Biblical Theology; Minneapolis: Fortress, 1992), 183. Likewise Henk Vroom suggests an approach to Scripture in which "the message of a text with its own particularities is used to clarify one's present life"; "Religious Hermeneutics, Culture, and Narratives," *Studies in Interreligious Dialogue* 4 (1994): 203.

61. Quoted in Albert C. Outler, "Toward a Postliberal Hermeneutics," *Theology Today* 42 (Oct. 1985): 290 (emphasis original).

the *imago Dei* is here undertaken with a view to its fruitfulness for developing an ethics of power rooted in a theological model of the self as empowered agent of compassion that would be serviceable for the Christian community in envisioning its calling in an increasingly violent and brutal world.

The Problem of Subjectivity

The question, however, inevitably arises as to whether it is appropriate to approach the study of the *imago Dei* with a preselected meaning in mind. In particular, isn't the royal-functional interpretation of the *imago Dei* inevitably just one more subjective reading of the biblical text? By this I do not mean that the royal-functional interpretation is simply idiosyncratic or that the acceptance of this model of the *imago Dei* is relatively recent. Indeed, there are examples of this interpretation occurring well before the twentieth century, though admittedly not in the theological mainstream. But that is not a fundamental problem, as if the minority status of this tradition of *imago* interpretation would be a deterrent. The exceptional competence of the twentieth-century Old Testament scholars who worked on the royal interpretation would certainly lay those fears to rest. The problem is more basic: how do we know that the royal interpretation, even granted the competence of Old Testament scholars, is a faithful reading of Genesis 1:26–27?

The question is particularly urgent since I have already highlighted the tendentiously subjective nature of the various substantialistic and relational interpretations of the image that have been proposed over the centuries, especially their dependence on extrabiblical paradigms of being human. But rather than be inspired to confidence by the clarity with which I note the tendentiousness of these interpretations, I am troubled. As Tom Wright points out in the section on epistemology of his *New Testament and the People of God*, interpreters typically see the interpretations of others as hopelessly subjective and their own as objectively true; they are antirealists about beliefs they disagree with and naive realists (whatever their disclaimers) about their own beliefs.[62]

But, beyond this general caution (which I take to heart), the fact that the royal-functional interpretation has found a ready hearing in our day among those in the Calvinian tradition ought to give me pause, since this tradition seems almost preconditioned to acceptance of this view by its accent on the sovereignty of God, which Canadian histo-

---

62. N. T. Wright, *The New Testament and the People of God* (Minneapolis: Fortress, 1992), 51.

rian W. Stanford Reid calls the "material principle" of Calvinism.[63] It is further significant that those most receptive to the royal interpretation in the Calvinian camp tend to be Kuyperians, who are attracted to the world-transformative vision of Abraham Kuyper.[64] That the royal interpretation of the image clearly supplies an important justification for the Kuyperian vision simply confirms the essential subjectivity of the interpretive enterprise. As one influenced by the Kuyperian tradition, who is moreover aware of the ubiquity of power (as both ontological category and social reality), it seems only natural that I would be drawn to an interpretation of the *imago Dei* as the human vocation to exercise authorized power in the world on God's behalf.

But my suspicions are deepened considerably when I consider one group of Reformed Christians that has recently latched onto the royal-functional interpretation of the image. Representing the extreme right wing of Calvinism, the growing religious movement in the United States (and to some extent in Canada and the United Kingdom) known as Theonomy or Christian Reconstruction not only propounds a postmillennial eschatology of progress, but claims a royal reading of the *imago Dei* as legitimation of its program for "reconstructing America" along theocratic lines, with full implementation of Old Testament legislation and sanctions.[65] A commentary on Genesis by a leading Reconstructionist is thus aptly—and ominously—entitled *The Dominion Covenant*.[66]

Even the undoubted competence of those Old Testament scholars who propose the royal interpretation today does not allay my suspicions, as if their research would put the validity of this interpretation on firmer

---

63. W. Stanford Reid, "Calvinism," in *The New International Dictionary of the Christian Church* (ed. J. D. Douglas; 2nd ed.; Grand Rapids: Zondervan, 1978), 180. Reid designates the authority of Scripture as Calvinism's "formal principle."

64. Nicholas Wolterstorff discusses this world-transformative emphasis in his *Until Justice and Peace Embrace* (Grand Rapids: Eerdmans, 1983), chap. 1.

65. The two foundational texts of Christian Reconstruction are Rousas John Rushdoony, *Institutes of Biblical Law* (Nutley, NJ: Craig, 1973), and Greg L. Bahnsen, *Theonomy in Christian Ethics* (Nutley, NJ: Craig, 1977). For a helpful summary of the movement, see Rodney Clapp, *The Reconstructionists* (2nd ed.; Downers Grove, IL: InterVarsity, 1990).

66. Gary North, *The Dominion Covenant: Genesis* (Tyler, TX: Institute for Christian Economics, 1982), esp. 27–28 on the *imago Dei*. It is also somewhat troubling that a version of the royal-functional interpretation found ready acceptance among Renaissance humanists of the fifteenth century. According to Renaissance historian Charles Trinkaus, this interpretation of the *imago Dei* functioned both to call into question the static, hierarchical (heteronomous) understanding of humanity's role in the cosmos that had been prevalent in medieval Europe and to legitimate the new, dynamic, optimistic (verging on autonomous) sense of the human condition that was emerging in the Italian Renaissance; see *In Our Image and Likeness*, esp. the summaries in his foreword (1.xii–xxvii) and conclusion (2.761–74).

footing.[67] The reason it does not allay my suspicions is twofold. First of all, even Old Testament scholars are subjective persons, who have various theological commitments and utilize particular scholarly paradigms in their interpretation of texts and sifting of evidence. It would be illusory to think that Old Testament scholars, unlike theologians (or naive believers), simply read texts objectively. To complicate matters, Old Testament studies is presently in a massive ferment, with a plurality of conflicting paradigms in evidence, where much is up for grabs.[68] But, second, in order to interpret the *imago Dei*, Old Testament scholars tend to cast their nets far afield—to ancient Near Eastern parallels. Not only are these proposed parallels in need of careful adjudication to see which are most relevant, but such parallels can only suggest, and not on their own justify, the interpretation of the image as rule in Genesis 1.[69] Thus, while such parallels function as an important clue in suggesting a prima facie connection of image with rule, this needs to be corroborated (and nuanced) by careful study of Genesis 1 itself.

But this appeal to the Genesis text, in the face of the undeniable subjectivity I have highlighted in the history of previous interpretation, should not be taken as harboring the naive belief that *this* time we will get the text right. My appeal to the text does not trade on some false ideal of unattainable objectivity, as if this interpreter (or any other) could simply read off what the text really says, independent of one's own biases, idiosyncrasies, race, gender, social location, ideological context, or religious and theological commitments.[70] On the contrary, my reading of the Genesis text is (like every reading, whether by a systematic

67. Some of these scholars are themselves Calvinian, such as Kline, de Groot, Stek, and myself, which provides a further complication.

68. For a recent account, see Rolf Rendtorff, "The Paradigm Is Changing: Hopes—and Fears," *Biblical Interpretation* 1 (1993): 34–53.

69. There are, furthermore, many unresolved problems regarding how this ancient Near Eastern notion could function as a plausible background to Genesis 1 (requiring a hypothetical reconstruction of the sociohistorical context of the Genesis text) as well as the matter of the precise nature of what Genesis 1 means to say vis-à-vis this ancient Near Eastern notion (I attempt such a reconstruction in part 2).

70. For further discussion of these matters (from a feminist perspective), see Joan Borsa, "Towards a Politics of Location: Rethinking Marginality," *Canadian Woman Studies/Les Cahiers de la Femme* 11 (1990): 36–39; and Adrienne Rich, "Notes Towards a Politics of Location," in *Blood, Bread, and Poetry: Selected Prose, 1979–1895* (New York: Norton, 1986), 210–32. For a male "androcritical" discussion of these matters (in relation to biblical scholarship), see Daniel Patte, "Acknowledging the Contextual Character of Male, European-American Critical Exegesis: An Androcritical Perspective," in *Reading from This Place*, vol. 1: *Social Location and Biblical Interpretation in the United States* (ed. Fernando F. Segovia and Mary Ann Tolbert; Minneapolis: Fortress, 1995), 35–55. See also David Jobling, *1 Samuel* (Berit Olam: Studies in Hebrew Narrative and Poetry; Collegeville, MN: Liturgical Press, 1998), chaps. 1–2. These two chapters, which are the prelude to Jobling's postmodern

theologian or biblical scholar) undeniably a *construal*, ineradicably influenced by my own preunderstandings and prejudices.

The Positive Role of Subjectivity

What then is the status of my appeal to the Genesis text? And how do I hope to fare any better than previous interpreters in determining its meaning? Indeed, what is the meaning of a text? Although an extended hermeneutical reflection is clearly beyond the scope of this study, some preliminary account needs to be given of these matters.

First of all, it needs to be said that the admission of subjectivity does not disqualify one's interpretation, as if there were some other (more viable) hermeneutical alternative waiting in the wings. To treat subjectivity per se with suspicion betrays what Richard Bernstein calls "Cartesian anxiety," the residual (perhaps unacknowledged) nostalgia for the sort of objective certainty that Descartes aspired to achieve in the *Meditations*.[71] This aspiration, though now widely recognized as unattainable (and illegitimate), still exercises a profoundly unsettling influence over the sense of epistemic security among many scholars across a wide spectrum of disciplines in the contemporary academy. It further tempts many scholars who acknowledge the inevitable subjectivity of the interpretive process to search for some objective method that would limit or adumbrate this subjectivity.

Rather than be debilitated by Cartesian anxiety—or thinking that there is some methodological cure for bias—we should embrace the ineradicable subjectivity of the human condition as a positive value, without which interpretation would be impossible. Subjectivity is not just inevitable; it is constitutive of the hermeneutical enterprise. One can see nothing without standing in a particular place. Apart from a social, religious, ideological location, with all its bias, there would simply be no point of entry for any interpretation. Our prejudices are thus valuable.[72] In the case of the Calvinian (and more particularly Kuyperian) tradition, the very uniqueness and specificity of the Reformational worldview and theological stance may well provide an impor-

---

reading of 1 Samuel, raise all the important questions of social location, subjectivity, context, and ethics that are usually hidden in studying a biblical text.

71. Richard Bernstein, *Beyond Objectivism and Relativism: Science, Hermeneutics, and Praxis* (Philadelphia: University of Pennsylvania Press, 1983), 16–20.

72. Precisely by limiting what we see, our prejudices enable us to see. On the constitutive role of prejudices in the hermeneutical enterprise, see Hans-Georg Gadamer, *Truth and Method* (trans. and ed. Garrett Barden and John Cumming; New York: Crossroad, 1984), 245–53.

tant opening on the Genesis text, alerting interpreters in this tradition to elements of the text that other interpreters are blind to or at least ignore as unimportant.

This does not mean that only those with the "correct" preunderstandings will be able to discern the "true" meaning of this text. Interpretation is not a fixed, unidirectional matter. It is dynamic and dialogical; texts can talk back. One's original understandings and prejudices are often changed by encounter with the text and also by listening to other traditions of interpretation. "Conversion" happens. What Martin Heidegger calls the hermeneutical circle is not closed and certainly not vicious.[73] It is, indeed, more like a spiral than a circle, since interpreters typically do not end up in precisely the same place they begin.

But the dialogical character of interpretation further suggests that a text does not have one fixed, legitimate true meaning, waiting passively to be discovered. Indeed, the meaning of a text does not strictly speaking reside in the text at all, but is always a product of an encounter between the text and an interpreter or a community of interpreters. Whether the interpretive community is a faith community or a scholarly guild, every such community works with preconceptions and paradigms that both limit and enable what meanings they see. Textual meaning (even of the Bible) is thus neither singular nor static, but is necessarily multiple and changes over time.[74] This simply acknowledges the social, historical, traditioned nature of the interpretive process, which is increasingly being recognized in our postmodern context.

It is my acknowledgment of the inevitable (inter)subjectivity of the hermeneutic enterprise that led me to begin this study of the *imago Dei* by addressing the history of interpretation and the present state of the question. Yet this chapter cannot claim to be a *status quaestionis* in any traditional sense. For the assumption of a *status quaestionis*—namely, that one has surveyed the history of a problem, elucidated the issues at stake, and assessed recent contributions—makes sense only in a clearly delimited field or discipline, where there is some sort of agreement, or at least meaningful debate or conversation, about the issues at stake. This is not the case with the *imago Dei*.

To begin with, interpretation of the *imago Dei* covers two and a half millennia and crosses the boundaries of two religious traditions: Juda-

73. The notion of the hermeneutical circle goes back to Heidegger's analysis of the circularity of *Dasein* in *Being and Time* (trans. John Macquarrie and Edward Robinson; New York: Harper & Row, 1962), for example, 27–28, 194–95, 362–64.

74. It may even be misleading to speak of *the* (singular) royal interpretation of the image, as if Renaissance humanists, Kuyperian Calvinians, and contemporary Old Testament scholars mean the same thing by their use of the metaphor of rule to describe the human vocation.

ism and Christianity.[75] To adequately discuss and situate this history of interpretation would require, minimally, expertise in Second Temple, talmudic, and medieval rabbinic Judaism as well as in the history of Christian theology and exegesis from patristic to modern times, including Christian speculation by nontheologians such as the humanists of the Italian Renaissance, among whom the *imago Dei* was prominent. This expertise is well beyond the capacity of any single scholar. It constitutes simple honesty to admit this. Yet most scholars surveying the history of interpretation of the *imago Dei* typically focus on a singular tradition or discourse (for example, Christian theology) and ignore all others as if they did not exist.

But to this historical and interreligious expertise must be added the ability to cross current disciplinary boundaries in the Christian theological curriculum, since the *imago Dei* is important not only in systematic theology, but also in contemporary Old Testament and New Testament scholarship. The *imago Dei* has, furthermore, become an important topic for reflection today outside the boundaries of the academic theological curriculum, being thematized by a variety of thinkers and writers concerned about the ethical implications of the doctrine in the contemporary world. Thus, in addition to theologians and biblical scholars, the conversation has been joined by a variety of feminists, ecologists, historians, and scientists.[76] Or, rather than speaking of a conversation being joined, it may be more accurate to say that the conversations have proliferated; they have certainly been historically multiple, often separated by academic discipline, faith community, or historical epoch. Any facile assertion, therefore, that one unified history of interpretation concerning the *imago Dei* could be adequately surveyed in a single chapter leads to the rejoinder, *Whose* conversation? *Which* history?[77]

This chapter thus neither claims nor attempts to be a traditional survey of the state of the question of the *imago Dei*. It could, however, be called with some justification a postmodern *status quaestionis* in that its approach to the issues partakes of typically postmodern characteristics such as a self-consciously selective, nontotalizing stance and awareness of the plurality and heterogeneity of relevant conversations and of the necessity for disciplinary debordering. The underlying reason for this

---

75. This assumes that we are limiting ourselves to interpretation of Genesis 1:26–27. The notion of *imago Dei* is, of course, found widely in religious and philosophical writings that have no explicit connection to the Bible.

76. This broader conversation, focusing on ethical issues raised by the *imago Dei* as rule, will be addressed in part 3 below.

77. Alluding, of course, to Alasdair MacIntyre's *Whose Justice? Which Rationality?* (Notre Dame, IN: University of Notre Dame Press, 1988), in which he challenges the Western modernist tradition of objective neutrality.

nontotalizing selectivity is the concern to take seriously the historically conditioned subjectivity that characterizes all interpretation, including this study of the *imago Dei*.

Toward a Hermeneutics of Mutuality

Yet in contrast to one common trend of postmodern hermeneutical practice, I do not believe that all meanings derivable from a text (or arising from the encounter of text and interpreter) are equally legitimate.[78] Although acknowledging that "legitimacy" is always a matter of subjective judgment (and thus fraught with risk), I affirm that texts have their own integrity that must be respected by the interpreter. It is entirely appropriate to judge that some interpretations (and interpretive traditions) do violence to particular texts, submerging and assimilating the text's alterity to the interpreter's heavy-handed preconceptions or deconstructive whimsy.

And beyond isolated interpretations of particular texts that may constitute extreme examples of a lack of respect for the text's alterity, it is worth noting that the mainstream of hermeneutical theory has historically conceptualized interpretation as "mastery" and "appropriation." Even Ricoeur, whose hermeneutical theory calls for the reader initially to let go of control and be displaced by the text, writes that "to 'make one's own' what was previously 'foreign' remains the ultimate aim of all hermeneutics."[79] Language like this leads Richard Palmer to describe many contemporary hermeneutical theories as "rape theories of interpretation."[80]

As an alternative to such interpretive violence, as well as to the unattainable ideal of objectivity (which imagines that we must forfeit our subjectivity), I propose to practice what James Olthuis describes as a hermeneutic of mutuality or connection—even of love.[81] Wright also

78. I say "practice" advisedly, since I know of no reputable hermeneutical theory that advocates an understanding of legitimate textual meaning as literally infinite. Yet it is my experience of academic conferences that more and more highly idiosyncratic readings of particular texts are being offered as legitimate simply because they are *someone's* readings, no matter how loosely anchored in the texts they claim to be readings of.

79. Paul Ricoeur, *Interpretation Theory: Discourse and the Surplus of Meaning* (Fort Worth: Texas Christian University Press, 1976), 91.

80. Richard Palmer, *Hermeneutics* (Chicago: Northwestern University Press, 1969), 247. It is not my intent to single out Ricoeur for special criticism here. And it is possible that Palmer's comments are somewhat excessive, although he documents well the language of mastery in hermeneutical theory.

81. James H. Olthuis, "Otherwise than Violence: Towards a Hermeneutics of Connection," in *The Arts, Community, and Critical Democracy* (ed. Lambert Zuidevaart and Henry Luttikhuizen; Cross-Currents in Religion and Culture; London: Macmillan, 2000), 137–64.

uses the metaphor of love to describe the interpretive process: "The lover affirms the otherness and the reality of the beloved. Love does not seek to collapse the beloved in terms of itself."[82]

In such a hermeneutic (as in any significant relationship between persons), *I bring myself fully* to the interpretive process, acknowledging my full-bodied subjectivity as a gendered, temporal, socially and culturally located person with a particular array of faith commitments (and much else besides). I do not hold any of this back in an attempt to practice an illusory objectivity. Rather, I approach the interpretive task with a "robust . . . sense of self,"[83] bringing my interests and questions (theological and otherwise) to the text of Genesis 1 that I might engage it fully, from where I stand. One of the specific things that this means is that I am willing to treat the text of Scripture as a full-fledged conversation partner in the contemporary theological task of developing a doctrine of the *imago Dei*.

Yet my willingness to put contemporary theological questions to the text is not meant to overwhelm it. A frank acknowledgment of subjectivity does not justify a stance of interpretive mastery or control. On the contrary, I bring myself to the text *precisely to listen to what it is saying*. The paradox, however, is that attentive listening for the voice of a text (just like listening to a person) is necessarily a subjective act. I must interrogate the text of Genesis 1 and intentionally listen for its answers if I desire to be impacted by its meaning.[84]

This means, of course, that not all my assumptions and questions about the text will turn out to be equally valuable. Opening oneself up to the voice of a text over time will inevitably result in the suggestion of new questions and avenues for research, as the text increasingly has its own say. This has certainly been my experience in studying the *imago Dei*. Although the sort of interpretive questions I put to the text of Genesis 1 were undoubtedly shaped initially by the Kuyperian tradition and later by the discipline of Old Testament studies (and arguably even my answers have been informed by those sources), none of this has been in any simplistic, predetermined fashion. Rather, my interpretation of

---

82. Wright, *New Testament and the People of God*, 64.

83. Olthuis, "Otherwise than Violence," 149.

84. What I am suggesting is similar to what Wright refers to as an epistemology of "critical realism." It is "a way of describing the process of 'knowing' that acknowledges *the reality of the thing known, as something other than the knower* (hence 'realism'), while also fully acknowledging that the only access we have to this reality lies along the spiralling path of *appropriate dialogue or conversation between the knower and the thing known* (hence 'critical'). . . . Knowledge, in other words, although in principle concerning realities independent of the knower, is never itself independent of the knower"; *New Testament and the People of God*, 35 (emphasis original).

the *imago Dei* has developed through a sustained, complex dialogue between my own theological preunderstandings and the text of Genesis 1, mediated by the diverse, changing field of Old Testament scholarship. In this dialogue, which can be understood as an exercise in *faith* (my initial assumptions about the *imago Dei*) seeking *understanding* (an investigation and clarification of these assumptions by interaction with the text and with Old Testament scholarship), my initial assumptions about the *imago Dei* have both been confirmed and profoundly transformed.

The remaining chapters of this book testify to my developing dialogue with the meaning of the *imago Dei* in Genesis 1—first as I explore the text and its symbolic world (in chapter 2), then as I investigate the ancient Near Eastern background of the image (in part 2), and finally as I put specific ethical questions about the use of power to the Genesis text (in part 3), questions that arise precisely from my ongoing conversation with this very text.

2

The *Imago Dei* in the Symbolic World of Genesis 1

I t is my purpose in this chapter to attend to the meaning of the *imago Dei* in its primary literary context. First of all, I will engage in a close reading of Genesis 1:26–28—the most immediate literary subunit in which the *imago Dei* is first mentioned—to see what light a linguistic-syntactical study of these verses sheds on the idea that humans are created in God's image. But this careful focus on details will then need to be supplemented by an examination of Genesis 1:1–2:3 as the broader literary context within which 1:26–28 is placed, to see how this larger literary unit—in the context of its shared symbolic world with other biblical texts—might inform the meaning of the image.[1]

1. Although it is still possible to find Old Testament scholars treating Genesis 2:4a as the concluding literary boundary of the creation story, it is now widely recognized (in my opinion, correctly) that 2:4a ("these are the generations of the heavens and the earth"; NRSV) does not *conclude* the account in Genesis 1, but *begins* the next episode in Genesis, the paradise/fall story of Genesis 2–3. The classic argument for 1:1–2:3 as the boundaries of the literary unit is Frank Moore Cross, *Canaanite Myth and Hebrew Epic: Essays in the History of the Religion of Israel* (Cambridge: Harvard University Press, 1973), 301–5. An early, influential study that treats 1:1–2:3 as a coherent literary unit is Bernhard W. Anderson, "A Stylistic Study of the Priestly Creation Story," in *Canon and Authority: Essays*

It is typical of many classic exegetical studies of the *imago Dei* (whether commentaries or essays) to focus on the level of linguistic minutiae, engaging in word studies of *ṣelem* (image) and *dĕmût* (likeness) either to search for the words' core or root meaning (a strategy characteristic of older studies) or to examine their semantic range (in accordance with more recent developments in linguistics) to see how this bears on an interpretation of the image. Although such word studies have been done by many scholars, some with considerable sophistication, these have produced very little by way of results. Thus even James Barr and John F. A. Sawyer conclude their highly technical linguistic studies with the claim that the precise meaning of the *imago Dei* is unspecified in the biblical text (or at least unattainable by the interpreter).[2] Whereas Barr examines the semantic field of Hebrew words meaning "image, likeness, similarity" that would have been available to the presumed sixth-century or fifth-century priestly author/editor of Genesis to determine why he chose *ṣelem* and *dĕmût*, Sawyer investigates the meaning of the phrase *image of God* in the context of the primeval history (Genesis 1–11). What is laudable about such studies is that they attempt to place their linguistic analysis in the context of larger textual units (in one case Genesis 1–11, in the other the whole book). In one important way, however, both studies strike me as being unnecessarily shortsighted, in that they examine the various philological and semantic issues in isolation from both the explicit syntax of Genesis 1:26–28 and the wider symbolic world of 1:1–2:3.

Although, in my opinion, neither a narrowly linguistic nor a syntactical approach to Genesis 1:26–28 yields conclusive results, such focused study is a necessary foundation for broader literary and intertextual approaches to the text. In what follows, I will first address the linguistic or philological question of the meaning of the words for "image" and "likeness" in the text. Then I will examine important and debated aspects of the text's syntax, to see how larger verbal units contribute to the meaning of the image. Finally, I will turn explicitly to 1:1–2:3 as the wider literary context of the *imago Dei*. Here I will explore the basic literary patterns of the text, both for the stylistic characteristics and rhetorical effects of these patterns and for the background symbolic

---

in *Old Testament Religion and Theology* (ed. George W. Coats and Burke O. Long; Philadelphia: Fortress, 1977), 148–62, repr. in Anderson's *From Creation to New Creation: Old Testament Perspectives* (Overtures to Biblical Theology; Minneapolis: Fortress, 1994), 42–55.

2. See James Barr, "The Image of God in the Book of Genesis—A Study of Terminology," *Bulletin of the John Rylands Library* 51 (1968): 11–26; John F. A. Sawyer, "The Meaning of בְּצֶלֶם אֱלֹהִים ('In the Image of God') in Genesis i–xi," *Journal of Theological Studies* 25 (1974): 418–26.

world that the text shares with many other Old Testament texts, since this shared symbolic world would color the meaning of Genesis 1 and the *imago Dei* for ancient readers of the text. This interpretive movement, from textual details to broad patterns within the text and ultimately to a shared intertextual symbolic world, is rooted in the conviction that no text (or idea) is an island. Rather, every text is informed by—even constituted by—other texts and ultimately by a network of ideas, many of them tacit, that are shared by the culture of the text. Attention to these ever-widening contexts is thus meant to illumine what Genesis 1 could plausibly mean when it says that God made human beings in his image and likeness.

The basic question that will be continually before us is this: What does a contextual reading of Genesis 1:26–28 disclose about the *imago Dei*? Specifically, does the text suggest an interpretation of the image as rule, thus providing exegetical confirmation for the near consensus of opinion in current Old Testament scholarship?

The Semantic Range of "Image" and "Likeness"

The most obvious starting point for a detailed textual study of the *imago Dei* is to determine the meaning of *selem* (image) and *děmût* (likeness) in Genesis 1:26–27 by examining their semantic range in the Hebrew Bible. What do such word studies yield? First of all, it becomes clear that *selem* and *děmût* are not all that common in Scripture. *Selem* occurs only seventeen times in the Hebrew Bible (besides the incidence of its Aramaic cognate in Daniel 2–3), while *děmût* occurs twenty-five times in the Hebrew Bible. But second, and more importantly, such word studies yield notoriously inconclusive results.

Selem describes humans created as the "image" of God (Genesis 1:26, 27 [twice]; 9:6) and (in a possibly derivative sense) Seth's relationship to (or affinity with) his father Adam (5:3).

The word, however, primarily designates three-dimensional cult statues of various false gods, which are all roundly condemned in the Old Testament (Numbers 33:52; 2 Kings 11:18; 2 Chronicles 23:17; Ezekiel 7:20; 16:17; Amos 5:26).[3] *Selem* also designates three-dimensional representations that are not cult statues of deities: (raised-relief) wall carvings of Babylonian soldiers (Ezekiel 23:14) and golden copies of the mice and tumors that afflicted the Philistines and that were offered as a guilt offering to YHWH to avoid judgment (1 Samuel 6:5 [twice],

---

3. The Aramaic cognate *ṣělēm/ṣalmāʾ* is also used eleven times in the narrative of Daniel 3:1–18 for the cult statue that Nebuchadnezzar erected.

11).[4] This range of usage certainly supports Walter Kaiser's conclusion that *ṣelem* means "carved or hewn statue or copy."[5]

Yet, to complicate matters, *ṣelem* is also used in a somewhat different sense in two Psalms (39:6 [MT 39:7]; 73:20) to describe human life as fleeting and insubstantial, resulting in translations like "shadow, phantom, fantasies, dream image." Whereas the majority of occurrences seem to indicate something concrete, tangible, or "plastic," here we find a shift in meaning from concrete representation to unreal appearance or mere semblance (*only* an image, we would say), a shift that is evident also in some uses of Greek *eikōn* and Latin *imago*.[6] If we were to reach for a feature common to both senses of *ṣelem*, perhaps we would settle on (visible) "form" (whether solid or insubstantial).

Dĕmût (like *ṣelem*) is used of humans as the "likeness" of God (Genesis 1:26; 5:1) and (again, like *ṣelem*) of Seth's affinity with Adam, his father (5:3).

In the vast majority of references, however, *dĕmût* is used as a general term of comparison between two things and is rendered by a statement that one thing had the "appearance" or "form" of another or else by phrases such as "like, as, something like, similar to," and so on (Psalm 58:4 [MT 58:5]; Isaiah 13:4; 40:18; Ezekiel 1:5 [twice], 10, 13, 16, 22, 26 [three times], 28; 8:2; 10:1, 10, 21, 22; Daniel 10:16). Significantly, most of these so-called abstract uses of *dĕmût* are found in Ezekiel, and they tend to cluster around the prophet's visions of YHWH in Ezekiel 1 (ten times) and Ezekiel 10 (four times), where they function to deliteralize the various elements of the vision, to remove what the prophet "saw" from too close an association with his terms of comparison.

This abstract use of the term leads biblical scholars to the commonplace tactic of distinguishing *ṣelem* from *dĕmût* by claiming that the physical, concrete connotation of *ṣelem* (whereby humans are visible or bodily images of God, an analogy with a cult statue of a deity) is intentionally modified in Genesis 1:26 by the more abstract *dĕmût*, which functions to prevent either an overly physicalistic understanding of the image or too close an identification of the human image with its divine archetype.[7]

4. In a similar manner, the Aramaic cognate *ṣĕlēm/ṣalmā* is used five times in Daniel 2:31–35 to describe the giant statue in Nebuchadnezzar's dream (which does not seem to be a cult image) and once for Nebuchadnezzar's own face or visage (3:19).

5. Walter Kaiser Jr., *Towards an Old Testament Theology* (Grand Rapids: Zondervan, 1978), 76.

6. See D. J. A. Clines, "The Etymology of Hebrew *Ṣelem*," *Journal of Northwest Semitic Languages* 3 (1974): 23.

7. This distinction goes back ultimately to Paul Humbert's influential word studies of *ṣelem* and *dĕmût* in his "Études sur le récit du paradis et de la chute dans la Genèse,"

Although it is true that there are no unequivocal biblical uses of *dĕmût* to designate a cult statue, which might be taken as support for the above interpretation, matters are not that simple, since *dĕmût* is used on occasion in Scripture for a concrete representation or copy of something (2 Kings 16:10; 2 Chronicles 4:3; Ezekiel 23:15). This concrete usage is paralleled by a 1979 excavation at Tell Fekheriyeh in Syria that unearthed a ninth-century B.C.E. statue with an inscription containing Aramaic cognate equivalents of both *selem* and *dĕmût* (and the Akkadian cognate of *selem*) as synonymous terms designating the statue.[8]

A further complication to the idea that the abstract *dĕmût* qualifies the concrete *selem* when they are used together in Genesis 1:26 is that they are used together *in reverse order* to describe Seth's relationship to Adam in 5:3 (is *selem* qualifying *dĕmût* here?), and each term also appears *by itself* to denote humanity's special status vis-à-vis God (*selem* in 1:27 and 9:5; *dĕmût* in 5:1).[9] This variation suggests either that the terms mutually qualify each other or that they may not be used in the early chapters of Genesis with clearly distinguishable meanings at all.

Neither is further precision concerning the meaning of these terms available if we examine the prepositional prefixes *beth* and *kaph* in the compound words *bĕsalĕmēnû* (*in* our image) and *kidĕmûtēnû* (*according to* our likeness), since these show a variation in usage similar to that of *selem* and *dĕmût*. While Genesis 1:26–27 and 9:6 link *beth* with *selem* (four times) and *kaph* with *dĕmût* (once), the prepositions are switched in 5:1–3, where we find *beth* with *dĕmût* (twice) and *kaph* with *selem* (once). Apart from the quite inconclusive debate about the precise nuances of the prepositions themselves (since each preposition can also

---

Mémories de l'université de Neuchâtel 14 (1940): 153–75, esp. 165, cited by J. Maxwell Miller, "In the 'Image' and 'Likeness' of God," *Journal of Biblical Literature* 91 (1972): 293. Whereas Humbert himself thought that *selem* clearly referred to a physical resemblance between humanity and God, which *dĕmût* was introduced to modify, other scholars who use a version of his argument often ignore the physical interpretation. See, for example, Barr, "Image of God in the Book of Genesis," 24; Friedrich Horst, "Face to Face: The Biblical Doctrine of the Image of God" (trans. John Bright), *Interpretation* 4 (1950): 259–60; Walther Eichrodt, *Theology of the Old Testament* (trans. J. A. Baker; Philadelphia: Westminster, 1967), 2.122–23. An exception is Ludwig Köhler, who agrees with Humbert on this point; "Die Grundstelle der imago-Dei-Lehre, Gen. 1:26," *Theologische Zeitschrift* 4 (1948): 16–22.

8. For an account of this inscription, see A. R. Millard and P. Bordreuil, "A Statue from Syria with Assyrian and Aramaic Inscriptions," *Biblical Archeologist* 45 (1982): 135–41.

9. Miller ("In the 'Image' and 'Likeness' of God," 301, 304) argues that in Genesis 1:26 *selem* was intentionally introduced to modify the objectionable implications of *dĕmût* and that in 9:6 it replaced *dĕmût*, since this word, by its assonance with Hebrew *dām* (blood), may have recalled Mesopotamian notions of humanity created from divine blood (Mesopotamian accounts of the creation of humanity are addressed in chapter 4).

mean simply "as"), there is simply no agreement on the significance of this variation.

Two relevant conclusions follow from this preliminary word study. First, neither *ṣelem* nor *dĕmût* is univocal; on the contrary, they each have a range of meanings (they are, like most words, polysemous), and just because *ṣelem* tends toward the concrete and *dĕmût* toward the abstract in most of their occurrences in the Hebrew Bible, this tells us nothing about the specific sense in which the writer of Genesis 1:26–27 (or 5:1 or 9:6) used the terms. As Jacques Doukhan puts it:

> Indeed, to seize the exact meaning which lies in each word of the text is hardly possible. The author is free and therefore he may use his words with connotations of his own, and even use the same word with various shades of meaning within the text. Recent works in linguistics have brought out this living character of the *parole*, making the lexicon no more the primary reference tool but reducing it to a secondary supporting tool.[10]

But, second, even if we could decide the question of abstractness versus concreteness, these word studies of *ṣelem* and *dĕmût* (though important as background work) still do not disclose exactly what the resemblance or likeness of humanity to God consists in.

To approach such a disclosure, we need to move from philology to syntax, from analysis of isolated words to larger verbal units, for it is at the level of phrases and sentences that significant meaning resides. Reading Genesis 1:26–28 at this level yields three specific observations that are commonly made about the image, all of which warrant further examination. The first observation is that the image is associated in 1:26 with God speaking in the first-person plural, something that God does nowhere else in Genesis 1. The second observation is that the image is associated in 1:26 (and possibly 1:28) with the exercise of human power over the nonhuman world. And the third observation is that the image is associated in 1:27 with the creation of humanity as "male and female." How exactly does a study of the syntax of these verses help us clarify these three sets of associations? Answering this question will demonstrate the value of close attention to the text, but will also suggest ways in which we need to move beyond the exegetical details of these verses to wider interpretive contexts, including the Genesis 1 creation account as a whole and still other biblical texts that shed light on the meaning of these verses.

10. Jacques B. Doukhan, *The Genesis Creation Story: Its Literary Structure* (Andrews Doctoral Dissertation Series; Berrien Springs, MI: Andrews University Press, 1978), 17.

Is "Male and Female" a Clue to the Image?

Let us begin with the reference to "male and female," which occurs in the context of a brief poem inserted in an otherwise prose text:

> So God created humanity in his image,
>   in the image of God he created him,
>   male and female he created them. (Genesis 1:27)

Does the third line of this poem mean, as Karl Barth claims, that "male and female" is what *defines* the image? Or is it simply that the image (whatever it consists in) is found in both men and women? Or is there some other connection?

Even if the image were indeed defined by the phrase *male and female*, it would still be unclear what exactly this means for a doctrine of the *imago Dei*. Barth takes this phrase as a clue to the fundamentally relational character of humanity, claiming that human beings are God's image precisely in their interpersonal, intercommunal character (extrapolating of course well beyond "male and female" relationships, literally understood).[11] Phyllis Trible, however, takes this same phrase as a clue to the idea that what we call stereotypically male and female characteristics equally reflect God's character, and she uses this interpretation to ground an examination of "feminine" characterizations of God in the Old Testament.[12]

Without denying the value of Barth's insight into human relationality or Trible's fruitful exploration of biblical metaphors, it needs to be said that these interpretations of Genesis 1:27 are misguided, for two reasons. First of all, they depend on taking the third line of 1:27 as a case of roughly synonymous parallelism with the first two lines (or at least with the second line). Apart from the important question whether even Hebrew poetic doublets really constitute strict synonymous parallelism (Robert Alter claims that by his count synonymous restatement characterizes less than one-quarter of all the poetic doublets in the Bible), it is clear that the third line in three-line Hebrew poetic units typically does not repeat a previous idea, but more usually serves a progressive function, introducing a new thought.[13] It is thus doubtful,

---

11. Karl Barth, *Church Dogmatics*, vol. 3: *The Doctrine of Creation*, part 1: *The Work of Creation* (trans. J. W. Edwards, O. Bussey, and Harold Knight; Edinburgh: Clark, 1958), 194–97.

12. Phyllis Trible, *God and the Rhetoric of Sexuality* (Overtures to Biblical Theology; Philadelphia: Fortress, 1984), 16–21.

13. Robert Alter, *The World of Biblical Literature* (San Francisco: Basic Books, 1992), 177–78.

on syntactical grounds, that "male and female" specifies in any way the nature of the image.

But the second reason these interpretations of 1:27 are misguided is that "male" (*zākār*) and "female" (*nĕqēbâ*) are biological, not social, terms and thus cannot support either the notion of human relationality or culturally male/female characteristics. Whereas the creation story of Genesis 2 uses the social categories *ʾîš* (man) and *ʾiššâ* (woman, wife), the terms *zākār* and *nĕqēbâ* from 1:27 are used of the animals that Noah brought into the ark in the flood account (6:19; 7:9) specifically to designate that they were pairs capable of reproduction. Not only, then, does the phrase *male and female* in 1:27 not define the content of the image in social-relational terms at all, but its role is anticipatory, looking ahead and preparing us for 1:28, where human beings (having been created biologically male and female in 1:27) are blessed with fertility and commissioned by God to reproduce, in order that they might fill the earth and subdue it.[14]

The Relationship of Image and Rule

This brings us to the second observation about our text that warrants investigation, namely, the unquestionable connection or association in Genesis 1:26 between *image/likeness*, on the one hand, and *rule*, on the other. In the report of God's decision to create humanity, God says, "Let us make humanity in our image, according to our likeness, *and let them rule* [*wĕyirdû*] over the fish of the sea, and over the birds of the air, and over the livestock, and over all the earth, and over everything that moves upon the earth." Whatever the precise semantic range of *ṣelem* and *dĕmût*, their side-by-side occurrence in this verse with "rule" (*rādâ*) is not by chance. The importance of rule is further highlighted by the recurrence of *rādâ* two verses later (1:28), along with the verb "subdue" (*kābaš*). Having thus created humanity in the divine image, God pronounces a blessing on the human creature: "Be fruitful and increase, and fill the earth, and subdue it [*wĕkibšuhā*], and rule [*ûrĕdû*] over the fish of the sea, and over the birds of the air, and over every living thing that moves upon the earth" (1:28). What exactly do these verses mean? And how does the ascription of power to humanity relate to creation in God's image?

14. See Phyllis A. Bird's excellent discussion of these matters in "Sexual Differentiation and Divine Image in the Genesis Creation Texts," in *The Image of God: Gender Models in Judaeo-Christian Tradition* (ed. Kari Elisabeth Børresen; Minneapolis: Fortress, 1995), 10–11, 22–23 n. 16; idem, "'Male and Female He Created Them': Gen 1:27b in the Context of the Priestly Account of Creation," *Harvard Theological Review* 74 (1981): 146–50.

We should first note that the verb *rādâ* is often linked with kingship in the Old Testament (it is used along with *mālak* [to reign] and *māšal* [to govern] to describe characteristically royal activity). Although it does not always have a royal sense (it is used of authority over slaves in Leviticus 25:43, 46, 53 and over laborers in 1 Kings 5:15 [MT 5:30]; 9:23; and 2 Chronicles 8:10; and possibly for the treading of a wine press in Joel 3:13 [MT 4:13]—though this may well be a different verb, *yārad* [to go down]),[15] *rādâ* is used of the rule of a king or other political leaders in 1 Kings 4:24 (MT 5:4); Psalm 72:8; 110:2; Isaiah 14:6; and Ezekiel 34:4.

Significantly, this last reference, Ezekiel 34:4, draws on the metaphor of shepherding, which was a standard image for a king in the ancient Near East. This intersection of royal and pastoral metaphors is particularly relevant for Genesis 1:26, 28, where *rādâ* occurs with various categories of animal life as its object, including *bĕhēmâ*, which is usually translated "cattle" or "livestock" and typically refers to domesticated animals. Significantly, however, humanity is called to exercise power also over "the birds of the air," "the fish of the sea," and indeed over "everything that moves upon the earth"—a rather comprehensive assignment. While Norbert Lohfink is likely correct that the text envisions "the domestication of animals in all spheres of reality: in the water, in the air, and on the earth,"[16] this must be understood as an unfinished, open-ended task and is applicable (well beyond the intentionality of the author) to other forms of the utilization of animal life for human benefit, besides domestication, strictly conceived (it may be applied, for example, to scientific study of the genetic code).[17] Whatever the details of applicability, however, James Limburg is undoubtedly correct when he suggests that the use of *rādâ* here extends an originally political ideal to the relationship of humans with the nonhuman creation.[18]

The verb *kābaš*, which occurs in 1:28, is a broader term than *rādâ*, without specific royal connotations, and in many contexts it seems to have a harsh or violent meaning. Even its use in Micah 7:19 for the forgiveness of sins probably has the sense of crushing them underfoot (which calls to mind the cognate noun *kebeš*, which means "footstool" in 2 Chronicles 9:18). More typically, *kābaš* is used of the defeat or con-

15. Norbert Lohfink, "'Subdue the Earth?' (Genesis 1:28)," in his *Theology of the Pentateuch: Themes of the Priestly Narrative and Deuteronomy* (trans. Linda M. Maloney; Minneapolis: Fortress, 1994), 11.

16. Ibid., 12.

17. The ethical question of the limits of human dominion is addressed in part 3 below.

18. James Limburg, "The Responsibility of Royalty: Genesis 1–11 and the Care of the Earth," *Word and World* 11 (1991): 14–30.

quest of enemies (2 Samuel 8:11), a man's (illegitimate) sexual relations
with a woman (Esther 7:8), the enslavement of human beings (Jeremiah
34:11, 16; Nehemiah 5:5; 2 Chronicles 28:10), and the control of land
after military conquest (Joshua 18:1; Numbers 32:22, 29; 1 Chronicles
22:18).

Whereas in those texts that refer to the exercise of power over persons
the actions involved certainly seem violent, in texts having to do with
subduing land/earth (which are probably the most relevant to Genesis
1), there is no implication of a violent or adversarial relationship to
the land/earth per se. Indeed, Deuteronomy 3:20 and 31:3 and Joshua
1:15, which are often thought to be Deuteronomic texts parallel to the
priestly texts Numbers 32:22 and 32:29 (all of which refer to Israel's
possession of the promised land), do not utilize kābaš, but yāraš, which
means simply "to take possession of" in a neutral sense, without any
particularly violent connotations.[19] Thus, while kābaš can indeed be used
in reference to violent acts of subjugation and conquest, the word itself
does not have an intrinsically violent meaning, but rather expresses the
general idea of bringing something or someone under control by the
exercise of power (whether by conquest, subjugation, or administration
depends on the context).

In Genesis 1:28 kābaš refers, minimally, to the right of humanity to
spread over the earth and make it their home. Since the earth has already
sprouted with vegetation in 1:12 and plants for human consumption
are mentioned in 1:29, kābaš may even anticipate human cultivation
of the earth by agriculture. Indeed, both the domestication of animals
(represented by rādâ) and cultivation of the earth (represented by kābaš)
are fundamental human functions that become quite explicit later in
the primeval history.[20]

The use of the verbs rādâ and kābaš thus suggests that the characteristic human task or role vis-à-vis both the animal kingdom and the earth
requires a significant exercise of communal power, and the primacy of
rādâ paints the human vocation with a distinctly royal hue.

The question then arises as to what exactly the relationship is between
image and rule in the text. Many scholars identify the imago Dei with rule

19. Lohfink, "Subdue the Earth?" 10.
20. In the MT both rādâ and kābaš occur with the earth as their objects in 1:26 and
1:28 respectively, thus suggesting that here at least the terms are interchangeable. The
Syriac, however, replaces "over all the earth" in 1:26 with "over all the wild animals of
the earth," thus reserving rādâ for humanity's relation to animals and kābaš for humanity's
relation to the earth. The Syriac here evidences a harmonizing tendency, by including a
category of land animals created earlier on the sixth day and next mentioned in the
paradise/fall story of Genesis 2–3, but omitted by the MT in 1:26. This harmonizing reading
is followed by the New American Bible and the NRSV.

without further ado. Thus Robert Davidson, noting that "context is the safest guide to meaning," asserts that "image and likeness are defined by what follows, to rule."[21] Likewise H. D. Preuss concludes that the meaning of the likeness to God in 1:26 "emerges only from the broader context (v. 28) and is explained as a cooperative sharing in dominion."[22] Many interpreters who deny that the image is simply equivalent to rule nevertheless take this verse to mean that rule is an important subsidiary component of the image, typically related to the image as its result or consequence. But this is not exactly a justified reading of the syntax of 1:26, since a Hebrew jussive with unconverted *wāw* (*wĕyirdû*, and let them rule) that follows a cohortative (*naʿăśeh*, let us make) always expresses the intention or aim of the first-person perspective (singular or plural) represented by the cohortative. The syntax, in other words, points to "rule" as the *purpose*, not simply the consequence or result, of the *imago Dei*.[23]

But even if we take 1:26 as a purpose statement, in the sense that humanity is created in God's image explicitly *to rule* (as the New English Bible has it) or *so that* they might have dominion (which agrees with the Dutch translation "opdat" in *Nieuwe Vertaling*), image and rule, while more closely linked, are not thereby syntactically equivalent. Syntax alone, in other words, does not permit us to define the image by its purpose. Nevertheless, by paying attention to the occurrence of similar purpose statements accompanying the creation of two other sets of creatures in Genesis 1, we will see that syntax does not tell the whole story.[24] We must inquire, in other words, about the place of 1:26

21. Robert Davidson, *Genesis 1–11* (Cambridge Bible Commentary; 3rd ed.; Cambridge: Cambridge University Press, 1980), 25.

22. H. D. Preuss, "דָּמָה *dāmāh*; דְּמוּת *dĕmûth*," in *Theological Dictionary of the Old Testament* (ed. G. Johannes Botterweck and Helmer Ringgren; trans. John T. Willis, Geoffrey W. Bromiley, and David E. Green; Grand Rapids: Eerdmans, 1978), 3.259. David Tobin Asselin likewise claims that "man is God's image because he shares God's power and dominion over creation"; "The Notion of Dominion in Genesis 1–3," *Catholic Biblical Quarterly* 16 (1954): 282. And Georges M. Landes writes that the image refers to "the endowment of humanity with the capacity to represent the divine rule and authority over the animals and natural world"; "Creation and Liberation," in *Creation in the Old Testament* (ed. Bernhard W. Anderson; Issues in Religion and Theology 6; Philadelphia: Fortress, 1984), 146.

23. On this grammatical point see Thomas O. Lambdin, *Introduction to Biblical Hebrew* (New York: Scribner, 1971), §107c. See also Ian Hart, "Genesis 1:1–2:3 as Prologue to the Book of Genesis," *Tyndale Bulletin* 46 (1995): 319–20.

24. In an analogous case, the limitations of a linguistic-syntactical approach are admitted by Brian Dodd for the vexed question in New Testament studies of how we are to decide whether "the faith of Jesus Christ" in the Pauline writings should be taken christologically (Christ's faith/faithfulness) or anthropologically (our faith in Jesus Christ): "Ultimately, the question is decided for an interpreter not primarily on philological or exegetical

54

in the larger symbolic world evoked by the rhetoric of the Genesis 1 creation account.

Thus we note in 1:6 that God creates the firmament (*rāqiaʿ*) to separate the waters above from the waters below. That this is not extrinsic to the firmament, but defines the nature of this particular creature, is suggested by the very conception of Hebrew *rāqiaʿ* as a firm (hence Latin *firmamentum*), transparent, bell-shaped dome or air bubble that keeps the cosmic waters at bay, thus opening up a habitable space for earthly life to flourish.[25] The firmament is by definition a separator; simply by existing it already fulfils its purpose of separating the waters.

The purpose of the sun and moon is analogous, though more complex: to separate day from night (1:14) or light from darkness (1:18); to serve as signs to mark seasons, days, and years (1:14); to be lights in the sky (1:15); to give light on earth (1:15, 17); and to govern the day and night (1:16, 18). Although modern cosmology might regard this as hopelessly geocentric and anthropocentric, from the perspective of the text these statements describe the intrinsic purpose of these two luminaries, which cannot be separated from their existence. And this is further indicated by their never being called sun and moon in Genesis 1, but simply "the greater light" and "the lesser light" (1:16), thus rhetorically highlighting their function in the created order.[26]

These two examples of creatures in 1:6 and 1:14–18 whose existence is explicitly defined by their function or purpose thus sets up the expectation, or leads to the presumption, that the royal function or purpose of humanity in 1:26 is not a mere add-on to their creation in God's image, separable in some way from their essence or nature. On the contrary, rule defines the image as its "permanent implication."[27] I am thus inclined to agree with D. J. A. Clines that while rule may well be grammatically only the purpose and not the definition of the image in 1:26, an initial look at

---

grounds but on the level of the hermeneutical spiral where Pauline theology is reconstructed and tested against Pauline usage and then tested again"; see Brian Dodd, "Romans 1:17— A *Crux Interpretum* for the Πίστις Χριστοῦ Debate?" *Journal of Biblical Literature* 114 (1995): 472–73.

25. The *rāqiaʿ* is said to be poured out like a molten mirror in Job 37:18 and is described as shiny in Ezekiel 1:22 and Daniel 12:3.

26. I am not at this point arguing that the author intentionally refrains from naming the luminaries to highlight their function. Rather, I am reading the text for its rhetorical effect. Possible reasons why the luminaries are not named are dealt with in chapters 5 and 7.

27. The phrase is from D. J. A. Clines, describing the purpose of the firmament in relation to its existence and character as firmament; "The Image of God in Man," *Tyndale Bulletin* 19 (1968): 97. If rule is indeed a "permanent implication" of the image, such that one cannot be the image of God without exercising rule, then from the point of view of sentential logic, image and rule are equivalent.

the overall rhetorical world of the text suggests that it is a necessary and inseparable purpose and hence virtually constitutive of the image.[28]

The Meaning of "Let Us"

The third observation about the syntax of Genesis 1:26–28 that warrants examination is the strange, much debated occurrence of the first-person plurals ("let *us* make humanity in *our* image, according to *our* likeness") that introduce the creation of humanity in 1:26. "Let us make" (*na⁽ăśeh*) is a cohortative of the verb *⁽āśâ*, which here takes the place of the jussives ("let there be x" or "let x do y") that are the typical form of God's fiats in Genesis 1. What does this switch from the third-person singular to the first-person plural signify?

These plurals have been interpreted as a remnant of polytheistic mythology (referring to the gods of the Canaanite or Mesopotamian pantheon), an adumbration of the Trinity (Augustine's suggestion) or at least of a plurality within the Godhead (proposed by Barth), or a request to the earth to aid in creating humanity (one of many rabbinic suggestions), as well as plurals of deliberation or of majesty.[29] While there is only ambiguous evidence for pronominal or verbal plurals of deliberation and majesty in the Hebrew Bible[30] and while God's address to the earth in Genesis 1:11 and 1:24 takes the form of jussives (in the third-person singular), not cohortatives (in the first-person plural), and explicitly names the earth, there may, however, be some truth to interpretations that promote the idea of some sort of plurality in the divine realm. To specify the sort of plurality involved, however, will require us to move beyond the parameters of Genesis 1 to other biblical texts that provide a clearer glimpse of the symbolic world behind these strange plurals. A careful intertextual reading of the plurals in 1:26 suggests that God here addresses the heavenly court or divine council of angels, a reading first suggested in rabbinic commentary on Genesis 1, going back to the Targum Pseudo-Jonathan.[31]

---

28. Ibid., 95–98. The same point is made by W. H. Schmidt, *The Faith of the Old Testament: A History* (Philadelphia: Fortress, 1983), 198.

29. Gerhard F. Hasel, "The Meaning of 'Let Us' in Gn. 1:26," *Andrews University Seminary Studies* 13 (1975): 58–66; Clines, "Image of God in Man," 63–69; Claus Westermann, *Genesis: A Commentary* (trans. John J. Scullion; Minneapolis: Augsburg, 1984), 1.144–45; Bruce Vawter, *On Genesis: A New Reading* (Garden City, NY: Doubleday, 1977), 53–54.

30. For a discussion of some of these ambiguous examples, see Clines, "Image of God in Man," 65–66, 68.

31. Targum Pseudo-Jonathan rests on a tradition going back to pre-Christian times, though its final form is probably sixth century C.E. For a recent translation, see Michael Maher (trans.), *Targum Pseudo-Jonathan: Genesis* (Aramaic Bible 1B; Collegeville, MN: Liturgical Press/Michael Glazier, 1992).

In many biblical texts, God's throne room is associated with a heavenly court of angelic beings, who are royal messengers of the cosmic king and who function as God's attendants or counselors, aiding in the administration of his kingdom.[32] Old Testament texts that refer to the heavenly court are both late and early, poetic, prophetic, and historical, and include Job 1:6; 2:1; 5:1; 15:8; 38:7; Psalm 29:1; 82:1; 89:5–7 (MT 89:6–8); 95:3; 96:4 (= 1 Chronicles 16:25); Psalm 97:7; Exodus 15:11; 2 Samuel 5:22–25; 1 Kings 22:19; Isaiah 6:2, 8; Jeremiah 23:18, 21–22; Ezekiel 1; 3:12–13; 10; Daniel 4:17 (MT 4:14). In Isaiah 6, the attendants of "the king, YHWH of hosts" are the winged seraphim, while in Ezekiel's vision of God's chariot throne (Ezekiel 1, 3, 10) the winged creatures are described but not named—which is also true of the vision of John in Revelation 4–5, when the heavens are opened and the seer is granted a glimpse of the proceedings in God's throne room.[33]

In Genesis 1, however, the main action does not occur in the heavens. Rather, the dramatic movement of the text is from the heavens (days 1 and 4) to the waters (days 2 and 5) to the earth (days 3 and 6), which is the focus for four of God's eight creative acts.[34] This may explain why on day 6, which foregrounds the *earth*, there is no explicit vision (or mention) of *heavenly* beings. Yet their presence is alluded to by the shift from third-person jussives in God's first seven creative acts to the otherwise cryptic cohortative ("let us make") in the eighth act.

Indeed, there is a similar first-person plural in Isaiah's vision, when YHWH asks, on behalf of both himself and the seraphim, "Whom shall I send? And who will go for *us*?" (6:8). Even the vacillation between singular and plural in Isaiah's vision echoes the variation in Genesis 1, where 1:26 has "in *our* image," yet 1:27 has "in *his* image."[35]

32. The most lucid study of the heavenly court in relation to Genesis 1:26 is Patrick D. Miller Jr., *Genesis 1–11: Studies in Structure and Theme* (Journal for the Study of the Old Testament Supplement 8; Sheffield: JSOT Press, 1978), chap. 1. See also idem, "Cosmology and World Order in the Old Testament: The Divine Council as Cosmic-Political Symbol," *Horizons in Biblical Theology* 9 (1987): 53–78; H. H. Rowley, "The Council of Yahweh," *Journal of Theological Studies* 45 (1944): 151–57; Gerald Cooke, "The Sons of (the) God(s)," *Zeitschrift für die Alttestamentliche Wissenschaft* 76 (1964): 22–47; and E. Theodore Mullen Jr., *The Divine Council in Canaanite and Early Hebrew Literature* (Harvard Semitic Monographs 24; Chico, CA: Scholars Press, 1980), part 2: "The Divine Council in Canaanite and Early Hebrew Literature."

33. The royal function of angels is also assumed in the New Testament in Jude 6, which mentions "angels who did not keep their own rulership."

34. This progression is especially noted by Anderson, *From Creation to New Creation*, 49–50.

35. In Ezra 4:18 we find a similar shift between plural and singular in reference to a human king and his royal court: "The letter that you sent to us has been read . . . before me" (NRSV).

That angelic beings are not foreign to the author of Genesis 1 is indicated by the occurrence of similar first-person plurals in 3:22 and 11:7 (both of which are usually regarded unproblematically as referring to the heavenly court) and by the explicit mention of cherubim in 3:24 and "sons of *ʾĕlōhîm*" in 6:1–4 (the latter being an expression that refers to angels in Job 38:7). And beyond these references in the primeval history, we have the frequent appearance of angels throughout Genesis in the stories of the ancestors. It is thus difficult to understand the force of Claus Westermann's objection that the priestly author of Genesis 1 was simply unacquainted with the notion of the heavenly court.[36] If the author of Genesis 1 was indeed responsible for editing the entire book into its final form (as is widely thought by critical scholars), or even the primeval history alone (Genesis 1–11), Westermann's objection does not seem plausible.[37] On the contrary, it is more than plausible that in Genesis 1 (like Isaiah 6) God shares with angelic courtiers the decision to commission the human agent for a significant earthly task.

But the association of angelic beings with the commissioning of humanity finds an even clearer parallel in Psalm 8, a text that reflects a conceptual milieu or symbolic world similar to that of Genesis 1. Having praised YHWH as creator of all things and wondering at the insignificance of humanity in the vast universe, the psalmist goes on to describe the human vocation in even more explicit royal terminology than Genesis 1 does:[38]

> You made them [humans] little lower than *ʾĕlōhîm*
>   and crowned them with glory and honor.
> You made them rulers over the works of your hands;
>   you put everything under their feet:
> all flocks and herds,
>   and the beasts of the field,
> the birds of the air,
>   and the fish of the sea,
>   all that swim the paths of the seas. (Psalm 8:5–8 [MT 8:6–9])

Not only does the psalm use language evocative of a royal coronation to portray the elevated status of humanity as ruler (from the verb *māšal*)

---

36. Westermann, *Genesis*, 1.144–45.

37. Vawter (*On Genesis*, 54) not only claims that the priestly writer would have rejected the popular mythology of angels, but he even goes so far as to dismiss the plurals of Genesis 11:7 and Isaiah 6:8 as mere rhetorical devices for God's own self-address.

38. Although the psalm's references to humanity in Psalm 8:5–8 (MT 8:6–9) are in the masculine singular (referring back to "man" and "son of man" in 8:4 [MT 8:5]), I render these singulars as plurals in the interests of gender inclusivity.

over God's works,[39] but it boldly dares to compare insignificant humanity to God. The psalm does this both implicitly and explicitly. Whereas the name of the creator-king is "majestic [ʾaddîr] in all the earth" and God's "splendor [hôd] is above the heavens" (8:1 [MT 8:2]), humanity is said to be crowned/adorned with an analogous "glory" (kābôd) and "honor" (hādār) for terrestrial rule (8:5 [MT 8:6]).[40] This implicit comparison, which uses terms with royal connotations to describe both God and the human creature,[41] is made explicit when the psalmist asserts that humans are godlike or almost divine, which is the import of having been made "little lower than ʾĕlōhîm."

Although the plural noun ʾĕlōhîm is the usual Hebrew word for God in the Old Testament, it can also refer, depending on the context, to false gods or the angelic host (other "divine" beings). This is why the Septuagint of Psalm 8:5 (MT 8:6) renders ʾĕlōhîm by Greek angelous, which the New International Version follows in its translation: "the heavenly beings."[42] That ʾĕlōhîm here is likely a reference to the heavenly court (or is intentionally ambiguous, referring to both God and the heavenly host) is indicated by the somewhat clumsy use of ʾĕlōhîm in a sentence that would more naturally read "little lower than yourself," since the psalm otherwise consists in direct second-person address to God (and addresses God as YHWH, not ʾĕlōhîm).

It is even possible that the imago Dei references in Genesis 1 and 9 share the same intentional ambiguity as Psalm 8. For example, the occurrence of the phrase ṣelem ʾĕlōhîm in Genesis 9:6 is somewhat jarring if the phrase means "image of God," since "his image" would have been the more natural construction. It may have both God and angels

---

39. Literally, God causes humanity to rule (the hiphil of māšal). The hiphil of mālak, a related verb, is a common expression for the installation of a king (or queen), especially in historical narratives (Judges 9:6, 16, 18; 1 Samuel 8:22; 12:1; 15:11, 35; 2 Samuel 2:9; 1 Kings 1:43; 3:7; 12:20; 16:16, 21; 2 Kings 8:20; 10:5; 11:12; 14:2; 17:21; 21:24; 23:30, 34; 1 Chronicles 11:10; 12:31; 23:1; 28:4; 29:22; 2 Chronicles 1:8, 9, 11; 10:1; 11:22; 22:1; 23:11; 26:1; 33:25; 36:1, 4, 10; Esther 2:17; Isaiah 7:6; Hosea 8:4). The hiphil of māšal is, however, quite rare, occurring only in Psalm 8:6 (MT 8:7) and Daniel 11:39 for the appointment of rulers. A related expression, to set or place (śîm) someone as ruler (mōšēl, the participle from māšal), is used of Joseph's appointment as ruler over Egypt in Genesis 45:8 and Psalm 105:21.

40. Note also the parallel between God's name being majestic in all the earth (8:1, 9 [MT 8:2, 10]) and the universal scope of human governance (all occurs twice in 8:7–8 [MT 8:8–9]).

41. The meaning and use of these terms in the Bible is discussed by Marc Zvi Brettler, God Is King: Understanding an Israelite Metaphor (Sheffield: JSOT Press, 1989), 57–72; and Øystein Lund, "From the Mouth of Babes and Infants You Have Established Strength," Scandinavian Journal of the Old Testament 11 (1997): 92–96.

42. Likewise, the New Jewish Publication Society translation (1999 revision) has "divine beings," with "angels" listed as the alternative, marginal reading.

in its purview. And 1:27 uses both *"his* image" and "image of *ʾĕlōhîm"* in parallel lines, which on the surface sounds redundant, unless *ʾĕlōhîm* includes both God and the heavenly court. This possible nuance leads Sawyer to translate 1:27 as: "So God created the man with a resemblance to Himself; / With a resemblance to divine beings He created him."[43] It is thus possible that not only Psalm 8 but also Genesis 1:27 and 9:6 may be comparing humans not just to the creator but to the divine/heavenly realm in general, thus suggesting a broad analogy between the cosmic king, his royal angelic courtiers, and his earthly human vice-regent.[44] That is, beyond suggesting that God consulted with angels to create humanity ("let us make"), Genesis 1 may include the notion that humans are created in the likeness of angels. "Image of *ʾĕlōhîm"* in 1:27 would thus appropriately reflect God's decision to create humanity ("in *our* image, according to *our* likeness") in 1:26.

It is fascinating that even the Genesis 2–3 paradise/fall story seems to understand a certain similarity between humans and angels. The latter text uses the very same verb to describe the purpose of both. While *ʾādām* is placed in the garden to till/work and "keep" (*šāmar*) it (2:15), the cherubim are placed at the east of the garden to "guard" (*šāmar*) the way to the tree of life (3:24). In this case, however, it may not be humans imaging angels, since the cherubim seem to take over the human vocation that was forfeited through sin. Thus when *ʾādām* is expelled from the garden, all that is left to do is to "till" or "work" the ground (3:23). The task of keeping or guarding the garden has been passed on to others.[45]

This intertextual reading of the plurals in Genesis 1:26 thus suggests the presence of an (adumbrated) royal metaphor in the background of the text, in which God is pictured as ruling the cosmos from his heavenly throne room, attended by angelic courtiers and emissaries. The presence of this background metaphor, along with the explicit syntax of 1:26–28, in the context of the functional, purpose-oriented rhetoric of

---

43. Sawyer, "Meaning of אֱלֹהִים בְּצֶלֶם," 424.

44. This is affirmed in the Jewish tradition by Rashi, Ibn Ezra, and the *Midrash Rabbah* (on Genesis 17:4; 8:11). It is even recorded that Rabbi Nathan said that humans are like angels in having understanding, walking erect, and speaking Hebrew; see *The Fathers according to Rabbi Nathan* (trans. Judah Goldin; Yale Judaica Series 10; New Haven: Yale University Press, 1955), chap. 37, cited by Edward Mason Curtis, *Man as the Image of God in Genesis in the Light of Ancient Near Eastern Parallels* (Ph.D. dissertation; University of Pennsylvania, 1984), 36, 73 (nn. 129–30).

45. Jarl Fossum documents a widespread ancient Jewish belief not only that God consulted with angels in creating humanity, but specifically that humans were created in the image of angels and even that the angels helped in the creation of humanity; "Gen. 1,26 and 2,7 in Judaism, Samaritanism, and Gnosticism," *Journal for the Study of Judaism* 16 (1985): 203–20.

Genesis 1, leads to the exegetical conclusion that the *imago Dei* refers to humanity's office and role as God's earthly delegates, whose terrestrial task is analogous to that of the heavenly court. In 1:26–28, that task is understood as the exercise of significant power over the earth and its nonhuman creatures (likely including the agricultural cultivation of land and the domestication of animals—which together constitute the minimal historical requirements for organized human society or culture). Imaging God thus involves representing and perhaps extending in some way God's rule on earth through the ordinary communal practices of human sociocultural life.

From Exegesis to Intertextuality

Having engaged in an initial linguistic-syntactical study of Genesis 1:26–28, supported by brief excursions into the text's wider literary and conceptual contexts, it is now my task to address, in a more focused way, the contribution of these wider contexts to the meaning of the *imago Dei*. Specifically, I am interested here in the question of how God is portrayed or "rendered" in 1:1–2:3.[46]

The portrayal of God in the Genesis 1 creation account is important both for a canonical reading of Scripture and as a clue to interpreting the *imago Dei*. First of all, the placement of Genesis 1 at the start of the biblical canon, as the preface or overture to the Bible as a whole, is of immense significance for anyone interested in reading the Bible as a coherent (though obviously complex) macrostory or metanarrative of redemption.[47] This placement alone requires those who take Scripture as normative to treat this portrayal as paradigmatic for the character of the God disclosed in the rest of the Bible.

But the portrayal of God in Genesis 1 is crucial more specifically because of the clear assertion of 1:26–27 that humanity is created to be God's image and likeness. Whatever else it might mean, this suggests minimally that the human vocation is modeled on the nature and actions of the God portrayed in Genesis 1. One way, therefore, to focus our question about whether the image refers to rule is to ask whether God, in whose image humanity is created, is portrayed as a ruler in the

---

46. For the term *rendered*, see Dale Patrick, *The Rendering of God in the Old Testament* (Philadelphia: Fortress, 1981).

47. On the significance of the canonical opening of Scripture for reading the biblical story of redemption, see J. Richard Middleton and Brian J. Walsh, *Truth Is Stranger Than It Used to Be: Biblical Faith in a Postmodern Age* (Downers Grove, IL: InterVarsity/London: SPCK, 1995), chaps. 5–6.

Genesis 1 creation story. An affirmative answer to this question will provide important corroboration for our exegesis so far.

My approach to answering this question in the remainder of this chapter will be in terms of a two-step process. First, I will pay particular attention to the two main literary patterns by which Genesis 1:1–2:3 is structured. These are the *fiat* pattern, which stylistically frames each of God's eight creative acts, and the pattern of two corresponding *panels* of four creative acts each, spread out over six days, with an introduction (prior to day 1) and a conclusion (day 7). These literary patterns will initially be explored for the rhetorical effect of their stylistic and compositional artistry, especially in order to discern how they portray God's creative activity and the nature of the world that God creates. The mutually intersecting images of creation by the word (represented literarily by the fiat pattern) and creation by fabrication or artistry (represented by the pattern of corresponding literary panels) are sometimes linked by critical biblical scholars to two hypothetical creation traditions that have been merged in Genesis 1, namely, an older *Tatbericht* (a deed-oriented creation account) that was later edited to fit the framework of a more recent *Wortbericht* (organized around God's fiats).[48] Whatever the merits of this tradition-critical claim, there is certainly no tension between these representations of God's creative activity in the text as it stands.[49] The putative sources or traditions have been melded into a coherent, unified creation account of the "articulation" of the cosmos (to use Gabriel Josipovici's wonderful pun, which alludes to both images).[50]

However, to fully grasp the significance of these literary patterns and the rhetorical world that they evoke requires us (as in the case of the

48. First proposed by Bernhard Stade, *Biblische Theologie des Alten Testaments* (Tübingen: Mohr, 1905–11), 1.349; and Friedrich Schwally, "Die biblischen Schöpfungsberichte," *Archiv für Religionswissenschaft* 9 (1906): 159–75.

49. Many Old Testament scholars, however, perceive these putative traditions to be in conflict. Thus Julian Morgenstern ("The Sources of the Creation Story—Genesis 1:1–2:4," *American Journal of Semitic Languages and Literatures* 36 [1920]: 169–212) claims to discern not only stylistic clumsiness in the juxtaposition of the two traditions in the present text, but also incompatible conceptions of deity in the two traditions. Thus he asserts that the later *Wortbericht* "fits but poorly" into the earlier *Tatbericht* (175) and that "the two conceptions are theologically too divergent and contradictory to be held by one single writer, or even one group or school of writers" (171). Even contemporary Old Testament scholar James L. Crenshaw writes that "within the first account of creation (1:1–2:4a) earlier traditions remain unassimilated, for eight acts of creation are here forced into a strange pattern calling for seven days, and creation by a word vies with creation by deed"; *Story and Faith: A Guide to the Old Testament* (New York: Macmillan/London: Collier Macmillan, 1986), 39.

50. Gabriel Josipovici, *The Book of God: A Response to the Bible* (New Haven: Yale University Press, 1988), 70 (also 68, 74). My thanks to David Jobling for pointing out this reference.

perplexing plurals of 1:26) to go beyond the text of Genesis 1 to the shared symbolic world that Genesis 1 participates in and draws upon—a symbolic world testified to and embodied in other biblical texts. No text, not even Genesis 1, is a self-contained, autonomous entity, but is related to and constituted by its relations to other texts—a phenomenon usually called "intertextuality" by literary scholars.[51] And my reading of the literary patterns and portrayal of God in 1:1–2:3 can appropriately be called an intertextual reading. *Intertextuality,* however, is a blanket term that covers a wide range of textual relationships and quite diverse interpretive strategies in contemporary biblical studies. It is important, therefore, to clarify what sort of intertextual reading I will engage in here and why this particular form of intertextuality is the most fruitful for my purposes.

Among the many different sorts of intertextual relationships that may be examined, the most explicit is *quotation,* which is the intentional citation of one text by another. But an intertextual relationship may be intentional yet implicit, as in the case of *allusion.* Both of these sorts of intertextual relationships among biblical texts fit what Michael Fishbane calls "inner-biblical exegesis"[52] and constitute examples of "diachronic" intertextuality, in that they involve an intentional and historically situated use of an earlier text (the *traditum*) by a later text (the *traditio*), whether explicit or implicit.

Not all intertextual relationships, however, are clearly intentional.[53] Whereas it is becoming increasingly popular in contemporary (postmodern) biblical studies to juxtapose just about any concatenation of texts—biblical or otherwise, ancient or contemporary—to see what rhetorical effects are produced, I am not interested here in such "wild" intertextuality, that is, intertextual relationships that exist only in the mind of the contemporary reader.[54] More significant for my purposes

51. The term (in French) was coined by Julia Kristeva in the 1960s, in essays where she introduced the work of Russian literary critic Mikhail Bakhtin. See especially Kristeva, "Word, Dialogue, Novel," in her *Desire in Language: A Semiotic Approach to Literature and Art* (ed. Leon S. Roudiez; New York: Columbia University Press, 1980), 64–91, repr. in *The Kristeva Reader* (ed. Toril Moi; Oxford: Blackwell, 1986), 34–61.

52. Michael Fishbane, "Inner-Biblical Exegesis: Types and Strategies of Interpretation in Ancient Israel," in his *Garments of Torah: Essays in Biblical Hermeneutics* (Bloomington: Indiana University Press, 1989), 3–18; and idem, *Biblical Interpretation in Ancient Israel* (Oxford: Clarendon, 1985), esp. chap. 14. Fishbane is dependent on a prior use of this phrase by Nahum Sarna, "Psalm 89: A Study in Inner-Biblical Exegesis," in *Biblical and Other Studies* (ed. A. Altmann; Brandeis Texts and Studies; Cambridge: Harvard University Press, 1963), 29–46.

53. Indeed, Kristeva's use of the term *intertextuality* was most decidedly not referring to intentional citation or allusion.

54. I am not ruling out the validity and importance of such intertextuality, merely noting that it is not relevant to my purpose here. Indeed, I combine attention to intertextual allusion with wild intertextuality in "From the Clenched Fist to the Open Hand: A

is what Richard Hays calls intertextual *echo*, a term that describes a form of intertextuality where there is no clearly decidable intentional use of one text by another, yet where there seems to be some sort of connection and one that would make sense to ancient readers (as in the relationship of much of the Pauline writings to the Old Testament Scriptures).[55] Although in many of the cases that Hays explores, Paul may be using phrases and ideas from the Old Testament without always being aware of it simply because he knows the texts so well, Fishbane draws attention to the possibility that thematic similarity between two texts might simply reflect "a shared stream of linguistic tradition" or "common *Wortfeld* [that] provides a thesaurus of terms and images" that both texts are able to draw upon and utilize for their own purposes.[56]

Daniel Boyarin articulates a similar notion of intertextuality when he proposes that, beyond paying attention to intentional citation and allusion, we need to be aware that textual meaning is constrained by "cultural codes," by which he means the conscious or unconscious worldview or "ideology of the culture" in which authors, texts, and readers are always embedded, since these affect the meaning of a text.[57] Boyarin here draws on historian Hayden White's analysis of how even contemporary historiographic works gain an "explanatory effect" (an excess of plausibility and significance) beyond "the formal explanations they may offer of specific historical events," by implicitly appealing to "archetypical story forms" or "patterns of meaning."[58]

These notions of a "common *Wortfeld*," shared "cultural codes," and "patterns of meaning" are combined in Gershon Hepner's analysis of a form of intertextuality "based on connections that reflect linguistic, esthetic, cultural or ideological contexts of the linked texts . . . which does not depend on authors of the texts knowing each other."[59] This

---

Postmodern Reading of the Twenty-Third Psalm," in *The Strategic Smorgasbord of Postmodernity: Literature and the Christian Critic* (ed. Deborah Bowen; Waterloo, ON: Wilfrid Laurier University Press, forthcoming), chap. 17.

55. Richard B. Hays, *Echoes of Scripture in the Letters of Paul* (New Haven: Yale University Press, 1989), esp. 1–33.

56. Fishbane, *Biblical Interpretation in Ancient Israel*, 288.

57. Daniel Boyarin, *Intertextuality and the Reading of Midrash* (Indiana Studies in Biblical Literature; Bloomington: Indiana University Press, 1990), 12.

58. Hayden White, *Tropics of Discourse: Essays in Cultural Criticism* (Baltimore: Johns Hopkins University Press, 1978), 58, quoted by Boyarin, *Intertextuality and the Reading of Midrash*, 85–86.

59. Gershon Hepner, "Verbal Resonance in the Bible and Intertextuality," *Journal for the Study of the Old Testament* 96 (2001): 25. Hepner is here explaining the work of Jay Clayton and Eric Rothstein, "Figures in the Corpus: Theories of Influence and Intertextuality," in *Influence and Intertextuality in Literary History* (ed. Jay Clayton and Eric Rothstein; Madison: University of Wisconsin Press, 1991).

particular sort of intertextuality does not assume any form of intentional citation of one text by another; rather, it "focuses on the text as part of a larger system and on the reader's matrix of associations."[60]

For my part, I am interested—in the rest of this chapter—in something along the lines of what Hays, Fishbane, Boyarin, and Hepner articulate. Specifically, I propose to examine Genesis 1 in connection with other Old Testament texts that seem to share a common conceptual milieu or gestalt of terms and images, to see how these texts might illumine Genesis 1. To use Hepner's terminology, Genesis 1 is surely "part of a larger system," whether that system is thought of as the historical and cultural situation of the text's author or the biblical canon as a whole or something in between. Since I am not claiming that Genesis 1 intentionally cites or alludes to other biblical texts nor am I addressing here the historical context in which Genesis 1 was written (and I thus make no assumptions about the priestly writer or his theology, reconstructed from other P texts), it is possible to understand my appeal to a broader intertextual "system" as a form of "synchronic" canonical intertextuality. As a postcritical, Christian reader of Genesis 1 who certainly takes this text as an integral part of the biblical canon, I am willing to accept this description of my project—with two provisos.

First, I do not intend to read Genesis 1 in the light of the entire biblical (or even Old Testament) canon, since this would simply be beyond the scope of this book. Rather, I plan to investigate rather limited portions of the biblical canon, focusing on texts where I discern some sort of plausible conceptual relationship to Genesis 1 in that they inhabit a similar conceptual framework or symbolic world. In our case, many of these will be creation texts from elsewhere in the Old Testament that use images and language similar to that of Genesis 1.

Second, although canonical approaches to Scripture are typically attempts to read widely disparate texts together, without assuming any particular historical understanding of such texts, I must emphasize that canon is neither a contemporary nor an atemporal construct, but rather an ancient readerly phenomenon. A canonical reading is thus not entirely synchronic, but partakes of a certain diachronic aspect. And beyond this general diachronic aspect, I am interested in an intertextual, canonical reading of Genesis 1:1–2:3 that explores the plausible and likely meanings that the text might have had for ancient readers, what Hepner calls "the reader's matrix of associations." Without arguing specifically that the author or readers of Genesis 1 knew the particular intertexts I will examine, but assuming that they did share a broadly similar cultural context and symbolic world, the more lim-

---

60. Hepner, "Verbal Resonance in the Bible and Intertextuality," 25.

ited (diachronic) aim of my intertextual reading is to discern how the literary patterns by which Genesis 1 is structured would depict God's creative activity in clearly recognizable ways for informed readers of this ancient text.

Admittedly, some intertextual readings can seem like flights of hermeneutical fantasy, guided only by the unrestrained whimsy of the interpreter. Thus, we find Stephen Moore's intertextual reading of the *imago Dei* in Genesis 1 in terms of, on the one hand, medieval Jewish midrashic and mystical speculation about God's corporeality and, on the other, contemporary body-building literature.[61] Although I admire the rigorous ethical impetus behind Moore's attempt "to fashion a critical midrash on the hypermasculinity of the biblical Yahweh,"[62] his reading of the *imago Dei* is less an exposition of the biblical text and more a work of "hermeneutical virtuosity" that "observe[s] no criteria other than the exhilarating thrill of an interpretive tour de force," to use the words of A. K. M. Adam.[63] I intend, by contrast, to engage in literary analysis of 1:1–2:3, supplemented by a comparatively restrained use of other Old Testament texts at appropriate junctures, in order to clarify the symbolic world of Genesis 1, thereby elucidating the text's portrayal or rendering of the God in whose image humanity is created. After examining the literary patterns in Genesis 1 for their rhetorical impact and symbolic world, I will reflect on implications for a contemporary understanding of the *imago Dei*.

Creation by the Word

One of the clearly distinctive features of Genesis 1 is its portrayal of God creating by his word. This image is conveyed literarily by the recurring fiat pattern, which first appears in 1:3–4: "And God said, 'Let there be light!' And there was light. And God saw that the light was good." Each of God's other creative acts in Genesis 1 is also framed by a similar literary pattern, typically of three basic elements: God's *fiat or word* ("and God said, 'Let there be x'" or "and God said, 'Let x do y'"), followed by an *execution report* ("and it was so") and an *evaluation report*

---

61. Stephen D. Moore, "Gigantic God: Yahweh's Body," *Journal for the Study of the Old Testament* 70 (1996): 87–115, which was expanded into a larger study: *God's Gym: Divine Male Bodies in the Bible* (New York: Routledge, 1996).

62. Moore, "Gigantic God," 115.

63. A. K. M. Adam, *What Is Postmodern Biblical Criticism?* (Guides to Biblical Scholarship; Minneapolis: Fortress, 1995), 64–65. Although Adam is referring here to "transgressive" inter*disciplinary* readings (he calls them "undisciplined" readings; 62), his comments are applicable also to inter*textual* readings such as Moore's.

("and God saw that it was good").[64] Technically, the text contains two quite different sets of execution reports. Whereas the first type reports that "it was so" (or, in one case, that "there was light"), the second type reports some specific action of God (making, creating, or separating). The second type either occurs in lieu of the first type (in one instance, on day 5) or (more typically) it supplements the first type. According to tradition critics, the first type of execution report is derived from the *Wortbericht*, while the second is derived from the *Tatbericht*.

The rhetorical impact of this recurring pattern that portrays God creating by mere speech evokes, as Dale Patrick and Allen Scult put it, the "authorial" power and sovereignty of the creator.[65] Their contemporary image of God as an "author" with absolute power over his creative "work" finds its ancient counterpart in the royal metaphor. Like a powerful king whose word is law, God brings new creatures into being simply by decreeing their existence. Whether this image is an extrapolation from the edicts and decrees of human rulers (for example, Genesis 42:18–20; 2 Kings 12:4–5; Ezra 1:2–4; 6:3–5; 7:23) or is derived from ancient Near Eastern mythopoeic models, like the Egyptian god Ptah bringing creatures into being by speaking first in his heart and then with his tongue (in the *Memphite Theology*)[66] or the Mesopotamian god Marduk first creating and then destroying a constellation by his mere word (in *Enuma Elish* 4.19–27),[67] *creatio per verbum* clearly portrays God as supreme in power and authority.

This is certainly congruent with how other Old Testament texts understand creation by the word. Thus Psalm 33:6 asserts that "by the word of YHWH the heavens were made" and goes on in 33:9 (which shares some vocabulary with Genesis 1) to describe God's creative activity:

> He spoke [ʾāmar] and it was [hāyâ],
> He commanded [ṣiwwâ] and it stood firm [ʿāmad].

While the first line of Psalm 33:9 uses the same verbs found in the fiats and execution reports of Genesis 1 ("and God said [ʾāmar] . . . and it was [hāyâ] so"), the second line interprets these fiats as God's commands.

---

64. There is, however, some variation in this pattern, such that certain execution and evaluation reports are missing or displaced or else occur in reverse order. The significance of these variations is addressed in chapter 7.

65. Dale Patrick and Allen Scult, *Rhetoric and Biblical Interpretation* (Sheffield: JSOT Press, 1987/Almond Press, 1990), 115.

66. For a recent translation see Miriam Lichtheim, *Ancient Egyptian Literature: A Book of Readings*, vol. 1: *The Old and Middle Kingdoms* (Berkeley: University of California Press, 1973), 54.

67. The result of this remarkable feat is Marduk's acclamation as king of the gods (*Enuma Elish* 4.28–29). The word for "constellation" (*lumāsu*) was previously misread as "garment" (*lubāsu*) in some older translations.

Similar terminology occurs in Psalm 148:5–6, where the psalmist calls on creatures to praise YHWH's name:

> For he commanded [*ṣiwwâ*] and they were created [*bārāʾ*],
> he established [*ʿāmad*] them forever and ever,
> he gave a decree [*ḥoq*] that cannot be transgressed.

The characterization of God's speech that effects creation as God's authoritative *command* or *decree* is significant for suggesting an underlying analogy in these texts between *creatio per verbum* and God's covenantal law given to Israel, which is pervasively referred to as commandments, statutes, ordinances, decrees, and so on.

Admittedly, this analogy between creation and covenant is only implicit in Psalm 33 and Psalm 148. It surfaces more explicitly, however, in Psalm 147. Three times (once in each stanza) this psalm connects God's providential activity toward the nonhuman creation with God's care for Israel. The same God, in other words, is active in what we would call nature and history. In the first stanza (147:1–6), YHWH's intimate knowledge and care of the stars (147:4–5) is sandwiched between his care for the brokenhearted exiles and the lowly in Israel (147:2–3, 6). In the second stanza (147:7–14), YHWH not only nurtures the earth and feeds the animals (147:7–9), but also protects Zion and grants its people shalom (147:10–14). The final stanza (147:15–20), however, is distinctive in making this connection by utilizing the notion of God's *word*. First, the change of seasons is portrayed as effected by YHWH's speech (the winter snows in 147:15–17, the spring thaw in 147:18). Then, without breaking stride—in the same breath, so to speak—the psalmist shifts to what seems to be a new topic: the Torah revealed to Israel. The transition between 147:18 and 147:19 is rhetorically seamless:

> He sends forth his word [*dābār*], and melts them;
> he makes his wind blow, and the waters flow.
> He declares his word [*dābār*] to Jacob,
> his statutes [*ḥuqqôt*] and ordinances [*mišpāṭîm*] to Israel.

While this shift from creation to covenant might seem like a giant leap to our modern, Western consciousness (with our ingrained split between nature and history), the transition is an effortless one within the psalm. It works only because of an assumed analogy between God's relationship to the human and the nonhuman worlds. This analogy provides the theological basis for the application of covenantal terms like *ḥoq/ḥuqqôt* (decree, statute), or its related verb *ḥûq*, and *mišpāṭîm* (judgments, ordinances) to God's providential relationship to creational phenomena, such as the deep or the sea (Proverbs 8:27, 29), the heavens (Job 38:33), the rain (Job 28:26), or all creatures (Psalm 119:91).

This analogy also underlies Genesis 9, which boldly uses the term *covenant* (*bĕrît*) not only for God's relationship with Noah and his family, but also for God's relationship with the earth itself (9:13) and with every living thing (9:11, 12, 15, 16, 17). Jeremiah 33 likewise draws upon the language of *bĕrît*, explicitly comparing the Davidic covenant with God's pledge of faithfulness to day and night and to heaven and earth:[68]

> Thus says YHWH: If you could break my covenant [*bĕrît*] with the day and my covenant [*bĕrît*] with the night, so that day and night would not come at their appointed time, only then could my covenant [*bĕrît*] with my servant David be broken. . . . Only if I did not establish my covenant [*bĕrît*] with day and night, and the statutes [*ḥuqqôt*] of heaven and earth, would I reject the offspring of Jacob and of my servant David. (Jeremiah 33:20–21, 25–26)

If it is indeed plausible to regard texts such as these as harboring an implicit (and sometimes explicit) analogy between God's dealings with creation and with Israel, then it may be possible to pick up echoes of God's covenantal relationship to Israel even in the threefold fiat pattern of Genesis 1. Whereas the creational fiats ("let there be x") echo to the stipulations or laws of the Mosaic covenant (whether given at Sinai or renewed in Deuteronomy) and whereas the execution reports ("and it was so") suggest the notion of covenantal obedience (there is no hint of disobedience yet in this primal kingdom), the evaluation reports ("and God saw that it was good") have their analogy in the covenant sanctions, at least the first set of such sanctions, namely, the blessing that God pronounces on the people's obedience (the parallels to the curses for disobedience do not occur until the story of the fall in Genesis 3). Later in Scripture, after human disobedience becomes entrenched, this disobedience is distinguished from the positive response that God receives from nonhuman creatures in Jeremiah 8:7, which vividly portrays migrating birds as observant keepers of Torah:

> Even the stork in the sky
>   knows its seasons,
> and the turtledove, swallow, and crane
>   keep the time of their coming;
> but my people do not know
>   the ordinance of YHWH.

68. Jeremiah 31:35–36 also describes God's pledge of faithfulness to the created order in similar language, though without using the term *bĕrît*.

One way in which this analogy between creation and covenant may be significant for interpreting the portrayal of God in Genesis 1 is that YHWH's covenant with Israel is usually understood as a distinctly *royal* figure. Although there is certainly no unanimity concerning historical influence here, it is widely recognized that the Deuteronomic (and perhaps Sinai) covenant has numerous formal parallels with ancient Near Eastern (either Hittite or Assyrian) suzerainty-vassal treaties whereby a conquering king (the suzerain) enters into a relation of sovereignty with a conquered nation (the vassal).[69] These treaties are royal instruments of international political administration, and their structural similarity to the covenant that YHWH enters into with Israel testifies to the pervasive political metaphor of God as king throughout the Old Testament.[70]

An intertextual reading of the threefold fiat pattern in Genesis 1 thus suggests that God is here portrayed as authoritatively sovereign over all creation. As John Stek puts it: "God's first acts . . . , his sovereign creating acts, are depicted as the initial edicts of the Great King by which he founded and ordered his kingdom."[71] In the rhetorical world

69. In these treaties the suzerain is typically called the Great King, an epithet used of King Sennacherib of Assyria by his envoy in Isaiah 36:4, 13. Although the term is never used for any Israelite king, it is used in Psalm 47:2 (MT 47:3) and Malachi 1:14 in connection with God's lordship over the nations and in Psalm 95:3 in reference to God as creator of the cosmos. A classic example of a suzerainty treaty is that between the Hittite King Murshili and his Amurru vassal Duppi-Teshub (*ANET* 203–5, trans. A. Goetze). For a discussion of ancient Near Eastern treaty forms and their relevance to the Old Testament, see George E. Mendenhall, "Covenant Forms in Israelite Tradition," *Biblical Archeologist* 17 (1954): 50–76; Dilbert R. Hillers, *Covenant: The History of a Biblical Idea* (Baltimore: Johns Hopkins University Press, 1969); Klaus Baltzer, *The Covenant Formulary in Old Testament, Jewish, and Early Christian Writings* (trans. David E. Green; Philadelphia: Fortress, 1971); J. A. Thompson, *The Ancient Near Eastern Treaties and the Old Testament* (London: Tyndale, 1964); Meredith G. Kline, *Treaty of the Great King* (Grand Rapids: Eerdmans, 1963); R. Frankena, "The Vassal-Treaties of Esarhaddon and the Dating of Deuteronomy," *Oudtestamentische Studiën* 14 (1965): 122–54; and Moshe Weinfeld, "Traces of Assyrian Treaty Formulae in Deuteronomy," *Biblia* 46 (1965): 417–27.

70. Although the formal parallels between the Mosaic covenant and ancient Near Eastern suzerainty treaties are widely recognized, the issue of derivation is hotly debated. For dissenting voices and critical surveys of the various positions, see Dennis J. McCarthy, *Treaty and Covenant: A Study in Form in the Ancient Oriental Documents and in the Old Testament* (Analecta biblica 21; Rome: Pontifical Biblical Institute Press, 1963); idem, *Old Testament Covenant: A Survey of Current Opinions* (Oxford: Blackwell, 1972), 65–72; E. W. Nicholson, *Exodus and Sinai in History and Tradition* (Richmond: John Knox, 1973), chap. 2; R. E. Clements, *Prophecy and Tradition* (Oxford: Blackwell, 1975), chap. 2. Without claiming that the *origin* of Israel's notion of covenant lies in the suzerainty treaties, it seems relatively clear to me that at some point in its history Israel used elements of the treaty form to express YHWH's relationship to Israel.

71. John H. Stek, "What Says the Scripture?" in *Portraits of Creation: Biblical and Scientific Perspectives on the World's Formation* (ed. Howard Van Till et al.; Grand Rapids:

of Genesis 1 the very existence of creatures constitutes their obedient response or conformity to the divine will. God therefore judges their existence *good* (the juridical function being a typical component of kingship in the ancient Near East).[72] Thus the recurring evaluation reports, when taken in conjunction with the pattern of divine fiats and execution reports, suggest that creation constitutes a covenantal kingdom in which each creature is willingly subject to the word of the creator-king. Here we find an echo of Psalm 148:8, which speaks of "stormy winds that fulfill God's word" (or in the New International Version's picturesque phrase: "that do his [God's] bidding"), and 119:91, which claims that "all things are your servants" (NRSV) The underlying picture is of God as cosmic ruler of a harmonious, well-functioning realm.[73]

God as King?

While the fiat pattern of Genesis 1 may well portray creation as covenantally related to the creator, even as obedient to the creator's word, is this really equivalent to a depiction of God as king? This question is important to raise explicitly for many reasons.

First of all, there is some debate concerning whether the covenant of God with Israel in the Old Testament is really historically indebted to the suzerainty-vassal treaties or even (the question of historical dependence aside) whether Israel's covenant is analogous to such treaties. While suzerainty-vassal treaties in the ancient Near East were certainly political in character, and many Old Testament scholars understand some sort of conceptual relationship between them and the Mosaic covenant (such that "love" for YHWH in Deuteronomy is typically interpreted as *loyalty* or *allegiance*),[74] Frank Moore Cross claims to detect in the biblical covenant language not political, but kinship, associations.[75] If Cross is correct, this calls into question my suggestion that

---

Eerdmans, 1990), 234. For a good literary analysis of the royal metaphor in Genesis 1:1–2:3, see 221–42, 250–62.

72. That God as creator-king will judge the earth is emphasized in Psalm 96:10–13.

73. Besides Psalm 96:10, God is also portrayed as creator-king quite explicitly in 95:3–5.

74. William L. Moran, "The Ancient Near Eastern Background of the Love of God in Deuteronomy," *Catholic Biblical Quarterly* 25 (1963): 77–87, repr. in *Essential Papers on Israel and the Ancient Near East* (ed. Frederick E. Greenspahn; New York: New York University Press. 1991), 103–15.

75. Frank Moore Cross Jr., *From Epic to Canon: History and Literature in Ancient Israel* (Baltimore: Johns Hopkins University Press, 2000), 3–21.

God's covenantal relationship with creation in the Old Testament is a royal figure.

The second reason for raising the question whether God is portrayed as king in Genesis 1 is that God is never actually called "king" (*melek*) or any clearly identifiable synonym for king (such as shepherd) in the text, nor is God the subject of any explicit verbs of ruling (whether *mālak*, *rādâ*, or *māšal*). Indeed, the royal metaphor in Genesis 1, if it is there at all, is certainly not overpowering. It is, on the contrary, somewhat implicit and adumbrated. In this, Genesis 1 is simply in line with the rest of the Pentateuch (and the Former Prophets), which do not typically name God "king" (perhaps to distinguish God's reign from the flawed human institution of kingship).[76] This is in contrast to the Psalms and the Latter Prophets, which often explicitly and enthusiastically name YHWH as king.[77] One hypothesis that tries to explain this phenomenon is that the Pentateuch (and Former Prophets) might represent a theological distancing from the classic picture in some parts of the Old Testament (and the ancient Near East) of the divine warrior-king who conquers primordial chaos to create the world (a picture found in Israel's poetic literature).[78] If the divine warrior is indeed the central royal metaphor for God in the Old Testament, or at least the metaphor associated with explicitly naming God "king," then it makes sense that the distance between this picture and the portrayal of God in Genesis 1 would involve a deemphasis or attenuation of the explicit metaphor of God as king in the text.[79]

But the presence of the royal metaphor in Genesis 1 does not depend on its explicitness. Here we do well to heed the methodological caution of Marc Brettler in his important study *God Is King: Understanding an Israelite Metaphor*.[80] Based on an investigation of the nature of metaphor indebted to Paul Ricoeur (among others), Brettler notes that the absence of the words for "king" or "rule" in a given text of the Hebrew Bible does not

---

76. The only references to God as "king" (*melek*) in the Pentateuch are found in Numbers 23:21 and Deuteronomy 33:5 (both poetic texts); the only reference in the Former Prophets is in 1 Samuel 12:12. God is said to "reign" (*mālak*, the cognate verb) in Exodus 15:18 (a poetic text) and 1 Samuel 8:7 and to "govern" (*māšal*) in Judges 8:23. Significantly, the two nonpoetic texts explicitly contrast God's rule with that of human kingship.

77. For references, see Tryggve N. D. Mettinger, *In Search of God: The Meaning and Message of the Everlasting Names* (trans. Fredrick H. Cryer; Philadelphia: Fortress, 1988), 116.

78. See chap. 6 (below) for further analysis of the divine warrior in the Old Testament in relation to Genesis 1.

79. See ibid., 92–122; and Jörg Jeremias, *Das Königtum Gottes in den Psalmen: Israels Begegnung mit dem kanaanäischen Mythos in den Jahwe-König-Psalmen* (Göttingen: Vandenhoeck & Ruprecht, 1987).

80. Brettler, *God Is King*, 23.

necessarily indicate that the metaphor of kingship is also absent, as long
as the text ascribes to God typical royal actions or characteristics.[81]

Among the indications for the royal metaphor in Genesis 1 are the
strange plurals in God's speech of 1:26. As we have seen, these suggest
the presence, however adumbrated, of the heavenly court, which is quite
definitely a royal figure, associated with God as king in the Old Testament. Furthermore, and consistent with the presence of the heavenly
court, Genesis 1 portrays God assigning spheres of authority or rule to
creatures—not only the (obvious) commission to humanity to rule and
subdue the earth and its creatures (1:26, 28), but also the delegation to
the sun and moon of a "governing" (*māšal*) function over day and night
or light and darkness (1:16, 18). This delegation of power fits perfectly
with the picture of God as king in the text and gives further confirmation
to the presence of the royal metaphor in Genesis 1. It is even possible,
as Stek suggests, that God's namings of the various temporal and spatial
regions (day, night, sky, sea, earth) are royal acts, equivalent to the assertion of lordship over these cosmic realms, and that the provision of
vegetation for the animals and humanity in 1:29–30 might well reflect
the royal assignment of food at the king's table.[82]

Then there is the prominent portrayal of God creating by his word.
Even if Cross is correct in his discernment of kinship, not political/king-
ship, associations in the biblical covenants, it ought to be noted that
kinship relations (certainly in the ancient world) involve the arrangement
and exercise of significant power. The motif of God's kinship-relationship
with creation in Genesis 1, especially one that is established and constituted by mere speech, is an image of great power and authority. Thus,
even if covenant does not have a clear royal flavor, the presence of the
fiat pattern in Genesis 1 portrays God as immensely powerful and as
some sort of governor or administrator of the universe of creatures,
with whom he is in significant relationship.

There is, however, another reason for explicitly questioning whether
God is portrayed as ruler in Genesis 1, namely, the presence of the verb

81. Brettler also notes that not all of the regalia, actions, or characteristics that were
typical of ancient Near Eastern (or Israelite) kings are applied to the biblical God. That
is, the Bible attests to a *selective* application of the metaphor of kingship to YHWH. Martin
Buber, likewise, argues that divine kingship in ancient Israel is detectable in the Bible,
even where God is not named king, by the pervasive notion of God as the one who *leads*
the people (from bondage, through the wilderness, in battle, back from exile, etc.), modeled
on the old Semitic notion of tribal leadership; see Buber's *Kingship of God* (trans. Richard
Scheimann; New York: Harper & Row, 1967), esp. 23, 44–45, 99–107.

82. Stek, "What Says the Scripture?" 232–323. Biblical texts that refer to the royal
provision of food include Genesis 43:34; 47:22; 2 Samuel 9:7, 13; 19:28 (MT 19:29); 1
Kings 2:7; 2 Kings 25:29–30; Jeremiah 52:33–34.

bārāʾ (to create) in 1:1, 21, 27; 2:3. According to Gerhard von Rad, *bārāʾ* precludes the notion of any possible analogy between God and humanity in the text. Von Rad actually makes two claims about *bārāʾ* in his commentary on Genesis, one of which is no longer followed by scholars.[83] First, because *bārāʾ* never occurs with any mention of prior material that is used in the act of creation, von Rad infers (erroneously) that the term might refer to *creatio ex nihilo* (there is, instead, somewhat more justification to claim that it refers to creative acts of radical newness). But von Rad's claim about the preclusion of any divine-human analogy draws on the second well-known fact about *bārāʾ*, namely, that it is never used of human creative activity in the Old Testament. Rather, God is the only subject of the verb in all its biblical occurrences. From this von Rad draws his widely influential conclusion that "the verb was retained exclusively to designate the divine creative activity. . . . It means a creative activity, which on principle is without analogy."[84]

But von Rad's conclusion concerning the incomparability of God's creative activity is not, strictly speaking, a required inference from the known word usage of the approximately fifty occurrences of *bārāʾ* in the Old Testament. It is at most a likely probability based on this word usage. But even this probability is directly and immediately contradicted by the statement in Genesis 1 that humans are "created" (*bārāʾ*) in God's image and likeness (which would be an oxymoron if von Rad were correct). Indeed, *bārāʾ* in 1:27 is functionally equivalent to (or synonymous with) *ʿāśâ* (to make) in 1:26, a verb clearly used of both God and humans. The most that could legitimately be inferred from *bārāʾ* being reserved for God's creative activity in the Old Testament is that the presence of this verb in Genesis 1 qualifies or limits any divine-human likeness or analogy portrayed in the text, protecting it from full identification.[85]

But there is a final reason for raising the question of the presence of the royal metaphor in the text, namely, because it is possible that we as readers may have simplistic understandings of this metaphor, particularly as applied to God's creative activity. For some contempo-

83. Gerhard von Rad, *Genesis: A Commentary* (trans. John H. Marks et al.; rev. ed.; Philadelphia: Westminster, 1972), 48–49.

84. Ibid., 49. A similar conclusion is articulated by Jan Bergman, Helmer Ringgren, Karl-Heinz Bernhardt, and G. Johannes Botterweck, "בָּרָא *bārāʾ*," in *Theological Dictionary of the Old Testament* (ed. G. Johannes Botterweck and Helmer Ringgren; trans. John T. Willis; rev. ed.; Grand Rapids: Eerdmans, 1977), 2.242–49.

85. Hence the conclusion suggested by Bruce C. Birch, Walter Brueggemann, Terence E. Fretheim, and David L. Petersen that while the Old Testament commonly uses analogies of human creating for God's creative activity, *bārāʾ* suggests that "no earthly analogy adequately portrays God's creative activity"; see *Theological Introduction to the Old Testament* (Nashville: Abingdon, 1999), 47.

rary readers, notions of God as king are colored by the history—or by contemporary experience—of the European monarchy. We may think the metaphor has to do either with despotism and the abuse of privilege or with superficial pomp and ceremony. Others may be misled by theological speculation about deterministic divine omnipotence or by modern, Western (Newtonian) notions of ineluctable natural law by which God governs the universe. One particular interpretive problem we face is that our highly differentiated notion of the office of king (as separate from that of judge or priest, for example) may mislead us either into not recognizing the royal metaphor when it occurs or into artificially delimiting its presence in the text in ways that ancient readers would never have considered doing.

God as Artisan

While I do not believe there is any significant question of the presence of the royal metaphor in Genesis 1, this metaphor must not be understood simplistically, but rather as a complex metaphor, incorporating elements that we might not usually think of as relevant to kingship. Alternatively, we could say that Genesis 1 utilizes a set of intersecting or mixed or overlapping metaphors to describe God's creative activity. Superimposed on and integrated with the picture of God speaking creation into being is the metaphor of God as designer and artificer, constructing with care, attention, obvious pleasure, and self-investment (as a good artist) a coherent, harmoniously functioning cosmos, according to a well-thought-out plan. This characterization of God as maker or artisan is rhetorically embodied in the superb literary artistry of the creation story, which moves from a preparatory statement in 1:1–2, through six "days" of God's work, to the seventh climactic day (2:1–3), when God "rests" (*šābat*), satisfied, having completed his work.

Since at least the eighteenth century, biblical scholars have noted that God's creative days are divided into two triads or panels of three days each (see fig. 4). The first panel (days 1–3) has to do largely with God engaging in acts of division or separation, by which the various regions or spaces or realms of the created order are brought into being, while the second panel (days 4–6) has to do with God filling these regions with living (or at least mobile) beings.[86] It is even suggested that these two panels (of regions and occupants) correspond to the introductory state-

---

86. Henri Blocher traces the observation of this symmetry or correspondence back to Johann Gottfried von Herder; see Blocher's *In the Beginning: The Opening Chapters of Genesis* (trans. David G. Peterson; Downers Grove, IL: InterVarsity, 1984), 51.

FIGURE 4

The structure of literary panels in Genesis 1:1–2:3

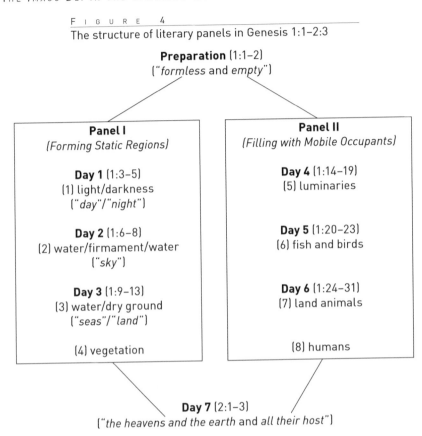

Preparation (1:1–2)
(*"formless and empty"*)

Panel I
(Forming Static Regions)

Day 1 (1:3–5)
(1) light/darkness
(*"day"/"night"*)

Day 2 (1:6–8)
(2) water/firmament/water
(*"sky"*)

Day 3 (1:9–13)
(3) water/dry ground
(*"seas"/"land"*)

(4) vegetation

Panel II
(Filling with Mobile Occupants)

Day 4 (1:14–19)
(5) luminaries

Day 5 (1:20–23)
(6) fish and birds

Day 6 (1:24–31)
(7) land animals

(8) humans

Day 7 (2:1–3)
(*"the heavens and the earth and all their host"*)

ment in 1:2 that the earth was "formless" (*tōhû*) and "empty" (*bōhû*).[87] Although *tōhû wābōhû* probably functions as a hendiadys, meaning something like "an empty wasteland," and certainly has an onomatopoeic sense (which might be conveyed by expressions like "hurly burly" or "helter skelter"),[88] there could very well be a third level of meaning, suggesting that the act of divine creation consists in God bringing form and structure to that which was formless (panel 1) and filling with living or mobile creatures that which was empty (panel 2). Genesis 2:1 thus provides a fitting conclusion (almost an inclusio) to the creation story

87. M. J. Lagrange, "Hexameron (Gènese 1 à 2,4)," *Revue biblique* 5 (1896): 382, cited by Blocher, *In the Beginning*, 51 n. 45.

88. Victor P. Hamilton suggests a series of possible onomatopoeic translations in *The Book of Genesis: Chapters 1–17* (New International Commentary on the Old Testament; Grand Rapids: Eerdmans, 1990), 108. *Le tohu-bohu* has even entered French vocabulary as an onomatopoeic expression meaning a state of confusion; Josipovici, *Book of God*, 60.

in its summary statement that "the heavens and the earth were created" (panel 1) "and all their host" (panel 2).[89]

Whether Genesis 1:2 and 2:1 can be made to bear this particular interpretation, the division into two triadic panels seems quite secure. Thus, on days 1–3 (the first panel), God separates light from darkness and names these realities "day" and "night" (day 1); then separates the waters above from the waters below by a firmament or transparent dome and names this dome "sky" or "heaven" (day 2); then separates the waters below from dry ground and names them "seas" and "earth" (or "land") respectively (day 3). Corresponding to days 1–3, we have days 4–6 (the second panel), on which God fills precisely the static spaces or domains of the first panel with the mobile creatures that appropriately inhabit them. So, on day 4, corresponding to the separation of light and darkness on day 1, God sets sun, moon, and stars in the sky (which are mobile, though not living, creatures); corresponding to the separation of sky and waters on day 2, God fills the waters with fish and the sky with birds on day 5; and corresponding to the separation of dry land from the waters on day 3, God fills this land with land animals of all sorts, including humans, on day 6. And running through the correspondences is an observable progression, repeated in each panel, from heaven (days 1 and 4) to waters (days 2 and 5) to earth (days 3 and 6).[90]

Whereas days 1–2 and days 4–5 each contain one single act of creation, this beautifully simple pattern of correspondences is complicated (beautifully) by days 3 and 6, each containing two acts. So we have eight creative acts, each introduced by a divine decree or fiat, spread over six days. Specifically, on day 3 we find both the separation of dry land from the waters (act 3) and the growth of vegetation on the dry land (act 4). And corresponding to the emergence of dry land on day

89. This reading of Genesis 2:1 is prefigured in the famous medieval distinction between God's work of separation (*opus distinctionis*) on days 1–3 and his work of adornment or embellishment (*opus ornatus*) on days 4–6 (for example, Thomas Aquinas, *Summa Theologiae*, part 1, Q. 65a, answer to objection 1). The medieval distinction, however, is between separation and adornment (as opposed to filling) and seems to be based on the Vulgate's mistranslation (following the Septuagint) of Hebrew *ṣābā'* (in context *ṣĕbā'ām*, their host) by Latin *ornatus*. It seems that the translators of the Septuagint misread *ṣābā'* (host, company, army) as *ṣĕbî* (beauty, glory, adornment). The New International Version tries to capture something of both senses in its translation of *ṣābā'* in Genesis 2:1 as "vast array." Robert Alter (*Genesis: Translation and Commentary* [New York: Norton, 1996], 7) and Everett Fox (*The Five Books of Moses* [Schocken Bible 1; New York: Schocken, 1995], 17) also render *ṣābā'* as "array."

90. Anderson observes this progression from heaven to waters to earth; *From Creation to New Creation*, 42–55. Anderson uses the word *panel* in his study to refer to each creative day, while I use *panel* to refer to the two corresponding triads of days.

3, we have on day 6 the creation first of land animals (act 7) and then of humans, a special kind of land animal (act 8), while the provision of vegetation for food to both humans and animals at the end of day 6, which falls somewhat outside the pattern, corresponds to the growth of this vegetation on day 3.

This (complex) pattern of correspondences illustrates not only the obvious point that Genesis 1 is a carefully constructed piece of litera-ture, but—if form reflects content in any significant way—that creation itself is depicted as a carefully constructed work. In particular, the literary pattern of corresponding panels suggests that one impor-tant dimension of this careful construction is an architectonic plan, implemented by stages. In this plan, the stages are interconnected and linked, so that earlier stages (habitable regions and vegetation) are preparatory for the later (mobile creatures that will inhabit these regions and feed on this vegetation), and the result is a complex, though coherent, whole.

The text, then, by its careful literary artistry, evokes a creator-God carefully constructing an artful world according to a well-thought-out plan for the benefit of creatures. This is a wise artisan, attentive to the details of his craft and pleased with both the stages or process of fabrica-tion (hence the recurring refrain, "God saw that it was good"; Genesis 1:4, 10, 12, 18, 21, 35) and the overall outcome (which God judges "very good"; Genesis 1:31). These refrains thus serve to indicate not only the obedience of creatures to the creator-king, but also the satisfaction of the divine artisan with his workmanship.

What Is God Making?

But we may inquire further into just *what* the divine designer and artisan is making in Genesis 1. A world, yes. But what kind of world? A preliminary answer is suggested by the common portrayal of the cosmos in the Old Testament as a building (see fig. 5). Often pictured with a vault or roof overhead (the firmament or the heavens) resting on "pil-lars" (*ʿammûdîm*; from *ʿāmad*, to stand), which are usually the moun-tains, the world is founded securely upon the primeval waters (see, for example, Job 9:6, 8; 26:11; 37:18; Psalm 75:3 [MT 75:4]; 1 Samuel 2:8). Thus verbs of building are often used for the act of creation, especially *yāsad* and *kûn*, which have a largely overlapping semantic range and are rendered variously "to establish, found, secure, make firm."[91] God

---

91. Other verbs for God's creative activity that portray God as builder include *bānâ* (to build), *yāṣar* (to form, shape), *ʿāśâ* (to make), and *nāṭâ* (to stretch out).

is said to have founded or established or secured the earth, the heavens, the vault upon the earth, the pillars of the earth, the deep, and so on (Proverbs 3:19; 8:27; Psalm 33:7; 75:3 [MT 75:4]; 104:5; 119:90; Job 28:26; 38:4; Isaiah 48:13; 51:13, 16; Zechariah 12:1; Amos 9:6). We even find references to the "foundations" of the mountains, the heavens, or more usually the earth.[92] This latter expression also turns up in many New Testament texts (for example, Matthew 13:35, 25:34; John 17:24; Ephesians 1:4; Hebrews 9:26).

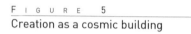

F I G U R E   5

Creation as a cosmic building

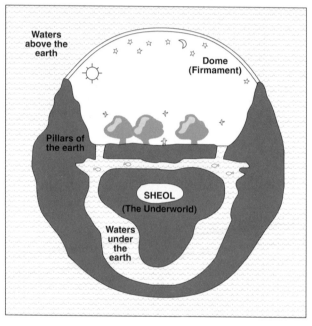

Source: Barry L. Bandstra, *Reading the Old Testament: An Introduction to the Hebrew Bible* (2nd ed.; Belmont, CA: Wadsworth, 1999), CD-ROM.

By the time of the New Testament "the foundations of the earth" is arguably a dead metaphor, referring simply to the origin of the world (thus the NRSV often translates "foundations" simply as "beginning"). But the metaphor is very much alive in the Old Testament. Take Job 38:4–7, for example, where YHWH questions Job about creation:

92. Usually *môsād* (from *yāsad*), as in Deuteronomy 32:22; 2 Samuel 22:8, 16; Psalm 18:7, 15 (MT 18:8, 16); 82:5; Proverbs 8:29; Isaiah 24:18; 40:21; Jeremiah 31:37; Micah 6:2.

> Where were you when I established [*yāsad*] the earth?
>   Speak if you have understanding.
> Do you know who fixed its dimensions
>   or who measured it with a line?
> Onto what were its bases sunk?
>   Who set its cornerstone
> when the morning stars sang together
>   and all the sons of *ʾĕlōhîm* shouted for joy?

While the building metaphor is prominent in Job 38, a more subtle example is found in Proverbs 3:19–20:

> YHWH founded [*yāsad*] the earth by wisdom [*ḥokmâ*],
>   he established [*kûn*] the heavens by understanding [*tĕbûnâ*];
> by his knowledge [*daʿat*] the deeps were divided
>   and the clouds drop down dew.

Remarkably similar language is used later in Proverbs for the building of a house:

> A house is built [*bānâ*] by wisdom [*ḥokmâ*],
>   and is established [*kûn*] by understanding [*tĕbûnâ*].
> By knowledge [*daʿat*] are its rooms filled
>   with all precious and beautiful things. (Proverbs 24:3–4)

Not only does the presence of these two texts in the same biblical book suggest an analogy between a well-built house and God's primordial construction of the cosmos, but Proverbs 24:3–4 clearly replicates the two panels of the Genesis 1 creation story (structure and filling). The idea behind these two panels—establishing a cosmic structure as habitable space—is clearly present in Genesis 1.

This idea of a habitable cosmic structure is reflected in Isaiah 45:18, a prophetic text with an elaborate identification formula for God:

> For thus says YHWH, who created the heavens,
>   he is God, who formed the earth and made it,
>   he established [*kûn*] it;
> he did not create it a waste [*tōhû*],
>   but formed it for habitation:
> I am YHWH and there is none else.

This text, which shares language with Genesis 1—not only *tōhû*, but also "create," "make," "heavens," and "earth"—identifies YHWH as the creator, and this is taken to mean precisely that God constructed a world fit for habitation.

Although the earth can once again become *tōhû* and revert to a state of precreation chaos as a result of God's judgment (as in the great flood in Genesis 6–9), many creation texts assert that due to God's word, wisdom, faithfulness, power, or rule, the world is presently constituted as a secure, dependable cosmic structure.

Interestingly, many texts that speak of cosmic dependability also combine the metaphor of God as artisan with that of God as ruler (creating by his word). Thus Psalm 119:89–91 asserts:

> YHWH exists forever;
>> your word [*dābār*] stands firm in the heavens,
>> your faithfulness is to all generations.
> You have established [*kûn*] the earth and it stands [*ʿāmad*];
>> they stand [*ʿāmad*] to this day according to your ordinances
>> [*mišpāṭîm*],
>> for all things are your servants.

The stability and trustworthiness of the cosmic building is here portrayed as equivalent to the obedient response of creatures to their cosmic ruler. Proverbs 8:27, likewise, uses creation-by-making and creation-by-word metaphors as parallel representations of God's creative activity as personified Wisdom testifies about her presence at the beginning of creation:

> I was there when he [God] established [*kûn*] the heavens,
> when he decreed [*ḥûq*] the horizon upon the face of the deep.

Even Job 38, which I previously cited for its vivid picture of creation as a building (38:4–6), combines this with a reference to the presence of the heavenly court (38:7), which is a royal metaphor.

But perhaps the most explicit combination of royal and building metaphors for God's relationship to the created order is found in Psalm 93:1–2:

> YHWH reigns [*mālak*],
>> he is robed in grandeur;
> YHWH is robed,
>> he is girded with strength.
> The world stands firm [*kûn*];
>> it cannot be shaken.
> Your throne stands firm [*kûn*] from of old;
>> you are from eternity.

In other words, it is due precisely to God's exercise of royal power that there is a stable, dependable cosmic structure.[93]

If we read these various creation texts together with Genesis 1, an underlying picture emerges of a stable, structured, habitable world constituted in response to God's royal decrees. The world is both a kingdom over which God rules and a cosmic building where a variety of creatures may live fruitfully together and flourish.

Creation as a Cosmic Sanctuary

But is it possible to specify further the metaphor of the world as a cosmic structure? Suppose we press the question, *what sort of building is God making in Genesis 1?* Although not immediately obvious, the unequivocal answer given from the perspective of the rest of the Old Testament is this: God is building a *temple.* The notion of the cosmos as temple has its roots in the ancient Near Eastern worldview, in which temples were commonly understood as the royal palaces of the gods, in which they dwelled and from which they reigned. Furthermore, creation, followed by temple building and then divine rest, is a central theme in Mesopotamian, and perhaps Ugaritic, mythology (both Marduk and Baal have temples built for them after their conquest of the chaos monster).[94]

In the Old Testament, perhaps the most important text for our purposes is the oracle recorded in Isaiah 66:1–2. Attributed by many scholars to Third Isaiah, this oracle calls into question the postexilic attempts of pious Jews to rebuild the Jerusalem temple (which had been destroyed by the Babylonians):[95]

> Thus says YHWH:
> Heaven is my throne
>   and earth is my footstool.
> Where could you build a house for me?

93. There is, in general, a striking connection between kingship and building in the Bible and the ancient Near East. Thus Solomon is portrayed as a builder in 1 Kings 5–10, constructing both palace and temple (see also Ecclesiastes 2:4–6), while the *Gilgamesh Epic* opens with reference to the monumental building projects of the ancient Sumerian king Gilgamesh. On the king as builder, see Brettler, *God Is King*, 116–18.

94. It is unclear if Baal's combat, followed by rest and temple building, is genuinely cosmogonic in the sense of having to do with the original creation of the world or merely the preservation and renewal of the annual cycle of nature.

95. On the historical context of Third Isaiah (that is, Isaiah 56–66), see Paul D. Hanson, *The Dawn of Apocalyptic* (2nd ed.; Philadelphia: Fortress, 1978); and idem, *The People Called: The Growth of Community in the Bible* (New York: Harper & Row, 1985), chap. 8.

What place could serve as my dwelling?
All this was made by my hand,
    And thus it all came into being
        —declares YHWH.

The text does not say that God has no need for a temple, merely no need
for a humanly constructed one, since God has already (by his own "hand")
built a cosmic sanctuary, and that should be sufficient. And this sanctuary in which God dwells is also portrayed as God's palace, from which
God reigns—hence the language of throne and footstool. The cosmic
temple, in other words, is clearly equivalent to God's kingdom.[96]

A similar understanding of the cosmic sanctuary underlies the earlier
Isaiah's vision in the Jerusalem temple (in the year that Uzziah, the human
king, died) of "the [divine] king, the LORD of hosts" (6:5). "I saw the Lord,"
says the prophet, "high and exalted" (6:1). Indeed, YHWH is so highly
exalted that only "the hem of his robe filled the temple" (6:1). The scale
of the vision is staggering. This is the cosmic ruler, who simply cannot be
contained by the sanctuary on Zion. By implication, then, and consistent
with 66:1–2, YHWH is enthroned in heaven over all the earth.

Besides the implicit notion of a cosmic sanctuary, many other features
of the vision in Isaiah 6 are significant for interpreting the royal metaphor
in Genesis 1. The first is that just as Isaiah's vision of YHWH issues in
the commissioning of the prophet to speak God's word to Judah, so the
depiction of God in Genesis 1 serves to introduce the creation and commissioning of humanity to represent the divine purposes on earth.[97]

But a further aspect of Isaiah's vision in Isaiah 6 that may well be significant for reading Genesis 1 is the title "LORD of Hosts" (YHWH *ṣĕbāʾôt*)
by which Isaiah names God. This name is characteristically associated in
the Hebrew Bible (as Tryggve Mettinger shows) with the notion of God
reigning as king in the context of the heavenly court, and this is symbolized by the presence of the cherubim throne in the Jerusalem temple.[98]
It may therefore be significant that Genesis 2:1 concludes the account of
creation with these words: "Thus the heavens and the earth were completed,
and all their host [*ṣābāʾ*]." Although *ṣābāʾ* (which is typically thought to

96. Note how Isaiah 65:17–25 draws on language from Genesis 1 in its promise of a
"new heavens and new earth" that God is about to "create."

97. Perhaps the recalcitrance of the people to whom the prophet is sent and his difficult
mission of rendering them blind, deaf, and hardened by his message (Isaiah 6:9–13) even
finds an echo in the primordial call of humanity to "subdue" the earth (Genesis 1:28), a
verb with admittedly harsh connotations.

98. Mettinger, *In Search of God*, 123–57. In connection with the meaning of the name,
we find Hezekiah praying to YHWH of Hosts precisely before the cherubim throne (Isaiah
37:14–20).

be the singular of *ṣĕbāʾôt* in the divine name) usually refers either to an earthly army or to the heavenly host (whether angelic or planetary), here it seems to include the totality of heavenly and earthly mobile creatures. Its occurrence in Genesis 1 thus stands out as quite unusual and serves as a linguistic echo of the regnant God, YHWH *ṣĕbāʾôt*, king of the cosmic temple, whose presence indwells heaven and earth.[99]

But the notion of cosmos as temple in Genesis 1 is suggested more specifically by the prominence of sevens in the creation story. Indeed, beyond the seven days of creation, we have in 1:1–2:3 seven execution reports ("and it was so"), seven evaluation reports ("and God saw that it was good"), the occurrence of both "God" and "earth" in multiples of seven (35 and 21, respectively), and word counts in multiples of seven for the entire text (469 words), the seventh day (35 words), and the precreation preamble in 1:1–2 (21 words: 7 words in 1:1 and 14 words in 1:2).[100]

Although the significance of the sevenfold (heptadic) structure of Genesis 1:1–2:3 has often puzzled Old Testament scholars over the years, this literary framing of the creation story resonates with a plethora of other sevens found throughout the Old Testament primarily in cultic contexts. Rarely noticed by Christian (especially Protestant) exegetes, this is widely recognized in Jewish commentary, from Josephus, through the Talmud, to present scholarly literature on the Hebrew Bible. Thus we have the seven-day Feast of Tabernacles (in the seventh month of the Israelite year) and Solomon's dedication of the newly built temple in Jerusalem during this feast (1 Kings 8:2). Solomon's dedication speech, furthermore, is structured in seven petitions (8:31–32, 33–34, 35–37a, 37b–40, 41–43, 44–45, 46–53), and the building of the temple took seven years (6:38). The heptadic structure of Genesis 1:1–2:3 thus seems to have cultic, liturgical significance and may well be associated in some way with the Jerusalem temple.[101]

---

99. Even if *ṣābāʾ* and *ṣĕbāʾôt* are not etymologically related (as is possible), the linguistic echo is still undeniable. On the significance of even unintended verbal resonances of unrelated words, see Hepner, "Verbal Resonance in the Bible and Intertextuality," 3–27.

100. For an extensive account of the presence of sevens in Genesis 1:1–2:3, see U. Cassuto, *A Commentary on the Book of Genesis*, vol. 1: *From Adam to Noah* (trans. Israel Abrahams; Jerusalem: Magnes, 1961), 12–15.

101. The association of Genesis 1 with the Jerusalem temple may actually be more of a contrast than a similarity. Although the cosmos as God's sanctuary is appropriately compared to the tabernacle (both are built in response to God's explicit command), the cosmic sanctuary may be more appropriately *contrasted to* (rather than compared with) the Jerusalem temple. Not only does the idea of building the temple come from David's (not God's) initiative, so that its acceptance by God is a divine concession from the outset (2 Samuel 7:1–16), but the temple later came to have an ideological function as a false guarantee of Judah's security and was thus subject to prophetic critique (Jeremiah 7:1–15; Isaiah 66:1–2). This very contrast between tabernacle and temple is found in Stephen's speech in Acts 7:44–51, which also quotes Isaiah 66:1–2.

But this association of the number seven with temples extends beyond the Old Testament to other ancient Near Eastern cultures. Thus we find an inscription by Gudea, ancient Sumerian king of Lagash (twenty-second century B.C.E.), concerning a seven-day dedication festival for one of his temples.[102] And, interestingly enough, the building of Baal's temple in the Ugaritic myth took seven days.

But more important than these (perhaps inconclusive) associations are the significant structural and thematic parallels between the creation account in Genesis 1 and the account of the construction of the taber-nacle (God's mobile house or dwelling) in the book of Exodus. Whereas it is standard scholarly opinion that Genesis 1 has its origins in Priestly circles in Israel, this somewhat hypothetical claim is bolstered by the well-documented parallels between the Genesis 1 creation account and tabernacle construction.[103]

Although it would take us too far afield to go into all of these paral-lels, let me cite a few.[104] God's instructions to Moses about building the tabernacle in Exodus 25–31 occur in seven distinct speeches,[105] and the

102. This inscription is preserved on the Gudea Cylinder B.18.19 and Statue B.7.30. For an English translation, see George A. Barton, *The Royal Inscriptions of Sumer and Akkad* (New Haven: Yale University Press/London: Oxford University Press, 1929), 253, 187.

103. The plausibility of these parallels is substantially independent of source-critical theories, like that of Joseph Blenkinsopp, concerning the contours of the putative priestly document, which Blenkinsopp claims stretches from the Genesis 1 creation story to the building of the tabernacle in Exodus; "The Structure of P," *Catholic Biblical Quarterly* 38 (1976): 275–92. I am fundamentally agnostic about all source-critical theories of the composition of the Pentateuch, not because I do not think the text is composite, but because I do not think it is possible to reconstruct the sources with any degree of confidence.

104. Besides Blenkinsopp's important study, I culled these parallels from Eric E. Elnes, "Creation and Tabernacle: The Priestly Writer's 'Environmentalism,'" *Horizons in Biblical Theology* 16 (1994): 144–55; Jon D. Levenson, *Creation and the Persistence of Evil: The Jewish Drama of Divine Omnipotence* (San Francisco: Harper & Row, 1988; rev. ed. Princeton: Princeton University Press, 1994), esp. 66–99; Terence E. Fretheim, *Exodus* (Louisville: John Knox, 1991), 268–72; Meredith G. Kline, *Images of the Spirit* (Grand Rapids: Baker, 1980), 13–34; John G. Gammie, *Holiness in Israel* (Overtures to Biblical Theology; Minneapolis: Fortress, 1989), 9–44; Moshe Weinfeld, "Sabbath, Temple, and the Enthronement of the Lord: The Problem of the Sitz im Leben of Genesis 1:1–2:3," in *Mélanges bibliques et orientaux en l'honneur de M. Henri Cazelles* (ed. A. Caquot and M. Delcor; Kevelaer: Butzon & Bercker/Neukirchen-Vluyn: Neukirchener Verlag, 1981), 501–12; Arthur Green, "Sabbath as Temple: Some Thoughts on Space and Time in Judaism," in *Go and Study: Essays and Studies in Honor of Alfred Jospe* (ed. Raphael Jospe and Samuel Z. Fishman; Washington, DC: B'nai B'rith Hillel Foundations, 1980), 287–305; Josipovici, *Book of God*, 90–107.

105. The seven speeches in Exodus 25–31, each of which is introduced with the words "YHWH spoke to Moses," are (1) 25:1–30:10; (2) 30:11–16; (3) 30:17–21; (4) 30:22–33; (5) 30:34–37; (6) 31:1–11; and (7) 31:12–17. The cycle of speeches is concluded with 31:18, which notes that "God finished speaking with Moses on Mount Sinai" (NRSV).

seventh speech is devoted to the theme of Sabbath observance, which is there rooted in God's rest on the seventh day.[106] Corresponding to the sevenfold appearance of "and it was so" and of "God saw that it was good" in Genesis 1, indicating that the world was constructed according to the divine intention, the account of the building of the tabernacle (Exodus 35–40) contains two sets of sevenfold occurrences of the expression "just as the LORD commanded Moses," again indicating the correspondence of the end product with God's intent.[107] Even the concluding statements in each account about the completion of "all the work" of creation and tabernacle-building are remarkably similar.[108]

Many other correspondences could be cited, including the extreme care taken in describing the intricacy of the tabernacle construction in Exodus that parallels the careful literary artistry of the Genesis creation account, but let me highlight one more crucial correspondence. The unusual (and much debated) expression *rûaḥ ʾĕlōhîm* (Spirit of God) mentioned in Genesis 1:2 does not occur often in the Pentateuch. One of its rare appearances is in Exodus 31, in the account of the building of the tabernacle, where it is said that Bezalel, the master craftsman who had oversight of the tabernacle construction, was filled with the *rûaḥ ʾĕlōhîm* (31:3; 35:31) and was thus granted wisdom and skill in all kinds of crafts and artistry.

Besides providing an important verbal link between creation and the construction of the tabernacle, the occurrence of *rûaḥ ʾĕlōhîm* in Genesis 1 might well indicate the guiding presence and wisdom of the creator overseeing the construction of the cosmic sanctuary (note the similar portrayal of wisdom in Proverbs 8:22–31).[109] This reading of Genesis 1:2, of course, flies in the face of those who argue that *rûaḥ ʾĕlōhîm* means simply a "great/mighty wind" (taking *ʾĕlōhîm* as a su-

---

106. The seventh speech concludes with YHWH explaining that the sabbath is "a sign forever between me and the people of Israel that in six days the LORD made heaven and earth, and on the seventh day he rested, and was refreshed" (Exodus 31:17 NRSV).

107. Exodus 39:1, 5, 7, 21, 26, 29, 31; 40:19, 21, 23, 25, 27, 29, 32. This does not count similar expressions that function to summarize the obedience of other individuals or the people as a whole in "everything" or "all" their work (38:22; 39:32, 42, 43; 40:16).

108. There is even a parallel between God's concluding blessing of the seventh day (Genesis 2:3) and Moses's concluding blessing of the people (Exodus 39:43). The overlap in terminology between the summaries of completion in Genesis 2:1–3 and the Exodus texts (Exodus 39:32, 42, 43; 40:16, 33) include the verbs *ʿāśâ* (to make, do) and *kālâ* (to complete) and the noun *mĕlāʾkâ* (work). The word for *work* in the phrase *all the work* is, however, represented by *mĕlāʾkâ* in Genesis 2:2–3 and Exodus 39:43 and by *ʿăbōdâ* in Exodus 39:32 and 39:42.

109. Hamilton notes that "this key phrase unites, via an intertextual allusion, world building and tabernacle building, the creation of a world and the creation of a shrine"; *Genesis*, 1.112.

perlative).[110] Indeed, while *rûaḥ* can certainly mean "breath," "wind," or "spirit" and *ʾĕlōhîm* may sometimes be a superlative, all occurrences of the compound expression *rûaḥ ʾĕlōhîm* in the Old Testament refer to *God's* breath/wind/spirit.[111] In other words, the connection between Genesis 1 and Exodus 31 suggests that *rûaḥ ʾĕlōhîm* in Genesis 1:2 is not a reference to a precreation chaos (implied in the notion of a mighty wind or storm) but rather to God's creative presence hovering in the wings. Thus the precreation presence of the *rûaḥ ʾĕlōhîm* might signal that God is "holding his breath" (so to speak), getting ready to vocalize creation into being ("let there be"). This would be consistent with the connection between God's creative word and breath according to Psalm 33:6: "By the word of YHWH the heavens were made, / and all their host by the breath of his mouth." It is significant that the section of this psalm that deals with creation (33:6–9) recapitulates precisely the pattern of Genesis 1 in moving from the heavens (days 1 and 4) to the waters (days 2 and 5) to the earth (days 3 and 6).

Beyond the association of word and breath, however, the presence of the *rûaḥ ʾĕlōhîm* in Genesis 1 might even suggest that the newly completed cosmic sanctuary would then be indwelt precisely by this divine presence (as the glory of YHWH filled the tabernacle when it was completed in Exodus 40:34). Thus Nahum Sarna suggests that *rûaḥ* in Genesis 1:2 might be "a term heralding the arrival of God, expressing His immanence, or symbolizing His presence."[112] This possibility does not depend on the supposed theology of the priestly writer (indeed, on some critical accounts, it is contradicted by this theology),[113] but arises from reading Genesis 1 in connection with a text like Isaiah 66:1–2, where God is said to be enthroned in heaven over the earth. That this is an image of God's immanence becomes clear when we reflect on Terrence Fretheim's astute suggestion that heaven, where God's throne or dwelling is often said to be located, does not transcend creation, but is structurally part of the created cosmos in Israel's worldview. As Fretheim explains, "The heavens

110. Such as von Rad, who thinks it means "terrible storm"; *Genesis*, 49.

111. Besides Genesis 1:2; Exodus 31:3; 35:31, the compound expression *rûaḥ ʾĕlōhîm* occurs in Genesis 41:38; Numbers 24:2; 1 Samuel 10:10; 11:6; 19:20, 23; Ezekiel 11:24; 2 Chronicles 15:1; 24:20.

112. Nahum Sarna, *Genesis* (JPS Torah Commentary: Philadelphia: Jewish Publication Society, 1989), 6 (this is one of three possible interpretations of *rûaḥ* in Genesis 1:2 that Sarna proposes; see also 353 n. 9).

113. Thus William P. Brown, following a source-critical understanding of the P document in the Pentateuch, claims that in the priestly theology God's presence does not indwell the cosmos, but only the tabernacle; *The Ethos of the Cosmos: The Genesis of Moral Imagination in the Bible* (Grand Rapids: Eerdmans, 1999), 86. Brown may indeed be correct here concerning priestly theology. But if this is so, it raises the question whether Genesis 1:1–2:3 differs from this theology (and perhaps even calls it into question).

(or semantic equivalents) thus become a shorthand way of referring to the abode of God *within* the world."[114] We even have a text like Jeremiah 23:24, where YHWH critiques any attempt to limit the divine presence by asserting, "Do I not fill heaven and earth?" (NRSV).

If the cosmos can be understood as indwelt by the creator, then the language of Psalm 119:91 ("all things are your servants"; NRSV) might well refer not only to the obedience of creatures to their cosmic ruler, but also to liturgical service in the cosmic sanctuary. This is consistent with Psalm 148, which exhorts all creatures—humans, angels, animals, even the sun, moon, mountains, and trees—to praise the creator, as if all creatures constituted a host of worshipers in the cosmic temple, over which God is exalted as king. This picture of creation as a cosmic temple also suggests the appropriateness of humanity as God's image in the symbolic world of Genesis 1. For just as no pagan temple in the ancient Near East could be complete without the installation of the cult image of the deity to whom the temple was dedicated, so creation in Genesis 1 is not complete (or "very good") until God creates humanity on the sixth day as *imago Dei*, in order to represent and mediate the divine presence on earth.[115]

But another interesting analogy between God's construction of the cosmos and the account of the building of the tabernacle in Exodus sheds further light on the *imago Dei*—namely, the role of Bezalel, the master craftsman. As overseer of tabernacle construction, Bezalel is filled (Exodus 31:3) with "wisdom" (*ḥokmâ*), "understanding" (*tĕbûnâ*), and "knowledge" (*daʿat*), precisely the same triad by which God is said to have created the world in Proverbs 3:19–20. To this is added that Bezalel is filled with "all crafts" or "all works" (*kol-mĕlāʾkâ*), the very phrase used in Genesis 2:2–3 for "all the works" that God completed in creation. Therefore, not only does the tabernacle replicate in microcosm the macrocosmic sanctuary of the entire created order, but these verbal resonances suggest that Bezalel's discerning artistry in tabernacle-building images God's own construction of the cosmos. Bezalel's Spirit-filled craftsmanship, which imitates God's primordial wise design and construction of the cosmos, is functionally equivalent to the *imago Dei*.

Even Bezalel's position of administrative oversight and authority in tabernacle-building is significant as a reflection of God's lordship in creation. Beyond the typical ancient Near Eastern association of rul-

---

114. Terence E. Fretheim, *The Suffering of God* (Overtures to Biblical Theology; Philadelphia: Fortress, 1984), 37 (emphasis original).

115. I am indebted for this insight to Rikki E. Watts, "On the Edge of the Millennium: Making Sense of Genesis 1," in *Living in the LambLight: Christianity and Contemporary Challenges to the Gospel* (ed. Hans Boersma; Vancouver, BC: Regent College Publishing, 2001), 148; and Scott N. Morschauser, "Created in the Image of God: The Ancient Near Eastern Background of the *Imago Dei*," *Theology Matters* 3.6 (Nov.–Dec. 1997): 3.

ers with building projects, this receives confirmation if we examine the only occurrence of *rûaḥ ʾĕlōhîm* between Genesis 1:2 and Exodus 31:31 in the Hebrew Bible. In Genesis 41:38–39 the Egyptians recognize the presence of *rûaḥ ʾĕlōhîm* in Joseph, since God has made him discerning and wise. Significantly, Joseph's Spirit-filled wisdom is associated in the text with his position of royal authority. Whereas Bezalel's wisdom empowers him for overseeing the construction of the tabernacle, Joseph is made pharaoh's second-in-command and placed over the entire land of Egypt (41:40–46). The associations between Spirit, wisdom, and power are thus quite clear and suggest that human rule and subduing of the earth in Genesis 1 involves an element of artful discernment in the service of the (cultural) shaping and transformation of the world, in imitation of God's wise acts of ordering and crafting what was originally formless into a habitable cosmic structure.

Implications for the *Imago Dei*

The conclusion toward which this chapter moves is thus twofold. On the one hand, careful exegesis of Genesis 1:26–28, in conjunction with an intertextual reading of the symbolic world of Genesis 1, does indeed suggest that the *imago Dei* refers to human rule, that is, the exercise of power on God's behalf in creation. This may be articulated in two different, but complementary, ways. Said one way, humans are *like God* in exercising royal power on earth. Said in another way, the divine ruler *delegated* to humans a share in his rule of the earth. Both are important ways of expressing the meaning of the *imago Dei*. The first expression—the notion of likeness to the divine ruler—suggests the image as "representational," indicating a *similarity or analogy* between God and humans. The second expression—the delegation of, or sharing in, God's rule—suggests the image as "representative," designating the responsible *office and task* entrusted to humanity in administering the earthly realm on God's behalf. But these expressions are not simply alternative; they are integrally connected. It is precisely *because* the representational aspect of the image consists in a functional similarity or analogy between God and humanity, specifically concerning the exercise of (royal) power, that the image can be articulated also as representative, referring to the human office of representing God's rule/power in the world.[116] A royal-functional reading of the *imago Dei* is therefore essentially confirmed.

116. Our interpretation so far seems to favor the reading of the preposition *beth* in *bĕṣalmēnû* (in our image) as a so-called *beth essentiae*, such that humans are created *as* God's image (a rather clear use of *beth essentiae* is found in Exodus 6:3, where God states,

On the other hand, this reading is significantly nuanced. Whether in the ancient Near East or the Bible in general or in Genesis 1:1–2:3 in particular, the meaning of "rule" goes well beyond our contemporary hermeneutical preconceptions. The royal metaphor (and thus the *imago Dei* as rule) does not exclude—but integrally includes—wisdom and artful construction. The God who rules the creation by his authoritative word is also the supreme artisan who constructs a complex and habitable cosmic structure. This portrayal of God as artisan might suggest that God's twofold creative activity of separation and filling (represented by the two panels of creative days in Genesis 1) is replicated in the twofold task assigned to humanity in 1:28 ("fill the earth and subdue it"), though here the order is reversed. That is, humans are called to imitate or continue God's own twofold creative activity by populating and organizing (in a manner appropriate to humans) the unformed and unfilled earth (which presents a partial parallel to the *tōhû wābōhû* of 1:2). God has, in other words, started the process of forming and filling, which humans, as God's earthly delegates, are to continue. Even the reverse order of this twofold activity makes sense since humans must first reproduce before they can engage in the task of organizing/subduing the earth.[117]

Whether this particular twofold stylistic correspondence is intended by the text, the human task of exercising power over the earth is nevertheless modeled on God's creative activity, which, in Genesis 1, is clearly developmental and formative, involving the process of transforming the *tōhû wābōhû* into an ordered, harmonious cosmos. By implication, then, the human calling as *imago Dei* is itself developmental and transformative and may be helpfully understood as equivalent to the labor or work of forming culture or developing civilization. Besides the definitive human task represented in 2:15 by the agricultural metaphor (to "till" and "keep" the garden), which is a paradigmatic form of organizing and transforming the environment into a habitable world for humans, we may note the pervasive interest throughout the primeval history in human cultural achievements and technological innovations such as city-building (4:17; 11:1–9) and nomadic livestock-herding, music, and metallurgy (4:20–22). The human task thus reflects in significant ways the divine artisan portrayed in Genesis 1 as artfully constructing a world.

But the *imago Dei* also includes a priestly or cultic dimension. In the cosmic sanctuary of God's world, humans have pride of place and

---

"I appeared to Abraham, Isaac, and Jacob *as* El Shaddai"). For an extended discussion of the complicated linguistic issues here, see Clines, "Image of God in Man," 70–80.

117. For an excellent analysis of the cultural mandate in Genesis 1:28 in connection with the *imago Dei*, see A. M. Wolters, "The Foundational Command: 'Subdue the Earth!'" in *Year of Jubilee; Cultural Mandate; Worldview* (Study Pamphlet 382; Potchefstrom: Institute for Reformational Studies, 1999), 27–32.

supreme responsibility, not just as royal stewards and cultural shapers of the environment, but (taking seriously the temple imagery) as priests of creation, actively mediating divine blessing to the nonhuman world and—in a postfall situation—interceding on behalf of a groaning creation until that day when heaven and earth are redemptively transformed to fulfill God's purposes for justice and shalom.[118] The human vocation as *imago Dei* in God's world thus corresponds in important respects to Israel's vocation as a "royal priesthood" among the nations (Exodus 19:6).[119] As we shall see in chapter 3, this conclusion is fundamentally confirmed by the ancient Near Eastern background of the image.

118. Indeed, we may say that due to the disobedience of humanity (God's priestly representatives on earth) the divine presence does not fully indwell the world. We thus await the day when God's glorious presence will redemptively fill the earth "as the waters cover the sea" (Isaiah 11:9; Habakkuk 2:14).

119. Instead of the traditional picture of the *imago Dei* as a mirror (reflecting God), we should understand it as more like a *prism* refracting the concentrated light of God's glory through a multitude of human sociocultural activities, as we interact with our earthly environment.

PART 2

The Social Context of the Image

3

An Ancient Near Eastern Background for the *Imago Dei*

Having examined the meaning of the *imago Dei* in the context of the symbolic world of Genesis 1, it is now our task to explore the social and historical world behind the text, to see what light this might shed on the meaning of the image. It is not my intent to claim that knowledge of the historical context of the text is strictly necessary for understanding the meaning of the image. In the field of Old Testament studies, any reconstruction of a text's historical context is largely a matter of hypothesis and plausibility. Reconstructing the historical context of Genesis 1 is particularly difficult, since there is little that could reliably indicate its date or provenance. The meaning of the image, thus, cannot be made to depend on something as tenuous as a particular historical reconstruction. Nevertheless, exploration of the possible historical background and social context of the text may well deepen the understanding of the *imago Dei* that we have arrived at on other grounds.

Given the propensity of Old Testament scholars to seek the background of the image of God by recourse to ancient Near Eastern parallels, it is incumbent upon us to examine—and critically evaluate—these putative parallels for their value in shedding light on Genesis 1. In this task a significant conversation partner will be Edward Curtis, whose 1984 doctoral dissertation *Man as the Image of God in Genesis in the Light of Ancient Near Eastern Parallels* is the most comprehensive sifting of the evidence to date and constitutes a helpful guide to the lay of the land.[1] Although I read the evidence somewhat differently from Curtis, interaction with his arguments will be important for clarifying my own position concerning a Mesopotamian background for the biblical *imago Dei*.

The question of parallels between the Bible and extrabiblical material is, of course, immensely complex in terms of methodology. As Helmer Ringgren articulates the matter, many fundamental questions remain to be answered in any comparative study: "What is a parallel, and what use do we make of it? What does it mean in its original context? How has it found its way into the Bible? What does it mean in its biblical context?"[2] Whereas it is the task of the present chapter and chapter 4 to sift and then utilize relevant parallels in reconstructing a plausible social context for the biblical *imago Dei* (roughly equivalent to Ringgren's first three questions), chapter 5 will focus on the implications of these parallels for interpreting what the Old Testament means by the *imago Dei* (equivalent to Ringgren's final question).

In the secondary literature on the *imago Dei* in Genesis 1, four sets of ancient Near Eastern data are typically adduced as possible parallels to the biblical notion: (1) a reference in the *Gilgamesh Epic* that describes Enkidu as an image (or double) of Gilgamesh the king; (2) two references in Egyptian wisdom literature to the creation of humans as the images of a god; (3) the widespread practice of Egyptian and Mesopotamian kings setting up statues or images of themselves in lands where they are physically absent; and (4) Egyptian and Mesopotamian references to kings (and sometimes priests) as the image of various deities.

These four sets of parallels are of quite different types. Whereas the first two sets of parallels constitute a few specific texts that are thought to have influenced Genesis 1, the last two sets draw upon a large range of texts (indicative of widespread ideology and practice in the ancient world) that could have influenced Genesis 1. Furthermore, there are serious linguistic

1. Edward Mason Curtis, *Man as the Image of God in Genesis in the Light of Ancient Near Eastern Parallels* (Ph.D. dissertation; University of Pennsylvania, 1984). The dissertation was supervised by biblical scholar and ancient Near Eastern specialist Jeffrey Tigay. Curtis's basic findings are briefly summarized in his "Image of God (OT)," in *The Anchor Bible Dictionary* (ed. David Noel Freedman et al.; New York: Doubleday, 1992), 3.389–91.

2. Helmer Ringgren, "The Impact of the Ancient Near East on Israelite Tradition," in *Tradition and Theology in the Old Testament* (ed. Douglas A. Knight; Philadelphia: Fortress, 1977), 32–33.

and/or historical difficulties in treating the first two sets as relevant for interpreting the biblical *imago Dei*. Nevertheless, it will be helpful for us to examine each set of possible parallels on its own merits.[3]

The Image as Counterpart

One rather prominent text sometimes cited as a parallel to the biblical *imago Dei* is the *Gilgamesh Epic*, which was certainly well known in biblical times. The specific reference occurs at the start of the epic and concerns the wild man Enkidu, who is created as a *zikru* or image of King Gilgamesh of Uruk. Due to Gilgamesh's uncontrollable libido, whereby he claims the right to have sex with all women in Uruk, the city is in chaos. When the people of Uruk complain to the gods, they in turn appeal to the creator-goddess Aruru to provide a companion for Gilgamesh, one in whom he would meet his match and who would thereby be able to contain, or sublimate, his urges:[4]

> The great Aruru they called:
>   "Thou, Aruru, didst create [the man];
> Create now his double [*zikru*];
>   His stormy heart let him match.
> Let them contend, that Uruk may have peace!"
> When Aruru heard this,
>   A double [*zikru*] of Anu she conceived within her.
> Aruru washed her hands,
>   Pinched off clay and cast it on the steppe.
> [On the step]pe she created valiant Enkidu,
>   Offspring . . . , essence of Ninurta. (1.2.30–35)

Friedrich Horst, in his Barthian reading of the *imago Dei*, cites this passage in support of the notion that humanity is created as a relational "counterpart" to God ("corresponding" to the divine), in much the manner that Genesis 2 describes the creation of woman as a helper suitable for the man.[5] Although it is clear from the epic that Enkidu is indeed

---

3. I am indebted to Richard A. Henshaw, professor emeritus of Old Testament at Bexley Hall, Rochester, NY, for helpful critical comments on the present chapter.

4. Translation from E. A. Speiser, "The Epic of Gilgamesh," in *ANET* 74.

5. Friedrich Horst, "Face to Face: The Biblical Doctrine of the Image of God" (trans. John Bright), *Interpretation* 4 (1950): 265. The *Gilgamesh Epic* is also claimed in support of a relational reading of the image by V. Maag, "Sumerische und babylonische Mythen von der Erschaffung des Menschen," *Asiatische Studien* 8 (1954): 85–106, cited by Claus Westermann, *Genesis: A Commentary* (trans. John J. Scullion; Minneapolis: Augsburg, 1984), 1.154.

something like Gilgamesh's counterpart (he is Gilgamesh's physical match, and they become inseparable friends), this reading of the *zikru* passage suffers from many problems.

First, the sense of the Akkadian term *zikru* here is disputed. It typically means "word, name, command, utterance" (related to *zakāru*, to speak) and not "image," as is recognized by even Horst.[6] The notion of image, if present, would then be derivative, possibly in the sense that one's name is an image or double of oneself. By extension, therefore, Enkidu could perhaps be a "second" Gilgamesh (or "double," as Speiser translates it).[7]

Alternatively, one could arrive at a similar notion by a quite different route. According to A. Leo Oppenheim, we are to interpret *zikru* not in relation to *zakāru*, but rather against the background of an ancient lexical series that equates Sumerian NÍG.SAG.ÍL.LA with Akkadian *zu-kur-ru*.[8] Curtis notes that NÍG.SAG.ÍL.LA is usually translated in Akkadian by *puḫu* or *andanānu*, both of which mean "substitute," and thus suggests that if we transfer this meaning to the use of *zikru* here, it might indicate that Enkidu is Gilgamesh's counterpart. Curtis himself, however, ultimately rejects this interpretation.[9]

Beyond the particular linguistic difficulties of this interpretation, it is unclear in whose image Enkidu is to be created (or whose substitute he is), since the relevant word is missing from line 30 (indicated by the term *the man* in square brackets). In the absence of the relevant word, various translators offer different possibilities. While Alexander Heidel supplies the name "Gilgamesh," both Stephanie Dalley and Oppenheim have "mankind," and Speiser (above) leaves it more ambiguous with "the man."[10]

---

6. See *CAD* Z 112–16 for the range of meanings.

7. This seems to be the reasoning behind *CAD* Z 116b, which agrees with Speiser vis-à-vis the *Gilgamesh Epic* and cites another Akkadian text that uses *zikru* in this way (*CAD* Z 116c). The interpretation of Johannes Hehn could be seen as a variant of this; he claims that the use of *zikru* indicates that Aruru is called upon to create someone deserving of Gilgamesh's *name*, hence someone *like* him; "Zum Terminus 'Bild Gottes,'" in *Festschrift Eduard Sachau* (ed. Gotthold Weil; Berlin: Reimer, 1915), 46.

8. The lexical series (basically an ancient Sumerian-Akkadian dictionary) is known as *Nabnitu*. See A. Leo Oppenheim, "Mesopotamian Mythology II," *Orientalia* n.s. 17 (1948): 23–24 n. 5, cited by Curtis, *Man as the Image of God*, 174, 238 n. 355.

9. Curtis, *Man as the Image of God*, 174 (citing *CAD* Z 153b). Among the reasons Curtis (127–28) suggests for doubting that this interpretation is relevant to the meaning of the image of God in Genesis 1 is that Akkadian already has a word for image (*ṣalmu*) that is cognate to Hebrew *ṣelem* and the word *puḫu* (substitute) is used with *ṣalmu* to mean substitute image/statue (*ṣalam pūḫi*).

10. See Alexander Heidel, *The Gilgamesh Epic and Old Testament Parallels* (2nd ed.; Chicago: University of Chicago Press, 1949), 18; Stephanie Dalley, *Myths from Mesopotamia: Creation, the Flood, Gilgamesh, and Others* (Oxford: Oxford University Press, 1989), 52; and Oppenheim, "Mesopotamian Mythology II," 23 n. 4. Although Oppenheim translates *zikru* as "substitute," his suggestion that the missing word here is "mankind" militates

To further complicate matters, the text says that in response to the request to create a *zikru* of Gilgamesh or humankind, Aruru conceives a *zikru* of Anu (the sky-god and patron-god of Uruk). It is only after this (mental) conception that she actually creates Enkidu from a piece of clay. *Zikru* may thus be more accurately translated in the second instance as "idea" or "mental image" (in accordance with which one shapes the actual plastic work), with the text indicating that in this particular case the goddess modeled her idea on Anu.

This interpretation seems to be corroborated by a similar use of *zikru* in the Akkadian myth *Descent of Ishtar to the Underworld*, a much truncated version of the famous older and longer Sumerian work that described the goddess Inanna's descent into the underworld. As in the *Gilgamesh Epic*, the creation of a particular person in the Ishtar myth is proposed in response to a crisis, although this time the crisis is widespread infertility (indeed, lack of all sexual intercourse) on earth, which resulted from the imprisonment of Ishtar (goddess of fertility) in the underworld by her sister, the goddess Ereshkigal. Having been implored to intervene, Ea (the god of wisdom) determines to rescue Ishtar by sending someone who, unlike most human males (exactly how is unclear and thus debated in the literature), will be able to enter and return from the underworld unscathed:

> Ea in his wise heart conceived an image [*zikru*],
> And created Asushunamir, a eunuch. (lines rev. 11–12)[11]

Whereas the language of the *Gilgamesh Epic* specified a *zikru* first of Gilgamesh (or humankind) and then of Anu, in the Ishtar text it is unclear just whose image Asushunamir might be, unless *zikru* refers to the mental image that Ea has of the yet-to-be-created Asushunamir.

---

against the counterpart notion, since Enkidu is not (on his reading) the substitute/ counterpart of Gilgamesh.

11. Translation from E. A. Speiser, "Descent of Ishtar to the Nether World," in *ANET* 108. Translations other than "eunuch" have been proposed for *assinnu*, the term describing Asushunamir's status. His name literally means "his appearance is bright" (Dalley, *Myths from Mesopotamia*, 158) or "he is resplendent as he comes forth" (Benjamin R. Foster, *Before the Muses: An Anthology of Akkadian Literature*, vol. 1: *Archaic, Classical, Mature* [Bethesda, MD: CDL, 1993], 407), and this has been understood to mean that he is (besides being a eunuch, proposed by Speiser, acknowledged as a possibility by Dalley), a good-looking playboy (Dalley) or an impersonator, possibly a male prostitute or transvestite (Foster). Richard A. Henshaw, in the context of examining the many, complex uses of the term in Mesopotamian literature, suggests that the *assinnu* in the *Descent of Ishtar to the Underworld* is "of in-between sex [that] made him impervious to the sexual rites and power that Ereshkigal, following the example of her sister, could impose upon him"; *Female and Male: The Cultic Personnel: The Bible and the Rest of the Ancient Near East* (Princeton Theological Monographs; Allison Park, PA: Pickwick, 1994), 288.

But if this understanding of *zikru* as mental image is correct and is transferable to the *Gilgamesh Epic*, how Enkidu could be a counterpart to Gilgamesh is unclear.

There is, however, one final way to read *zikru* that might give some credence to the counterpart notion. In his translation of the Ishtar text, Benjamin Foster plays on the sense of *zikru* as "word" and renders it as "(what was) called for."[12] Many scholars (including Dalley) likewise translate the second use of *zikru* in the *Gilgamesh Epic* as the "word" of Anu, possibly in the sense that Aruru's conception of Enkidu is "what Anu commanded."[13] If we transfer this meaning to the first use of *zikru* in the *Gilgamesh Epic*, we could possibly speak of Enkidu as Gilgamesh's counterpart, in the sense of a creation that was apt or appropriate to him (just what was called for). But this interpretation is highly tenuous and has not been, to my knowledge, suggested as the basis for the counterpart notion.[14]

To complicate matters even further, however, Dalley proposes a quite different meaning for the first use of *zikru* in the *Gilgamesh Epic*. Whereas Oppenheim suggests that the missing Akkadian word in line 30 was *amēlûtu* (mankind), Dalley conjectures that the missing word was *zikru/zikaru* (man, male). Based on this conjecture, she suggests that the use of *zikru* in the following line was meant to be a pun with the missing word.[15] Hence she translates *zikru* in line 31 of the *Gilgamesh Epic* rather neutrally as "someone" and in the *Descent of Ishtar to the Underworld* simply as "a person."[16]

---

12. Foster, *Before the Muses*, 1.407.

13. This is the suggestion of Curtis, *Man as the Image of God*, 238 n. 357. Dalley's rendering is found in *Myths from Mesopotamia*, 52.

14. Indeed, this interpretation is directly contradicted by Andrew George's reading of the text, even though he understands *zikru* to mean something close to Dalley's proposal (in the sense of Anu's idea or what he thought of). George takes the first use of *zikru* (in line 31) as referring not to Gilgamesh at all, but (like the second use) to Anu. He bases this on what he takes to be a stanza missing from the standard version of Gilgamesh (but preserved in a fragment of an older version) that refers to the people's complaint coming first to Anu, who responds by telling them to ask Aruru to create someone to vie with Gilgamesh. He thus translates "now fashion/create his *zikru*" in line 31 (line 96 in his numbering) as "now fashion what Anu has thought of!" If this reconstruction is correct, it totally invalidates the notion of Enkidu as a counterpart of Gilgamesh. See Andrew George, *The Epic of Gilgamesh: The Babylonian Epic Poem and Other Texts in Akkadian and Sumerian* (London: Penguin, 1999), 4.

15. Dalley, *Myths from Mesopotamia*, 126 n. 9, 161 n. 12. Jeffrey Tigay cites an older fragment of the *Gilgamesh Epic* that has the word *a-wi-lam* (man, mankind) at this point; *The Evolution of the Gilgamesh Epic* (Philadelphia: University of Pennsylvania Press, 1982), 192–93, 266.

16. Dalley (*Myths from Mesopotamia*, 52) translates *zikru* as "someone" in *Gilgamesh Epic* line 31 and as "word(?)" in line 35, although her insertion of a question mark indicates

Given the uncertainty of the above issues of translation and interpretation (Jeffrey Tigay, in perplexity, leaves *zikru* untranslated),[17] it would be extremely unwise to treat the *Gilgamesh Epic* as a reliable indicator of the meaning of the *imago Dei* in Genesis. Indeed, Genesis, by comparison, is a model of clarity, and if they were to be compared, we might ironically suggest that Genesis more plausibly sheds light on the *Gilgamesh Epic*!

Egyptian Wisdom Literature

A more plausible parallel, by comparison, consists in two famous Egyptian wisdom texts (both of which contain admonitions or instructions addressed by fathers to sons) that refer to the creation of humans as images of the divine. The first such reference typically cited is found in the *Instruction for Merikare*, a treatise on kingship by an unknown king addressed to his son Merikare, dating from the twenty-second century B.C.E., during the so-called First Intermediate Period, after the fall of the Old Kingdom:[18]

> Well directed are men, the cattle of the god. He made heaven and earth according to their desire, and he repelled the water-monster. He made the breath of life (for) their nostrils. They who have issued from his body are his images [*snnw*]. He arises in heaven according to their desire. He made for them plants, animals, fowl, and fish to feed them. (lines 131–33)[19]

Since it is extremely common in the royal ideology of ancient Egypt (recorded in a variety of literary texts and inscriptions) for various pharaohs to be called the image of a particular god, the *Instruction for*

---

her uncertainty: "Now create someone for him, to match(?) the ardour(?) of his energies!" (line 31); "When Aruru heard this, she created inside herself the word(?) of Anu" (line 35). Dalley's translation of the relevant line in the *Descent of Ishtar to the Underworld* reads simply: "Ea, in the wisdom of his heart, created a person" (158).

17. See his discussion of the matter in *Evolution of the Gilgamesh Epic*, 266–76.

18. During the First Intermediate Period, Egypt was divided by rival dynasties in the north and south, reigning from Herakleopolis and Thebes, respectively. The writer of the *Instruction for Merikare* seems to be a northern pharaoh (evident from comments he makes to his son about how to treat the southern region, in lines 71–76).

19. Translation from John A. Wilson, "The Instruction for King Meri-Ka-Re," in *ANET* 417. Miriam Lichtheim's translation (*Ancient Egyptian Literature: A Book of Readings*, vol. 1: *The Old and Middle Kingdoms* [Berkeley: University of California Press, 1973], 106) is not substantially different from Wilson's rendering: "Well tended is mankind—god's cattle, / He made sky and earth for their sake, / He subdued the water monster, / He made breath for their noses to live. / They are his images, who came from his body, / He shines in the sky for their sake; / He made for them plants and cattle, / Fowl and fish to feed them."

Merikare is sometimes cited as an example of the "democratization" of this ideology.[20] Whether this atypical (and admittedly remarkable) application to the entire human race of what is typically an elitist image turns out to be a significant parallel to Genesis 1 is something we shall have to investigate. However, that the *Instruction for Merikare* predates by some five hundred years any attested reference to an Egyptian pharaoh as an image of a god suggests that the notion of democratization is anachronistic when applied to this text without further proof.

The second Egyptian wisdom text (over half a millennium later) is the *Instruction of Ani*, which consists in exhortations from Ani, a scribe or wisdom teacher, to his son Khonsuhotep about proper living. The father's wisdom instruction is then followed by three rounds of dialogue wherein the son replies to the instruction and is replied to, in turn, by the father (who gets the last word). In the son's second reply, where he protests his father's likening a receptive student to a domesticated animal, we find the *imago Dei* reference:

> Men are in the image of the god <in> their custom of hearing a man in regard to his reply. It is not the wise alone who is in his image [*snnw*], while the multitude are every kind of cattle.[21]

Here we find two separate uses of the image of god. Whereas the first functions as an ethical or behavioral ideal for the father or wisdom teacher to follow (he should act like the gods in listening), the second is applied to the entire human race (and not just to the wise) to assert their dignity.

Although R. J. Williams's translation of the *Instruction of Ani* is cited by both Curtis and Tigay[22] in their discussions of the text as a possible parallel to Genesis 1, Miriam Lichtheim's rendering is quite different at one important point:[23]

> Man resembles the god in his way
> If he listens to a man's answer.
> ⌜One (man) cannot know his fellow,⌝
> If the masses are beasts.

20. For example, Westermann, *Genesis*, 1.35.

21. Translation from R. J. Williams, "Scribal Training in Ancient Egypt," *Journal of the American Oriental Society* 92 (1972): 221.

22. Curtis, *Man as the Image of God*, 196 n. 66; Jeffrey H. Tigay, "The Image of God and the Flood: Some New Developments," in *Studies in Jewish Education and Judaica in Honor of Louis Newman* (ed. Alexander M. Shapiro and Burton I. Cohen; New York: Ktav, 1984), 173.

23. Miriam Lichtheim, *Ancient Egyptian Literature: A Book of Readings*, vol. 2: *The New Kingdom* (Berkeley: University of California Press, 1976), 145.

Although this translation does not alter the general, overall point or sense of Williams's rendering, in that both translations have the son protesting an elitist pedagogy by affirming the dignity of the masses, it is significant that Lichtheim's use of half-brackets indicates that the text is here partially broken. Furthermore, her translation of the broken text, while suggesting that the masses are not to be regarded as beasts, does not utilize the image at all.

Instead, Lichtheim (whose translations of Egyptian texts have become widely accepted as standard) translates the relevant word *snnw* as "fellow," not "image," and takes "his" as a reference not to the god, but to "man" or "one (man)."[24] What this divergence of translation signals is that while *snnw* as used here is identical in form to that used in the *Instruction for Merikare* for image, it may well be a different word entirely, from *snw* (two), whereas *snnw* in the *Instruction for Merikare* is from *snn* (image, likeness, statue).[25] This does not mean that the translation "image" must be rejected, only that the matter is not straightforward.[26]

If we follow Lichtheim's translation, we have a single use of the idea of image or resemblance to the divine in the first half of the *Instruction of Ani* quotation, used as something like an ethical norm by the son, in order to call the father to task for his elitist, top-down pedagogy. This is not technical image terminology applied to the entire human race. Rather, what we have is an ad hoc functional appeal from the student that the teacher treat him with dignity, since even the gods listen to humans. It is doubtful, however, on the strength of this translation alone that the *Instruction of Ani* could be legitimately cited (as is sometimes done) as a text promoting democratization of the royal Egyptian image of god.

If, on the other hand, we follow Williams's (contestable) translation, we get a second use of the image in the latter half of the quotation, namely, the application of a technical term for image to the masses in order to assert their dignity and right to be heard when they dissent from the instruction of the wise. This second use could legitimately be called a democratized image of God and would indeed provide a remarkable parallel to the image in Genesis 1.

Thus the *Instruction for Merikare* and possibly the *Instruction of Ani* (on one reading) seem to proclaim, in a manner reminiscent of Genesis

24. Lichtheim's "one (man)" corresponds to Williams's "alone," and she renders Williams's "the wise" not as a noun (or substantive adjective) but by the verb "know."

25. Curtis, *Man as the Image of God*, 92–93.

26. Indeed, some scholars recognize the distinction between the two words, yet render it "image" or "equal"; for example, Curtis (*Man as the Image of God*, 92), who cites Erik Hornung, *Conceptions of God in Ancient Egypt* (trans. John Baines; Ithaca: Cornell University Press, 1982), 138.

1, the dignity and exalted stature of humanity by recourse to a notion of the image of god (though this dignity is not explicitly royal in either *Merikare* or *Ani*).

The *Instruction for Merikare*, however, is further significant for containing many other parallels to the Genesis 1 creation story, all of which occur in the immediate vicinity of the image.[27] First of all, like the creator in Genesis 1, the god in *Merikare* is clearly said to have created heaven and earth. His repelling of the water monster is a possible parallel to God's dividing of the waters on the second and third days of creation.[28] Furthermore, the god here provides the breath of life for human nostrils (a parallel with 2:7) and gives both plants and animals for food to humanity, a variation of God's assignment of a vegetarian diet for humanity in Genesis 1.

It is thus undeniable that many of the ideas in *Instruction for Merikare* parallel those in Genesis 1. Parallel ideas, however, do not constitute historical influence. And without some sort of historical connection between Genesis 1 and either of these texts (or the ideas therein), it does not make sense to utilize them to interpret the biblical notion of *imago Dei*.

Indeed, a historical connection seems unlikely for many reasons. First of all, neither the *Instruction for Merikare* nor the *Instruction of Ani* is contiguous in time with any period in the history of Israel as a nation. Whereas the main manuscript of the *Instruction for Merikare* (Papyrus Leningrad 1116A) is dated in the Eighteenth Dynasty (second half of the fifteenth century B.C.E.), the original text was composed in the twenty-second century, a millennium before the exodus from Egypt and four hundred years before the time that Abraham is supposed to have lived. The date of the *Instruction of Ani* is somewhat less clear. The primary manuscript (a papyrus) derives from the Twenty-first or Twenty-second Dynasty (eleventh to eighth centuries B.C.E.), and it is suggested that the text was composed in the unstable period following the religious revolution of Akhenaten, which would place it in the reign of Tutankhamen, at the end of the fifteenth century B.C.E.[29] Yet the title of the work is preserved in a fragmentary tablet in the Berlin museum,

27. There are other differences between the two texts. Whereas the *Instruction for Merikare* describes the human race as the god's cattle, the *Instruction of Ani* explicitly rejects the derogatory notion of humans being mere beasts. It is further significant that the *Instruction for Merikare* associates being the god's image with generation from the god's body, while the *Instruction of Ani* makes no mention of this notion.

28. An alternative translation ("he suppressed the greed of the waters") is given by R. O. Faulkner, "The Teaching for Merikare," in *The Literature of Egypt: An Anthology of Stories, Instructions, and Poetry* (ed. William Kelly Simpson; rev. ed.; New Haven: Yale University Press, 1973), 191.

29. Curtis, *Man as the Image of God*, 147.

which describes Ani as a scribe of "the Palace of Queen Nefertari."
If this is Ahmes Nefertari, wife of Ahmose I, the first pharaoh of the
Eighteenth Dynasty, the text's origin would be placed in the early sixteenth century B.C.E.[30] Either of these dates would put the *Instruction
of Ani* before the traditional date of the exodus (usually thought to be
the thirteenth century).

Of course, early dating of these texts does not in itself rule out historical influence on Genesis, as long as the relevant ideas were propagated
in later times either by accessible textual copies or by oral tradition. The
trouble is that both the *Instruction for Merikare* and the *Instruction of
Ani* are distinctly atypical texts, proposing ideas that were common in
Egypt only when applied to the pharaoh, not to the mass of humanity
(with the *Instruction for Merikare*, this goes well beyond the image). It is
suggested that the unusual ideas they contain are perhaps to be explained
from both texts being derived from transitional times of political crisis,
when the old social order and the ideology that underpinned it were in a
state of destabilization.[31] This certainly fits the historical circumstances
of the *Instruction for Merikare*, though it would be true only of the later
date for the *Instruction of Ani* (which would place the text in the upheaval
following Akhenaten's unpopular reforms, in which he exalted himself
even beyond previous pharaohs in claiming an exclusive relationship
to the divine as sole interpreter and priest). If the earlier date is correct,
however, it is more likely that the democratization of the image in the
Instruction of Ani (if it is there at all) has its basis in the son's own experience of marginalization by his scribal father's elitist attitudes.[32] But
whatever the source of the ideas concerning the creation of humanity
in the image of god in both texts, these ideas found no ready home in
later Egyptian thought. Indeed, not only the texts, but also their ideas,
were roundly suppressed.[33]

30. Lichtheim, *Ancient Egyptian Literature*, 2.135, 136, 145 n. 1.

31. Curtis, *Man as the Image of God*, 146–48.

32. This is, of course, all hypothetical. Not only is it unclear if this notion is to be found
in the *Instruction of Ani*, we do not know if the son's objections are the record of a genuine
disagreement or merely a pedagogical device used in this wisdom text to add an element
of realism. Neither do we know if "father" and "son" are meant here literally or are
synonyms for "teacher" and "pupil."

33. The argument in favor of these texts influencing Genesis 1 suffers from analogous
problems to the claim that Akhenaten's famous *Hymn to the Aten* historically influenced
Psalm 104 (a claim made, for example, by J. H. Breasted, *The Dawn of Conscience* [New
York: Scribner, 1933], 366–70). While both the hymn and the psalm certainly contain
numerous parallel ideas concerning creation (as well as, it must be said, many dissimilar
ones), it is particularly difficult to explain how a single, atypical, suppressed text such as
the hymn, dating from an earlier historical period, could have come to influence the
writing of a biblical psalm.

A further point counts against the influence of the *Instruction for Merikare* on Genesis 1, namely, its association of image with the notion of generation from the body of a god. This notion of divine generation (applied here, atypically, to all humanity, though common in later Egyptian royal ideology as a description of the pharaoh's origins) is conceptually alien to the worldview of the Old Testament (and to Genesis 1), which studiously avoids concepts and metaphors of biological relationship between God and humanity or between God and Israel.[34] It is hardly likely, therefore, in view of the above factors, that either the *Instruction for Merikare* or the *Instruction of Ani* is a source of the image of God in Genesis 1. But if either of these isolated texts (or their ideas) did, in fact, influence the notion of *imago Dei* in Genesis, it is still quite unclear what light they shed on the interpretation of the biblical text.

Statues of Kings in Distant Lands

A third set of possible parallels to the biblical *imago Dei* is the common practice of ancient Near Eastern kings setting up images or statues of themselves in lands where they were physically absent as a symbol of their rule over these lands. Although there is no specific reference here to the image of a *god* (except insofar as a king might be viewed as quasidivine), this parallel, if valid, suggests that humanity in Genesis 1 functions as the authorized representative on earth of the divine creator-king.[35]

An early use of this analogy is found in the writings of the Antiochine church father Theodore of Mopsuestia (350–428 C.E.). Drawing not specifically on ancient Near Eastern parallels, but presumably on his own observations of fourth-century Roman imperial practice, Theodore describes humanity as the image of God in terms of "a statue erected in the center of the royal residence," explains T. Jansma. "After having built a city the king erects a statue to be honoured by the citizens. So God after having finished the creation set man as His image that all creatures in rendering service to him should pay honour to their Creator."[36]

---

34. This of course raises the interesting question of the place of *difference* or *distinctiveness* in comparative study of Israel and the ancient Near East, a topic that will be addressed in chapter 5.

35. In this analogy the divine king could perhaps be thought of as requiring representation on earth since he is enthroned in the heavens.

36. T. Jansma, "Investigations into the Early Syrian Fathers on Genesis: An Approach to the Exegesis of the Nestorian Church and to the Comparison of Nestorian and Jewish Exegesis," *Oudtestamentische Studiën* 12 (1958): 127.

Today this parallel is appealed to with increasing frequency (much more often than either the *Gilgamesh Epic* or the Egyptian wisdom texts) as the crucial clue to the *imago Dei* in Genesis. Thus John F. A. Sawyer, who actually *denies* the validity of a royal interpretation of the image, is nevertheless forced to cite this particular parallel (which he calls an "attractive theory") in order to critique it.[37] And Walter Brueggemann claims: "It is now generally agreed that the image of God reflected in human persons is after the manner of a king who establishes statues of himself to assert his sovereign rule where the king himself cannot be present."[38]

Although this possible parallel to the biblical *imago Dei* is very often cited in the secondary literature, it is noteworthy that most of these citations are filtered through a *single source*, namely, Gerhard von Rad, who popularized the notion in at least three places.[39] Von Rad in turn cites as *his* source for the idea an earlier article by Wilhelm Caspari.[40]

Yet, despite the filtering of this idea through limited sources, the ancient practice of kings setting up images of themselves in distant lands is quite well attested, both in inscriptions on the statues themselves and in royal documents describing the practice.[41] But while this practice is certainly well attested, its meaning is disputed. Thus J. Maxwell Miller argues that it is not at all clear that the purpose of these images was to represent the absent king's authority. Miller suggests, rather, that study of the statues' inscriptions indicates that they were understood more generally as memorials to the kings and their accomplishments.[42] This

---

37. John F. A. Sawyer, "The Meaning of בְּצֶלֶם אֱלֹהִים ('In the Image of God') in Genesis i–xi," *Journal of Theological Studies* 25 (1974): 421.

38. Walter Brueggemann, *Genesis* (Interpretation; Atlanta: John Knox, 1982), 32.

39. Gerhard von Rad, *Genesis: A Commentary* (trans. John H. Marks et al.; Old Testament Library; rev. ed.; Philadelphia: Westminster, 1972), 60; Gerhard Kittel, Gerhard von Rad, and Hermann Kleinknecht, "εἰκών," in *Theological Dictionary of the New Testament* (ed. Gerhard Kittel; trans. Geoffrey W. Bromiley; Grand Rapids: Eerdmans, 1964), 2.392; and Gerhard von Rad, *Old Testament Theology*, vol. 1: *The Theology of Israel's Historical Traditions* (trans. D. M. G. Stalker; New York: Harper & Row, 1962), 146.

40. Wilhelm Caspari, "Imago divina Gen i," in *Zur Theorie des Christentums: Festschrift für R. Seeberg* (Leipzig, 1929), 197–208.

41. Besides numerous inscriptions on the statues themselves, surviving literary records of many Neo-Assyrian kings describe the practice. For Ashurnasirpal's accounts in his annals (discovered at Kalhu [= biblical Calah]) of his fashioning and setting up such images, see Daniel David Luckenbill, *Ancient Records of Assyria and Babylonia*, vol. 1: *Historical Records of Assyria from the Earliest Times to Sargon* (repr. New York: Greenwood, 1968), #443, #445, #446 (pp. 145, 146, 147). For a similar claim by Ashurnasirpal's son Shalmaneser III, see #558 (p. 201).

42. J. Maxwell Miller, "In the 'Image' and 'Likeness' of God," *Journal of Biblical Literature* 91 (1972): 296.

finds some confirmation in the judgment of Curtis that images of kings were sometimes set up simply as memorials.[43]

But what makes the matter quite complicated is that images of kings were used in the ancient Near East for multiple purposes, in quite varied contexts, as Curtis points out.[44] Thus, for example, many Mesopotamian kings (as well as private individuals) placed statues of themselves in temples, before cult images of the gods in order to represent their perpetual attitude of supplication to the deity in question.[45] These "votive or dedicatory statues"[46] conveyed the king's gratitude to the god for past favors and served to remind the god of his faithful servant, in effect prompting the god to bless and prosper the king in all his endeavors. Furthermore, in Mesopotamia images of kings were sometimes deposited in the foundations of buildings, likely for votive purposes (they were visible, presumably, to the god alone). In a few cases, there are even images of Mesopotamian kings before cult statues that came to be treated as minor divinities in their own right, before which offerings were made (probably by association with the cult statue). And there is mention of an image of the king used in the so-called substitute king ritual (either along with or instead of the more usual human substitute).[47]

Yet Curtis does allow that statues of kings were also set up in distant lands as symbols of the king's authority over conquered territory. This is clearest in the case of Egyptian pharaohs, whose statues in conquered lands served to mediate the king's power from its concentrated seat in the royal palace to the borders of the empire. These royal statues were thought to effectively control or hold back the forces of chaos in those areas most distant from the center of the empire and thus most vulnerable to Egypt's enemies.[48] Curtis, however, does not think that the purpose of such statues is quite as clear in the case of Mesopotamian kings, although he suggests that the statues most likely represented the king's presence and authority in some general way.[49]

To illustrate how complicated it is to interpret such matters, we may take the case of the statute of King Adad-iti (or Had-yitʾî) found at

43. Curtis, *Man as the Image of God*, 118. He refers specifically to Egyptian kings here.

44. See the quite extensive, representative list of statues of Mesopotamian kings listed in *CAD* Ṣ 80a–82a.

45. The case of Esarhaddon is cited by D. J. A. Clines, "The Image of God in Man," *Tyndale Bulletin* 19 (1968): 83 (citing *CAD* Ṣ 81a). Curtis's examples include, besides Esarhaddon, statues of Ishtarduri, Ammiditana, Shalmaneser III, and Adad-iti; *Man as the Image of God*, 121–23.

46. Curtis, *Man as the Image of God*, 121, 123.

47. Ibid., 124–28.

48. Ibid., 117–18.

49. Ibid., 119.

Tell Fekheriyeh (in modern Syria) in 1979. According to the bilingual inscription on the statue, it was set up to acknowledge the blessing of the god Adad (or Hadad) on the king and to signal the king's rule over the Assyrian province of Guzan (the statue was "for perpetuating his throne, for the length of his rule"). Especially significant about this inscription is that it contains the Aramaic equivalents of both *selem* and *děmût* and the Akkadian equivalent of *selem* as synonymous terms designating the statue.[50] Thus it seems to provide a very apt parallel to the *imago Dei* in Genesis 1. Yet because the inscription on the statue also states that it was "for hearing his prayer, for accepting his words" (the statue's hands are clasped in an attitude of prayer), Curtis classifies it as a votive image.

It may well, however, have served a dual purpose, both reminding the deity of the devoted king's gratitude and symbolizing his authority over the conquered realm, as W. Randall Garr argues.[51] Indeed, this accords with the general conclusion of Bertil Albrektson concerning Mesopotamian royal inscriptions (whether on buildings or statues and regardless of whether such inscriptions were intended to be read by others). According to Albrektson, Mesopotamian royal inscriptions served primarily the cultic purpose of glorifying the gods (indeed, they were often addressed to the gods), but this was not separated from the king's military or political exploits, since as the deputy and representative of the god on earth, the king's exploits *were* the god's exploits. Cultic and political purposes were fused.[52]

Yet, despite the lack of clarity about the precise significance of all cases of this ancient Near Eastern royal practice, the general sense certainly has to do with the statue representing, in some way, the absent king. Since this representative notion is intrinsic to the ancient Near Eastern understanding of images, it seems quite plausible to regard the practice of kings setting up images of themselves as a legitimate parallel to the creation of humans as the image of God in Genesis.

50. For an account of this inscription, see A. R. Millard and P. Bordreuil, "A Statue from Syria with Assyrian and Aramaic Inscriptions," *Biblical Archeologist* 45 (1982): 135–41.

51. W. Randall Garr argues for this dual purpose based on the usage of the words for "likeness" and "image" in the Aramaic portion of the inscription. He takes them as coreferential and semantically similar, but pragmatically distinct, such that "likeness" expresses a petitionary, votive function (toward the god), while "image" expresses sovereignty and majesty (toward the people); "'Image' and 'Likeness' in the Inscription from Tell Fakhariyeh," *Israel Exploration Journal* 50 (2000): 227–34. Curtis himself seems to imply that a dual purpose is possible; *Man as the Image of God*, 218 n. 210.

52. Bertil Albrektson, *History and the Gods: An Essay on the Idea of Historical Events as Divine Manifestations in the Ancient Near East and in Israel* (Lund: Gleerup, 1976), 43.

Nevertheless, an even more plausible parallel consists in ancient Near Eastern royal ideology texts that describe various kings (and sometimes priests) as the image of a god. Not only is this by far the most widely cited set of ancient Near Eastern parallels for the notion of the *imago Dei* in Genesis 1, but these texts have the advantage of being quite numerous, and the ideology in which the texts are grounded is relatively well understood. Furthermore, it is possible that the practice of kings setting up images of themselves is itself connected with this ideology.

Although some of these royal ideology image texts were cited in relation to the biblical image of God as far back as 1915 by Johannes Hehn,[53] the significance accorded to these texts by Old Testament scholars can be traced to the influential studies of Werner Schmidt and Hans Wildberger in the mid-1960s.[54] Since the studies of Schmidt and Wildberger,[55] many other scholars have increased the fund of relevant references, particularly in the case of the Egyptian texts, so much so that it would be impractical to cite these all individually.

The Image of God in Egyptian Royal Ideology

A recent, representative sampling of relevant Egyptian texts, however, is found in Curtis's doctoral dissertation. Culled from a variety of sources, the texts that Curtis cites designate at least eighteen different Egyptian pharaohs as the image of a god (with sometimes over a dozen references for one particular pharaoh).[56] Although these texts range from the Middle Kingdom (Pharaoh Rahotep in 1640 B.C.E.) to Ptolemaic times (Ptolemy V Ephiphanes, from a 196 B.C.E. inscription, a copy of which is preserved

53. Johannes Hehn, "Zum Terminus 'Bild Gottes,'" in *Festschrift Eduard Sachau* (ed. Gotthold Weil; Berlin: Reimer, 1915), 36–52. Hehn cites only *Mesopotamian* image texts and that he uses these to shed light on the image primarily in the *New Testament*.

54. See Werner H. Schmidt, *Die Schöpfungsgeschichte der Priesterschrift* (2nd ed.; Neukirchen-Vluyn: Neukirchener Verlag, 1967), esp. 127–49; idem, *The Faith of the Old Testament: A History* (trans. John Sturdy; Philadelphia: Westminster, 1983), esp. 182–206; and also Hans Wildberger, "Das Abbild Gottes: Gen. 1,26–30," *Theologische Zeitschrift* 21 (1965): 245–59, 481–501. Not only did Schmidt and Wildberger come to their conclusions about the importance of the comparative material at about the same time, but it seems that they arrived at their conclusions independently (see Wildberger's comment on 501 n. 184, where he makes passing reference to Schmidt's 1964 publication).

55. For their discussion of these references, see Schmidt, *Schöpfungsgeschichte der Priesterschrift*, 137–40; idem, *Faith of the Old Testament*, 195–96; and Wildberger, "Das Abbild Gottes," 253–54, 484–91.

56. For the list of Egyptian kings, see Curtis, *Man as the Image of God*, 86–96, 226–28 n. 262, 368 n. 53. For his discussion of the ideology behind the texts, see 143–55. Curtis admits that his list is representative, not exhaustive.

on the Rosetta Stone), the majority of these references date from the New Kingdom, specifically the fifteenth to twelfth centuries B.C.E. The most common designation seems to be the image of Re (the primary name for the sun-god, national deity of Egypt), but the pharaoh is also commonly called the image of Amon-Re, Horus, Atum, and Amon, and we often find expressions that qualify "image" with "living" or "holy" and some that do not name the god in question.

To give a few examples, Pharaoh Ahmose I (1550–1525 B.C.E.) is described as "a prince like Re, the child of Qeb, his heir, the image of Re, whom he created, the avenger (or the representative), for whom he has set himself on earth."[57] Queen Hatshepsut (1479–1457 B.C.E.) is described as "superb image of Amon; the image of Amon on earth; the image of Amon-Re to eternity, his living monument on earth."[58] Amenhotep II (1427–1400 B.C.E.) is described variously as "image of Re," "image of Horus," "image of Atum," "holy image of the lord of the gods," "foremost image of Re," "holy image of Re," "holy image of Amon, image of Amon like Re," and so on.[59] Amenhotep III (1390–1352 B.C.E.) is addressed by Amon as "my living image, creation of my members, whom Mut bare to me." Amenhotep III is also addressed by Amon-Re: "You are my beloved son, who came forth from my members, my image, whom I have put on earth. I have given to you to rule the earth in peace."[60] Merenptah (1213–1203 B.C.E.) is described as the "child and likeness of the Bull of Heliopolis."[61] And Nebneteru, an official of court and temple, refers to Osorkon II (874–850 B.C.E.) by the circumlocution "the palace," when he writes: "He [Amon] introduced me to the palace in private, / So that I saw Horus in his image."[62] Such citations could be easily multiplied. They serve to highlight that it was quite typical, especially in the New Kingdom, to understand the Egyptian pharaoh as the image of a god.

To understand the meaning and function of this idea, we need to grasp something of the wider ideology of kingship in Egypt. Central to this ideology was the divinity of the pharaoh, by which he was set apart from all other human beings. In the words found on the tomb of the vizier Rekhmire, from the Eighteenth Dynasty: "What is the king of Upper and

57. Cited by Clines, "Image of God in Man," 85 (parenthesis original). In this paragraph the names and dates of the pharaohs have been changed from the sources cited to conform to the most recent scholarly conventions.

58. Curtis, *Man as the Image of God*, 226.

59. Ibid., 227.

60. Both references to Amenhotep III are cited by Clines, "Image of God in Man," 85.

61. Curtis, *Man as the Image of God*, 228.

62. Miriam Lichtheim, *Ancient Egyptian Literature: A Book of Readings*, vol. 3: *The Late Period* (Berkeley: University of California Press, 1980), 19.

Lower Egypt? He is a god by whose dealings one lives, the father and the mother of all men, alone by himself, without an equal."[63] Both artistic and inscriptional evidence shows that in all periods of pharaonic Egypt, the reigning king is thought of as the son and offspring of the gods, authorized by his divine birth to rule Upper and Lower Egypt (indeed, the world) on behalf of the gods. Typically (though not exclusively) thought of as the incarnation of Horus during his life (and identified with Osiris in death, so that the successor to the throne becomes the next incarnation of Horus, the son of Osiris), the reigning pharaoh is the bond and intermediary between the gods and the earthly realm. Not only are all courtly and priestly officials understood to be assigned their positions by the direct delegation of pharaoh, but it is due to his effective potency and his rule according to *ma'at* (truth, justice, or cosmic order) that there is harmony in the social realm, military victory against Egypt's foes, and fertility in the land (the regular inundations of the Nile, whereby it renews the parched land, are specifically attributed to the efficacy of the pharaoh's rule).[64]

The notion of the pharaoh as an image of a god must be understood in this context. In one sense, the notion of image is but one among many other ways of expressing the pharaoh's divine origin and kinship to the gods. The notion is distinctive, however, in that it picks up specifically on the central *function* of the king, namely, his cultic, intermediary function of uniting the earthly and divine realms. The pharaoh was thought, in a fairly strong sense, to be a physical, local incarnation of deity, analogous to that of a cult statue or image of a god, which is also such an incarnation. Indeed, of eight Egyptian words for "image" that were used to describe the king in the extant texts, seven are also used to designate cult statues.[65] "The king as the living image of god was," Curtis explains, "like the cult statue, a place where the god manifested himself and was a primary means by which the deity worked on earth."[66]

63. Quoted in Henri Frankfort, *Kingship and the Gods: A Study of Ancient Near Eastern Religion as the Integration of Society and Nature* (Chicago: University of Chicago Press, 1948), 47.

64. For a comprehensive statement of Egyptian royal ideology, upon which the preceding summary is based, see Frankfort, *Kingship and the Gods*, chaps. 1–4. In Frankfort's own summary: "Pharaoh was not a mortal but a god. This was the fundamental concept of Egyptian kingship, that Pharaoh was of divine essence, a god incarnate; and this view can be traced back as far as texts and symbols take us. It is wrong to speak of a deification of Pharaoh. His divinity was not proclaimed at a certain moment, in a manner comparable to the *consecratio* of the dead emperor by the Roman senate. His coronation was not an apotheosis but an epiphany" (5).

65. These terms are *ḥntj, šsp, twt, sšmw, snn, sḫm*, and *tjt*. The exception, *mjtj*, is a more general term for a likeness or comparison between two things; Curtis, *Man as the Image of God*, 87–96 (also 149–53).

66. Ibid., 152.

Just as cult statutes functioned as intermediaries between the god and the people, supposedly able to pronounce oracles and cure sickness, so the king as the image of the god was thought to mediate the god's presence and power on earth. This function of the king as the gods' high priest and primary cultic intermediary helps explain why, besides the numerous royal image of god texts, there are also a few texts that refer to Egyptian priests as the image of a god.[67]

Mesopotamian Image of God Texts

In contrast to the plethora of extant Egyptian image of god texts, the few Mesopotamian texts cited by Schmidt and Wildberger have been only marginally supplemented and are, overall, far less numerous than their Egyptian counterparts.[68] Specifically, only six extant Mesopotamian texts refer to a king,[69] and one refers to a priest explicitly as the image (or likeness) of a god (although there are also cases of various kings being compared to a god, without using image terminology; see the next section below). One of the relevant image texts dates from the thirteenth century B.C.E., while the others are from the seventh century, and all but one use *ṣalmu*, the Akkadian cognate of Hebrew *ṣelem*.

The oldest of these texts is the famous *Tukulti-Ninurta Epic*, composed to glorify the exploits of the Middle Assyrian king Tukulti-Ninurta I (1244–1208 B.C.E.), especially his defeat of the Babylonian king Kashtiliash I, when Tukulti-Ninurta captured the cult statue of Marduk (the national god of Babylon) and transported it to the Assyrian capital of Ashur (where it remained for a century). In the epic the king is said to have been born of the gods, gestated in the divine womb, and exalted to a rank second only to the warrior-god Ninurta, who is the firstborn son

67. Curtis makes reference to a Memphite priest of Ptah in the New Kingdom and a late-Ptolemaic priest of Amon, as well as to priests in the Eleventh and Twelfth Dynasties; ibid., 92, 94, 153.

68. Gunnlaugur A. Jónsson (*The Image of God: Genesis 1:26–28 in a Century of Old Testament Research* [trans. Lorraine Svendsen; rev. Michael S. Cheney; Coniectanea biblica Old Testament Series 26; Stockholm: Almqvist & Wiksell, 1988], 141) incorrectly claims that Wildberger "quotes a long series of [Mesopotamian] texts in which the king is described as 'the image of God.'" Not only is this generally impossible, since the list of extant Mesopotamian image texts is actually quite short, it is simply inaccurate, as a look at Wildberger, "Das Abbild Gottes," 253–54, ascertains. Possible reasons for this paucity of Mesopotamian texts will shortly be addressed.

69. Biblical scholars typically cite as parallels only five references to Mesopotamian kings as image of a god. A sixth Mesopotamian image text is relevant, but I have not yet seen it cited in this connection.

of the high god Enlil.[70] In this context, namely, a description of the king's divine origin and status, we find the following line (as translated by Foster): "It is he who is the eternal image of Enlil, attentive to the people's voice, the counsel of the land."[71]

Although W. G. Lambert's translation agrees with Foster's in suggesting that the king is like the god both in listening to his people (attentive to their voice) and in advising them (he is their counsel),[72] other translations repeat the preposition *to*, thus treating *the voice of the people* and *the counsel of the land* as two phrases in apposition: "attentive to the voice of the people, to the counsel of the land" (Peter Machinist) or "attentive to the voice of the people, to the mood of the land" (Jeffrey Tigay).[73]

While both possible meanings involve a functional analogy between the king and the god (that is, the king is thought to act in a manner like the god), the immediate context of this line does not consist in descriptions of the king's attention to his people. The context is, rather, overwhelmingly dominated by a vivid portrayal of Tukulti-Ninurta's warlike splendor that destroys his enemies and causes all other kings to fear him. In this he is explicitly compared to the gods Adad and Ninurta (gods of storm and war), though without the actual term *image* (*ṣalmu*). The text reads: "When he thunders like Adad, the mountains tremble; / And when he raises his weapons like Ninurta, the regions (of the world) everywhere are thrown into constant panic."[74] A quite plausible overall interpretation is that the king is the image of Enlil (and possibly Adad and Ninurta also) in virtue of both his divine birth and his attentive care of his people, which is expressed precisely in his destruction of Assyria's enemies.

All of the other extant Mesopotamian image texts are Neo-Assyrian in provenance (that is, the copies we possess are Neo-Assyrian), and, unlike the *Tukulti-Ninurta Epic*, they do not associate the image with divine gestation or birth. One of these texts, a letter from a priest or cultic official to a seventh-century Assyrian king (either Esarhaddon or Ashurbanipal), is recorded on a tablet that is seriously broken, so that neither the beginning nor the end of the letter is preserved. And while

70. Foster, *Before the Muses*, 1.209–29 (1.10–23, based on the earlier line numbering of R. Campbell Thompson); W. G. Lambert, "Three Unpublished Fragments of the Tukulti-Ninurta Epic," *Archiv für Orientforschung* 18 (1957): 38–51 (1.Y.2–15).

71. Foster, *Before the Muses*, 1.213 (Foster's line 18; Lambert's line 10).

72. Lambert, "Three Unpublished Fragments of the Tukulti-Ninurta Epic," 51.

73. Peter Machinist, *The Epic of Tukulti-Ninurta I: A Study in Middle Assyrian Literature* (Ph.D. dissertation; Yale University, 1978), quoted in Curtis, *Man as the Image of God*, 81; Tigay, "Image of God and the Flood," 172.

74. Machinist's translation, quoted in Curtis, *Man as the Image of God*, 81.

there are even some broken sections of the relevant text, the gist is nevertheless clear. After inquiring about the king's decision on various cultic matters, the writer exhorts the king to send his response, noting that "[the king, my lord], is the [ima]ge of Marduk. The word of [the king], my lord, [is] just as [final] as that of the gods."[75] Here the writer uses two expressions to characterize the king's authority: he describes him as the god's image (*ṣalmu*) and compares the authority or finality of his word to that of a god (using a simile). This suggests that image here expresses a functional similarity between the king and the god, whereby the king speaks with the god's authority as his representative.[76]

Another relevant text is a letter from a Neo-Babylonian astrologer, Asharedu the Older, to an unnamed seventh-century Assyrian king in whose court the writer serves. In the context of describing the dependence of the court officials (including the writer) on the king's disposition, Asharedu states: "The king of the world is the very image of Marduk: when you have been angry with your servants we have suffered the anger of the king, our lord, but we have also experienced the king's favor."[77] On the face of it, either the king's anger or the king's favor is being compared with that of the god Marduk (or possibly the comparison intends both). While R. Campbell Thompson, in an older translation, associates only the king's anger with his imaging Marduk,[78] Simo Parpola's reconstruction of Assyrian royal ideology leads to the opposite conclusion. In his reconstruction, the Assyrian king's judgments, which he executed as the image of Shamash (god of justice), had to be tempered by acts of mercy, which he enacted as the image (*ṣalmu*) of Marduk (god of mercy).[79] Yet attention to the fuller context of the quotation suggests that both characteristics are being compared. Thus, in Hermann Hunger's recent translation we read: "The wisest, merciful Bel, the warrior Marduk, became angry at night, but relented in the morning. You, o king of the world, are an image of Marduk; when you were angry with your servants, we

75. Translation from Steven W. Cole and Peter Machinist (eds.), *Letters from Priests to the Kings Esarhaddon and Assurbanipal* (State Archives of Assyria 13; Helsinki, Finland: Helsinki University Press, 1998), 43 (letter #46, lines rev. 11–12).

76. This is my own interpretation; I have not seen this text cited by Old Testament scholars as a parallel to the biblical *imago Dei*.

77. Quoted by Tigay, "Image of God and the Flood," 172.

78. R. Campbell Thompson, *The Reports of the Magicians and Astrologers of Nineveh and Babylon in the British Museum*, vol. 2: *English Translations, Vocabulary, Etc.* (London: Luzac, 1900), lxii (report #170): "O King! thou art the image of Marduk, when thou art angry, to thy servants! When we draw near the king, our lord, we shall see his peace!"

79. Simo Parpola (ed.), *Letters from Assyrian and Babylonian Scholars* (State Archives of Assyria 10; Helsinki, Finland: Helsinki University Press, 1993), xvii.

suffered the anger of the king our lord; and we saw the reconciliation of the king."[80]

Significantly, three of the remaining four Neo-Assyrian references come from the stylus of Adad-shumu-usur (ca. 740–665 B.C.E.), a court astrologer and *āšipu* (a cultic official, usually understood as an exorcist-priest) at the royal court in Nineveh. Adad-shumu-usur was the personal *āšipu* and close confidant of Neo-Assyrian King Esarhaddon (who reigned 680–669 B.C.E.), and references to the image of god are found in three letters or memoranda he wrote to Esarhaddon.[81]

One of these letters, which can be dated to 670 B.C.E., urges the king, who seems to have been ill at the time, not to remain indoors, fasting (perhaps engaging in certain rites of mourning) for longer than the sun would be hidden each day. The reasoning behind this is that the king is the image of Shamash (the sun-god and god of justice):

> Why, today already for the second day, is the table not brought to the king, my lord? Who (now) stays in the dark much longer than Šamaš, the king of the gods; stays in the dark a whole day and night, and again two days? The king, the lord of the world, is the very image of Šamaš. He (should) keep in the dark for half a day only.[82]

Although there are some uncertainties of translation (for example, Parpola's "for the second day" is rendered by Robert Pfeiffer as "a second time today"), the basic point seems clear.[83] Esarhaddon is exhorted to

80. Hermann Hunger (ed.), *Astrological Reports to Assyrian Kings* (State Archives of Assyria 8; Helsinki, Finland: Helsinki University Press, 1992), 189 (letter #333, lines obv. 4–6 and rev. 1–6).

81. Adad-shumu-usur was one of seventeen scholars in what Parpola calls the king's "inner circle" and authored fifty-six extant letters or reports to the king on medicine, magic, astrology, and other topics; *Letters from Assyrian and Babylonian Scholars*, xxv–xxvi. He came from a high-ranking scribal family in the continuous employ of the Assyrian royal court for some two and a half centuries. For further details on Adad-shumu-usur, see Simo Parpola, *Letters from Assyrian Scholars to the Kings Esarhaddon and Assurbanipal*, part 2: *Commentary and Appendices* (Kevelaer: Butzon & Bercker/Neukirchen-Vluyn: Neukirchener Verlag, 1983), xv–xix. On the office of the *āšipu*, see Henshaw, *Female and Male*, 145–47.

82. Parpola, *Letters from Assyrian and Babylonian Scholars*, 159 (letter #196, lines obv. 14–20 and rev. 1–6), published earlier in idem, *Letters from Assyrian Scholars to the Kings Esarhaddon and Assurbanipal*, part 1: *Texts* (Kevelaer: Butzon & Bercker/Neukirchen-Vluyn: Neukirchener Verlag, 1970), 113 (letter #143).

83. Robert H. Pfeiffer's translation (*State Letters of Assyria* [New Haven: American Oriental Society, 1935; repr. New York: Kraus, 1967], 188) is as follows: "Why should not a meal be served before the king my lord a second time today? Whoever mourns for Shamash, the king of the gods, mourns for a day, a whole night and again two days. The king, the lord of countries, is the (very) image of Shamash; for half a day only should he put on mourning" (letter #264). For another translation that agrees with

live up to his privileged identity as the image (*ṣalmu*) of Shamash, by imitating the sun's behavior. Since the sun is obscured for only half a day (that is, at night), the king ought not fast in the dark for more than half a day. Rather, he ought to be publicly visible to those who depend on his light/justice. The image of god, like that in the *Instruction of Ani*, thus functions here as a behavioral norm, to which one ought to conform.

Another letter from Adad-shumu-usur to King Esarhaddon thanks him for granting a favor that the astrologer-priest had previously requested. Adad-shumu-usur praises both Esarhaddon and his father, Sennacherib, for the benevolence they have shown to him and his family throughout his years of service to the royal court. After quoting a line from a letter that the king had previously written to him, he describes both kings (Esarhaddon and Sennacherib) as the image (*ṣalmu*) of Bel (Akkadian for "lord," a reference to Marduk):

> As to what the king, [my lord] wrote me: "I have heard from the mouth of my father that you are a loyal family, but now I know it from my own experience"—the father of the king, my lord, was the very image of Bel, and the king, my lord, is likewise the very image of Bel.[84]

Although the use of the image of god here could simply be a hyperbolic form of flattery expressing the writer's gratitude (indeed, it is typical in royal correspondence to begin by addressing the king with list of exalted, quasidivine epithets), Adad-shumu-usur might be making a more specific functional comparison. That is, the king has acted like Marduk precisely in his benevolence.

In the final letter from Adad-shumu-usur to Esarhaddon, the priest quotes what seems to be a proverb about the human condition (although precisely where the proverb ends is debated), and this is followed by his own comment about the king's likeness (*muššulu*) to a god. Although the cognate for *ṣelem* is not used here, it is noteworthy that *muššulu* is cognate to the Hebrew noun *māšāl* (proverb), and the participle (*môšēl*) derived from this root is used in the Bible as a synonym for *děmût*.[85]

Pfeiffer on the above point, see Leroy Waterman, *Royal Correspondence of the Assyrian Empire*, part 1: *Translation and Transliteration* (Ann Arbor: University of Michigan Press, 1930), 7 (letter #5).

84. Parpola, *Letters from Assyrian and Babylonian Scholars*, 181 (letter #228, lines obv. 14–19). Pfeiffer's translation is almost identical: "As to what the king my lord wrote me, 'From the lips of my father I have heard that you are a loyal family, but now I know it, I have seen it.' The father of the king my lord was the (very) image of Bel, and the king my lord is likewise the (very) image of Bel"; *State Letters of Assyria*, 120 (letter #161).

85. See Tigay, "Image of God and the Flood," 171, for the relationship of these cognate terms. On *muššulu*, see *CAD* M 281b.

Yet the text suffers from a myriad of interpretive problems, the least of which is the extent of the proverb. This is Parpola's translation: "The well-known proverb says: 'Man is a shadow of god.' [But] is man a shadow of man too? The king is the perfect likeness of the god."[86] Apart from reading the second sentence as a question, which is not generally followed by other translators, the translation is quite literal. But what exactly does it mean?

One common way of reading the text is to take the proverb as a general description of the human condition, to which is added a comment contrasting this to the king's privileged status. Thus the proverb would state (minimally), "Man is a shadow of god,"[87] to which the priest adds "but the king is the (very) image of a god" (Pfeiffer), or "the king [in contrast] is a likeness of a god" (Tigay).[88] On this reading, Adad-shumu-usur is contrasting the general human condition (as the god's shadow) with the status of the king (who is the god's image or likeness). It is even possible, depending on how one translates the text *between* these two lines, to see a three-tiered social order here. Thus Pfeiffer renders the entire section as, "Man is the shadow of a god, a slave is the shadow of a man; but the king is the (very) image of a god."[89] Clines's translation is similar: "A (free) man is as the shadow of god, the slave is as the shadow of a (free) man; but the king, he is like unto the (very) image of god."[90] But the word for "slave" does not actually occur in the text. Rather, the middle section states that (or possibly asks whether, as in Parpola) a man is a shadow of a man—presumably referring to different men.

But even those interpretations that simply contrast humanity with the king are misguided if they take the term *shadow* as negative or derogatory. Instead, we should note the very specific positive meaning of the phrase *the shadow of the king* in the immediately preceding context of the contested lines, in other letters of Adad-shumu-usur, and in other Assyrian writings, where it consistently denotes royal protection and favor.[91]

86. Parpola, *Letters from Assyrian and Babylonian Scholars*, 166 (letter #207, lines rev. 9–13).

87. Pfeiffer, *State Letters of Assyria*, 234 (letter #345); and Tigay, "Image of God and the Flood," 171, have, similarly, "Man is a shadow of a god." Parpola's earlier translation in *Letters from Assyrian Scholars*, 1.113 (letter #145), is slightly different: "Man is [only] a shadow of a god."

88. Pfeiffer, *State Letters of Assyria*, 234 (letter #345); Tigay, "Image of God and the Flood," 171.

89. Pfeiffer, *State Letters of Assyria*, 234 (letter #345).

90. Clines, "Image of God in Man," 84.

91. See Frankfort, *Kingship and the Gods*, 406–7 n. 35; A. Leo Oppenheim, "Assyriological Gleanings IV: The Shadow of the King," *Bulletin of the American Schools of Oriental Research* 107 (1947): 7–11. Curtis cites these sources and this line of argument approvingly (*Man as the Image of God*, 176, 238 nn. 365–66), thus implicitly challenging the interpretation

Thus Oppenheim (who also takes the extent of the proverb differently than most) translates the text rather wordily as follows: "'The *amêlu* (lives in) the shadow of god, and mankind (in the) shadow of the *amêlu*' (and) *amêlu* means 'king' (in this context) because he (i.e., the king) is (for us human beings) just like a god!"[92] On this reading, not only is "shadow" taken as a positive term, but the proverb (underlined above) is interpreted as applying to the king, who is the *amêlu* (understood here to mean the primal or ideal human). But even if the proverb is taken as applying to humanity generally, as most take it, the text makes perfect sense: humanity lives under the protection of the god (the proverb) and also under the protection of a human being, the king (two different referents for *amêlu*), since the king is the likeness of a god.

Whereas all of these interpretations emphasize the king's exalted status vis-à-vis the masses, a positive reading of "shadow" also specifies in what way the king is like a god. On this interpretation, Adad-shumu-usur's point is that the king *functions* as protector of humanity *just as* the god is the protector of humanity (or the protector of the king, on Oppenheim's reading), since the king is the god's likeness.

Besides these six references to Assyrian kings, an important reference to a priest or cultic official (significantly, an *āšipu*) as the image of a god occurs in an incantation text preserved on the tablets of the *bīt mēseri* series (2.225–26). While the tablets themselves date from seventh-century Assyria, the language is thought to be older (although the precise date and place of origin are uncertain). The text in question has a lot to say about images, both describing various images that were used to drive away evil from a sick man and noting that images of the two guardians, Ea and Marduk, were placed on the right and left of the entrance to the *bīt mēseri* (house of healing). Then comes the line: "The spell (recited) is the spell of Marduk, the exorcist-priest [*āšipu*] is the image [*ṣalmu*] of Marduk."[93] The point seems to be that in the act of incantation, the priest's word has the power and authority of the god. In this functional

---

of his own dissertation advisor, Jeffrey Tigay. It is intriguing that Curtis was likely working on his doctoral dissertation at the same time that Tigay was writing his essay "The Image of God and the Flood: Some New Developments" (the dissertation was approved in 1984, the same year the essay was published).

92. Oppenheim, "Assyriological Gleanings IV," 9 n. 6 (parentheses original, underlining added).

93. Translation from Tigay, "Image of God and the Flood," 172. Instead of "spell" and "exorcist-priest," other scholarly renderings include "exorcism" and "priest" (Clines, "Image of God in Man," 84) and "conjuration" and "conjurer" (Phyllis A. Bird, "'Male and Female He Created Them': Gen 1:27b in the Context of the Priestly Account of Creation," *Harvard Theological Review* 74 [1981]: 142 n. 34). Tigay, Clines, and Bird all cite as their source G. Meier, "Die zweite Tafel der Serie bīt mēseri," *Archiv für Orientforschung* 14 (1941–44): 151–52.

analogy, the priest stands in as Marduk's representative for purposes of the exorcism.

Mesopotamian Royal Ideology

There are many things to note about these Mesopotamian image of god texts. First of all, they clearly support—like the Egyptian texts—a *functional* notion of the image. Yet, on the surface, the particular function designated by this notion seems different in the two cultures. While the Mesopotamian king (or priest) is compared to a god by virtue of some specific discernable royal (or priestly) action or behavior (such as attentiveness, authority, mercy, anger, public visibility, benevolence, protection), in Egypt the image of god seems to be a more standardized royal concept, designating the pharaoh's cultic function as a decisive manifestation of the gods on earth. That is, while the Egyptian references suggest the image as *representative*, designating the office and status of the king, the Mesopotamian references suggest a *representational* notion of the image, which Tigay calls a "metaphorical usage" of the image.[94]

Does this mean that there is some significant difference about the idea of the king as image of god between the two cultures? Or do both ideas have a similar *basis*, in a representative notion of the image, to which is *added*, in Mesopotamia, a representational notion, with the result that certain behavioral characteristics of the king are specified? That primarily kings are said to be the image of a god in both Mesopotamia and Egypt suggests a prima facie similarity. Indeed, the specific metaphorical characteristics highlighted in the Mesopotamian references all have to do with the exercise of power. As Phyllis Bird puts it, "In both royal and priestly designations the human representative is viewed above all as one possessing the power and authority of the god, whether for weal or woe."[95] It is therefore plausible to infer that the reason why Mesopotamian kings are described as the image of a god is due to the office they hold in Mesopotamian society, an office similar to that of their Egyptian counterparts, as cultic intermediaries and representatives of the gods on earth. This also explains why the term could be applied to priests, who were also cultic intermediaries and representatives.

The plausibility of this inference about the basis of the Mesopotamian image of god is corroborated by the standard Mesopotamian notion

94. Tigay, "Image of God and the Flood," 177. Tigay also classifies the image of god in the Egyptian *Instruction of Ani* as metaphorical (173).
95. Bird, "Male and Female He Created Them," 142 n. 34.

of the king as the gods' authorized deputy or viceroy on earth. This notion of the king as deputy of the gods goes back, as Albrektson documents, to ancient Sumerian times and is central to the royal ideology of Babylonia and Assyria over a stretch of some thirteen centuries.[96] It is expressed even in the titles of Babylonian and Assyrian kings, who are called *šakkanakku* (Sumerian GÌR.NITA) or *šaknu*, both of which mean "deputy, vice-gerent, governor."[97] While *šakkanakku* of the gods (or more usually of a particular god) is a title of Mesopotamian kings from Old Babylonian to Neo-Babylonian times,[98] *šaknu* of Enlil is most commonly used of Assyrian kings, both early and late.[99] These titles signify that the king "is the deputy of the god on earth . . . executing divine decisions, an instrument in the hand of the real ruler."[100]

But beyond specific titles, Mesopotamian kings are often portrayed in various literary and inscriptional texts as acting on behalf of the gods, as their representative and intermediary on earth. Thus the ancient Sumerian King Ziusudra who survived the flood (the Sumerian equivalent of biblical Noah) is described as a "lustration priest" and a "seer" in the *Eridu Genesis* (also known as the *Sumerian Flood Story*), which illustrates, according to Thorkild Jacobsen, the ancient Mesopotamian idea that "the king was, as priest-king, mediator between the people and the gods."[101] A typical statement of the combination of political and cultic tasks assigned to Mesopotamian kings by the gods is a stone tablet at Sippar concerning the Babylonian king Nabu-apla-iddina (ninth century): To Nabu-apla-iddina "the great lord Marduk entrusted the righteous sceptre, the shepherding of the peoples, to avenge Akkad, to make cities habitable, to found sanctuaries, to prepare reliefs, to put in order rites and cult objects, to establish regular sacrifices, to increase offerings" (2.29–3.10).[102] In these political and cultic duties, the king represents the interests—and mediates the rule—of Marduk on earth.

---

96. Albrektson, *History and the Gods*, chap. 3.

97. Ibid., 45.

98. Albrektson cites Adad-nirari I (thirteenth century), who describes himself as "the viceroy of the gods," and Shalmaneser III (ninth century) and Ashurbanipal (seventh century), both of whom are called viceroy of the god Ashur (ibid.). More informally, Nebuchadnezzar II (sixth century) says to Marduk, "I am indeed your faithful *šakkanakku*" (46).

99. Albrektson (ibid., 46–47) cites Shamshi-Adad I (nineteenth century), Adad-nirari I, Shalmaneser I, and Tukulti-Ninurta I (thirteenth century), and Esarhaddon (seventh century) as examples.

100. Ibid., 47.

101. Thorkild Jacobsen, "The Eridu Genesis," *Journal of Biblical Literature* 100 (1981): 523.

102. Albrektson, *History and the Gods*, 48–49.

A similar understanding of the king as viceroy of the gods is assumed in a letter of Adad-shumu-usur to Esarhaddon that refers to a favorable liver omen prediction or extispicy, where the gods predict the character of the king's reign:

> Aššur, [the king of the gods] called the name of [the king], my lord, to the kingship of Assyria, and Šamaš and Adad, through their reliable extispicy, confirmed the king, my lord, for the kingship of the world. A good reign—righteous days, years of justice, copious rains, huge floods, a fine rate of exchange! The gods are appeased, there is much fear of god, the temples abound; the great gods of heaven and earth have become exalted in the time of the king, my lord.[103]

In this description of the king's reign, which is characterized by justice, fruitful rainfall, and cultic piety—and also by widespread procreation, mercy to the condemned, and care for the hungry (lines obv. 16–rev. 3)—we see the common Mesopotamian assumption that when the king rules well both the social and natural orders of life are fruitful and blessed, and through this the gods are exalted. The king is the one who represents and mediates the gods' blessing on earth.

Thus an inscription of Esarhaddon implicitly identifies the king's authority with that of the god who commissioned his rule. Referring to the rebellion of Sidonian King Abdi-milkutti, Esarhaddon says that the rebel king "did not fear my lordship and did not obey the word of my lips but trusted the rolling sea and threw off the yoke of (the god) Ashur."[104] Rebelling against the king's word is thus functionally equivalent to throwing off the yoke of the god.

Adad-shumu-usur makes a similar judgment in a letter to Esarhaddon, where he endorses a suggestion the king had previously made by stating: "(By contrast) what the king, my lord, said is as perfect as the (word of) the god."[105] Here, instead of using the metaphor of image (or likeness) to compare the king to a god, the priest uses a simile, which amounts to much the same thing.[106] Tigay himself cites another simile that compares a king with a god, treating it as virtually equivalent to

103. Parpola, *Letters from Assyrian and Babylonian Scholars*, 177–78 (letter #226, lines obv. 5–15). For an older translation, see Pfeiffer, *State Letters of Assyria*, 118 (letter #160).

104. Albrektson, *History and the Gods*, 49 (parentheses original).

105. Parpola, *Letters from Assyrian and Babylonian Scholars*, 156 (letter #191, lines rev. 6–7). For another translation, see Waterman, *Royal Correspondence of the Assyrian Empire*, 5 (letter #3).

106. One of the Mesopotamian image of god texts cited earlier used this very simile (a comparison with the god's word) as equivalent to the image.

107. Tigay, "Image of God and the Flood," 172, citing *CAD* I 92.

the metaphorical image of god: "His lord, the king, looked favorably upon him, with a shining face, like a god."[107] Another simile, quoted by Frankfort, occurs in a prayer or petition directed to the gods and to the king, who are implored in parallel fashion for mercy:

> May the god who rejected me help me!
> May the goddess who [resented me] have pity on me!
> May the shepherd, the sun of men (the king),
>   who is like the god (be gracious to me)![108]

This functional similarity of god and king, which is documented in many Mesopotamian texts, is vividly illustrated in a famous wall relief of King Ashurnasirpal that pictures the god Ashur suspended in a winged solar disk above the king. Both when Ashurnasirpal draws his bow and when he lets it fall, the god's actions in heaven duplicate those of the king on earth. Thus Albrektson concludes: "The identity of divine and royal deed is patent."[109] But this is perhaps an overstatement. The issue is not identity, but similarity.

To put it another way, the king is the *image* of the god. That is, the widely attested functional similarity between king and god in Mesopotamia (whereby the king *represents* the god by virtue of his royal office and is portrayed as *acting like* the god in specific behavioral ways) provides the necessary background for understanding the extant descriptions of the king as the image of a god in the Mesopotamian references we have examined.

It is my judgment that the description of ancient Near Eastern kings as the image of a god, when understood as an integral component of Egyptian and/or Mesopotamian royal ideology, provides the most plausible set of parallels for interpreting the *imago Dei* in Genesis 1. If such texts—or the ideology behind them—influenced the biblical *imago Dei*, this suggests that humanity is dignified with a status and role vis-à-vis the nonhuman creation that is analogous to the status and role of kings in the ancient Near East vis-à-vis their subjects. Genesis 1, and not the Egyptian wisdom texts previously cited, thus constitutes a genuine democratization of ancient Near Eastern royal ideology. As *imago Dei*, then, humanity in Genesis 1 is called to be the representative and intermediary of God's power and blessing on earth.

But what are we to make of Westermann's famous objection that this analogy (as proposed in the work of Wildberger and Schmidt) is

---

108. Frankfort, *Kingship and the Gods*, 309.
109. Albrektson, *History and the Gods*, 49.
110. Westermann, *Genesis*, 1.153. This is actually the second of three objections (153–54) that Westermann gives to the interpretation of Wildberger and Schmidt. Not only are

"inconceivable" and that the priestly writer "could not possibly think of a human being as standing in the place of God on earth"?[110] Since nothing in Genesis 1 prevents this interpretation (and much suggests it), it is likely that Westermann finds it difficult to entertain this possibility because his reasoning is constrained by a particular hypothetical reconstruction of the priestly theology. For all his scholarly erudition, Westermann seems merely prejudiced against the idea because of a prior construct. By way of contrast, William Brown, who also thinks that Genesis 1 is part of the priestly writing, nevertheless treats Genesis 1 with more literary integrity and thus discerns exactly what Westermann thinks is impossible in 1:26–28. "Such language, at the very least," he explains, "transfers the tasks and trappings of royalty and cult, the offices of divine representation and habitation, to humanity."[111] If Brown's conclusion is correct, this set of parallels from ancient Near Eastern royal ideology essentially confirms the interpretation of the *imago Dei* suggested in chapter 2 through a reading of the image in terms of its own symbolic world.

Egyptian or Mesopotamian Influence?

The question then arises, however, as to *which* image of god notion—the Egyptian or the Mesopotamian—constitutes the better parallel. This involves exploring the question of historical influence: Can we determine whether the notion of humanity as image of God in Genesis 1 is indebted primarily to the Egyptian or Mesopotamian notion of the king as image of a god? And does such a decision really matter all that much?

On the one hand, a decision in favor of Egyptian or Mesopotamian influence might impact our conclusions concerning when the idea entered Israel's worldview (Egyptian and Mesopotamian influence might be more likely in different historical periods). This, in turn, might affect our reconstruction of the social context or rhetorical situation being addressed by the image in Genesis 1. This reconstruction may, in turn, influence our interpretation of what the author of Genesis 1 was trying to communicate by means of the *imago Dei*.

On the other hand, however, a choice in favor of Mesopotamia or Egypt is not necessarily decisive for the particular sociohistorical context

---

none of the objections convincing, in my opinion, but the other two seem to get their force from Westermann's prior commitment to a particular reconstruction of the theology of P.

111. William P. Brown, *The Ethos of the Cosmos: The Genesis of Moral Imagination in the Bible* (Grand Rapids: Eerdmans, 1999), 44.

that gave rise to Genesis 1, since an ancient idea may well be used at a later date (with transformed meaning), and indeed Israel had significant cultural contact with both Egypt and Mesopotamia over long periods of time. Furthermore, given that the ideas in biblical texts were likely passed down by oral tradition within Israel prior to their reduction to writing, the relevant Egyptian or Mesopotamian influence may have taken place long before the actual text of Genesis 1 was written. So the matter is highly complex.

Also complex is the question whether we should treat the numerous references to the king as image of a god in Egyptian texts over an immense period of time, compared to the relatively few extant Mesopotamian texts, as prima facie evidence that Egyptian royal ideology is the source of the biblical image of God. To answer this question we need to address some other, subsidiary questions: Why are the extant Mesopotamian references to kings as the image of a god so few, especially when compared with the multitude of Egyptian references? Further, why are the Mesopotamian references all limited to Assyrian kings and then mostly in the Neo-Assyrian period? Why, for example, are there no extant references to Babylonian kings as the image of a god from approximately the same period?[112]

Curtis treats the paucity of references in the archeological record to Mesopotamian kings as the image of a god as an accurate indication of the popularity (or lack thereof) of the idea in Mesopotamian culture. "The small number of references to people as the image of god in Mesopotamia," he explains, "clearly indicates that the term never played as significant a role in Mesopotamian thought as it did in Egypt."[113] But this is a clear non sequitur on many counts.

First of all, the geographical region corresponding to ancient Mesopotamia is notorious for the relative rarity of manuscript finds from the second half of the second millennium B.C.E. (approximately the period when we find most of the Egyptian references to kings as the image of a god). Then, to further complicate matters, even though Babylonia was the dominant cultural power of the region for an entire millennium, there are simply no large extant collections of Babylonian tablets comparable

112. I am not identifying Mesopotamian culture simply with the empires of Assyria and Babylonia in their prime. Apart from the massive inheritance of ancient Sumer, a full account of what is known of Mesopotamian culture would have to examine the Isin-Larsa period, Mari with its Amorite influence, the Nuzi texts with their Hurrian background, late Babylonian texts with their Greek influence, and others. My focus, however, is limited by the precise issue being addressed.

113. Curtis, *Man as the Image of God*, 155.

114. Foster, *Before the Muses*, 1.8–10, 205. The letters of Adad-shumu-usur are all from the Nineveh site.

to the famous Assyrian collections from sites like Nineveh, Ashur, Kalhu (= biblical Calah), or Sultantepe.[114] This means, for example, that sixth-century Neo-Babylonian texts, which might in principle supplement the testimony of extant seventh-century Neo-Assyrian texts, are significantly underrepresented in the archeological record. The caution, therefore, of H. W. F. Saggs that "the random nature of archaeological discovery may result in gaps in the evidence and false emphases" is certainly applicable to references to Mesopotamian kings as the image of god.[115] Or as Gary Knoppers puts it, "Absence of evidence does not constitute evidence of absence."[116]

But even if the archeological record were complete, it would be extremely perilous to limit the reconstruction of an ideology or worldview to textual sources alone, as if every influential idea in a people's cultural life must find written attestation, especially in a predominantly oral culture. In the case of Mesopotamian kings as image of a god, although the archeological record is spotty, this notion fits well with what we know of the Mesopotamian royal ideology. Indeed, even if the few extant textual references to Assyrian kings (and a priest) as the image of a god were all that ever did exist, Mesopotamian royal ideology (both Babylonian and Assyrian) suggests that the fundamental *idea* behind the king as the god's image is standard.

But Curtis demurs. His judgment that the king as image of god was never an important idea in Mesopotamia is not grounded solely in the rarity of textual references. He claims also a lack of conceptual fit with Mesopotamian royal ideology.[117] According to Curtis, although there is a strict parallel between the notion of the cult image and the king in Egypt—which allows the pharaoh to be called the image of a god—there is no such parallel in Mesopotamia. There, although the cult image is understood much as it was in Egypt—as the dwelling place or incarnation of a god—this understanding is in significant discontinuity with the notion of Mesopotamian kingship, in which the king is viewed not as a divine incarnation, but as a mortal with godlike qualities, raised above his fellows by election or adoption to quasidivine sonship.

115. H. W. F. Saggs, *The Encounter with the Divine in Mesopotamia and Israel* (London: Athlone, 1978), 18.

116. Gary N. Knoppers, "The Vanishing Solomon: The Disappearance of the United Monarchy from Recent Histories of Ancient Israel," *Journal of Biblical Literature* 116 (1997): 30. Although Knoppers is addressing the paucity of archeological evidence for Solomonic Israel, and not for Babylonian civilization, his comments are relevant: "It is a fundamental methodological error to confuse impoverishment of archaeological remains with impoverishment of culture" (41).

117. Curtis, *Man as the Image of God*, 154–55, 166, 170–71.

Curtis here draws on Henri Frankfort's influential analysis in *Kingship and the Gods: A Study of Ancient Near Eastern Religion as the Integration of Society and Nature*. In a summarizing statement, Frankfort comments:

> The texts and usages which we have examined hitherto bear witness to a single conception of rulership: the Mesopotamian king was a mortal charged with the crushing burden of leading mankind in its servitude. Although his divine election endowed him with a potency surpassing that of ordinary men . . . it did not approximate him to the gods.[118]

A classic example of such a king is Gilgamesh, ruler of ancient Uruk, who is portrayed in the epic that bears his name as a man plagued with the anguished burden of mortality. This burden leads him to embark upon a heroic quest to attain eternal life, a quest in which he ultimately fails.

It is this near-canonical distinction between Egyptian kings, who were thought to be divine, and Mesopotamian kings, who were mere mortals, that Curtis appeals to when he writes: "The term image of god would be an appropriate one to apply to a divine king since the god was alive and active in his image, but the term would not have been especially appropriate to describe a Mesopotamian king who was in fact a mortal."[119]

There is, of course, an element of truth to this distinction between Egyptian and Mesopotamian royal ideology.[120] Yet it can be misleading to overemphasize it. While it is important to note the distinction for the sake of historical accuracy, Egyptian and Mesopotamian notions of kingship are remarkably similar when compared, for example, to modern secular conceptions of political authority (or even the remnants of titular monarchy in Europe or the Middle East). The functional identity between the king and the god in Mesopotamia, which I have already sketched, should make that clear. Even Gilgamesh, for all his mortality, is characterized in the epic as a combination of divine and human (two-thirds god), and his larger-than-life portrayal renders a character with near-absolute power over his subjects (1.2.1).

Frankfort himself qualifies his own summarizing comment on Mesopotamian kingship by examining the ways "in which the polarity be-

118. Frankfort, *Kingship and the Gods*, 295.
119. Curtis, *Man as the Image of God*, 155.
120. This distinction is now very commonly made. For example, Schmidt notes that in Mesopotamia "the king is not god incarnate, but appointed, elected and blessed by God"; *Faith of the Old Testament*, 183.
121. Frankfort, *Kingship and the Gods*, 295. The evidence in this paragraph and the following two is examined by Frankfort on pp. 295–312.

tween the human and the divine appears as suspended or destroyed" in the person of the Mesopotamian king.[121] Thus he notes that the divine determinative (the dingir sign) was used before the names of some Mesopotamian kings during their own lifetimes.[122] In the First Dynasty of Babylon, also, personal names of individuals often incorporated names of kings on analogy with the well-known function of divine names as a component of personal names. Furthermore, some Sumerian kings in the Third Dynasty of Ur were, partway through their reigns, deified and worshiped as gods in the temples of cities over which they had extended their suzerainty. Steven Cole and Peter Machinist, however, suggest that this practice was not limited to Ur III, but began prior to that in the period of Early Dynastic Lagash and continued in the Old Babylonian period (in both Babylonian cities and at Mari) and in the Neo-Assyrian period.[123] Yet even then, these are relatively sporadic practices over a period of some two thousand years and do not characterize all known Mesopotamian kings.

More significant, claims Frankfort, is the prominent cultic role of the Mesopotamian king as the bridegroom of the goddess Ishtar in the annual *hieros gamos* (sacred marriage), which was thought to refructify nature. In the Sumerian form of the ritual the king was clearly thought of as the god Tammuz. In the theology underlying this ritual, which is attested well beyond it, the Mesopotamian king is associated with the powers of nature.[124] Thus he is often called "the sun" or credited with the prosperity, fertility, and welfare of the land.

Furthermore, notes Frankfort, Mesopotamian kings were frequently referred to as the child or son of various gods, and various gods were referred to as the mother or father of the king. While the variety of deities said to be so connected to any given king suggests that this kinship was not meant literally, the king was clearly associated with the realm of the divine in a manner appropriate to his exalted status as the gods' intermediary or viceroy—I would dare to say image—who represents their rule on earth.

More fundamental, however, than these considerations is the sharing by Egyptian and Mesopotamian kings (as this chapter has already shown) of a similar cultic function in mediating and representing the

122. Curtis himself acknowledges that this practice is found among certain kings of the Akkad period, most kings of the Neo-Sumerian period, and a few Old Babylonian and Kassite kings; *Man as the Image of God*, 156.

123. See Cole and Machinist, *Letters from Priests to the Kings Esarhaddon and Assurbanipal*, xiv–xv (for summary) and xxii–xxiii nn. 13–30 (for documentation).

124. While the sacred marriage between the gods is attested in various times and places in Mesopotamia, whether the king participated in the sacred marriage outside ancient Sumer is debated by scholars.

gods on earth. Thus, even if Curtis is correct that the Mesopotamian king "was not set apart from his fellow man *by nature*," as was the Egyptian king, but rather "had been *chosen* by the gods as king and *endowed* with kingship by the gods," this does not vitiate the fundamental similarity of function that they shared.[125] Whether grounded in nature or grace (if we may so put it), it is the intermediary or representative function of Egyptian and Mesopotamian kings that provides the basis for referring to such kings as the image of a god.

But even apart from the possibility that Curtis's excessive dependence on Frankfort's distinction causes him (perhaps unintentionally) to downplay the divine character and function of Mesopotamian kings, we ought to wonder whether his interpretation of Mesopotamian cult images is skewed in the opposite direction. Were cult images in Mesopotamia really understood to be literal incarnations of the gods, divine by nature, like Egyptian pharaohs? Perhaps we need to apply here Frankfort's own caution about "the peculiar fluidity which the concept of divinity possessed in Mesopotamian . . . religion."[126] Indeed, Mesopotamian cult images turn out, upon examination, to provide a rather good parallel to the office and function of Mesopotamian kings, and an understanding of such images may well shed light on the meaning of humanity as God's image in Genesis 1.

As is now well known, Mesopotamian cult images were consecrated by means of an elaborate ritual, accompanied by incantations, typically known as the "mouth-washing" or sometimes the "mouth-opening" ritual (in Akkadian *mīs pî* or *pit pî*, respectively).[127] Although the *mīs pî* is a commonly attested ritual, used in many other contexts in the ancient Near East (for all sorts of purposes), forms of the ritual designed for the consecration of a cult statue (reconstructed from Assyrian and Babylonian texts found at Nineveh, Ashur, Sultantepe, Hama, Babylon, and Sippar) suggest that it functioned as an initiation or transition rite,

---

125. Curtis, *Man as the Image of God*, 159 (emphasis added).

126. Frankfort, *Kingship and the Gods*, 306.

127. A similar ritual was also used for consecrating Egyptian cult statues. See David Lorton, "The Theology of Cult Statues in Ancient Egypt," in *Born in Heaven, Made on Earth: The Making of the Cult Image in the Ancient Near East* (ed. Michael B. Dick; Winona Lake, IN: Eisenbrauns, 1999), 123–210.

128. Christopher Walker and Michael B. Dick, "The Induction of the Cult Image in Ancient Mesopotamia: The Mesopotamian *mīs pî* Ritual," in *Born in Heaven, Made on Earth: The Making of the Cult Image in the Ancient Near East* (ed. Michael B. Dick; Winona Lake, IN: Eisenbrauns, 1999), 67–68. See also Walker and Dick's expanded study, *The Induction of the Cult Statue in Ancient Mesopotamia: The Mesopotamian Mis Pi Ritual* (State Archives of Assyria Literary Texts; Helsinki, Finland: Neo-Assyrian Corpus Project, 2001).

using "language of gestation and birth to ritually recreate the cult statue as the god."[128]

In an extant *mīs pî* text for the consecration and vivification of an image of Shamash, for example, the image, carved out of tamarisk wood and overlaid with precious metals, was—while still in the workshop—ritually denied to be a human product.[129] Then, in a nightlong ceremony that took place by the riverbank (symbolizing the primordial waters) and in an orchard (representing the primeval forest), the image was—by means of various incantations and symbolic actions—ritually regressed to a time prior to its crafting by human hands. By this process it was effectively "transubstantiated," to use Jacobsen's vivid analogy, much as the host is consecrated in classical Roman Catholicism, so that it was, for the worshipers, no longer simply a physical object.[130] Michael Dick similarly, in an extensive study of the *mīs pî* ritual, compares the understanding of the consecrated image to the "theology of the 'real presence' of Jesus within the Eucharist."[131] The result of the *mīs pî* is that the carefully carved and decorated statue is said to be born of the gods and becomes the living presence of deity on earth. The mode of this presence, as both Jacobsen and Dick indicate, was distinct from either a merely symbolic reminder of deity or the actual, literal god.

The name of the ritual is itself significant. As a line in one of the incantations explicitly proclaims: "This statue cannot smell incense, drink water, or eat food without the Opening of the Mouth!"[132] The ritual, in other words, is understood as efficaciously vivifying the image, so that its various orifices are opened and it may speak, hear, see, and even (in a certain sense) walk. Testimony to belief in this vivification, once the *mīs pî* had been performed, is seen in the cult images being usually clothed and served two meals a day; and they were sometimes visited by other cult images (transported, of course, by priests).

129. This ritual text is examined in some detail by Thorkild Jacobsen, "The Graven Image," in *Ancient Israelite Religion: Essays in Honor of Frank Moore Cross* (ed. Patrick D. Miller Jr., Paul D. Hanson, and S. Dean McBride; Philadelphia: Fortress, 1987), 15–32. In both their article and their book (see previous note), Walker and Dick give the full text of this ritual, as well as two other ritual texts and various incantation texts used in the ritual.

130. Jacobsen, "Graven Image," 23.

131. Walker and Dick, "Induction of the Cult Image," 57 n. 2. This is specifically identified as a comment by Dick, who mistakenly calls it a Catholic doctrine. However, the doctrine of "real presence" is typically an Anglican interpretation of the Eucharist (going back through John Calvin to a pre-Thomist way of addressing the question).

132. *When the God Was Made* line 43, from Sultantepe tablet 200. Walker and Dick suggest this as the single most crucial line for understanding the ritual; "Induction of the Cult Image," 114.

The salient point for our purposes, however, is that Curtis's distinction between the cult image and the Mesopotamian king is too harshly drawn. Neither the king nor the cult statue was by nature divine. The cult statue was thought to *become* a divine image by choice of the gods, and this transition was mediated by human agency (artisans, priests, and sometimes the king himself). Even then the image was not simply identified with the god (nor was the god's presence limited to the image). Thus both the ritual consecration and the resulting "transubstantiation" of Mesopotamian cult images provide a most apt parallel to the election, adoption, and installation of the Mesopotamian king as the authorized intermediary of the gods on earth. It is this fundamental similarity between cult images and kings in Mesopotamia that most likely provides the basis for applying the term *ṣalmu* (the standard term for a cult image) to various Mesopotamian kings.

It is difficult to understand why Curtis distinguishes so sharply between the cult image and the king, since he himself admits that the creation of humanity in Genesis 2 (where God first makes then vivifies Adam by breathing the breath of life into his nostrils) likely echoes the *mīs pî* ritual.[133] If this very "earthy" portrayal of human creation in the Bible may contain an analogy with cult statues, what would be the problem with comparing Mesopotamian kings with cult statues? If, indeed, Genesis 2 echoes the *mīs pî*, it seems likely that the creation story in Genesis 1 also contains such an analogy (not only is it more royal than the Genesis 2 story, but it actually uses the term *image*).[134]

But if Mesopotamian royal ideology cannot be disqualified a priori, on either archeological or conceptual grounds, as a potential conduit of the image of god from the ancient Near East to Genesis 1, how do we decide which ideology—the Egyptian or Mesopotamian—is the most likely candidate? Is there any positive evidence to which we could turn?

---

133. Curtis suggests the comparison between Genesis 2 and *mīs pî* in his *Man as the Image of God*, 363 n. 28, and "Image of God (OT)," 390. This connection is also suggested by Catherene L. Beckerleg, "The Creation, Animation, and Installation of Adam in Genesis 2:7–25," paper read to the Hebrew Scriptures and Cognate Literature section at the annual meeting of the Society of Biblical Literature, November 21, 1999, in Boston, MA.

134. Curtis even implies a fundamental similarity between cult images and some *priests*, since he thinks that the *āšipu* in the *bīt mēseri* series was ritually identified with the cult image of Marduk mentioned earlier in the incantation text; *Man as the Image of God*, 161.

The Plausibility of Mesopotamian Influence

An initial (though inconclusive) consideration for a Mesopotamian source for the biblical *imago Dei* is that Hebrew *ṣelem* is cognate to Akkadian *ṣalmu*, the term specifically used in the Mesopotamian references (it is possible that the comparison of kings with cult images led to the use of this word). A further linguistic consideration, although admittedly not compelling, is that some uses of *ṣelem* and its Aramaic cognate *ṣĕlēm/ṣalmāʾ* are associated with Mesopotamia in the Bible.[135] Thus *ṣelem* is used of visual representations of Neo-Babylonian soldiers in Ezekiel 23:14 and refers to images of Babylonian or Assyrian gods in Amos 5:26, while the seventeen occurrences of *ṣĕlēm/ṣalmāʾ* in Daniel 2–3 are all associated with Babylon, with eleven of them designating the cult statue erected by Nebuchadnezzar II.

Of perhaps more significance is that, as Schmidt points out, the image of God "seems to be a fixed technical term" in both Genesis and the Mesopotamian references (which is not the case in Egypt).[136] Genesis 1:27; 5:1; and 9:6 all have "image/likeness *of God*," even when "*his* image/likeness" might be more appropriate syntactically. This corresponds to the formulations in the Mesopotamian texts: "image of Enlil," "image of Marduk," "image of Bel," "image of Shamash," or "likeness of a god." The Egyptian references, by contrast, do not always use "image/likeness of god" as a standardized epithet, but rather contain a more varied and flexible set of expressions, including "my image" (or "his image"), often in combination with "holy image," "living image on earth," and so on.[137] Although Schmidt's observation is certainly suggestive, it can hardly be conclusive evidence, given the small number of extant references in Genesis and the Mesopotamian literature.

A more decisive consideration is the widely recognized Mesopotamian character of the primeval history (Genesis 1–11), in which references to the image of God appear.[138] Without going into a great deal of detail at this point, we may note the following well-known connections or parallels between the primeval history and Mesopotamian literature.[139]

---

135. This is duly noted by Curtis, *Man as the Image of God*, 340, 365 n. 39, 376 n. 106.

136. Schmidt, *Faith of the Old Testament*, 195.

137. Ibid., 195–96.

138. A helpful overview of the Mesopotamian background of the primeval history is Stephanie Dalley, "The Influence of Mesopotamia upon Israel and the Bible," in *The Legacy of Mesopotamia* (ed. Stephanie Dalley; Oxford: Oxford University Press, 1998), 64–68.

139. Many of these parallels will be explored in chapters 4–5 for their contribution to an interpretation of the *imago Dei* in the context of the primeval history.

First of all, numerous scholars have discerned parallels between Mesopotamian literature and the Genesis creation accounts. Thus, ever since Hermann Gunkel, comparisons between Genesis 1 and the creation account in the Babylonian *Enuma Elish* have been proposed. The most notable similarities include the development of an ordered cosmos out of a watery beginning, cognate words used for the watery deep (Hebrew *tĕhôm* in Genesis 1:2 and Akkadian *tiʾāmat* in the Babylonian account), the threefold classification of land animals (domestic, wild, and crawling), the broad sequence of creative events (specifically, the order of firmament, dry land, luminaries, and humans), the theme of divine rest after creation, and the important place given to the creation of humanity.[140] While none of these prove that the writer of Genesis 1 knew or was influenced by the text of *Enuma Elish*, there is an intriguing similarity of ideas here (along with some sharp contrasts as well).[141]

One particularly distinctive Mesopotamian emphasis in the creation accounts in Genesis 1–2 is the prominent focus on the creation of humanity. Whereas Egyptian creation accounts do not usually highlight the creation of human beings, Mesopotamian accounts typically include the creation of humans in the context of cosmic creation, that is, they describe the creation of a *peopled* universe.[142] Likewise, the creation of humanity out of the dust of the ground in Genesis 2 echoes many Mesopotamian texts (such as *Enki and Ninmah*, the *Atrahasis Epic*,

140. I selected these parallels from Gunkel's analysis in *Schöpfung und Chaos in Urzeit und Endzeit* (Göttingen: Vandenhoeck & Ruprecht, 1895), a portion of which is translated by Charles A. Muenchow as "The Influence of Babylonian Mythology upon the Biblical Creation Story," in *Creation in the Old Testament* (ed. Bernhard W. Anderson; Issues in Religion and Theology 6; Philadelphia: Fortress, 1984), 25–52; and from Alexander Heidel's more guarded sifting of the evidence in *The Babylonian Genesis: The Story of Creation* (2nd ed.; Chicago: University of Chicago Press, 1951), chap. 3.

141. Although Richard J. Clifford doubts that Genesis 1 is dependent on *Enuma Elish*, he suggests parallels with other lesser-known Mesopotamian texts and utilizes numerous parallels to interpret Genesis 2–11, which he thinks is based on the Mesopotamian genre of the creation-flood story; *Creation Accounts in the Ancient Near East and in the Bible* (Catholic Biblical Quarterly Monograph Series 26; Washington, DC: Catholic Biblical Association of America, 1994), 137–50.

142. This point is to be distinguished from Westermann's influential argument (followed by his student Rainer Albertz) that there are two fundamental types of Mesopotamian creation myths: creation of the whole and creation of the one, that is, cosmic creation accounts and human creation accounts. Westermann's distinction is fundamentally flawed, as Clifford cogently argues (*Creation Accounts*, 6, 151–53). For Westermann's viewpoint, see *Genesis*, 1.22–25, and *Isaiah 40–66* (trans. D. M. G. Stalker; Old Testament Library; Philadelphia: Westminster, 1969), 24–26. For Albertz's argument, see *Weltschöpfung und Menschenschöpfung: Untersucht bei Deuterojesaja, Hiob und in den Psalmen* (Calwer Theologische Monographier; Stuttgart: Calwer, 1974).

the *Gilgamesh Epic* [creation of Enkidu], the *Babylonian Theodicy*, and the *Descent of Inanna to the Underworld*) where humanity is said to be made by the gods out of clay. And the sequence, in Genesis 1:1–2:3, of the creation of humanity *followed by* divine rest is a distinctly Mesopotamian motif (found in, for example, *Enuma Elish*, *Atrahasis Epic*, and *Enki and Ninmah*). It is not a sequence typically associated with Egyptian creation accounts.[143]

An even more important parallel, however, is the evident similarity between the account of the great flood in Genesis 6–9 and Mesopotamian flood traditions. It is generally recognized that the flood story is not an indigenous Israelite tradition, but is of Mesopotamian origin. Not only are the Mesopotamian flood texts (such as the *Atrahasis Epic*, the *Gilgamesh Epic*, and the *Eridu Genesis*) considerably more ancient that the biblical account, but flooding was a recurring Mesopotamian problem, not typical of the Levant.

There are also specific parallels between the biblical account of the flood and some of the Mesopotamian texts. First is the basic shared story line of a human being warned by a god of an impending flood, with detailed instructions to build a boat to save his family and various animals. Beyond that, however, we find the unusual word for "pitch" (*kōper*) used in Genesis 6:14 that does not occur anywhere else in the Old Testament with this meaning, but that is cognate to Akkadian *kupru* in the Mesopotamian stories.[144] And not only do Noah, Atrahasis (the flood hero in the epic that bears his name), and Utnapishtim (the flood hero of tablet 11 of the *Gilgamesh Epic*) all offer sacrifices after the flood, but Noah and Utnapishtim both release the very same birds from the window of the ark/boat when the rains stop.

Beyond the flood story proper is an overall structural similarity between Genesis 1–9 and two Mesopotamian versions of the flood story, namely, the *Atrahasis Epic* and the shorter (and more fragmentary) *Eridu Genesis*. These texts all portray a universal history of the world beginning with creation and moving to the flood. But there are further specific parallels between Genesis 1–9 and the Mesopotamian texts. Both Genesis 1–9 and the *Eridu Genesis* insert genealogical lists between

143. The theme of divine rest after creation is known in Egyptian thought (as in the *Memphite Theology*), but it is not associated with the creation of humans. The distinctiveness of this Mesopotamian theme, found pervasively in both Sumerian and Akkadian texts, leads W. G. Lambert, who typically does not admit much external influence on Genesis, to claim that here "ultimate borrowing by the Hebrews seems very probable"; "A New Look at the Babylonian Background of Genesis," in *The Bible in Its Literary Milieu: Contemporary Essays* (ed. Vincent L. Tollers and John R. Maier; Grand Rapids: Eerdmans, 1979), 294.

144. Dalley, "Influence of Mesopotamia," 66.

the creation of humanity and the flood, whereas Genesis 1–9 and the *Atrahasis Epic* both portray the newly created humanity facing various threats, culminating in the great flood.

Isaac Kikiwada and Arthur Quinn specifically correlate the three threats to humanity in the *Atrahasis Epic* (plague, drought, and flood) with three threats in the primeval history (Cain's murder, Lamech's vengeance, and the flood itself).[145] Tikva Frymer-Kensky, however, focuses on a more significant internal parallel between Genesis 1–9 and the *Atrahasis Epic*, namely, the reason for the flood.[146] Whereas the flood in the *Atrahasis Epic* is generated by human overpopulation (the gods are disturbed by the noise made by the growing human race), in Genesis the reason for the flood is human violence, which fills and corrupts the earth. Corresponding to these differing articulations of the narrative problematics, we find different narrative resolutions in the two accounts: the postflood introduction of population-control mechanisms in the *Atrahasis Epic* (such as infertility, stillbirth, and miscarriage) and the institution of the law against murder (with sanctions) in Genesis 9:6.

Then there is the formal similarity between the genealogy in Genesis 5 and the *Sumerian King List*. Apart from both texts having very long ages for those listed prior to the flood (although the ages in the king list are substantially higher than in Genesis 5), a more fundamental conceptual convergence is suggested by the placement of references to humanity as God's image in Genesis 5:1–3 and 9:6. The restatement of the *imago Dei* theme (the first time after Genesis 1) at the start of the Genesis 5 genealogy further confirms a royal interpretation of the *imago Dei*, since the human race takes the place in the Genesis genealogy that the line of kings occupies in the *Sumerian King List*. Even the reassertion of the *imago Dei* in Genesis 9:6 finds its parallel in the statement in the *Sumerian King List* that kingship was again "lowered from heaven" after the flood (since the dynastic line had presumably been disrupted).[147]

A Mesopotamian background is also indicated by various geographical references and personal names in the primeval history.[148] The genealogy

---

145. Isaac M. Kikiwada and Arthur Quinn, *Before Abraham Was: The Unity of Genesis 1–11* (Nashville: Abingdon, 1985), 47–52. They actually attempt to correlate the *Atrahasis Epic* to Genesis 1–11, viewing Genesis 10–11 as equivalent to the semitragic resolution at the end of the *Atrahasis Epic*. I am inclined to think that Genesis 2–9 properly constitutes the parallel to the *Atrahasis Epic*, with Genesis 1:1–2:3 and Genesis 10–11 functioning as an editorial framework.

146. Tikva Frymer-Kensky, "The Atrahasis Epic and Its Significance for Our Understanding of Genesis 1–9," *Biblical Archeologist* 40 (1977): 147–55, esp. 151.

147. Noted by Miller, "In the 'Image' and 'Likeness' of God," 295 n. 20.

148. For the following discussion, see Dalley, "Influence of Mesopotamia," 66–67.

of Genesis 10, for example, lists a series of Babylonian and Assyrian cities in association with the ruler Nimrod, who is said to be "a mighty hunter before YHWH" (10:8–12). The text may preserve a reference to Nimrud, which was another name for the Assyrian royal city of Kalhu (= biblical Calah). The patron-deity of the city was the Sumerian god Ninurta, who was known as patron of the hunt. Indeed, Genesis 10 may even intend an abbreviated reference to the thirteenth-century Assyrian King Tukulti-Ninurta I (who was named after the god), the first Assyrian monarch to conquer Babylon. This might explain why 10:10–12 lists both Babylonian and Assyrian cities under Nimrod's rule: "The beginning of his kingdom was Babel, Erech [that is, Uruk], and Accad, all of them in the land of Shinar. From that land he went into Assyria, and built Nineveh, Rehoboth-ir, Calah, and Resen between Nineveh and Calah; that is the great city" (Genesis 10:10–12 NRSV).

Perhaps more centrally, however, Genesis clearly portrays human history as beginning in Mesopotamia, since the Tigris and Euphrates rivers are described as flowing out of the garden of Eden (Genesis 2:14). It is even possible that the building of the first city in Genesis 4 reflects an ancient Mesopotamian tradition about Eridu as the first city (found in many places, including the *Sumerian King List* and the *Eridu Genesis*). Although the text as we now have it posits Cain as the builder of the first city and notes that he names it after his son Enoch, it is possible that the text originally attributed the building of the first city to Enoch himself. Genesis 4:17 literally says: "Cain knew his wife and she conceived and bore Enoch, and he built a city and named it after his son Enoch." It is possible that the final word *Enoch* is a scribal addition meant to clarify who did the building since the sentence would otherwise be ambiguous. Although the text as it stands suggests that Cain is resisting his fate to be a wanderer on the earth, it is possible that the original text assumed that he did not settle down, but that Enoch built the first city, which would then be named after his son Irad, whose name seems to be a variant of Eridu.[149]

A final, important link between Mesopotamia and the primeval history is the concluding episode of that history, consisting in the tower of Babel story in Genesis 11:1–9 together with Abram's subsequent departure from Ur of the Chaldeans (11:31). The Babel account (which echoes the theme of the shift from a single language to multiple languages found in the Sumerian epic of *Enmerkar and the Lord of Aratta*) evidently preserves the memory of Mesopotamian cultural and political hegemony—and

---

149. Ibid., 67.

150. Dalley suggests that Shinar was the Kassite name for Babylonia in the Late Bronze Age (ibid.).

protests it in no uncertain terms. Mesopotamia is indicated both by the name Babel itself (*bābel* is simply the normal Hebrew word for Babylon) and by the locale where the city is built (the land of Shinar mentioned in Genesis 11:2 refers to southern Mesopotamia in 10:10, that is, the region of Sumer and Babylonia).[150] Likewise in the account of Abram's departure, the references to Ur (a prominent city in ancient Sumer) and the Chaldeans (Neo-Babylonian king Nebuchadnezzar II was ethnically Chaldean) are clearly Mesopotamian, although these references (anachronistically) unite very different historical periods.[151] Whatever the actual historical origin of the tower of Babel account,[152] in its present canonical location it provides a context for Abram's subsequent departure from Mesopotamia, thus connecting an account of human origins centered in Mesopotamia (Genesis 1–11) with stories of Israel's ancestors in the land of Canaan (Genesis 12–50).

These well-established, widely recognized connections between Mesopotamia and the primeval history suggest a clear presumption in favor of Mesopotamian influence on the *imago Dei* idea in Genesis 1. Curtis himself agrees that the cultural background for the primeval history is primarily Mesopotamian,[153] and he is constrained to admit that if the *imago Dei* in Genesis 1 is of Egyptian origin (as he believes), it is grafted into a creation story that is fundamentally Mesopotamian in character.[154] Indeed, Curtis's own arguments implicitly suggest Mesopotamian influence. If there really was such a significant gap between Egyptian and Mesopotamian kingship, as Curtis suggests, such that there was no ready home for the idea of the king as image of god in Mesopotamia, this makes it even more unlikely that the Egyptian image of god influenced the Bible directly (without the mediation of Mesopotamia), since

151. While Ur was an important Sumerian center in the third millennium B.C.E., it is not known whether the Chaldeans entered Babylonia prior to the first millennium, where we have clear evidence of this. It is possible that Genesis 11:1–9 critiques the entire project of Sumero-Akkadian (or at least Sumero-Babylonian) civilization under the rubric "Babel."

152. Dale S. De Witt suggests that the text is very early and refers historically to the demise of the Third Dynasty of Ur; "The Historical Background of Genesis 11:1–9: Babel or Ur," *Journal of the Evangelical Theological Society* 22 (1979): 15–26.

153. Curtis, *Man as the Image of God*, 356; 378 n. 114. This is also E. A. Speiser's opinion in *Genesis: Introduction, Translation, and Notes* (Anchor Bible 1; Garden City, NY: Doubleday, 1964), liv.

154. Curtis, *Man as the Image of God*, 377 n. 112, 378 n. 113.

155. Curtis even admits that although Egyptian influence would most likely be early, an early date "would not preclude the possibility that the expression 'image of God' came into Israel through Mesopotamian influence"; *Man as the Image of God*, 343.

156. Ibid., 167–70.

ancient Israel was closer to Mesopotamia than to Egypt, not only in its understanding of kingship, but also in its wider worldview.[155]

Curtis even provides a hypothesis for the origin of the idea of the king as the image of a god in the extant Mesopotamian texts.[156] Having noted, with the exception of the *Tukulti-Ninurta Epic*, the prominence of priests in the Mesopotamian references (three texts are written by an *āšipu*, while one designates an *āšipu* as the image of Marduk), Curtis suggests that the idea could have been introduced into Mesopotamian royal ideology precisely by such priests.[157] Not only did *āšipu* priests typically officiate at the mouth-washing ritual used in the consecration of cult images and thus were thoroughly acquainted with the theology of images,[158] but it is possible, he suggests, that they first applied the notion to a member of their own guild. In a manner similar to a cult image, the priest was thought to function in the exorcism as the intermediary of the god, therefore the spell recited carries the authority of the god's word. This functional analogy, Curtis postulates, would then have been applied to the Mesopotamian king by *āšipu* priests, who discerned a similarity between their own cultic function and the royal office.[159]

A Neo-Babylonian Exilic Background for the *Imago Dei*?

Although this is pure guesswork—at most a plausible hypothesis and not proof of anything—the association of cultic officials (*āšipu* priests) with the Mesopotamian image of god renders the significance of the *Priestly* authorship of Genesis 1 worth exploring. This tantalizing connection raises the question whether there is any merit to the traditional scholarly construct of an exilic, Neo-Babylonian date for the so-called priestly edition of the Pentateuch, of which Genesis 1 is usually thought to be a part. Specifically, was the author of Genesis 1 influenced by the Mesopotamian image of god during (or possibly soon after) the exile?

We may break this question down into three interconnected issues. First of all, is it reasonable to postulate that ideas similar to those found in the seventh-century Neo-Assyrian image texts formed part of Neo-Babylonian royal ideology in the sixth century, when Israel was in exile? Second, is it likely that the author of Genesis 1 (or any Israelite) had access to the relevant ideas of Mesopotamian royal ideology? And third, do we have

---

157. Ibid., 167. It is unclear if Asharedu is an *āšipu*. His precise cultic profession is unknown.

158. Ibid., 193 n. 28.

159. A further factor, Curtis adds, is that these priests possibly came into contact with the notion of Egyptian kings as the image of deity through Esarhaddon's invasion of Egypt in 671 B.C.E.

any evidence that indicates when Genesis 1 was written? In particular, are there any indications of an exilic (or possibly postexilic) date?

The first question is the easiest to answer. That Babylonia and Assyria may have shared the notion of the king as image of a god is highly likely, even in the absence of clear textual evidence. We have already seen that Assyria and Babylonia shared a similar royal ideology in which the king functioned as the cultic representative of the gods on earth. It is, furthermore, interesting to note that Asharedu, the author of one of the Mesopotamian image of god letters, is a Neo-Babylonian priest in the Assyrian royal court, and it is entirely possible that the *bīt mīseri* series preserves a Babylonian reference (scholars have not been able to date the text or decide its provenance with any certainty).

Beyond this, it is suggestive that Marduk (patron-god of Babylon) figures prominently in the Assyrian image of god references (in four of the seven references). Not only the *āšipu* priest in the *bīt mīseri* series, but also the unnamed Assyrian kings in two of the letters and Esarhaddon and Sennacherib in one of Adad-shumu-usur's letters are said to be the image of Bel/Marduk (and Shamash, mentioned in one of the references, is a deity of both Assyria and Babylon). The notion of *Assyrian* kings as the image of a *Babylonian* god may be due to the well-known allure of Babylonian culture even at a time of Assyrian political and military superiority.[160] This may also explain why both *Enuma Elish* and the *Atrahasis Epic*, which were originally Babylonian compositions, are known to us also in important Assyrian recensions—the result of cultural borrowing and adaptation. This cultural borrowing amply illustrates how much overlap there was of Babylonian and Assyrian cultural ideals.

Thus, along with a shared Mesopotamian royal ideology concerning the cultic role of kings and the Assyrian reworking of originally Babylonian compositions, it is quite plausible, even in the absence of written documentation, that the two cultures shared the specific notion of kings as the image of a god. If we take this together with the distinctive Mesopotamian background of ideas for the primeval history, it is certainly possible that the biblical *imago Dei* derives from a Neo-Babylonian context. It is important to be clear, however, that there is no documented proof of this. It is simply a reasonable assumption.

This leads to our second question, namely, whether the author of Genesis 1 (or any other Israelite) had access to the Mesopotamian notion of the king as image of a god. A negative answer might initially be

160. A. Leo Oppenheim addresses the complex influence of Babylonian civilization on Assyria in his *Ancient Mesopotamia: Portrait of a Dead Civilization* (Chicago: University of Chicago Press, 1964), 65–67, 166.

161. Ibid., 146–48.

suggested by Oppenheim's well-known opinion that Mesopotamian royal inscriptions (which praised the exploits of various kings and testified to their devotion to the gods) were never widely promulgated.[161] Such Babylonian and Assyrian royal inscriptions on bricks, cylinders, stone slabs, statues, and various gold and silver objects were not accessible to the general populace. Rather they were typically deposited in the wall or under the foundations of temples and palaces, to be read by the god alone or sometimes by the next king who had to restore the building. Likewise, royal inscriptions on wall reliefs addressed to the gods were in dark and hidden sections of the palace or in some other inaccessible location.

It is true, Oppenheim admits, that some royal inscriptions that proclaimed, in propagandistic form, the king's victories to the world are found on stelae set up in public venues. Yet he is loath to admit that even these were meant for public dissemination and reading. Oppenheim's argument is here based on the evident similarity in content between some inscriptions on stelae (for example, those of Ashurnasirpal II and Nabonidus) and buried inscriptions (for example, on the cylinder of Nebuchadnezzar II).[162] Since the buried inscriptions were not meant for public reading, Oppenheim doubts that the stelae were meant for that either. And if widely attested royal inscriptions were largely inaccessible to the public, as Oppenheim claims, this would likely be true also of the previously cited Neo-Assyrian letters from the king's elite cultic advisors, which mention the image of god. It is thus unlikely that any biblical author would have known the specific contents of such letters.

Yet matters are not as simple as Oppenheim portrays them. First of all, his argument from hidden inscriptions to supposedly public stelae could go the other way. That is, the similarity in content of some stelae and building inscriptions could be taken as indicating that the content of supposedly hidden royal inscriptions was sometimes made accessible.

In the second place, Peter Machinist persuasively shows that Isaiah, the eighth-century prophet, was intimately familiar with a variety of motifs from Neo-Assyrian royal propaganda (some of which is found on building inscriptions) and used these to great effect in his oracles against the Assyrian king and his army.[163] Whereas some of these motifs, he avers, could have been promulgated in visual propaganda (in the form of stelae set up in Judah by the Assyrian army)[164] or in oral pro-

162. Ibid., 148.

163. Peter Machinist, "Assyria and Its Image in the First Isaiah," *Journal of the American Oriental Society* 103 (1983): 719–37.

164. Machinist admits that none have been yet excavated in Judah, but they have been found in nearby Samaria and Ashdod (ibid., 731).

165. Ibid., 730.

paganda (such as the speeches made on the city wall to the Jerusalem populace by Sennacherib's field commander [*rab-šāqēh*] in 2 Kings 18–19 || Isaiah 36–37), the "rather precise correspondence to written Assyrian idiom"[165] that characterizes some of Isaiah's oracles "is enough to raise the distinct possibility that Isaiah's knowledge of Assyria was gained not merely from actual experience of the Assyrians in Palestine, but from official Assyrian literature, especially of the court."[166] The relevant point from Machinist's discussion for the question we are investigating is that some of the language that Isaiah uses to critique Assyria reflects extant (supposedly inaccessible) Neo-Assyrian royal inscriptions.[167] The implication is either that Isaiah knew these inscriptions directly or (more likely) that their content and language was in some way transmitted to a wider public as part of Assyrian royal propaganda.[168] Although the content of the propaganda is somewhat different in the case we are concerned with, there is good reason to think that the notion of the king as an image of a god (which is part of the widespread Mesopotamian ideology of the king as the gods' viceroy and cultic intermediary) would also be known beyond specific written texts. It is thus plausible that the author of Genesis 1 (whether writing in the exile or not) would have had access to this Mesopotamian notion.

Granted this initial plausibility, however, how do we move from the claim of Mesopotamian (or even Babylonian) influence on the biblical *imago Dei* to a fully reconstructed sociohistorical context for Genesis 1? Indeed, is such a reconstruction possible? How do we even begin to determine when the text was written?

One line of approach would be through pentateuchal source criticism. Although a great deal of what the older literature referred to as the

166. Ibid., 729.

167. Ibid., 722–28.

168. A similar argument for widespread knowledge of the content of Esarhaddon's building inscriptions (which functioned as part of his royal propaganda) is made by Barbara N. Porter, *Images, Power, and Politics: Figurative Aspects of Esarhaddon's Babylonian Policy* (Philadelphia: American Philosophical Society, 1993), 105–16, cited by John F. Kutsko, *Between Heaven and Earth: Divine Presence and Absence in the Book of Ezekiel* (Biblical and Judaic Studies from the University of California, San Diego; Winona Lake, IN: Eisenbrauns, 2000), 22–23.

169. See Rolf Rendtorff, "The Paradigm Is Changing: Hopes—and Fears," *Biblical Interpretation* 1 (1993): 34–53. It is telling that in Rendtorff's opening remarks for the Tradition History of the Pentateuch seminar during the 1991 annual meeting of the Society of Biblical Literature in Kansas City, MO, he was constrained to sum up the previous years' meetings by saying that not only had the scholars working on the topic not been able to come to any agreement on the tradition history of the Pentateuch, but they were not even agreed on what the proper questions were.

170. Julius Wellhausen, *Die Composition des Hexateuchs und der historischen Bücher des Alten Testaments* (4th ed.; Berlin: de Gruyter, 1963 [1st ed. 1876]); idem, *Prolegomena*

"assured results" of critical scholarship is presently in creative ferment (some would say outright chaos), where no single paradigm dominates the scene,[169] some critical scholars continue to hold a modified version of Wellhausen's documentary hypothesis, which claims that Genesis 1 is part of the final phase of the editing of the Pentateuch (really the Tetrateuch—Genesis through Numbers).[170] On this view, articulated most coherently in the twentieth century by Martin Noth, Genesis 1 belongs to the work of a priestly redactor or school (identified by the siglum P), working either in the exile or sometime after, whose hand is evident in parts of Genesis and in significant portions of Exodus, Leviticus, and Numbers and who propounded a distinctive theology and social program.[171]

Among those who hold to the existence of P, there are typically two different opinions about its literary nature. Especially since Noth's arguments, many scholars understand P as an originally independent source along with J (the Yahwist) and E (the Elohist), telling its own version of the primeval history, the ancestors of Israel, the exodus from Egypt, and the founding of the nation (hence references to the putative priestly document or writing), and conclude that (later) P editors combined this existing P document with those of J and E into the Tetrateuch we have today.[172] An alternative view, associated especially with Frank Moore Cross, is that P was never an independent source, existing alongside J and E, but simply provided a later redactional or editorial framework for these sources and supplemented these with various priestly additions

---

zur Geschichte Israels (3rd ed.; Berlin: Reimer, 1899 [1st ed. 1878]); idem, Prolegomena to the History of Ancient Israel (trans. J. S. Black and A. Menzies; repr. Cleveland/New York: World, 1957).

171. Martin Noth, Überlieferungsgeschichte des Pentateuch (2nd ed.; Darmstadt/Stuttgart: Kohlhammer, 1960 [1st ed. 1948]); idem, A History of Pentateuchal Traditions (trans. Bernhard W. Anderson; Atlanta: Scholars Press, 1981). For a user-friendly version of Noth's pentateuchal source analysis, see Anthony F. Campbell and Mark A. O'Brien, Sources of the Pentateuch: Texts, Introductions, Annotations (Minneapolis: Fortress, 1993).

172. Noth, History of Pentateuchal Traditions, 8–19. Whereas Noth thought that P was primarily a narrative source and that the various law collections were independent of P, many critical scholars view the P source as a combination of narrative and law.

173. Frank Moore Cross, Canaanite Myth and Hebrew Epic: Essays in the History of the Religion of Israel (Cambridge: Harvard University Press, 1973), 293–325.

174. The variations of source analysis are almost limitless and include, beyond the various documentary hypotheses, so-called supplementary and fragmentary hypotheses, which reject the existence of distinct J, E, and P documents and argue, instead, that the Pentateuch grew by a gradual accumulation of small units of tradition. For an account and critique of many of the major hypotheses, see R. N. Whybray, The Making of the Pentateuch: A Methodological Study (Journal for the Study of the Old Testament Supplement 53; Sheffield: Sheffield Academic Press, 1987).

and expansions.[173] But whatever the variations, the dominant critical view is that the P source and/or editor dates from either the exile (sixth century) or soon after the return from exile (fifth century).[174] I myself am agnostic about the existence of a putative P document of which Genesis 1 is supposedly a part. It is not that I dispute the existence of sources or an editorial framework in Genesis through Numbers or that I refuse to recognize distinctive priestly theological emphases throughout these books. Rather, I simply do not believe we have access to the relevant knowledge to reconstruct or date the sources of the Pentateuch with any degree of certitude.[175] To illustrate the difficulty of reconstructing the historical context of Genesis 1, it may be helpful to compare the standard notions of the P source as an exilic or postexilic document (or editorial framework) with the alternative point of view going back to Yehezkel Kaufmann[176] and followed by many scholars today—who do not, however, necessarily follow Kaufmann's arguments or conclusions in all details. Nevertheless, according to these scholars, much, if not most, of P is preexilic, originating from the seventh century or earlier.

Many who follow this line of interpretation take a linguistic route in seeking to determine the date of P. While the issue is highly complex, and not all those working on the question agree, many Hebrew scholars conclude that the language of those sections of the Bible typically identified as P has clear affinities with classical Biblical Hebrew (as found in much of the Hebrew Bible and in preexilic epigraphic remains

175. For a recent, sustained attempt to reconstruct the sources of Genesis, see David M. Carr, *Reading the Fractures of Genesis: Historical and Literary Approaches* (Louisville: Westminster John Knox, 1996).

176. Yehezkel Kaufmann, *The Religion of Israel: From Its Beginnings to the Babylonian Exile* (trans. and abridged by Moshe Greenberg; Chicago: University of Chicago Press, 1960), 175–200 (from *History of Israelite Religion* [8 vols.; Tel-Aviv: Bialik Institute-Duir, 1937–56], vols. 1–7 [Hebrew]).

177. For example, Gary Rendsburg, "Late Biblical Hebrew and the Date of P," *Journal of the Ancient Near Eastern Society* 12 (1980): 65–80; Ziony Zevit, "Converging Lines of Evidence Bearing on the Date of P," *Zeitschrift für die Alttestamentliche Wissenschaft* 94 (1982): 502–9; and the work of Avi Hurvitz cited in the following note. For scholars who think the language of P is exilic (somewhere between classical Biblical Hebrew and Late Biblical Hebrew) or has significant postexilic elements, see Robert Polzin, *Late Biblical Hebrew: Toward an Historical Typology of Biblical Hebrew Prose* (Harvard Semitic Monograph 12; Missoula, MT: Scholars Press, 1976); Baruch A. Levine, "Late Language in the Priestly Source: Some Literary and Historical Observations," in *Proceedings of the Eighth World Congress of Jewish Studies: Panel Sessions—Bible Studies and Hebrew Language* (Jerusalem: World Union of Jewish Studies, 1983), 69–82.

178. Avi Hurvitz, "The Usage of שֵׁשׁ and בּוּץ in the Bible and Its Implication for the Date of P," *Harvard Theological Review* 60 (1967): 117–21; idem, "The Evidence of Language in Dating the Priestly Code," *Revue biblique* 81 (1974): 24–56; idem, *A Linguistic Study of*

from Palestine) and not with Late Biblical Hebrew (found in postexilic biblical writings such as Ecclesiastes, Esther, Daniel, Chronicles, and Ezra–Nehemiah and in the Qumran texts).[177] Among the various arguments given in support of this conclusion are that certain technical cultic terms used in P either are replaced by other terms in the postexilic era or are used with a different meaning altogether.[178] I am not a linguist and thus certainly not competent to adjudicate this matter. However, the linguistic argument for a preexilic date for P among many reputable biblical scholars flies in the face of the standard critical view and therefore should give us pause.

But there are other reasons to think that P is preexilic. Whereas Wellhausen (and many source critics after him) thought that the priestly description of the tabernacle was really a coded way to refer to the postexilic Second Temple, it is telling that neither the dimensions of the tabernacle nor many of its accoutrements and institutions (for example, the ark of the covenant, the cherubim, the Urim and Thummim, the practice of anointing the high priest, and regulations for animal tithes) correspond to anything in the Second Temple period.[179] Furthermore, Moshe Weinfeld notes many places where Deuteronomy and Joshua quote, allude to, or rework various terms and texts typically attributed to P (from Genesis, Leviticus, and Numbers), yet the reverse is not true.[180] This suggests that P predates the book of Deuteronomy and the Former Prophets. But the strongest evidence for regarding P as preexilic is that Ezekiel (who prophesied during the Babylonian exile) critically engages priestly theology, even quoting and alluding to numerous P texts.[181]

While this certainly throws the classical claim for an exilic or postexilic date for P into confusion, none of it is actually decisive for the date of Genesis 1, since a preexilic date for even the majority of P does not

---

the Relationship between the Priestly Source and the Book of Ezekiel (Cahiers de la Revue biblique 20; Paris: Gabalda, 1982); idem, "The Language of the Priestly Source and Its Historical Setting—The Case for an Early Date," Proceedings of the Eighth World Congress of Jewish Studies: Panel Sessions—Bible Studies and Hebrew Language (Jerusalem: World Union of Jewish Studies, 1983), 86–93; idem, "Dating the Priestly Source in Light of the Historical Study of Biblical Hebrew a Century after Wellhausen," Zeitschrift für die Alttestamentliche Wissenschaft 100 (1988): 88–100.

179. Kaufmann, Religion of Israel, 175–200; Richard Elliott Friedman, The Exile and Biblical Narrative: The Formation of the Deuteronomistic and Priestly Works (Harvard Semitic Monograph 22; Chico, CA: Scholars Press, 1981), 45, 48.

180. Moshe Weinfeld, Deuteronomy and the Deuteronomic School (Oxford: Clarendon, 1972), 179–82.

181. Kutsko, Between Heaven and Earth, 11–13 and passim; and Hurvitz, Linguistic Study.

182. For an extended argument in favor of a preexilic date for P with later exilic redaction, see Friedman, Exile and Biblical Narrative, 44–132.

necessarily exclude later (exilic or postexilic) priestly editorial work on the Pentateuch.[182] Such later editorial work might well include the addition of Genesis 1 (whatever its origins) as a preface to the book of Genesis and/or to the entire Pentateuch. In other words, even if there was a (preexilic) P document, there is no certainty that Genesis 1 was a part of it.

Indeed, there is reason to doubt that Genesis 1 derives from the same priestly hand or tradition that is responsible for what is usually thought of as the P sections of Leviticus.[183] Without denying that Genesis 1 may be priestly in origin (given the cosmic temple notion we discussed in chapter 2), I note that there is significant tension between the worldview of Genesis 1, in which every stage and facet of creation is said to be "good," and the whole "very good" (Genesis 1:31), and the symbolic universe of Leviticus, which is predicated on maintaining distinctions "between the holy and the profane, and between the unclean and the clean" (Leviticus 10:10), implying varying levels of valuation within the created order. There are, of course, explanations that attempt to harmonize the levitical schema with Genesis 1, such as Mary Douglas's theory that unclean animals in Leviticus are those that do not fit clearly into any particular category of creation in Genesis 1.[184] One way of understanding this theory (which requires going beyond the actual text of the creation story) is to claim that Genesis 1 portrays a world in which "the sky was populated by noncarnivorous winged creatures. The earth was inhabited by four-legged creatures that chewed the cud and had cloven hooves. The sea was inhabited by creatures with scales and fins."[185] Given this very specific definition of what God is supposed to have created in Genesis 1 (which certainly goes beyond the text), animals that do not fit the above categories (for example, certain insects and mammals, as well as reptiles, crustaceans, and birds of prey) are regarded as unclean (Leviticus 11). What this attempted harmonization fails to reckon with, however, is the question of the origin of these unclean animals. The extraordinary implication here seems to be that God did not create large categories of presently existing animal life. This

183. While Leviticus 1–16 is usually regarded as P, Leviticus 17–26 (the Holiness Code) is typically assigned to a different priestly tradition (designated H). While it used to be traditional to regard H as earlier than P, the opposite is argued by Jacob Milgrom, *Leviticus 1–16: A New Translation with Introduction and Commentary* (Anchor Bible 3; New York: Doubleday, 1991), 13–29; and Israel Knohl, *The Sanctuary of Silence: The Priestly Torah and the Holiness School* (Minneapolis: Fortress, 1994).

184. Mary Douglas, *Purity and Danger: An Analysis of the Concepts of Pollution and Taboo* (London: Routledge & Kegan Paul, 1966), chap. 3.

185. Barry L. Bandstra, *Reading the Old Testament: An Introduction to the Hebrew Bible* (2nd ed.; Belmont, CA: Wadsworth, 1999), 148.

highly problematic implication underlies the criticism of the levitical schema in the story of the apostle Peter's rooftop vision in Acts 10:9–16. Having been exhorted in a vision to eat animals that are regarded as unclean according to the laws of Leviticus, Peter objects that he has never before eaten anything unclean or profane. He is then told by a heavenly voice: "What God has made clean, you must not call profane" (Acts 10:15 NRSV), which implicitly upholds the worldview of Genesis 1 against that of Leviticus 11.

Given the complexity of the question, then, whether the dating of P bears directly on Genesis 1, it is perhaps more relevant to consider that Genesis 1 seems to be presupposed in Jeremiah 4:19–27. In the middle of an oracle of judgment on seventh-century Judah, Jeremiah says: "I looked on the earth, and lo, it was waste and void [tōhû wābōhû]; / and to the heavens, and they had no light" (4:23 NRSV). Analogous to the P sections of the flood story in Genesis, where the separation of the waters on days 2 and 3 is undone, here we find a vision of the reversal of creation that describes the earth in its precreation state as tōhû wābōhû (Genesis 1:2) and mentions the absence of light in the heavens (1:3). If this is an allusion to Genesis 1 (and not just to the traditions that underlie it) and if the oracle is authentic to Jeremiah the prophet (whose oracles of judgment date from 627 through the fall of Jerusalem in 586), this excludes an exilic or postexilic date for Genesis 1.

But even if we could specify when Genesis 1 was written, this would not answer the question of when the image of god idea entered Israelite tradition. Not only is it possible that the ideas of Genesis 1 circulated in Israelite tradition prior to the actual writing of the text, but Mesopotamia and Israel were in contact by trade for the entirety of Israel's existence as a nation, and contact between Mesopotamia and Palestine extended back even into the Late Bronze Age (the narrative setting of the Abraham, Isaac, and Jacob stories). So, the image of god idea (if it indeed came from Mesopotamian royal ideology) may, in principle, have influenced Israelite oral tradition prior to any textual trace of it in Scripture.

Yet, if the idea entered Israelite tradition early, it is strange that the terminology does not show up in other places besides the three texts in Genesis (1:26–27; 5:1–3; 9:6). Thus, given the rather limited occurrence of the *imago Dei* in the Old Testament, it makes sense to think that the notion (or at least the terminology) was relatively new to Israelite thinking. It may even suggest that the Genesis image texts are themselves rather late. On the face of it, it seems unlikely that so fecund a notion as the *imago Dei*, if it were early, would receive no intrascriptural commentary whatsoever, given the general proclivity of the biblical writers to engage in such commentary and the later attraction of both Jewish and Christian commentators to the *imago Dei*. Nevertheless, it is unclear just how late this requires Genesis 1 to have been composed. It may well be compatible with a seventh-century date. And if it is not, it is still possible that the *imago Dei* may be an exilic addition to an earlier, preexilic version of the text.

In conclusion, then, while it is reasonable to think that the image of god was applied to Neo-Babylonian kings in the sixth century (when Israel was in exile) and it is entirely likely that Israelite authors (in the sixth century or before) were acquainted with Mesopotamian royal ideology, there is no clear evidence for an exilic or postexilic date for the image of God references in Genesis. Indeed, the evidence, if anything, points to a seventh-century date (or earlier) for Genesis 1. But even this is not definitive for the *imago Dei*, which could have been added to Genesis 1 later. Thus, while a sixth-century date cannot be definitely excluded for the transmission of the *imago Dei* from Mesopotamia to Israel, there is no explicit support for this. The evidence for dating is fundamentally ambiguous.[186]

It would be unwise, therefore, for us to limit ourselves to an exilic context for the purpose of interpreting the *imago Dei*. Rather, given the widely agreed upon Mesopotamian background of the primeval history, I will assume for the purposes of the argument what is no more than a plausible scenario, namely, that the author of Genesis 1 (whenever he lived) was acquainted (in either oral or written form) with the Mesopotamian notion of the king as image of a god (as a particular crystallization of royal ideology) and that he intentionally challenged this notion with the claim that all humanity was made in God's image.[187]

186. My thanks to Nik Ansell and Sylvia Keesmaat (both of the Institute for Christian Studies, Toronto) for pushing me on this matter.

187. It is even possible that the author of Genesis 1 knew only the general Mesopotamian royal theology (in which the king is the intermediary or viceroy of the gods) and put this together with the representative character of images (whether applied to cult statues, votive statues, statues of kings in distant lands, or Israel's own idol critique) and then made the decisive leap to the claim that humanity is God's authorized image on earth (without the benefit of ever seeing in writing—or even hearing of—any Mesopotamian king referred to as the *ṣalmu* of a god).

4

The Matrix
of Mesopotamian
Ideology

E ven though the Mesopotamian ideology of sacral kingship (which includes the notion of the king as image of a god) provides an appropriate background for understanding the biblical *imago Dei*, this ideology was not an isolated, freestanding element, but was embedded in a broader matrix of Mesopotamian ideology. Two particular aspects of this broader Mesopotamian ideology, beyond the unique status of the king, need to be addressed.[1]

First of all, since the unique status of the Mesopotamian king (as the gods' viceroy and image) is meant to distinguish him from the general populace and because Genesis 1 applies the *imago Dei* to humanity as a whole, it would be wise for us to examine the status of humanity in the Mesopotamian worldview. That is, in contrast to the king (and perhaps priests), how were ordinary human beings understood in ancient Mesopotamia? This chapter will thus examine various Mesopotamian creation accounts (both ancient Sumerian and later Akkadian accounts)

1. I am grateful to Richard A. Henshaw for his helpful advice on the ancient Near Eastern materials discussed in this chapter.

for their understanding of the human status and role in the cosmos. We will specifically explore how this understanding of humanity (in tandem with the notion of the king as cultic representative of the gods) functioned to undergird the Mesopotamian social order.

Second, we will examine the theme of the *Chaoskampf* or combat myth (the grounding of creation in primordial divine violence) in *Enuma Elish*, also known as the Babylonian *Epic of Creation*. Not only is this one of the central Mesopotamian texts that articulates the human purpose, but its great popularity, especially toward the middle of the first millennium B.C.E. in both Babylonia and Assyria, requires us to take a closer look at how some of its distinctive perspectives may have impacted the Mesopotamian worldview. This chapter will thus attempt to weave together the strands of Mesopotamian sacral kingship (including the king as image of a god), the status and role of humanity in Mesopotamian creation accounts, and the theology of primordial violence as found in *Enuma Elish*, to illumine the larger matrix of Mesopotamian ideology that would have mythically undergirded the empires of Babylon and Assyria. It is this ideological matrix that provides the appropriate background for interpreting the biblical *imago Dei* as a counterproposal about the human condition.

The terms *ideology* and *ideological*, which I have so far used without definition, require some clarification. *Ideology* is, of course, a loaded term, with a variety of contested meanings.[2] At its most fundamental level, I use the term to signify that the ideas in question are not free-floating, neutral concepts without ethical implications or sociocultural embodiment. On the contrary, the Mesopotamian ideas I will explore in this chapter form a coherent worldview that commends or shapes specific patterns of behavior and has historically functioned to legitimate the social order or political arrangement of actual societies in history.

There is, however, another sense to the word *ideology* that is relevant to my depiction of the Mesopotamian worldview, a sense that derives from Marx.[3] This is the pejorative sense of ideology as false or deceptive ideas that underwrite the oppressive circumstances of a people and serve as mystification or rationalization of these circumstances. I

2. For a helpful discussion of different meanings of "ideology," see A. K. M. Adam, *What Is Postmodern Biblical Criticism?* (Guides to Biblical Scholarship; Minneapolis: Fortress, 1995), 45–60, esp. 47–49.

3. See part 1 of Karl Marx and Frederick Engels, *The German Ideology* (London: Lawrence & Wishart/Moscow: Progress Publishers, 1965 [orig. 1846]), which begins with a sustained "materialist" critique of the "idealist" illusions of the Young-Hegelian philosophy. For a more accessible text, see *The German Ideology, Part One: With Selections from Parts Two and Three, Together with Marx's "Introduction to the Critique of Political Economy"* (ed. C. J. Arthur; New York: International Publishers, [1969]).

happen to believe that this understanding of ideology is also applicable to the Mesopotamian worldview.

Although in what follows I try to be fair in my descriptions of Mesopotamian mythic conceptions and social arrangements, I cannot claim to be neutral or unbiased, since my purpose is to paint a picture of what I take to be a fundamentally unjust ideology that required radical critique from a biblical perspective. I fully realize that my alignment *with* the biblical witness *against* the Mesopotamian worldview means that I have to accept fully that my own approach to the material is itself ideological in at least the first sense of the term. Whether my approach is ideological in the second sense also is for others to judge. There is, at any rate, no nonideological (that is, neutral) place to stand. Having already addressed the inevitable role of subjectivity in interpretation (in chapter 1), here I simply acknowledge my own biases and signal my intent to represent fairly the Mesopotamian worldview in the exposition that follows.

The Status of Humanity in Sumero-Akkadian Creation Accounts

The purpose and role of humanity in the cosmos is articulated in many Mesopotamian creation accounts, including lengthy Akkadian epic texts like the *Atrahasis Epic* and *Enuma Elish* as well as shorter Sumerian texts like *Enki and Ninmah* and *Ewe and Wheat*, and the bilingual (Sumerian/Akkadian) text known as *KAR 4*. These texts testify to a common Sumero-Akkadian creation theology in which humans are created to serve the gods, thus relieving them of their burdens. Typically this service, which includes the building and maintaining of temples, the provision of cultic sacrifices, and the upkeep of the irrigation and agricultural system upon which the temple economy depended, is viewed as the express purpose of human existence.

It might be helpful to think of the internal logic or conceptual interrelationship between the various elements of this complex service as follows: The fundamental human destiny and duty is to care for the needs of the gods, which is understood as the provision of housing and food for them. Whereas the duty to provide *housing* is equivalent to the building and maintenance of temples, the duty to provide *food* is equivalent to the daily sacrificial meals offered in the cult. These meals, however, require massive agricultural production, which in turn requires the maintenance of a complex system of irrigation canals.

Not every creation account expressed every dimension of this complex service. Whereas the human task to build and/or maintain temples as dwellings for the gods is noted in *Enuma Elish*, the task of feeding the gods with daily sacrifices is prominent in both *Enuma Elish* and in the flood section of the *Atrahasis Epic*. *Ewe and Wheat*, however, depicts human service of the gods in terms of agriculture, since this is necessary to sustain the daily sacrifices, while the need to keep the rivers and irrigation canals silt free (a task crucial to Mesopotamian agriculture, by which the gods' food was produced) is central to the *Atrahasis Epic* and to *Enki and Ninmah*. The myth known as *KAR 4* combines all these functions, in its multifaceted depiction of the human task (although its focus is on irrigation agriculture).

Although other Mesopotamian creation texts address the role and status of humanity in the cosmos, many are fragmentary and do not add substantially to the picture we can derive from the five I have chosen for exposition. These five, furthermore, have the benefit of being available in reliable recent translations by reputable scholars of Mesopotamian literature, and their main outlines are relatively well understood.

My purpose in the exposition that follows is thus not primarily to adjudicate the interpretation of these cosmogonies (as was necessary with many of the ancient Near Eastern parallels cited in chapter 3), but rather to explicate a broad consensus on relevant aspects of the Mesopotamian worldview that is articulated in them. There are, admittedly, a variety of controversial readings in the texts I have chosen for exposition, either having to do with sections missing in the original or the translation of obscure Akkadian or Sumerian terminology or syntax.[4] None of these, however, affects the basic interpretation of the myths, and only those interpretive questions that are essential for my argument will be addressed.[5] For the most part, then, my exposition will combine quotation of significant sections of the translated text with a coherent exposition of its ideas, in order both to give a flavor of the particular myth and to convey its notion of the human role and purpose in the world.

Atrahasis Epic

For the typical Mesopotamian understanding of human purpose, we would do well to begin with the account of the creation of humanity

4. This is particularly true in the Sumerian texts, as the Sumerian language is not as well understood as Akkadian.

5. The field of ancient Near Eastern studies—or even Mesopotamian studies alone—can be a minefield for biblical scholars. I am aware of how quickly new interpretations arise, based on new discoveries, new methodologies, and advances in understanding of relevant languages. It is inevitable that some of the analysis in this chapter will become outdated in a few years and will need to be updated. Nevertheless, I try to follow mainstream, reliable interpretations of the texts in question.

recorded on tablet 1 of the *Atrahasis Epic*.[6] Not only is this epic one of the longest and most famous Akkadian texts in existence today, but it was also one of the most popular texts in ancient Mesopotamia, as is evident from the different recensions of it that have turned up from Old Babylonian, Middle Babylonian, and Late Assyrian times, spanning approximately one thousand years.[7]

Although the plot of the *Atrahasis Epic* covers a great deal of ground, including the problem of human overpopulation and the gods' attempts to rectify this, culminating in the great flood (Atrahasis is the name of the flood hero, meaning "exceedingly wise"), the text begins with the situation before human beings existed, when the gods had to do their own work.[8] The epic (in the Old Babylonian version) opens with the following words:

> When gods were man,
> They did forced labor, they bore drudgery.
> Great indeed was the drudgery of the gods,
> The forced labor was heavy, the misery too much:
> The seven(?) great Anunna-gods were burdening
> The Igigi-gods with forced labor. (1.1–6)[9]

6. Recent English translations of the *Atrahasis Epic* are found in Stephanie Dalley, *Myths from Mesopotamia: Creation, the Flood, Gilgamesh, and Others* (Oxford: Oxford University Press, 1989), 1–38; Benjamin R. Foster, *Before the Muses: An Anthology of Akkadian Literature*, vol. 1: *Archaic, Classical, Mature* (Bethesda, MD: CDL, 1993), 158–201, a portion of which (the Old Babylonian text on pp. 160–85) is reprinted in *COS* 1.450–53. Older English translations may be found in W. G. Lambert and A. R. Millard, *Atra-ḫasīs: The Babylonian Story of the Flood* (Oxford: Clarendon, 1969); and *ANET* 104–6, 512–14 (trans. E. A. Speiser and A. K. Grayson).

7. The most complete form of the text is an Old Babylonian version, which claims to be written by the scribe Nur-Aya in the reign of the Babylonian king Ammi-saduqa (late seventeenth century B.C.E.).

8. Richard J. Clifford suggests that the *Atrahasis Epic* is an "anthological cosmology," combining creation and flood motifs based on earlier Sumerian works. The section on human creation is based on the Sumerian myth *Enki and Ninmah*, while the section on the flood may be based on the *Sumerian Flood Story* (also known as the *Eridu Genesis*); see *Creation Accounts in the Ancient Near East and in the Bible* (Catholic Biblical Quarterly Monograph Series 26; Washington, DC: Catholic Biblical Association of America, 1994), 74.

9. Translation from Foster, *Before the Muses*, 1.159, as are all further quotations of the *Atrahasis Epic* unless otherwise specified. Foster explains that the first line of the *Atrahasis Epic* is not intended literally, but is a metaphor meaning "when gods were (like) men" (159 n. 1). This agrees with Lambert and Millard's classic translation: "When the gods like men" (*Atra-ḫasīs*, 43). Even Dalley's variant translation, "When the gods instead of man" (*Myths from Mesopotamia*, 9), does not change the basic meaning, which is that prior to humanity the gods did what we now think of as human work.

The work—portrayed here as canal-digging[10]—was so laborious and burdensome that the Igigi, the lesser gods upon whom the labor had been imposed, burn their tools and go on strike, taking their grievance to the high god Enlil, who in this text has responsibility for earthly affairs. Having surrounded Enlil's house/temple at night and threatening hostility, the Igigi are finally given a hearing, and the Anunna-gods agree that the complaint is legitimate.[11] Anu himself declares:

> Why do we blame them?
> Their forced labor was heavy, their misery too much. (1.176–77)

A solution to the work stoppage and the Igigi's grievance is found only when Enki, the god of the subterranean freshwaters,[12] calls upon Mami (also known as Nintu), the mother goddess, to create humanity:

> Create a human being that he may bear the yoke,
> Let him bear the yoke, the task of Enlil,
> Let man assume the drudgery of god. (1.195–97)

But Mami/Nintu declines to attempt the task alone:

> It is not for me to do it,
> The task is Enki's.
> He it is that cleanses all,
> Let him provide the clay so I can do the making. (1.200–203)

Then follows a narrative in which, at Enki's direction, a god is slaughtered and his flesh and blood are mixed with clay by Mami/Nintu in order to create humanity. The name of the slain deity is given as We-ilu (perhaps a play on awêlu, man), and he is killed "along with his ṭēmu," a word of contested meaning that Foster renders "inspiration" (1.239).[13] The result of

---

10. The text goes on to mention the digging of watercourses, including the Tigris and Euphrates rivers, the digging of wells, and the draining of marshes (1.21–35).

11. Foster's "Anunna" is equivalent to "Anunnaki" in other translations. Originally this was a Sumerian term referring to the older deities, while "Igigi" referred to the younger gods. In later Mesopotamian myths, however, the terms evidence significant fluidity. Sometimes the Anunna/Anunnaki are distinguished from the Igigi, while in other myths there are two categories of Anunna/Anunnaki (major and minor, or pertaining to heaven and earth/underworld). The term *Igigi* can be likewise quite fluid, sometimes used interchangeably with *Anunna/Anunnaki*. The context will determine the referents. See the glossary in Dalley, *Myths from Mesopotamia*, esp. 318, 323.

12. Although it is an Akkadian work, the *Atrahasis Epic* utilizes the old Sumerian triad of ruling deities: Enlil (god of earth), Anu (god of heaven/sky), and Enki (god of the subterranean waters, portrayed as the friend of humans in many myths).

13. The meaning of *ṭēmu* will be examined later in this chapter.

this mixture of divine substance with clay is that the god's spirit (*ețemmu*) will remain a constituent part of human nature, memorialized in the pulsating of the human heart. When the clay mixture is prepared and humans are about to be fashioned, Mami announces to the gods:

> I have done away with your heavy forced labor,
> I have imposed your drudgery on man.
> . . . .
> I have released the yoke, I have [made] restoration. (1.240–41, 243)

At this the gods rush up in gratitude and kiss Mami's feet, naming her Belet-kala-ili or "Mistress-of-All-the-Gods" (1.245–47).

Once humans are birthed, with Mami as midwife, they begin to multiply. Although the text is fragmentary at this point, it seems that humans are put to work maintaining the canals and producing food:

> They made n[e]w hoes and shovels,
> They built the big canal banks.
> For food for the peoples, for the maintenance of [the gods]. (1.337–39)

This fragmentary reference to the human task is considerably clarified later in the *Atrahasis Epic*, in the flood section of the story, where humans multiply so greatly that their clamor disturbs the gods, particularly Enlil. Although various deities send first disease, then drought, to wipe out the human race, these calamities are averted when humans (at the suggestion of Enki, their creator) appease the gods in question by building temples in their honor and providing food offerings. In each case, the text says concerning the deity with primary responsibility for the calamity:

> The flour offering pleased him,
> He was shamed by the gift and suspended his hand. (1.409–10; 2.27–28)

But the third and final calamity, the great flood—initiated by Enlil and Anu—is of a different order and requires a different solution. Instead of suggesting that humans appease the gods, Enki (who has been ordered by the gods not to help humanity again) instructs Atrahasis surreptitiously (by speaking to a wall close to where Atrahasis is sitting) to build a boat and so escape annihilation. This Atrahasis does, bringing on board not only his family, but also many animals and birds, thus preserving their life.

After seven days and nights of the flood, however, the gods are in anguish. Whereas Enki and Mami grieve for the destruction of their human creations, the other gods have more pressing concerns. They have been without food offerings for an entire week:

> The Anunna, the great gods,
> Were sitting in thirst and hunger.
> . . . .
> Their lips were agonized with thirst,
> They were suffering pangs of hunger. (3.3.30–31; 3.4.21–22)

Indeed, when the flood subsides, the first thing Atrahasis does on dry land is to offer a sacrifice, which W. G. Lambert and A. R. Millard describe as "psychologically a good move," since it reminds the gods of their need for humans (and their folly in bringing the flood).[14] All the gods—except Enlil and Anu, who were still angry at Atrahasis's survival—immediately flock to the sacrificial meal:

> [The gods sniffed] the savor,
> They were gathered [like flies] around the offering. (3.5.34–35)[15]

Thus it turns out that Enki's rescue of Atrahasis from the flood was not purely philanthropic. The survival of the human race was meant to guarantee a continued supply of food. Addressing the assembly of gods, Enki declares: "I did it [indeed] for your sakes!" (3.6.18).

The purpose of humanity in the *Atrahasis Epic* is, therefore, clarified: Humans were created to relieve the gods of their toil in maintaining the canal system, which was essential for irrigation farming, and the ultimate purpose of this was so that the gods' needs might be met, specifically through regular cultic sacrifices.

Enki and Ninmah

In its account of human creation, the first tablet of the *Atrahasis Epic* is evidently dependent on the ancient Sumerian myth known as *Enki and Ninmah*, which is one of the oldest extant Mesopotamian creation texts.[16] The Sumerian myth, as we have it, seems to be a composite of two originally separate stories, the first (lines 1–43) describing the creation of humans to relieve the gods of their burdens, the second (lines 44–139) describing the creation of deformed or defective humans, the

---

14. Lambert and Millard, *Atra-ḫasīs*, 12.

15. Although the text is here broken, it is reconstructed from later repetitions of these lines.

16. Jacob Klein claims that it is the earliest Mesopotamian creation account; *COS* 1.516.

result of a contest by Enki and Ninmah, who were both drunk at the time. Although the second section of *Enki and Ninmah* is paralleled by the fragmentary conclusion to the *Atrahasis Epic* (where the creation of defective humans is viewed as a solution to overpopulation), our concern here is with the first section, which begins, as the epic does, with the time prior to humans.[17]

In those days, explains the text, the gods had to produce their own food and keep the canals silt free (line 10), presumably because the production of food (line 8) depended on the irrigation of fields (although this is not explicitly stated). The situation as portrayed in *Enki and Ninmah* anticipates the opening lines of the *Atrahasis Epic*:

> The senior gods did oversee the work,
>> while the minor gods were bearing the toil.
> The gods were digging the canals,
>> were piling up their silt in Ḫarali;[18]
> The gods were dredging the clay,
>> they were complaining about their (hard) life. (lines 9–11)[19]

Their complaint, although accompanied by much weeping, is unknown to the god Enki, who is sleeping in his subterranean chamber. It does, however, come to the attention of Nammu, Enki's mother, who rouses him and challenges him to find a solution to this problem (she even plants the seed of an idea in his mind):

> My son, arise from your bed;
>> and when you have searched out wise
>> counsel with your ingenuity,
> When you have fashioned a worker
>> comparable(?) to the gods,
>> may they relax from their toil! (lines 22–23)

In response, Enki asks Nammu to fashion humanity from clay taken from the subterranean freshwater chamber, utilizing other divine help-

---

17. For recent English translations of *Enki and Ninmah*, see Klein's abridged translation (lines 1–43, 52–82) in *COS* 1.516–18; Thorkild Jacobsen, *The Harps That Once . . . : Sumerian Poetry in Translation* (New Haven: Yale University Press, 1987), 151–66; and Samuel Noah Kramer and John Meier, *Myths of Enki, the Crafty God* (New York: Oxford University Press, 1989), 31–33 (Kramer's translation). For Kramer's earlier translation, see *Sumerian Mythology: A Study of Spiritual and Literary Achievement in the Third Millennium B.C.* (rev. ed.; New York: Harper & Brothers, 1961), 68–72.

18. Ḫarali was the gods' dwelling place prior to the creation of humanity.

19. Translation from Klein in *COS* 1.516, as are all further quotations of *Enki and Ninmah*.

ers that he has created, with the goddess Ninmah as midwife.[20] After this request, and just before the (fragmentary) account of the actual creation, Enki addresses Nammu as follows:

> My mother, after you decree his fate,
>   let Ninmah impose on him the burden. (line 37)[21]

This myth, like the later *Atrahasis Epic*, depicts the purpose of human creation as relieving the gods of their burdens by having humans take over the task of canal irrigation (on which agricultural production, and thus cultic offerings, ultimately depended).

Ewe and Wheat (LAHAR and Ashnan)

While the *Atrahasis Epic* and *Enki and Ninmah* share significant overlap in their accounts of human creation, the cosmological section of the Sumerian disputation text known as *Ewe and Wheat* (formerly called *Cattle and Grain* by scholars) differs in both narrative outline and details.[22] Taking its name from the functions of two female deities, Lahar (ewe) and Ashnan (wheat),[23] the cosmogony begins with a time when neither of the two existed, thus neither the gods nor humans had woven clothing (wool is associated with Lahar) or pre-

---

20. The precise identification of the other divine helpers is debated. The compound term is a combination of four Sumerian words (which in one bilingual version of the myth is replaced with the word for "womb"). This results in a variety of different interpretations by translators and commentators, including the possibility that it refers to the seven divine helpers named in lines 34–35, to the fourteen wombs mentioned in the Old Babylonian version of the *Atrahasis Epic* (that birthed seven males and seven females), or to a pair of birth goddesses or divine matrices, symbolizing the female ovaries (see Klein, in *COS* 1.517 n. 14; Clifford, *Creation Accounts*, 41 n. 61; Jacobsen, *Harps That Once*, 156 n. 7). None of this, however, affects the basic interpretation of the purpose of humanity in the myth.

21. The fragmentary account of human creation occurs in lines 38–43.

22. The cosmological introduction to the disputation text, which is the section that concerns us here, consists of lines 1–70. The disputation proper occurs in lines 71–178, while the verdict (where Wheat is judged superior to Ewe) is found in lines 179–92. The most recent English translation of the entire text (with commentary) is found in Bendt Alster and Herman Vanstiphout, "Lahar and Asnan: Presentation and Analysis of a Sumerian Disputation," *Acta sumerologica* 9 (1987): 1–143. An older, now outdated translation of part of the cosmological introduction is found in Kramer, *Sumerian Mythology*, 53–54, 72–73.

23. The title of the text is "U$_8$ and Ashnan." Although the Sumerian sign U$_8$ usually means "ewe," it may also be read as Lahar. The text is thus sometimes called "LAHAR and Ashnan," with the small caps designating the lack of certainty. But *Ewe and Wheat* will do for a title here.

pared food (mutton and milk are associated with Lahar; bread, beer, and field cultivation with Ashnan). Indeed, at that time people lived like animals:

> The people of those distant days,
> They knew not bread to eat;
> They knew not cloth to wear;
> They went about with naked limbs in the Land,
> And like sheep they ate grass with their mouth,
> Drinking water from ditches. (lines 20–25)[24]

Then, at the gods' Holy Hill, at the divine birthing place, Lahar and Ashnan are fashioned and the gods gather in their dining hall ready for a feast (lines 26–28). But there is a problem:

> Of the bounty of Ewe and Wheat
> The Godlings of the Holy Hill
> Partook, but were not sated.
> Of the sweet milk of their goodly sheepfold
> The Godlings of the Holy Hill
> Then drank, but were not sated. (lines 29–34)

This twofold repetition of "were not sated" most likely means that there was not sufficient food for them to consume (although it might mean that the gods liked the meal so much they couldn't stop eating).[25]

Then comes a summarizing statement, anticipating the narrative to come:

> And so, for their own well-being in the goodly sheepfold
> They gave them to mankind as sustenance. (lines 35–36)

Although the statement is somewhat cryptic, its meaning is that the gods gave Ewe and Wheat to the human race, thus providing them with the ability to produce food and clothing. The relevant point for our purposes is that this was both for the "sustenance" of humanity and for the "well-being" of the gods themselves, since humanity is now equipped with the ability to supply the gods' needs.

The text then narrates that Enki convinces Enlil to "send down Ewe and Wheat from the Holy Hill" (lines 40–42) to dwell among humans, with the result that the land now becomes full of abundance and well-

---

24. Translation from Alster and Vanstiphout, "Lahar and Asnan," as are all further quotations of *Ewe and Wheat*.

25. Ibid., 2.

being (lines 56–63). That this is not only for human benefit, but also accrues to the gods, is suggested by a comment placed at the conclusion of the description of this abundance. According to the text, by filling the storerooms and barns of the land, Ewe and Wheat thus "gladden the heart of An and the heart of Enlil" (line 64).

Although this could simply mean that the high gods selflessly rejoice in the bounty now bestowed on humanity,[26] Enki's motives in "sending down" Ewe and Wheat to humanity are (just as in the *Atrahasis Epic*) not purely philanthropic, indicated by the earlier summarizing statement. Thus, we find that even in a disputation text (not technically the genre of a creation myth), the standard Mesopotamian notion of the human purpose to provide for the needs of the gods is assumed.

KAR 4

In the bilingual (Sumerian/Akkadian) text designated *KAR 4*, the human purpose is explained in somewhat more detail.[27] The myth (which may have originally been written in Sumerian, although this is uncertain) begins with the gods, having established heaven and earth, reflecting together on what they will create next (lines 1–6). Taking their seat in the place of honor in the divine assembly (lines 7–9), the four chief gods (An, Enlil, Ninmah, and Enki, with Enlil as their spokesman), address the multitude of other gods (the Anunna):

> As they had already established the plan of the universe,
> And with the intention of preparing the irrigation system
> That was determined by the course of the Tigris and the Euphrates,
> <Enlil asked them,> "And now what are we going to do?
>   What are we going to make now?" (lines 10–13)

The Anunna's answer to Enlil reflects the motif in the *Atrahasis Epic* where a god is slain so that humans can be created:

26. The disputation section of the text certainly celebrates the extravagant bounty that Ewe and Wheat bring to humanity, as each tries to outdo the other in boasting.

27. The abbreviation *KAR 4* stands for text #4 in E. Ebling, *Keilschrifttexte aus Assur religiösen Inhalts* (Leipzig: Hinrichs, 1915–23). For a recent English translation, see Clifford's rendering of Samuel Noah Kramer's French translation in Clifford, *Creation Accounts*, 49–51, taken from Kramer and J. Bottéro, *Lorsque les dieux faisaient l'homme: Mythologie mésopotamienne* (Bibliothèque des histoires; Paris: Gallimard, 1989), 503–5. For an older English translation, see Alexander Heidel, *The Babylonian Genesis: The Story of Creation* (2nd ed.; Chicago: University of Chicago Press, 1951), 68–71. Quotations of *KAR 4* are from Clifford's translation; words in parentheses are Clifford's explanatory notes.

In the "Flesh-Growing Place" of Duranki (Nippur),
We are going to slay two divine *Alla* (NAGAR, reading uncertain),
And from their blood give birth to human beings! (lines 18–20)

The creation of humans is here located at Duranki, a sacred site in
the ancient city of Nippur (indicated by the translator's parenthetical
insertion), which some Sumerian traditions understand as the first
city founded by the gods. The reference to the two deities to be slain is
particularly brief and unelaborated, but Clifford suggests that these are
two worker gods who had rebelled against their duty to care for the irrigation system.[28] Whether Clifford's suggestion is correct, two humans
(named Ullegarra and Annegarra) are indeed created out of the blood
of the two slain gods.[29]

But the focus of the text is evidently on the gods' *purpose* in creating
humanity:

The corvée of the gods will be their corvée:
    They will fix the boundaries of the fields once and for all,
And take in their hands hoes and baskets,
To benefit the House of the great gods,
    Worthy seat of their high Dias! (lines 21–23)

Human work or service, directed to the sanctuary (the house of the
gods), is thus depicted as caring for the fields, which suggests agricultural production, and (given the stereotypical Mesopotamian reference
to hoe and basket) as brick-making, which suggests temple building or
repairs.

The text then goes on to foreground specifically the tasks of irrigation and agriculture:

They will add plot to plot;
They will fix the boundaries of the fields once and for all,
They will install the irrigation system . . .
To provide water everywhere
And thus make all kinds of plants to grow.
. . . .
Thus they will cultivate the fields of the Anunna,
Increasing the riches of the land,
And diverting the fresh water to the Great residence,
Worthy seat of the high Dias! (lines 24–29, 35–37)

28. Clifford, *Creation Accounts*, 51.
29. Their names are mentioned in line 31 and their actual creation in line 49.

As a capstone to the twofold task of maintaining the sanctuaries of the gods (briefly alluded to) and producing agricultural abundance (the central focus), humans are perpetually to perform the sacrificial duties associated with temples:

> Then will be celebrated worthily, day and night,
>   the feasts of the gods,
> according to the full plan that they have established—
> An, Enlil, Enki, and Ninmah, the chief gods. (lines 46–48)

The explicit purpose of humanity, as depicted in *KAR 4*, is thus to build and/or maintain temples to house the gods and especially to practice irrigation agriculture, thereby providing food for the gods' cultic meals.

Enuma Elish

When we turn to the account of human creation in *Enuma Elish* (also known as the Babylonian *Epic of Creation*), we find a story different in both narrative outline and details from the shorter Sumerian myths and also from the longer Akkadian *Atrahasis Epic*.[30] While the purpose of human creation in *Enuma Elish* certainly conforms to the general Mesopotamian notion that humans are created to relieve the gods of their burdens and to attend their needs, *Enuma Elish* is distinctive in the way it implicates this human purpose in a broader worldview of primordial violence.[31] This violence outstrips that found in the other creation myths we have examined. Although the gods indeed attempt violence against the human race in the *Atrahasis Epic*, culminating in the great flood and although both the *Atrahasis Epic* and *KAR 4* contain the motif of the slaughter of a god or gods to create humanity, the way *Enuma Elish* roots the present order of things in a violent origin is quite simply unprecedented among Mesopotamian creation myths.

Enuma Elish was an extremely popular work, attested in a variety of extant copies from the first millennium B.C.E., which includes Babylonian

30. Recent English translations of *Enuma Elish* may be found in Foster, *Before the Muses*, 1.351–402, the major portion of which is reprinted in *COS* 1.390–402; and Dalley, *Myths from Mesopotamia*, 228–77. Older English translations include Heidel, *Babylonian Genesis*, chap. 1; and *ANET* 60–72, 501–3 (trans. E. A. Speiser and A. K. Grayson).

31. In fact, W. G. Lambert claims that it is an idiosyncratic Mesopotamian text, even "sectarian and aberrant" compared to more typical Sumero-Akkadian creation accounts; "A New Look at the Babylonian Background of Genesis," in *The Bible in Its Literary Milieu: Contemporary Essays* (ed. Vincent L. Tollers and John R. Maier; Grand Rapids: Eerdmans, 1979), 289.

copies from the sixth century as well as Assyrian versions from the tenth and seventh centuries, one of which substitutes the name of the god Ashur for Babylonian Marduk. Although scholars used to think the work originated as far back as Old Babylonian times (when Marduk became the national god of Babylon),[32] W. G. Lambert persuasively argues that the notion of Marduk's supremacy over the other gods (especially the old Sumerian deities Anu, Enlil, and Ea) is not attested prior to a boundary stone calling Marduk "the king of the gods," which dates to the Isin II period, during the reign of Nebuchadnezzar I at the end of the twelfth century B.C.E.[33] A somewhat earlier date (sometime in the fourteenth to twelfth centuries, in the late Kassite period) is, however, proposed by some scholars.[34]

Whenever its date of composition, it is evident that *Enuma Elish* enjoyed immense popularity during the resurgent Neo-Babylonian Empire, evident from the numerous quotations and allusions to various aspects of the myth in sixth-century Babylonian texts, including learned commentaries on the fifty names of Marduk (listed on tablet 7) and especially its prominence at the Neo-Babylonian New Year Festival known as the Akitu, which celebrated the renewal of the cosmos and of the Babylonian sociopolitical order.[35]

The central event of *Enuma Elish*, as is well known, is the conquest of Tiamat, the ocean-goddess and leader of the "olden gods," by the young god Marduk (the patron-god of Babylon), through which he rises to kingship over the entire pantheon.[36] That this is the highlight of the myth is evident from its last two summary lines:

> Let them sound abroad the song of Marduk,
> How he defeated Tiamat and took kingship. (6.161–62)[37]

---

32. Heidel, *Babylonian Genesis*, 13–14.

33. Lambert's argument for dating *Enuma Elish* is found in "The Reign of Nebuchadnezzar I: A Turning Point in the History of Ancient Mesopotamian Religion," in *The Seed of Wisdom: Essays in Honour of T. J. Meek* (ed. W. S. McCullough; Toronto: University of Toronto Press, 1964), 3–13.

34. See Clifford, *Creation Accounts*, 83–84; and Dalley, *Myths from Mesopotamia*, 229–30.

35. Foster, *Before the Muses*, 1.352. The relationship of *Enuma Elish* to the Neo-Babylonian Akitu Festival will be examined later in this chapter.

36. For the expression, see Frank Moore Cross, "The 'Olden Gods' in Ancient Near Eastern Creation Myths," in *Magnalia Dei, the Mighty Acts of God: Essays on the Bible and Archaeology in Memory of G. Ernest Wright* (ed. Frank Moore Cross, Werner E. Lemke, and Patrick D. Miller Jr.; Garden City, NY: Doubleday, 1976), 329–38.

37. Quotations of *Enuma Elish*, unless otherwise indicated, are from Foster, *Before the Muses*, vol. 1.

The story, however, begins long before either the creation of humanity or the Marduk-Tiamat battle. It goes back to the time before the gods and recounts the original theogony, when the first two deities, Tiamat (the ocean) and her spouse Apsu (the freshwaters), are generated.[38] Tiamat and Apsu then bring forth the younger gods, among whom are three who will figure prominently in the myth: Anshar, his son Anu, and Anu's son Ea (the god of wisdom, also called Nudimmud). The noisy, exuberant play of these younger deities disturbs Tiamat and angers Apsu. Although mother Tiamat tries to calm him down, Apsu is intent on violence. But Ea gets wind of Apsu's intent and casts a spell to put him into a deep sleep. Ea then kills Apsu and builds his dwelling over him (reflecting that the Ea temple in Eridu was indeed built upon a freshwater lagoon called the Apsu). This is simply the first of three acts of primordial violence recounted in the myth.

In that very dwelling constructed above the dead Apsu, Marduk is born to Ea and his spouse Damkina. Soon the exuberant play of the young Marduk disturbs Tiamat. Encouraged by a group of other deities who remind her that Apsu has been murdered—and that she has done nothing to avenge him—Tiamat gathers an army of terrifying monsters to mount an all-out attack against the younger gods. To lead her troops, she appoints her new spouse Qingu, thus replacing the dead Apsu.

When the news of the impending attack reaches Anshar, the leader of the younger gods, he is terrified and in panic seeks a champion who can stand up to Tiamat. First Ea, then Anu, is sent out to deal with Tiamat. When both return cowed, the young, untried Marduk steps forward at Ea's prompting and lays down his terms. In exchange for defeating Tiamat and thus bringing peace and security to the gods, Marduk demands to be made their king:

> If indeed I am to champion you,
> Subdue Tiamat and save your lives,
> Convene the assembly, nominate me for supreme destiny! (2.157–59)

At a great banquet that Anshar convenes, the gods agree to Marduk's terms. When Marduk demonstrates his power by first destroying, then

---

38. Although it is traditional to interpret Tiamat as the primordial ocean/saltwater and her spouse Apsu as the primordial freshwater, a dissenting voice is found in Clifford, who argues that Tiamat and Apsu are simply a set of personified doublets of the primordial waters, with no salt/fresh distinction intended; *Creation Accounts*, 86, citing Sanford Goldfless, *Babylonian Theogonies: Divine Origins in Ancient Mesopotamian Religion and Literature* (Ph.D. dissertation; Harvard University, 1980), 127–30.

creating, a constellation by fiat (4.19–27),[39] the gods hail him as king
(4.28–29), equip him with weapons, and commission him:

> Go, cut off the life of Tiamat,
> Let the winds bear her blood away as glad tidings! (4.31–32)

Armed with powerful weapons and astride his storm-chariot, Marduk
leads the gods into battle. But Tiamat's spell scatters Marduk's forces,
and he is left to face her alone. The ensuing battle is then described in
vivid, even gruesome terms:

> Tiamat and Marduk, sage of the gods, drew close for battle,
> They locked in single combat, joining for the fray.
> The Lord spread out his net, encircled her,
> The ill wind he had held behind him he released in her face.
> Tiamat opened her mouth to swallow,
> He thrust in the ill wind so she could not close her lips.
> The raging winds bloated her belly,
> Her insides were stopped up, she gaped her mouth wide.
> He shot off the arrow, it broke open her belly,
> It cut to her innards, it pierced her heart.
> He subdued her and snuffed out her life,
> He flung down her carcass, he took his stand upon it. (4.93–104)

With Tiamat dead, Marduk captures her now-dispirited army of deities and monsters, including Qingu their leader, thereby,

> Having fully achieved Anshar's victory over his enemies,
> Valiant Marduk having attained what Nudimmud desired. (4.125–26)[40]

The glorification of violence in the myth is then intensified as Marduk,
in a fit of celebratory rage or victory fever, tramples upon Tiamat's
corpse, crushes her skull, cuts her arteries, and scatters her blood on
the winds, to the gods' great rejoicing.[41] Finally,

> He calmed down. The Lord was inspecting her carcass,
> That he might divide(?) the monstrous lump and fashion artful things
>   [niklātu]. (4.135–36)

---

39. The word for "constellation" (lumāšu) was previously misread as "garment" (lubāšu),
as Dalley explains in *Myths from Mesopotamia*, 275 n. 15. This misreading is reflected in
the earlier translations of Speiser and Heidel.

40. Nudimmud is the other name for Ea, Marduk's father.

41. In my opinion, the glorification of violence in *Enuma Elish* is extreme (almost
pornographic), and it is especially troubling that such violence is directed against a female
deity by a male god.

The word *niklātu*, rendered by Foster as "artful things," is an important thematic marker in *Enuma Elish*, for it is repeated when Marduk
later conceives his plan to create humanity. The term thus connects the
two acts of creation that Marduk engages in.[42]

Here the term designates Marduk's artful construction of the cosmos
out of Tiamat's dead body (pictured both as the carcass of a great beast
or dragon and as a body of water):

> He split her in two, like a fish for drying,
> Half of her he set up and made as a cover, (like) heaven.
> He stretched out the hide and assigned watchmen,
> And ordered them not to let her waters escape. (4.137–40)

Using the upper half of Tiamat's body, Marduk constructs his heavenly
sanctuary called Esharra (corresponding to the one below that Ea erected
over dead Apsu) and assigns the gods their positions in the various
constellations. Marduk then turns his attention to the remaining half
of Tiamat's corpse, using it to construct the earthly realm, including its
waterways and mountains:

> He set down her head and piled [   ] upon it,
> He opened underground springs, a flood was let flow(?).
> From her eyes he undammed the Euph[rates] and Tigris,
> He stopped up her nostrils, he left . . .
> He heaped up high-peaked mo[unt]ains from(?) her dugs.
> He drilled through her waterholes to carry off the catchwater.
> He coiled up her tail and tied it as(?) "The Great Bond." (5.53–59)

After Marduk is cleaned up from the dust and grime of battle, he
ascends his throne and receives homage from the gods:

> "Formerly [Mar]duk was 'our beloved son.'
> Now he is your king, pay heed to his command."
> Next all of them spoke and said:
> "'Lugaldimmerankia' is his name, trust in him!" (5.109–12)

Having slain Tiamat, created the cosmos, and been acclaimed
"Lugaldimmerankia," or "king of the gods of heaven and earth," the
stage is now set for Marduk's crowning act of creation, the second of his

---

42. Thorkild Jacobsen discusses the significance of the term *niklātu* (his rendering is
"ingenious contrivances") in a helpful commentary on the structure and plot of *Enuma
Elish* in *The Treasures of Darkness: A History of Mesopotamian Religion* (New Haven: Yale
University Press, 1976), 165–91.

"artful works" (*niklātu*). But transitional to the creation of humanity is
an episode of the story in which Marduk desires to build—on the newly
created earth—the city of Babylon as his permanent capital, with his own
temple, plus a multitude of other temples to function as hostels or tem-
porary stopping places for the gods in their travels between heaven and
earth. The gods enthusiastically affirm Marduk's building project.

The next section, however, which concludes tablet 5, is fragmentary,
so we cannot recount with any certainty the events that directly precede
the creation of humanity, at the beginning of tablet 6. It is not even clear
which gods are involved in the building, although the context suggests
that it is the imprisoned rebel gods who accompanied Tiamat.[43] In the
section where the text breaks off, either the gods devote themselves to
the building task, praising Marduk, or they complain that the job is too
difficult. Whichever it is, praise or complaint,

> When [Mar]duk heard the speech of the gods,
> He was resolving to make artful things [*niklātu*]. (6.1–2)

He explains his plan to Ea, his father:

> I shall compact blood, I shall cause bones to be,
> I shall make stand a human being, let "Man" be its name.
> I shall create humankind,
> They shall bear the gods' burden that those may rest. (6.5–8)

Ea, however, suggests that to facilitate this plan a god needs to be
slain:

> Let one, their brother, be given to me,
> Let him be destroyed so that people can be fashioned. (6.13–14)

Although, at one level, the slaughter of a god simply reflects a Mesopotamian theme common also to the *Atrahasis Epic* and *KAR 4*, this
slaughter takes on a distinctive meaning by virtue of its occurrence in a
myth celebrating primordial violence. Just as the cosmos is constructed
out of the dead body of the greatest enemy of Marduk, so the creation of
humanity requires the slaughter of a worthy foe. Marduk thus inquires
of the gods to discover who is most worthy of death:

---

43. Their identity is indicated by the final section of *Enuma Elish*, which celebrates
Marduk's fifty names. The text calls on the reader to exalt Marduk as Agaku (7.25): "Who
had mercy on the vanquished gods, / Who removed the yoke imposed on the gods, his
enemies, / Who, to free them, created mankind" (7.27–29).

> Who was it that made war,
> Suborned Tiamat and drew up for battle?
> Let him be given over to me, the one who made war,
> I shall make him bear his punishment, you shall be released. (6.23–26)

In anticipation of this promised freedom, the gods name Qingu as their war leader and even participate in his slaughter:

> They bound and held him before Ea,
> They imposed the punishment on him and shed his blood.
> From his blood he [Ea] made mankind,
> He imposed the burden of the gods and exempted the gods.
> After Ea the wise had made mankind,
> They imposed the burden of the gods on them!
> That deed is beyond comprehension,
> By the artifices of Marduk did Nudimmud create! (6.31–38)

Contrary to what one might expect, however, it is not humans but the gods who actually go on to build Babylon and its temples, including the Marduk temple (known as the Esagila). The unique human role is, however, articulated in terms of continuing what the gods started, by engaging in cultic service, and includes a building component:

> He [Marduk] shall appoint the black-headed[44] folk to serve him.
> Let the subject peoples be mindful that their gods should be invoked,
> At his command let them heed their goddess(es).
> Let their gods, their goddesses be brought food offerings;
> Let (these) not be forgotten, let them sustain their gods.
> Let their holy places be apparent(?),
>   let them build their sanctuaries. (6.113–18)

Enuma Elish thus joins with the *Atrahasis Epic* and earlier Sumerian creation myths in articulating a distinctive Mesopotamian conception of the role and purpose of human beings in the world. Indeed, there are many more references in both Sumerian and Akkadian literature to this distinctive role, which seems to have been simply assumed as part of background of Mesopotamian beliefs over an extremely long period of time.[45] In John Walton's summary, "the cuneiform literature everywhere agrees that people were created to do the work the gods were tired of doing and to provide for the gods' needs."[46] Specifically this

---

44. "Black-headed" is the standard designation for Mesopotamians.

45. A multitude of Mesopotamian texts articulating the human role in the cosmos is analyzed in Clifford, *Creation Accounts*, chap. 2 (on Sumerian texts) and chap. 3 (on Akkadian texts).

means, explains Alexander Heidel, that humanity was created because "the gods were in need of worshipers who would build and maintain their temples and who would bring offerings and sacrifices to them for the purpose of supplying their wants."[47] Or, as David Asselin puts it, the human destiny was "to serve the gods with libations and sacrificial meals, the cult of grand ceremony which they required in order to live as gods."[48] Similar comments could easily be multiplied to show widespread agreement among biblical and ancient Near Eastern scholars concerning the claims of Mesopotamian creation myths.[49]

Creation Myths as Legitimation of the Temple System

We would be remiss, however, in interpreting the Mesopotamian conception of human purpose as a freestanding theological idea, with no connection to actual social conditions. There is, on the contrary, a significant parallel between the claims of the various Sumero-Akkadian myths of human creation and the actual shape of Mesopotamian society. This parallel leads H. W. F. Saggs to explain that such myths were "not basically a comment on the nature of man [as an abstract doctrine] but an explanation of a particular social system, heavily dependent upon communal irrigation and agriculture, for which the gods' estates were primary foci of administration."[50]

As far as scholars can ascertain, Mesopotamian city-states (from ancient Sumerian times in the third millennium B.C.E.) were constituted by three distinct forms of social organization, which coexisted within each urban center with varying degrees of tension or competition:[51] (1) the community of free, private citizens of the city (usually organized

46. John H. Walton, *Ancient Israelite Literature in Context: A Survey of Parallels Between Biblical and Ancient Near Eastern Texts* (Grand Rapids: Zondervan, 1989), 29.

47. Heidel, *Babylonian Genesis*, 79.

48. David Tobin Asselin, "The Notion of Dominion in Genesis 1–3," *Catholic Biblical Quarterly* 16 (1954): 285.

49. Lambert and Millard, *Atra-ḫasīs*, 15; Edwin Mason Curtis, *Man as the Image of God in Genesis in the Light of Ancient Near Eastern Parallels* (Ph.D. dissertation; University of Pennsylvania, 1984), 187.

50. H. W. F. Saggs, *The Encounter with the Divine in Mesopotamia and Israel* (London: Athlone, 1978), 168.

51. A. Leo Oppenheim, *Ancient Mesopotamia: Portrait of a Dead Civilization* (Chicago: University of Chicago Press, 1964), 95; I. M. Diakonoff, "The Rise of the Despotic State in Ancient Mesopotamia" (trans. G. M. Sergheyev), in *Ancient Mesopotamia: Socio-Economic History* (ed. I. M. Diakonoff; Moscow: Nauka, 1969), 179–80. Benjamin R. Foster, "A New Look at the Sumerian Temple State," *Journal of the Economic and Social History of the Orient* 24 (1981): 225–41, makes clear the inadequacy of an earlier hypothesis among scholars of Mesopotamian history that all or most land in early Sumerian city-

into a manor system of large agricultural estates owned by a landed oligarchy, alongside smaller, family-owned plots of land worked by the households of free citizens); (2) the royal palace (that is, the household or estate of the ruler, which included royal officials and administrators, artisans, warriors, and agricultural laborers); and (3) the various temples of the major deities of the city (understood as the households or estates of the gods).

Although there were similarities between all three forms of social organization, there was a particularly important parallel between the institutions of temple and palace. "The deity," explains A. Leo Oppenheim, "is conceived as residing in his cella [the recessed shrine in which the cult statue was placed], to be fed, clothed, and cared for appropriately, just like the king on his dais."[52] Also like the king, adds Benjamin Foster, the god (via the cult statue) held court, was offered petitions for aid by various supplicants, settled lawsuits, and was on occasion carried in grand procession through the temple yards or the city streets.[53] Thus the cult statue "exercised on the divine plane all the functions associated with temporal human rulers."[54]

All these functions required (again on analogy with the king) a staff of appropriate personnel, which included temple administrators and various cultic officials or priests (as the primary attendants, officials, or courtiers of the god)[55] as well as artisans and a large number of serfs or vassals who did the necessary physical work, including agricultural production on the land owned by the temple. The fruits of this agricultural production were used by the temple first as sacrificial offerings for the gods, but also as income or rations for the temple personnel and workers on the temple estates, with the surplus either stored for future use or traded beyond the temple for materials and goods the temple needed.[56] In all this, it was the deity's partaking of

---

states was temple land, with all or most of the population working that land. This hypothesis, based on the work of Anton Deimel in the 1920s, is critiqued by Foster on several counts.

52. Oppenheim, *Ancient Mesopotamia*, 96. Oppenheim calls palace and temple the "great organizations" (187) of Mesopotamian society and compares them at length in his chap. 2.

53. Foster, *Before the Muses*, 1.33.

54. Ibid.

55. This is also the Old Testament notion of priests, argues Peter J. Leithart, "Attendants of Yahweh's House: Priesthood in the Old Testament," *Journal for the Study of the Old Testament* 85 (1999): 3–24. His thesis is that "fundamentally and throughout Israel's history priests were ministers, stewards, or administrators of Yahweh's house and his personal attendants" (12).

56. Oppenheim, *Ancient Mesopotamia*, 187.

the daily sacrificial meal that grounded the entire temple system.[57] Oppenheim explains:

> The Mesopotamian deity remained aloof—yet its partaking of the ceremonial repast gave religious sanction, political status, and economic stability to the entire temple organism, which circulated products from fields and pastures across the sacrificial table to those who were either, so to speak, shareholders of the institution or received rations from it. At any rate, the image is the heart and the hub of the entire system. His attendant worshipers lived from the god's table, but they did not sit down with him.
>
>   . . . [T]he critical point . . . was the act of consumption of food in the sacrificial repast. It represents the central *mysterium* that provided the effective *ratio essendi* for the cult practice of daily meals and all that it entailed in economic, social, and political respects.[58]

There was thus a significant convergence between the function of the cult image and the creation myths. Together, they provided a powerful, mutually reinforcing legitimation for the entire Mesopotamian temple system.

I. M. Diakonoff estimates, by extrapolating from trade and land documents dating from the twenty-fourth century B.C.E., that perhaps one-quarter of the total population of ancient Lagash (that is, 25,000 of an estimated 100,000 persons) lived and worked on the various temple estates of this ancient Sumerian city-state.[59] This is a very significant portion of the population, and it leads Oppenheim to comment that "such a large body of serfs—especially in the early (pre-Sargonic) temples as those of Lagash—should give considerable concern to the social historian."[60] Oppenheim correctly links this phenomenon to "a specific socio-ideological situation in which certain groups of the population expressed their relation to the deity in terms of menial service dedi-

---

57. We should not think of the sacrificial meal here as a "burnt offering" (which is how the popular imagination usually understands biblical sacrifice). The gods' cultic meals in ancient Mesopotamia were modeled on the meals served before the king, involving a complex table service, with various courses of beverages, meat, and fruit. The meal was accompanied by music, incense, and water for washing afterward. See Oppenheim, *Ancient Mesopotamia*, 188–89.

58. Ibid., 191.

59. Diakonoff estimates that these temple estates constituted one-sixth to one-fifth of the total land area claimed by Lagash (that is, about 500–600 out of 3,000 square kilometers); "Rise of the Despotic State," 173–76. Although Foster is generally positively disposed to Diakonoff's analyses, he cautions that there is disagreement among scholars of Mesopotamian history concerning just how much land in any specific city was owned by any specific group at any specific time in third-millennium Sumerian society; "New Look at the Sumerian Temple State," 230.

60. Oppenheim, *Ancient Mesopotamia*, 96.

cated to the god's household."[61] Strangely, however, Oppenheim does not directly connect this state of affairs to the Mesopotamian creation myths or to the ideas behind them (since this early period predates the actual written myths). Instead, he says: "What legal or pious fiction or what economic or social pressure conditioned this attitude, we shall probably never know."[62]

Oppenheim is right, of course, that we cannot reconstruct with any certainty the actual processes by which large groups of Mesopotamians actually came to believe that they owed the obligation of servitude to the gods (or even to what extent they actually internalized this temple propaganda). Nevertheless, his own claim that the feeding of the cult image was the *ratio essendi* of the entire temple system points in the direction of the Mesopotamian myths of human creation—or at least the worldview they embodied—as the crucial factor. This worldview clearly grounded the obligation of temple service in the order of creation, as the explicit *raison d'être* for human existence. These creation myths thus have a clear ideological function, serving to legitimate the social role of vast numbers of human beings as vassals of the gods and servants of the temple and the priesthood in ancient Sumer, Babylon, and Assyria, thus bolstering a sociopolitical arrangement characteristic of ancient Mesopotamian civilization for close to three thousand years.

Creation Myths as Royal Ideology

This is not to say that Mesopotamian society was static or underwent no significant change over the millennia. Diakonoff, for example, charts many societal shifts from the Early Dynastic period in ancient Sumer through to early Babylonian times. The most significant shift concerns the relationship of palace and temple. Whereas in the Early Dynastic period of ancient Sumer (twenty-eighth to twenty-fourth centuries B.C.E.) there was a significant distinction (even tension) between the institutions of civil government and the various temples—such that the temple estates operated independently of the ruler of the city—we find numerous successful attempts by particular rulers and dynasties over the next six hundred years to annex the temple estates and transform them into crown lands, that is, the personal property of the ruler.

Diakonoff charts four periods in particular where temples came under royal control, which are correlated with the rise of what he calls "despotic kingship" (that is, concentrations of royal power) in

61. Ibid., 97.
62. Ibid.

Mesopotamia.[63] While the first such period consisted in a few short-lived annexation attempts during the third Early Dynastic period (under Mesanepanda of Ur, Ententarzi of Lagash, and Ur-Nanshi of Lagash), the second is represented by the accumulation of royal power in the dynasty of Sargon of Akkad (2334–2279 B.C.E.), self-proclaimed "King of the Four Quarters of the World," who first united all Mesopotamia under a single hegemonic state (during the twenty-fourth and twenty-third centuries). Following a diminution of royal power after the Sargonids came the powerful third dynasty of Ur (twenty-second and twenty-first centuries), which later collapsed under the Amorites around 2000 B.C.E. Then followed four hundred years of the fluctuation of royal power, culminating in a massive concentration of power in the dynasty of Hammurapi of Babylon (1792–1750 B.C.E.), who united all Mesopotamia under the first (or Old) Babylonian Empire (which lasted until the early sixteenth century, when the Hittites sacked Babylon).

In all these cases where royal power and hegemony increased significantly beyond what previous Mesopotamian rulers had known, we find the temple estates coming under direct royal control and ownership. By Hammurapi's time there were no longer three forms of social organization or types of land in Babylon. Land was either royal land (owned by the king) or community land (owned by free citizens), and administrative power was limited to royal governmental bodies and community organs.[64] The temple estates, which had previously been autonomous, had become entirely subsumed under the auspices of the palace.[65]

Corresponding to the annexation of the temple by the palace, we find—in precisely these periods of the accumulation of royal power— the rise of religious, cultic legitimation of the power of the king. This legitimation includes the first claims to divine origin, election, and protection of the ruler and to the king's high priestly status, along with the occasional deification of particular kings.[66] Significantly, in the Ur III period taxation of the population becomes construed as obligatory sacrifice, and by Hammurapi's time all free citizens are understood to

63. Diakonoff, "Rise of the Despotic State," 189–201.

64. Ibid., 199–201.

65. Parallel to the phenomenon of the growing hegemony of the palace over the temple, Wolfram von Soden explains that the dominant king (*lugal*) in the periods of the Akkad and the Ur III dynasties diminished the traditional power and status of the independent princes/rulers (*ensi*) of the city-states that comprised the empire, "until Hammurabi finally put an end to the ancient institution"; *The Ancient Orient: An Introduction to the Study of the Ancient Near East* (trans. G. Schley; Grand Rapids: Eerdmans, 1994), 64.

66. Diakonoff, "Rise of the Despotic State," 195, 199. I discuss the cultic legitimation of the Mesopotamian monarchy in more depth in chapter 3.

be under obligation to serve in digging and maintaining the canal irrigation system, which the king supervised.[67]

Thus, by the time of the Old Babylonian Empire the religious legitimacy that the god's presence in the cult statue previously bestowed on the temple had accrued also to the person and rule of the king, the patron and sponsor of temples. The king therefore comes to assume a unique, unparalleled cultic status, including a high priestly role as mediator of social harmony and cosmic fertility from heaven to earth.[68] This legitimacy is significantly intensified throughout the later Middle Assyrian, Neo-Assyrian, and Neo-Babylonian empires.[69] Whereas Mesopotamian myths "had long been used to undergird the authority of sanctuaries and the hegemony of individual city-states," notes Bernard Batto, "the tendency to use myths for political propaganda reached a new plateau with the rise of the nation-states of Babylon and Assyria."[70]

That the notion of humanity created to serve the gods continued in prominence well beyond ancient Sumerian times, even in epochs characterized by a changed relationship between temple and palace, suggests that the meaning of this notion was quite flexible. Although creation myths that articulated the human purpose originally served to legitimate the role of those employed on the temple estates of ancient Sumer as vassals of the gods, the applicability of this notion to changing political circumstances represents a considerable broadening in how these myths were understood. This broadening was no doubt abetted by the nonspecific, universalizing rhetoric of the myths, which did not explicitly single out any particular group for vassalage to the gods, but spoke of humanity in general. This universalizing rhetoric not only allowed creation myths (whether older Sumerian or later Akkadian accounts) to function as temple ideology, but permitted them eventually to

67. Diakonoff, "Rise of the Despotic State," 196, 201.

68. One emblem of the king's unique status is what happened to the food of the sacrificial meal. Although all temple personnel and workers lived from the god's table, so to speak, in that the temple estates provided for their basic needs, the king was special. Texts indicate that after the cultic meal had been presented to the image, it was then sent directly to the king for his consumption. Although it is unclear as to whether this was a regular, daily practice or limited to special ceremonial occasions, Oppenheim explains that the food "was considered blessed by contact with the divine and capable of transferring that blessing to the person who was to eat it. This person was always the king"; *Ancient Mesopotamia*, 189.

69. Along with this religious legitimacy went great power. According to von Soden (*Ancient Orient*, 65), "after around 1500, there appear to have been only minimal institutional limitations on the power of the kings of Babylonia and Assyria."

70. Bernard Batto, "Creation Theology in Genesis," in *Creation in the Biblical Traditions* (ed. Richard J. Clifford and John J. Collins; Catholic Biblical Quarterly Monograph Series 24; Washington, DC: Catholic Biblical Association of America, 1992), 25.

be co-opted as part of Babylonian and Assyrian royal ideology in order to legitimate the entire social order, presided over by the king.

Thus, in a changed political situation, when the autonomy of the temple had become largely subsumed under the authority of the palace, myths of human creation may well have been understood as legitimating the service, not only of those who actually worked on the temple estates, but also of nontemple personnel beholden to the palace, and may even have been understood as claiming that all people (including free citizens) owed a universal human obligation to the gods, mediated by the king.

An important distinction, however, needs to be made at this point. Although Mesopotamian creation myths claimed that all people were created for the express purpose of serving the gods, the fact is that in all periods of Mesopotamian history some served in a position of privilege. Their service (not to be equated with servitude) elevated them above the ordinary masses and granted them an extraordinary dignity, accompanied by the benefits of social power. The obligation and service legitimated by Mesopotamian myths of human creation would thus have accrued in practice to the benefit and privilege of particular elite groups, including the priests who supervised the various cultic sites (and effectively controlled access to the divine) and especially the king, who was the primary representative and mediator of the will of the gods on earth. Mesopotamian creation myths thus worked in tandem with Mesopotamian royal ideology to solidify the king's authority. As Bertil Albrektson puts it:

> Through the chosen instrument, the king, the deity's purposes are carried out both in the political and social, and in the cultic domains. And because the king is nothing but a representative of the divine ruler, rebellion is not simply described as an act of disobedience towards a human master but is regarded as insubordination against the god himself.[71]

This privileged function of the king in Mesopotamian royal ideology (which is behind the image of god texts), together with the purpose of humanity as articulated in Mesopotamian creation myths, would have provided vigorous legitimation of the social hierarchy of ancient Babylon and Assyria. If the purpose of the mass of humanity is to serve the gods and if the king represents those gods as their son and image, then the gods are served precisely by serving the king, who wills the present social order.

71. Bertil Albrektson, *History and the Gods: An Essay on the Idea of Historical Events as Divine Manifestations in the Ancient Near East and in Israel* (Lund: Gleerup, 1976), 49.

The Significance of Creation from Divine Blood

On the surface, however, this ideological reading of humanity's servitude to the gods is gainsaid by the notion—found in some Mesopotamian creation myths—that humans were created from clay mixed with the blood of a slain god. That the veins of humanity flow with divine blood, despite their earthly form of clay, suggests to some commentators the high dignity of human beings in Mesopotamia (much as Gilgamesh was part god and part human). Whereas W. G. Lambert and A. R. Millard base a positive reading of divine blood in these myths on a presumed equivalence to the breath of life that God breathes into humanity in Genesis 2, David Asselin suggests that creation from divine blood is an apt parallel to the *imago Dei* in Genesis 1.[72] If indeed the creation of humans out of divine blood is intended to suggest the exalted dignity of the human race, this exaltation stands in significant tension with the menial function for which humans are created.[73] Thus, if a positive spin on the notion of divine blood turns out to be the correct reading, I would be constrained to regard this spin as mystification, articulated by Mesopotamian "spin doctors," in the service of the ideological legitimation of the royal-cultic status quo.

There are, however, good reasons to interpret the creation of humans out of divine blood not as an exaltation, but as a significant *devaluation*, of humanity. First of all, neither We-ilu nor Qingu (the deities killed in the *Atrahasis Epic* and *Enuma Elish*, respectively) appears in any known god lists, suggesting that they are not significant Mesopotamian deities in their own right. The creation out of their blood is thus likely a slight against human origins and status.[74]

Beyond this, however, the very fact that the creation of humanity requires the slaughter of a god should give us pause. This grounding of human creation in a primordial act of violence suggests neither an auspicious beginning nor an exalted nature for humanity. Furthermore, it is clear in *Enuma Elish* that Qingu, the god from whose blood humans are created, is—from the standpoint of the text's narrative logic—an evil or demonic deity. As the consort of Tiamat and leader of her forces, he is one of the archenemies of Marduk. The text thus attributes to humans, who are created from Qingu's blood, an essentially rebellious and degraded nature, much as the cosmos contains

72. Lambert and Millard, *Atra-ḫasīs*, 22; Asselin, "Notion of Dominion," 229 n. 7. Lambert and Millard make the connection based on the biblical idea that the life is in the blood (citing Leviticus 17:11).

73. As even Asselin, "Notion of Dominion," 285, admits.

74. Personal communication from Richard Henshaw.

within it an evil or chaotic principle, constructed as it is out of the dead carcass of Tiamat.[75]

The meaning of divine blood in the *Atrahasis Epic* and *KAR 4* is arguably more ambiguous, since the slain gods mentioned there are not explicitly identified as evil. Indeed, hardly anything is said of the slain gods in *KAR 4*. The deity in the *Atrahasis Epic*, however, is killed "along with his *ṭēmu*," and when humans are created out of his blood the result is that they embody the god's spirit (*eṭemmu*, a pun on *ṭēmu*). Although *ṭēmu* is usually translated "personality" or "intelligence,"[76] implying that humanity inherits this laudable divine attribute, William Moran suggests that the *ṭēmu* of the slain god, which rendered him a suitable victim, is better translated "plan" or "design," referring to the plan/design of the rebellious Igigi to overthrow Enlil. The slain god in the *Atrahasis Epic* is thus punished as the leader of an illicit rebellion, much as Qingu is slain for leading Tiamat's forces to war in *Enuma Elish*.[77] This interpretation is consistent with the negative connotations of *eṭemmu*, which has the sense of "spirit of the dead" or "ghost" (and is not associated with positive notions of vitality).[78] This more negative interpretation of human creation also informs Foster's translation of *ṭēmu* as "inspiration," namely, the inspiration for the Igigi's work stoppage.[79] Whereas killing the god with his *ṭēmu* puts an end to the immediate problem of the work stoppage, the need for any further rebellion on the part of the Igigi is eliminated by the creation of humanity to do the work they had balked at. In the logic of the myth, however, the trouble is not over, since the rebellious tendencies of the Igigi are passed on to humanity (by means of the divine blood), leading to the later human disturbance of the gods, which occasioned the flood as punishment.[80] The intradivine

75. For a negative reading of divine blood in *Enuma Elish*, see Saggs, *Encounter with the Divine*, 167; Heidel, *Babylonian Genesis*, 139–40; Curtis, *Man as the Image of God*, 188; Ralph W. Klein, *Israel in Exile: A Theological Interpretation* (Overtures to Biblical Theology; Philadelphia: Fortress, 1979), 128; and Douglas A. Knight, "Cosmogony and Order in the Hebrew Tradition," in *Cosmogony and Ethical Order: New Studies in Comparative Ethics* (ed. Robin W. Lovin and Frank E. Reynolds; Chicago: University of Chicago Press, 1985), 143, 146.

76. Lambert and Millard, *Atra-ḫasīs*, 59; Dalley, *Myths from Mesopotamia*, 15, 16.

77. William Moran, "The Creation of Man in Atrahasis I 192–248," *Bulletin of the American Schools of Oriental Research* 200 (1970): 52.

78. Saggs, *Encounter with the Divine*, 165–66. Curtis further points out that death and the afterlife were not positively conceived in Mesopotamia; *Man as the Image of God*, 185–86, 188.

79. Foster, *Before the Muses*, 1.166 n. 1. Curtis agrees with this interpretation (*Man as the Image of God*, 187), as does Batto, "Creation Theology in Genesis," 23.

80. Batto comments that "along with the blood of the slain rebel god, these primeval humans had inherited his spirit (*eṭemmu*) and his tendency to scheme (*ṭēmu*). Soon similar noises of rebellion began to emerge from their midst"; "Creation Theology in Genesis," 23.

chaos that had previously afflicted the divine realm has now shifted to the noisy, populous human race.

Although there is some residual ambiguity about the status of divine blood in the *Atrahasis Epic*, this is not the case in *Enuma Elish*, where the creation of humans has decidedly negative connotations. Just as the cosmos is fashioned out of the dead carcass of the primordial chaos monster, thus representing evil as intrinsic to the fabric of the world, always having to be repressed and controlled, so humanity is created from the blood of one of the chief enemies of Marduk, patron-god of Babylon, thus representing our "demonic" origin and essentially degraded and subservient status vis-à-vis the divine. Although it might be possible in *KAR 4* (and on one reading of the *Atrahasis Epic*) to see the divine blood pulsing through human veins as evidence of our elevated status in the cosmic scheme of things, the mythology of *Enuma Elish* proclaimed in no uncertain terms the servitude (even bondage) of humanity, "created out of evil substance,"[81] as cheap slave labor to do the "dirty work" of the lower gods.[82]

The Ideological Function of *Enuma Elish*

Although *Enuma Elish* may be, in some senses, an idiosyncratic Mesopotamian myth, and is not as old as the *Atrahasis Epic*, it is nevertheless based on older Mesopotamian traditions of the slaying of a monstrous primordial foe by a god who is then made ruler over the pantheon (this tradition is found in the *Myth of Anzu* and other fragmentary texts).[83] Furthermore, *Enuma Elish* came to exert considerable influence in Mesopotamian society, culminating in its evident popularity during the resurgent Neo-Assyrian and Neo-Babylonian empires of the seventh and sixth centuries B.C.E., respectively.[84] It is thus important to explore the

81. Knight, "Cosmogony and Order," 146.

82. Klein, *Israel in Exile*, 128.

83. The relationship of *Enuma Elish* to the *Myth of Anzu* will be examined later in this chapter. At least four different deities take this role in the extant versions of these two myths. In the Old Babylonian version of the *Myth of Anzu* the warrior-god is Ningirsu, while in the standard Babylonian version it is Ninurta. And while Marduk is the hero in the most versions of *Enuma Elish*, in one Assyrian version the warrior-god is Ashur. But other fragmentary Mesopotamian texts testify to a similar tradition, with other deities in the role of the warrior. One such text describes the victory of Tishpak (who is identified with Ninurta in some god lists) over a great serpent/lion (this text is called *The Slaying of the "LABBU"* by Heidel, *Babylonian Genesis*, 141–43; and *The Lion-Serpent* by Foster, *Before the Muses*, 1.488–89), and another describes a similar victory by Nergal over a monstrous serpent (Foster, *Before the Muses*, 1.486–87).

84. Lambert, who thinks *Enuma Elish* is an idiosyncratic Mesopotamian myth, nevertheless admits that "it happens to be the best preserved Babylonian document of its

inner logic—and the ethical and political implications—of the worldview embodied in *Enuma Elish*, since this worldview frames the meaning of human existence in Mesopotamia close to the period when Genesis 1 was likely written. Two dimensions of this Mesopotamian worldview are particularly important for our purposes.

The first is the notion of mimesis, which is not, however, limited to *Enuma Elish*, but is characteristic of the entire Mesopotamian worldview, embodied in its many mythic and cultic traditions. Mimesis here does not refer to a generalized notion of "imitation" (Greek *mimēsis*), but to the specific ideal (found in many ancient cultures, from ancient China and India to Mesoamerica and the ancient Near East) that for human sociopolitical life to achieve its best and highest form, society must replicate the divine pattern that the gods enacted in primordial time.[85] Sociopolitical order is thus thought of as a microcosm of the larger world of the gods and their founding of the cosmos, with some central urban site typically conceived as the navel of the world or the bond of heaven and earth.[86]

The mimetic ideal included two important practical implications. The first implication is that the ordering of the polis according to the divine model is conceived as a cultic or sacred act and that those who implement the divine pattern are royal-priestly intermediaries. This clearly provides the background for understanding the idea of the king as the gods' viceroy on earth, including the idea of the king as the image of a god.

The second implication of the mimetic ideal is that change tends to be prohibited and that social stability is the primary value, since any deviation from the original divine pattern constitutes regression. Although it is something of an overstatement, Mircea Eliade's classic statement that mimetic cultures (which he calls "archaic") were in "terror of history" does lift up the inherently conservative character of this worldview.[87] When we put together these two implications of the

---

genre simply because it was at its height of popularity when the libraries were formed from which our knowledge of Babylonian mythology is mostly derived"; "New Look at the Babylonian Background," 289.

85. Clifford notes that creation was the "privileged moment" in the Mesopotamian worldview, since the conditions that obtained at the beginning were thought to be constitutive of the present; *Creation Accounts*, 198.

86. On the mimetic ideal in a variety of cultures, see Mircea Eliade, *The Myth of the Eternal Return; or, Cosmos and History* (trans. Willard R. Trask; Princeton: Princeton University Press, 1954); Claude Lévi-Strauss, *The Savage Mind* (Chicago: University of Chicago Press, 1966), 217–44; and Merold Westphal, *God, Guilt, and Death: An Existential Phenomenology of Religion* (Bloomington: Indiana University Press, 1984), 194–218.

87. This is the title of ch. 4 (139–63) in Eliade, *Myth of the Eternal Return*.

mimetic ideal, it becomes clear that this worldview could function as a powerful ideological legitimation of the status quo of Mesopotamian society as divinely willed, where any resistance to those who mediate divine rule is excluded by definition as illegitimate.

But a second dimension of the Mesopotamian worldview as embodied in *Enuma Elish* is crucial to note for our purposes, namely, its violent dualism, which biblical scholars have traditionally called the *Chaoskampf* (Hermann Gunkel) and more recently the combat myth (John Day), the chaos-cosmos scheme (Pedro Trigo), and the myth of redemptive violence (Walter Wink).[88] What all these designations attempt to articulate is an understanding of reality where evil is at least equiprimordial with good and is perhaps even more basic. In the combat myth, evil—represented by primordial chaos—is vanquished so that goodness or righteousness, represented by cosmic order, might be established. The battle with chaos, even when it is associated with creation (as in *Enuma Elish*), is thus fundamentally a redemptive or salvific act, usually understood as defeating or restraining the forces of evil, in order that the cosmos might be constructed. By the nature of things, however, this redemptive ordering of the cosmos can never be final, since evil is intrinsic to the fabric of things, having always to be repressed and controlled lest it break forth and overwhelm the fragility of cosmic order.[89]

Paul Ricoeur, in his masterful study of *Enuma Elish*, discerns how the primordial act of violent cosmos-making in the Mesopotamian worldview, which he characterizes as a theology of holy war, becomes the mythic legitimation of Neo-Babylonian imperial expansionism, where the king, standing in for Marduk (as the image of Marduk), vanquishes the enemies of Babylon, who are regarded as the historical embodiments of the chaos monster.[90] As Ricoeur puts it, "Creation is a victory over an Enemy older than the creator; that Enemy, immanent in the divine, will be represented in history by all the enemies whom the king in his turn, as servant of the god, will have as his mission to destroy."[91] Babylon's

88. Hermann Gunkel, *Schöpfung und Chaos in Urzeit und Endzeit: Eine religionsgeschichtliche Untersuchung über Gen 1 und Ap Joh 12* (Göttingen: Vandenhoeck & Ruprecht, 1895); John Day, *God's Conflict with the Dragon and the Sea: Echoes of a Canaanite Myth in the Old Testament* (University of Cambridge Oriental Publications 35; Cambridge: Cambridge University Press, 1985); Pedro Trigo, *Creation and History* (trans. Robert R. Barr; Theology and Liberation Series; Maryknoll, NY: Orbis, 1991), 69–108; and Walter Wink, *Engaging the Powers: Discernment and Resistance in a World of Domination* (Minneapolis: Fortress, 1992), 13–31.

89. See chapter 6 for an extended discussion of the logic of cosmogonies characterized by the combat myth.

90. For Ricoeur's extensive analysis of *Enuma Elish*, see his *Symbolism of Evil* (trans. Emerson Buchanan; Boston: Beacon, 1969), 175–99, esp. 194–98.

91. Ibid., 182.

defeat of its enemies thus (re)establishes the sociopolitical cosmos in historical time, in imitation (mimesis) of the god's establishment of the broader cosmos in mythical time.[92]

The link between *Chaoskampf*, mimesis, and *imago Dei* is profoundly illuminated by one of the Mesopotamian texts examined in chapter 3. In the *Tukulti-Ninurta Epic* the Middle-Assyrian king Tukulti-Ninurta I was described as the image (*ṣalmu*) of the high god Enlil, second only to Enlil's firstborn son, Ninurta. In the context of this exalted description he is portrayed as conquering the enemies of Assyria in his capacity as the gods' appointed emissary on earth.

Significantly, a Mesopotamian mythic tradition prominently features the god Ninurta (after whom Tukulti-Ninurta I is named) conquering a primordial foe. In the *Myth of Anzu*, which embodies much of this tradition, Ninurta defeats the monstrous Anzu bird (who is said to be a product of the flood waters) in order to recover the tablet of destinies that the bird had stolen from Ninurta's father, Enlil, the king of the gods.[93] Although scholars disagree about many issues concerning the origins of ancient texts, there is growing consensus that the Marduk-Tiamat battle in *Enuma Elish* draws upon the battle of Ninurta with Anzu.[94] While the overall story lines are by no means identical, there are many structural and stylistic similarities between the *Myth of Anzu* and the section of *Enuma Elish* narrating the defeat of Tiamat and Qingu, including an unusual amount of quotation within quotation in both texts. These sections of the myths also share a basic plot in which various gods (three in the *Myth of Anzu*, two in *Enuma Elish*) are invited to battle a primordial monster and decline, followed by a champion who accepts (Ninurta, Marduk) and is initially distressed or disoriented by the first encounter. After regrouping, the champion is vic-

92. Ricoeur's analysis of the political function of the combat myth may be applicable also in other ancient Near Eastern cultures outside Mesopotamia. For example, the Egyptian combat myth known as *The Repulsing of the Dragon* was interpreted in ancient times as a mythic account to be historically enacted in military campaigns of the pharaoh against the enemies of the empire. For various versions of *The Repulsing of the Dragon*, see *ANET* 7, 11–12, 367 (this myth portrays the nightly struggle of the sun-god Re with Apophis the serpent, who tries to swallow him in the underworld, followed by Re's victory resulting in the birth of the new day). Although we have no evidence concerning the political implications of the Ugaritic combat myths, in which Baal conquers watery enemies, it is likely they had a similar function.

93. For an English translation of the *Myth of Anzu*, see Foster, *Before the Muses*, 1.461–85. The myth exists in an Old Babylonian and a Standard Babylonian version.

94. On the relationship between the *Myth of Anzu* and *Enuma Elish*, see W. G. Lambert, "Ninurta Mythology in the Babylonian Epic of Creation," in *Keilschriftliche Literaturen* (ed. Karl Hecker and Walter Sommerfeld; 32nd Rencontre assyriologique internationale; Berlin: Reimer, 1986), 55–60; Foster, *Before the Muses*, 1.24–25; and Clifford, *Creation Accounts*, 84–85.

torious in battle (utilizing the winds as a weapon) and is acclaimed with many names as king of all the gods.[95] Indeed, the similarities between *Enuma Elish* and the *Myth of Anzu* are so great that an extant hymn of Ashurbanipal to Marduk that contains numerous allusions to *Enuma Elish* actually attributes the killing of the Anzu bird to Marduk.[96]

The celebration of Ninurta's battle prowess in the *Myth of Anzu* is significant for our purposes when taken in conjunction with the *Tukulti-Ninurta Epic*, since Tukulti-Ninurta I is described in suprahuman terms as destroying all his enemies on the field of battle and is explicitly compared to Ninurta in his capacity as a divine warrior. When read in conjunction with the *Chaoskampf* embodied in the *Myth of Anzu* and *Enuma Elish*, the *Tukulti-Ninurta Epic* thus provides a clear example of a Mesopotamian king said to be the *image* of a god, mimetically imaging or representing the divine specifically in war.

But the *Chaoskampf* is replicated not only in the Assyrian/Babylonian policy of imperial expansionism (a policy that resulted, significantly, in the sixth-century captivity of Israel), it may also be discerned in the very structure of Mesopotamian society itself. Beyond providing legitimation for the forcible suppression of external chaos in the form of the enemies of the Babylonian or Assyrian Empire, the *Chaoskampf* could also serve to reinforce the hierarchical class structure by which the chaos internal to Mesopotamian society was suppressed and held in check.[97] The ideological division between the masses created for menial service to the gods and the privileged elites who control access to the gods as mediators of blessing constitutes an oppositional dualism that looks very much like an internal version of the chaos-cosmos scheme.

That an underlying oppositional dualism is shared by Mesopotamian imperial and domestic policy (if we may put it so) receives corrobora-

95. Some of the similarities of detail are particularly striking and suggest that *Enuma Elish* is dependent on the *Myth of Anzu*, rather than vice versa. Thus Marduk's use of a net against Tiamat does not make sense if she is the primordial ocean, but a net makes sense to fight a bird (and while no net is mentioned in the *Myth of Anzu*, it does come up in other Anzu traditions). Likewise, the tablet of destinies that Marduk takes from Qingu fits oddly in *Enuma Elish*, but is central to the plot of the *Myth of Anzu*, since the Anzu bird steals it from Enlil. Then there is the wind that bears Tiamat's blood away, probably in imitation of the wind that bears away Anzu's feathers after his defeat. Another possible imitation might be the eight specific monsters listed in association with Tiamat (known from a variety of Babylonian traditions), with the additional (unparalleled) mention of three generic groups of monsters (for a total of eleven), whereas eleven victories are associated with Ninurta in various traditions. For a discussion of these (and other) similarities, see Clifford, *Creation Accounts*, 84–85; and Lambert, "Ninurta Mythology," 56–58.

96. See Foster, *Before the Muses*, 1.25.

97. The application of the chaos-cosmos scheme to Mesopotamian society is solely my own analysis. I have not encountered any biblical or ancient Near Eastern scholars arguing this line.

tion from *Enuma Elish*, in which Marduk creates two sets of "artful things" (*niklātu*) by violent means. In *Enuma Elish*, both the cosmos and humanity are grounded in acts of violence in primordial time, involving the forcible imposition of order on a principle of recalcitrant chaos (whether Tiamat or Qingu). Whereas the violent founding of the cosmos provides mythic legitimation for Mesopotamian imperialism, the violence at the root of human creation contributes to the legitimation of the Mesopotamian social order in which the masses serve the temple and the king. It thus makes perfect sense to conclude that both the myth of Marduk's conquest of Tiamat and the notion of human creation out of Qingu's blood to serve the gods would have worked in tandem to reinforce Mesopotamian royal ideology. In this ideology, the king is the gods' privileged representative (or image) on earth, who mediates and enforces their will on both his enemies and his subjects.

The Neo-Babylonian Akitu Festival

The function of the combat myth as royal ideology receives important corroboration from the Mesopotamian New Year Festival known as the Akitu. Although the Akitu Festival was celebrated in numerous Mesopotamian cities from very ancient times and could be correlated with either the spring (vernal) or autumnal new year, our best evidence for the content of the festival dates from Neo-Babylonian times.[98] At this eleven-day Spring Festival, which began on the first day of Nisan (April), *Enuma Elish* was recited aloud in its entirety before the cult statue of Marduk on the fourth day of the celebrations, thus setting a vivid tone for the cosmic/political victory of order over chaos that the festival celebrated. Although not all aspects of the Akitu are well understood, at numerous points the Neo-Babylonian version of festival clearly reflects events recounted in *Enuma Elish* and had a definite royal-political component.[99] Indeed, the Babylonian king had such an

98. My description of the Neo-Babylonian Akitu Festival is dependent on the judicious summary given in J. A. Black, "The New Year Ceremonies in Ancient Babylon: 'Taking Bel by the Hand' and a Cultic Picnic," *Religion* 11 (1981): 39–59. See also Tikva Frymer-Kensky, "Akitu," in *The Encyclopedia of Religion* (ed. Mircea Eliade; New York: Macmillan, 1987), 1.170–72.

99. At one time scholars thought that the Babylonian Akitu Festival combined Marduk's conquest of chaos with an older myth of the release of a fertility deity from the underworld (a death-and-resurrection motif). But this was based on a misinterpretation of *KAR 143*, also known as *The Marduk Ordeal Text*. For a recent discussion, see Tikva Frymer-Kensky, "The Tribulations of Marduk: The So-Called 'Marduk Ordeal Text,'" *Journal of the American Oriental Society* 103 (1983): 131–41.

important role in the Akitu that if he was absent certain parts of the festival could not be celebrated that year.

The king's role begins on the fourth day when he sets out from Babylon for Borsippa, a ten-mile journey by river, in order to fetch the cult statue of Nabu (Marduk's firstborn son and patron-god of Borsippa). On the fifth day, the king returned from Borsippa by river to Babylon and disembarked at the banks of the Euphrates. Upon entering the temple dedicated to Marduk (known as the Esagila), the king was divested of his royal insignia (his staff, mace, crown, and ring) by a priest (a šešgallu), who struck him across the face. The priest then led the king into Marduk's shrine and made him kneel by pulling him by the ears. This ritual humiliation is understood by scholars as symbolizing the king's participation in the reversion to chaos before the reestablishment of order, which the coming of the new year represented.

The king then prayed a confession of innocence before Marduk, to the effect that he had honorably discharged his duties vis-à-vis Babylon and Marduk's temple. This confession is rooted in the king's traditional role as Marduk's high priest/mediator and as the protector/shepherd of the city. As J. A. Black explains, the king insists that "he has faithfully fulfilled the sacred duties of kingship and priesthood entrusted to him."[100] The šešgallu then recited an assurance that the king's prayer had been heard and that Marduk would bless his kingship, the temple, and the people. The political overtones are clear when the priest declares: "He [Marduk] will destroy your enemies, defeat your adversaries." Following this assurance, the priest reinvested the king with the insignia of royal office. Tikva Frymer-Kensky interprets the role of the king as follows: "The participation of the king, his abasement, and his reinvestiture indicate that royal power in Babylonia at this period was connected to the royal power of Marduk and that therefore both kingship and the organizational power of the universe were renewed and celebrated yearly at this Akitu festival."[101]

On the eighth day, the king, "taking Bel [that is, Marduk] by the hand," escorted the image of Marduk to the temple courtyard where it was enthroned under a canopy. They then proceeded to the "Shrine of Destinies" located within Nabu's sanctuary in the Esagila, where a divine assembly was ritually enacted (conforming to an episode in *Enuma Elish*), at which Marduk was acclaimed king of the gods (before their cult statues) and invested with supreme authority. This was the first "decree of destinies," by which the king's fate for the coming year was

100. Black, "New Year Ceremonies in Ancient Babylon," 54.
101. Frymer-Kensky, "Akitu," 171.

determined. The rule of Marduk and the Babylonian king were thus intimately intertwined.

Then the king once again "took Bel by the hand" and led him out of the temple precincts in a grand public procession through the streets of Babylon. This procession of the image of Marduk and all the cult statues of the visiting gods and goddesses, mounted on chariots, and accompanied by priests, musicians, and singers, "could easily," comments Black, "be turned by kings into an opportunity for the display of armed forces, tribute and prisoners."[102] Passing through Procession Street (with its immense turquoise walls decorated with mythical monsters), then past the Hanging Gardens and the Ishtar Gate, the procession exited the city and traveled by barge along the Euphrates to the Akitu temple, located outside the city limits (whose doors may have been decorated with battle scenes from *Enuma Elish*).[103]

When the procession of deities finally returned to Babylon on the eleventh day of the festival, a second divine assembly mentioned in *Enuma Elish* was reenacted in the "Shrine of the Destinies" within Nabu's sanctuary in the Esagila. This constituted the second "decree of destinies," at which the fate of the land of Babylon was determined.

The annual Akitu Festival in Neo-Babylonian times thus combined elements of *Enuma Elish*, with its distinctive emphasis on the conquest of chaos by which the cosmos was founded, with the king's traditional role as mediator and representative of the gods on earth. It constituted a grand ritual enactment of the annual renewal of the cosmos and the Babylonian social order in which the king had a prominent role as the authorized delegate of the gods.

The above analysis, not only of the Akitu Festival, but also of Mesopotamian imperial practice and the structure of Mesopotamian society, points to the ideological character of the Mesopotamian worldview. No element of this worldview—neither Mesopotamian sacral kingship (in which the king was thought of as the image of a god) nor the mythic claim that humans were created to serve the gods nor the *Chaoskampf* motif (by which the cosmos was understood to be grounded in primordial divine violence)—was a freestanding theological idea. Rather, through their complex interweaving these elements formed a powerful matrix of ideology that both legitimated and found concrete sociopolitical embodiment in the Babylonian and Assyrian empires. These empires boasted not only immense political and military might, but also signifi-

102. Black, "New Year Ceremonies in Ancient Babylon," 46.

103. We know from both literary and archeological evidence that the door of the Akitu temple in Ashur in Neo-Assyrian times was decorated with scenes of the defeat of Qingu (with Ashur in the place of Marduk); see ibid., 46.

cant architectural and cultural achievements, which contributed to their prestige in the ancient Near East. The challenge that Mesopotamian civilization, undergirded by its mythic ideology, would have constituted for Israel, and how Israel responded to this challenge through the *imago Dei*, will be explored in chapter 5.

5

Genesis 1–11
as Ideology
Critique

Having sketched, in chapter 4, the matrix of Mesopotamian ideology that legitimated and found embodiment in the empires of Babylon and Assyria, it is now my task to clarify the challenge that this ideology posed to ancient Israel and to read the biblical *imago Dei* as a response to this challenge, especially through its articulation of an alternative construal of the human condition. This counterideological reading will require going beyond Genesis 1 to the primeval history (Genesis 1–11). There are two reasons for this. First of all, the *imago Dei* is embedded in the primeval history at crucial junctures (1:26–27; 5:1; 9:6), such that the primeval history may be regarded as an important context for interpreting the *imago Dei*. But, second, the primeval history itself (and not just the *imago Dei*) has a distinctive Mesopotamian background (as we saw in chapter 3). It will be useful, therefore, to explore how Genesis 1–11 as a complex literary unit (undoubtedly composed of different sources) articulates a worldview (and especially an understanding of being human) alternative to that of ancient Mesopotamia, precisely by utilizing various Mesopotamian ideas and motifs.[1]

---

1. Lawrence A. Turner analyzes Genesis 1–11 as a coherent story (without denying its composite character) in his monograph *Announcements of Plot in Genesis* (Journal for the Study of the Old Testament Supplement 96; Sheffield: Sheffield Academic Press, 1990), 21–49. His analysis does not, however, address the Mesopotamian background of the text.

Although I will make some concluding comments on the difference it might make if the Neo-Babylonian exile were indeed the context in which this alternative worldview (crystallized in the *imago Dei*) was voiced or heard, my reading of the primeval history as ideology critique is not tied to an exilic/postexilic context or to any other particular historical situation (since the text is evidently composite, reflecting different historical situations). Rather, my reading of the primeval history is broadly applicable to an extended stretch of Israel's life in the shadow of Mesopotamian civilization. It will be my suggestion in what follows that Genesis 1–11 does not just embody a vision of humanity that happens to be distinctive vis-à-vis ancient Mesopotamia, but that it may be fruitfully understood as intentionally subversive literature, utilizing a distinctive vision of the human condition to call into question central elements of Mesopotamian ideology.

At the moment, however, this is simply an assumption on my part—and it is a particularly troubling assumption for many contemporary biblical scholars, who tend to be suspicious (and not without reason) of overblown claims for the distinctiveness of Israel or the Old Testament vis-à-vis the ancient Near East.

The Problem of the Distinctiveness of Israel

I am fully aware that the issue of how we are to relate a biblical text to its ancient Near Eastern background is extremely complex. Even if we have decided on plausible ancient Near Eastern parallels (chapter 3) and adequately sketched the broader Mesopotamian worldview (chapter 4) as a background to the *imago Dei* and the primeval history, there still remains the issue of the precise relationship of these parallels and this worldview to the biblical text. The most basic question for us is whether the biblical *imago Dei* (in the context of Genesis 1–11) is to be understood in fundamental continuity with the Mesopotamian material or in some sort of contrast to this material.

But this is merely a subspecies of the wider—and historically contentious—question of the relationship of the Old Testament (and Israel) to the ancient Near East in general. On this question, the history of scholarship is replete with prejudgments. The extremes are represented by the *Babel und Bibel* school in Germany at the end of the nineteenth century and the so-called Biblical Theology Movement in America during the 1940s and 1950s, with roots in earlier German scholarship.[2]

2. The notion of an American Movement, appropriately capitalized, goes back to Brevard S. Childs's critical analysis in his *Biblical Theology in Crisis* (Philadelphia: Westminster, 1970).

Although the position of the *Babel und Bibel* school has been thoroughly discredited for so long that it seems like an idiosyncratic aberration, in its heyday its foremost proponent—Friedrich Delitzsch—and his followers claimed the antiquity and superiority of Babylonian culture and literature and viewed Israelite culture and the biblical writings as a pale, decidedly inferior, later imitation.[3]

By way of contrast, the Biblical Theology Movement (associated above all in the United States with the writings of G. Ernest Wright) emphasized the radical discontinuity between the uniqueness of Israel's ethical monotheism and the debased polytheism of its neighbors.[4] Representatives of this position (whether in the American Movement, so-called, or among its German predecessors in the 1920s and 1930s) typically highlighted the supposedly linear view of time characteristic of the Bible, which valorized God's "mighty acts in history," versus the cyclical view of time of other ancient Near Eastern cultures, whereby the gods were deifications of the immanent forces and processes of nature.[5]

This understanding of the distinctiveness of the Bible vis-à-vis the ancient Near East has come under substantial critique for several important reasons.[6] It has become clear, first of all, that the history/nature dichotomy was a theological construct decisively influenced by neo-orthodox theology, particularly by Karl Barth's famous distinction between (historical) revelation and (natural) religion.[7] This does not in

---

3. For an account, see H. B. Huffmon, "*Babel und Bibel*: The Encounter between Babylon and the Bible," in *Backgrounds for the Bible* (ed. M. P. O'Connor and D. N. Freedman; Winona Lake, IN: Eisenbrauns, 1987), 125–36; and Omar Carena, *History of the Near Eastern Historiography and Its Problems: 1852–1985*, vol. 1: *1852–1945* (Alter Orient und Altes Testament 218.1; Kevelaer: Butzon & Bercker/Neukirchen-Vluyn: Neukirchener Verlag, 1989), 96–112.

4. See especially G. Ernest Wright, "How Did Early Israel Differ from Her Neighbors?" *Biblical Archeologist* 6 (1943): 1–20; and idem, *The Old Testament against Its Environment* (Studies in Biblical Theology 2; Chicago: Regnery/London: SCM, 1950). Maimonides may be regarded as a precursor of the Biblical Theology Movement in *The Guide for the Perplexed*, part 2, chap. 39, where he contrasted the Torah given through the prophet Moses with the merely human law of the Greeks and the "follies" or "ravings" of the Sabeans.

5. The popularity of the highly charged distinction between nature and history for understanding the uniqueness of biblical faith stems from Old Testament scholars Gerhard von Rad, Albrecht Alt, and Martin Noth and was so great that it pervaded the work of writers as diverse as Oscar Cullmann, T. C. Vriezen, Henri Frankfort, Walther Eichrodt, Markus Barth, James Smart, and Eric Voeglin.

6. For a recent account (and critique) of the Biblical Theology Movement, see Walter Brueggemann, *Theology of the Old Testament: Testimony, Dispute, Advocacy* (Minneapolis: Fortress, 1997), 15–49.

7. On the important historical and political circumstances that led Barth to formulate his dichotomy, see H. Martin Rumscheidt, *Revelation and Theology: An Analysis of the Barth-Harnack Correspondence of 1923* (Cambridge: Cambridge University Press, 1972).

itself invalidate the distinction, since conceptual constructs are inevitable in any interpretation of Scripture. More to the point, however, is that this particular construct falsifies the actual relationship between Israel (and the biblical materials), on the one hand, and the ancient Near East, on the other. This relationship, on the contrary, involves great areas of commonality and cultural sharing.[8] As Assyriologist W. G. Lambert, himself a proponent of (limited) biblical distinctiveness, puts it, "it is practically impossible to offer any clearly defined grounds for this view without raising a retort from some quarter that other nations shared in the aspect claimed as distinctive."[9]

Although many have raised their voices in critique of the history/nature distinction, perhaps no one has done more to elucidate its artificial character when applied to the ancient Near East than Berktil Albrektson. His brief but lucid study *History and the Gods* conclusively demonstrated (by representative citations of primary sources) that the putative "nature gods" of the ancient Near East were typically understood by ancient Near Eastern peoples to act in both nature and history (as we use the terms) and that these gods were often described in a manner fundamentally similar to the biblical portrayal of YHWH, as bringing historicopolitical judgment or blessing on people and nations.[10]

But if the history/nature distinction is not an adequate construct for expressing Israel's uniqueness vis-à-vis its neighbors, what about the possibility that biblical aniconism—the imageless nature of Israel's worship—might capture what is unique about biblical faith? Not only has it been a popular claim over the years that aniconism is central to the

---

Walter Brueggemann argues that while we may need to critique this influential distinction, we ought to respect the ethical discernment of the times (in Nazi Germany) that led Barth and others to utilize this distinction: "Thus I regard this period of scholarship and its governing assumptions not as a lapse, as some are wont to do, but as producing a body of work that we must continue to take seriously"; "Response to J. Richard Middleton," *Harvard Theological Review* 87 (1994): 282.

8. This was the (overstated) insight of the *Babel und Bibel* school. For a more reasonable, now classic, statement of commonality and cultural sharing see Morton Smith, "The Common Theology of the Ancient Near East," *Journal of Biblical Literature* 71 (1952): 35–47.

9. W. G. Lambert, "Destiny and Divine Intervention in Babylon and Israel," *Oudtestamentische Studiën* 17 (1972): 65.

10. Bertil Albrektson, *History and the Gods: An Essay on the Idea of Historical Events as Divine Manifestations in the Ancient Near East and in Israel* (Lund: Gleerup, 1976). While Albrektson refutes the alignment of history with the Bible and the alignment of nature with ancient Near Eastern religion by showing that both are "historical," Ronald Simkins, in a more recent study, challenges not only this caricature of the ancient Near East, but also the applicability of the distinction within the Bible itself; *Yahweh's Activity in History and Nature in the Book of Joel* (Ancient Near Eastern Texts and Studies 10; Lewiston: Mellen, 1991), 3–75.

uniqueness of biblical faith, but it might well be relevant to the notion that humans are the only legitimate *imago Dei*.

But then we have to reckon with Tryggve Mettinger's formidable cross-cultural study of aniconism in ancient Near Eastern cultures, which calls into question this claim to uniqueness.[11] Examining archeological data from a host of ancient Near Eastern cultures, including Mesopotamia, Egypt, Nabatea, pre-Islamic Arabia, Spain, the Phoenician-Punic world, and Bronze Age Syria (including Mari and Ebla), Mettinger finds abundant evidence for what he calls "material aniconism" and some evidence for "empty-space aniconism." Whereas the former refers to religious cults that utilize some sort of material that is clearly not a cult-statue to symbolize the divine presence, such as a standing stone (*maṣṣēbâ*), meteorite, or other nonrepresentational symbol, the latter refers to a cult that understands some open area or empty space as the locus of the deity's presence.

Noting that the idea of YHWH seated on the cherubim throne upon the ark of the covenant in the holy of holies is a clear Israelite example of empty-space aniconism, Mettinger draws our attention to the intriguing fact that empty-space aniconism was most prominent in Phoenicia and that Solomon employed Phoenicians to construct the Jerusalem temple in which the ark was housed. Although Mettinger thinks that Israelite empty-space aniconism predates Phoenician influence, he proposes that Israel's aniconism began with a material aniconic cult focused on standing stones or *maṣṣēbôt* (to which there is abundant archeological testimony, besides the biblical testimony itself) and that this was part of a significant and widespread West Semitic tradition of standing-stone aniconism found in Nabatea, Arabia, Phoenicia, and Syria.

Israel, however, moved beyond the de facto aniconism of this common West Semitic cultural tradition (which was quite tolerant of images) to an explicit iconoclasm, which Mettinger calls "programmatic aniconism." Thus both the Torah and the writing prophets come explicitly to condemn the construction and the use of cult statues—and even of standing stones—in Israel's worship. But this move beyond its neighbors is not, in Mettinger's opinion, strictly speaking unique to Israel, since the early material aniconism of Arabia seems to have led, in a parallel development, to the later, well-known programmatic aniconism of Islam.

The studies of Mettinger (on aniconism) and Albrektson (on divine action in history) do not mean that there are no significant differences between the Bible and the ancient Near East. Rather, they suggest that

11. Tryggve N. D. Mettinger, *No Graven Image? Israelite Aniconism in Its Ancient Near Eastern Context* (Coniectanea biblica Old Testament Series 42; Stockholm: Almqvist & Wiksell, 1995).

differences must not be simply assumed, but carefully investigated. This is an important point, not only because I intend to argue that the understanding of humanity as *imago Dei* in the primeval history is indeed distinctive (in an important sense) vis-à-vis the ideology of Mesopotamia, but also because there is an overwhelming tendency in contemporary scholarship to look askance at claims of distinctiveness for Israel or the biblical text. This is certainly an understandable response, given the overburdened claims for distinctiveness that have historically been made.

But rather than swing from one extreme to the other, we should take seriously William Hallo's objection to the designation *comparative* (as in "comparative studies") since it is an open question whether the relevant ancient Near Eastern parallels in any particular case will be more appropriately understood in *comparison* with, or in *contrast* to, the biblical materials one is investigating.[12] Although Hallo initially suggested the term *contrastive* in an attempt to supplement the one-sidedness of the designation *comparative*,[13] he has more systematically proposed a "contextual" approach as the broader, more inclusive rubric for understanding the Bible's complex (comparative/contrastive) relationship to its ancient Near Eastern setting.[14]

Hallo's approach, however, has an important methodological limitation. He himself distinguishes his own interest in "the written documentary testimony" of the ancient Near East from the more sociological approach to context evident in the work of Paul Hanson.[15] Whereas Hallo is content to stay at the level of comparing and contrasting ancient Near Eastern written materials (whether literary or inscriptional) with the Bible, Hanson is interested also in the "sociological context . . . visible behind the material."[16] My own approach to both the Bible and the ancient Near East has been decisively influenced by Hanson's

---

12. William W. Hallo, "Biblical History in Its Near Eastern Setting: The Contextual Approach," in *Scripture in Context: Essays on the Comparative Method* (ed. Carl D. Evans, William W. Hallo, and John B. White; Pittsburgh: Pickwick, 1980), 2. See also Shemaryahu Talmon, "The Comparative Method in Biblical Interpretation: Principles and Problems," in *Congress Volume: Göttingen 1977* (Vetus Testamentum Supplement 29; Leiden: Brill, 1978), 320–56.

13. See William W. Hallo, "New Moons and Sabbaths: A Case-Study in the Contrastive Approach," *Hebrew Union College Annual* 78 (1977): 1–17.

14. Note the use of the word *context* both in the subtitle of Hallo's essay, "Biblical History in Its Near Eastern Setting: The Contextual Approach," and in the title of the volume in which it appears, *Scripture in Context: Essays on the Comparative Method.*

15. Ibid., 2.

16. Paul D. Hanson, "Jewish Apocalyptic against Its Ancient Near Eastern Environment," *Revue biblique* 78 (1971): 33; idem, *The Dawn of Apocalyptic* (Philadelphia: Fortress, 1975).

work.[17] Both Hanson's writings and the extensive corpus of Walter Brueggemann[18] have been important resources for my own exploration of a sociopolitical or ideological reading of the *imago Dei* in Genesis. In a rough and ready way, we may say that a sociopolitical/ideological reading of biblical texts is attentive both to the text's rootage in a particular social context and to the text's social function, which may be to express and thus legitimate the current social order or to propose a critical alternative to the status quo.

The pioneers of such an approach to the Hebrew Bible are undoubtedly George Mendenhall and Norman Gottwald.[19] Although there are important methodological and substantive differences between them, as well as much that could be challenged in their work,[20] particularly useful for my reading of the biblical *imago Dei* is their shared thesis that the distinctiveness of YHWH vis-à-vis the gods of the ancient Near East is inextricably linked to the distinctiveness of Israel's egalitarian form of social organization that developed prior to the monarchy and is expressed in the memory of the exodus and the Sinai laws. Both Mendenhall and Gottwald argue that the formation of early, premonarchic Israel was

17. See especially the superb book by Paul D. Hanson, *The People Called: The Growth of Community in the Bible* (San Francisco: Harper & Row, 1986), repr. with a new introduction (Louisville: Westminster John Knox, 2002).

18. Walter Brueggemann's approach is developed most programmatically in *The Prophetic Imagination* (Philadelphia: Fortress, 1978), and with significant attention to methodology in three articles: "Trajectories in Old Testament Literature and the Sociology of Ancient Israel," *Journal of Biblical Literature* 98 (1979): 161–85; "A Shape for Old Testament Theology, I: Structure Legitimation," *Catholic Biblical Quarterly* 47 (1985): 28–46; and "A Shape for Old Testament Theology, II: Embrace of Pain," *Catholic Biblical Quarterly* 47 (1985): 395–415. The *Catholic Biblical Quarterly* articles are reprinted in Brueggemann's *Old Testament Theology: Essays on Structure, Theme, and Text* (ed. Patrick D. Miller; Minneapolis: Fortress, 1992), chaps. 1–2. I interacted with Brueggemann's approach in my "Is Creation Theology Inherently Conservative? A Dialogue with Walter Brueggemann," *Harvard Theological Review* 87 (1994): 257–77; for Brueggemann's reply, see "Response to J. Richard Middleton," *Harvard Theological Review* 87 (1994): 279–89.

19. Of George Mendenhall's and Norman Gottwald's many writings, the most important are Mendenhall's seminal, early article, "The Hebrew Conquest of Palestine," *Biblical Archeologist* 25 (1962): 66–87; and his later elaboration, *The Tenth Generation: The Origins of the Biblical Tradition* (Baltimore: Johns Hopkins University Press, 1973); and Gottwald's magnum opus of over nine hundred pages: *The Tribes of Yahweh: A Sociology of the Religion of Liberated Israel, 1250–1050 B.C.E.* (Maryknoll, NY: Orbis, 1979).

20. For exposition and criticism of Mendenhall and Gottwald, see Werner E. Lemke, "Interpreting Biblical History through the Eyes of Sociology and Politics: The Work of George Mendenhall and Norman Gottwald," *Conservative Judaism* 39 (1986): 67–80; Walter Brueggemann, "Israel's Social Criticism and Yahweh's Sexuality," *Journal of the American Academy of Religion Supplement Series* 45 (1977): 739–72; and idem, "The Tribes of Yahweh: An Essay Review," *Journal of the American Academy of Religion* 48 (1980): 441–51.

an intentional sociopolitical/ideological rebellion against the oppressive hegemony of Egypt and the Canaanite city-states (a phenomenon that Gottwald calls "retribalization"). Whether the various details of either Gottwald's or Mendenhall's historical and sociological reconstruction will stand the test of time, their central (shared) insight into the connection between Israel's understanding of God and its egalitarian form of life provided a foundation for a broad approach to the Bible (and ancient Near Eastern literature) that many other scholars find fruitful.[21]

It is important to note, however, that Mendenhall and Gottwald disagree profoundly on how we are to understand the precise nature of the connection between theological claim and social reality. Whereas Gottwald (utilizing a hybrid of Marxian class analysis and Durkheim's structural-functionalism) portrays this in quasimaterialist fashion as a one-way influence of sociopolitical formations on theology, such that YHWH becomes a mere "function" of (and cipher for) the egalitarian social order, Mendenhall asserts the priority of faith and the reality of the biblical God. In this he is joined by Brueggemann, who explicitly challenges Gottwald's assumption of monocausality, proposing instead a dialectical model in which theological claims do not just reflect, but can also generate, social formations.[22] Brueggemann thus formalizes and makes explicit Mendenhall's (typically unthematized) working assumption of a two-way influence between theological conceptions and the social order.[23]

A Nuanced Proposal of Distinctiveness

Brueggemann furthermore makes the intriguing suggestion, in a review of Gottwald's *Tribes of Yahweh*, that this sociological approach to the Bible provides a way "of giving substance and credibility to the now discredited 'mighty deeds of God' construct" (which was central to the

21. See the articles in *The Bible and the Politics of Exegesis: Essays in Honor of Norman K. Gottwald on His Sixty-fifth Birthday* (ed. David Jobling, Peggy L. Day, and Gerald T. Sheppard; Cleveland: Pilgrim, 1991); and *The Bible and Liberation: Political and Social Hermeneutics* (ed. Norman K. Gottwald and Richard A. Horsley; rev. ed.; Maryknoll, NY: Orbis/London: SPCK, 1993).

22. Lemke also objects to Gottwald's sociological determinism, which trivializes the reality of the biblical God; "Interpreting Biblical History," 80. At the 1999 annual meeting of the Society of Biblical Literature in Boston, MA (in a panel discussion honoring the twentieth anniversary of the publication of *The Tribes of Yahweh*), Gottwald orally "repented" of what he termed his earlier "scientism."

23. This modification is the central point of Brueggemann's "Tribes of Yahweh" and the burden of much of his work on Scripture. Hanson (*People Called*, 7–8) also works with a dialectical model similar to Brueggemann's.

Biblical Theology Movement) in that it grounds these deeds not in the problematic category of history (the unique and unrecoverable *hapax* that actually happened, which is endlessly debatable), but more firmly in broad sociological patterns of reality.[24] This distinction between history and sociology has relevance to my hesitancy in defining too specifically *the* (singular) historical context of Genesis 1, since there is no reliable way for us to determine when the text was written. We do, however, have sufficient understanding of the broad patterns of Mesopotamian society (and its legitimating ideology), which formed a significant part of the cultural landscape of the ancient Near East during the entire period in which Israel was developing its own culture and worldview.

But even more intriguing than Brueggemann's point about historical *hapax* versus sociological patterns is that the Mendenhall-Gottwald proposal in effect reformulates the insight of the Biblical Theology Movement regarding the distinctiveness of Israel in a manner that avoids altogether the artificial history/nature distinction. This ideologically sophisticated, sociological reappropriation of the notion of Israel's distinctiveness focuses not on free-floating theological claims about the supposed arena of divine action (nature or history), but on what sort of social order these claims legitimate or generate. If we were to apply this way of putting the question to the interpretation of the *imago Dei*, my own provisional formulation would be that the distinctiveness of Israel vis-à-vis the ancient Near East hinges not on whether the gods act in history, but on whether ordinary humans (and not just kings or priests) are allowed to be significant participants in the historical process.

A focus on the distinctiveness of Israel's social claims finds support in the comments of Frank Moore Cross, who certainly has no simplistic understanding of Israel's distinctiveness. On the contrary, Cross is renowned in the field of biblical scholarship for his groundbreaking volume *Canaanite Myth and Hebrew Epic*, which examined how Old Testament writers borrowed in fundamental ways from the culture, religion, and theology of their Canaanite neighbors in articulating their own faith.[25]

When asked in a 1991 interview, "What would you describe as new in Israel?" Cross unhesitatingly answered: "Israel's critique of kingship and temple."[26] Elsewhere in the interview Cross explained the idea of sacral kingship that Israel dissented from, connecting it to both the combat myth and the mimetic ideal:

24. Brueggemann, "Tribes of Yahweh," 445.

25. Frank Moore Cross, *Canaanite Myth and Hebrew Epic: Essays in the History of the Religion of Israel* (Cambridge: Harvard University Press, 1973).

26. Hershel Shanks (ed.), *Frank Moore Cross: Conversations with a Bible Scholar* (Washington, DC: Biblical Archaeology Society, 1994), 74.

A fundamental mythic pattern in Canaan and Mesopotamia describes the cosmos as emerging from theomachy, a conflict among the gods, in which kingship in heaven—and hence on earth—is established by the victory of the storm god, the god of fertility and life. Human society participates in these orders of creation because kingship on earth was rooted in divine kingship, which was properly unchanging and eternal.[27]

Notice, first of all, that Cross's articulation of Israel's distinctiveness is not limited to any particular historical period and is thus relevant to my reading of Genesis 1–11, no matter when the texts are dated. Second, Cross does not make the common mistake of characterizing the mimetic ideal as a variety of "nature religion." On the contrary, he is properly aware that ancient Near Eastern religion involves the postulation of a microcosmos-macrocosmos relationship between what we would call society/history, on the one hand, and nature, on the other—a widely recognized relationship that led to the telling phrase *the integration of society and nature* in the subtitle of Henri Frankfort's classic study *Kingship and the Gods*.[28] The theological-ethical problem with this integration (the microcosmos-macrocosmos relationship), from the perspective of biblical religion, is that the primordial paradigm in which the human social order is grounded, and to which it must conform (the cosmic polis of the gods), is fundamentally an *unjust* order. To embody this order in an actual society thus results in injustice at the human level.

In contrast to this ancient Near Eastern mythic pattern, explains Cross, stands ancient Israel,

with its rejection of the sacral claims of state and church and with its sustained prophetic critique of the mighty and wealthy—including priest and king—who oppressed the poor and the weak. Israel's attitudes towards its

27. Ibid., 75–76. Hanson (*People Called*, 16) has a similar analysis: "In the myth and ritual pattern associated with the cults of the major city-states and empires, we find a rigidly hierarchical conception of authority. The chief deity residing in the main temple was the absolute sovereign, whose rule was administered by the king. The authority of the king was in turn established by the ascription of divine attributes. This conception determined the sociopolitical structures of the state. Essential to social harmony was the obedient acceptance by each individual of his or her assigned station in life, be that as priest, free landowner, peasant, or slave."

28. Henri Frankfort, *Kingship and the Gods: A Study of Ancient Near Eastern Religion as the Integration of Society and Nature* (Chicago: University of Chicago Press, 1948). Another way of expressing the "integration of society and nature" in ancient Near Eastern religion is found in the title of Thorkild Jacobsen's famous essay on Mesopotamian religion: "The Cosmos as a State," in *The Intellectual Adventure of Ancient Man: An Essay on Speculative Thought in the Ancient Near East*, by Henri Frankfort et al. (Chicago: University of Chicago Press, 1946), 125–84, which became the basis for his later major study: *The Treasures of Darkness: A History of Mesopotamian Religion* (New Haven: Yale University Press, 1976).

rulers, and the unjust society they created, are unique in the ancient Near East, where deified kings and hierarchical class structure were assumed to be part of the order of creation.[29]

Cross's point here is not simply that the biblical writers had an idea of *God* that was different from their neighbors (although this is not excluded), but that they had different ideas about what sort of *social order* was ordained of God, namely, one that nurtured the flourishing of human life, rather than protecting the powerful at the expense of the weak.

Whereas this ideologically sophisticated version of the distinctiveness of Israel is not susceptible (in my opinion) to the criticism that it falsifies Israel's relationship to the ancient Near East (as the history/nature dichotomy did), it is nevertheless open to a major ethical criticism. Thus, it might be argued that this more recent understanding of distinctiveness, no less than the Biblical Theology Movement, perpetuates an us/them dichotomy that uncritically valorizes the religious tradition in which Western thought and culture are rooted (the Bible) and demonizes that which is other (the rich and varied cultures of the ancient Near East). This is an important issue that cannot be fully addressed here, although awareness of it pervades my own analysis that follows. Perhaps a step toward addressing the issue, however, is to realize that the distinction between the two forms of social claims (and practices) that Cross suggests does not separate Israel in any absolute way from the nations of the ancient Near East. On the contrary, as Cross's comments indicate, we should understand this distinction as operating also *within* Israel, thus providing the basis of an *internal* ideology critique (as found, for example, in many of the prophetic writings).[30]

The Mesopotamian Challenge to Biblical Faith

It is my discernment that the distinctive biblical insight into God's purposes for justice in the world, an insight originally forged in the crucible of Egypt and Canaan, is applied beyond its original cultural context to a critical engagement with Mesopotamian ideology in the literature of Genesis 1–11 (with its discernable Mesopotamian motifs). This engagement, which involved recontextualizing the stories of Israel's election, deliverance, and covenant in terms of universal human history

29. Shanks, *Frank Moore Cross: Conversations with a Bible Scholar*, 68.
30. See part 3 (below) for a discussion of how the nonviolent character of creation in Genesis 1 might serve to call into question the violence found within Scripture.

(and ultimately in terms of the creation of humanity and the cosmos), was accomplished through the use—and subversive transformation—of elements of Mesopotamian ideology, especially those that articulated an understanding of the purpose and status of humanity in the world.

Since we have already (in chapter 4) sketched some of the basic elements of Mesopotamian ideology and examined how these elements would have worked together to provide mythic legitimation of the Mesopotamian social order, here we need to try and understand the allure of Mesopotamia and why this impressive civilization, with its ideological underpinnings, would have constituted a challenge to Israelite faith that needed answering.

The civilization of Mesopotamia, stretching from the ancient Sumerians of the third millennium B.C.E. through the Babylonian and Assyrian empires of the second and first millennia B.C.E., constituted a truly impressive cultural achievement and was recognized as such throughout the ancient Near East. Drawing on and expanding A. Leo Oppenheim's classic notion of the Mesopotamian "stream of tradition,"[31] Stephanie Dalley helpfully documents both the cultural achievements of Mesopotamia and the impact of Mesopotamian culture upon many ancient Near Eastern cultures over a vast stretch of time.[32] These achievements include the invention of cuneiform, which is probably the first writing system ever developed. This system of wedge-shaped marks on clay tablets by which Sumerian was first written and that was later adapted for Akkadian (the Semitic language of Babylonia and Assyria), has been found throughout the ancient Near East in a variety of cultures due to Mesopotamian influence and itself constituted an important medium for the dissemination of Mesopotamian cultural ideals.

The rigorous system of scribal training developed in Mesopotamia, which utilized copying exercises from cuneiform texts, was imitated by other nations, and the prestige of the system was such that scribes outside Mesopotamia often adopted Babylonian names as a sign of their profession.[33] It is due to this widespread imitation that copies of the core cuneiform texts used in Mesopotamian scribal training have turned up in Iran, Anatolia, Egypt, Syria, Palestine, Transjordan, and the eastern Mediterranean,[34] and these texts testify to a variety of Meso-

31. A. Leo Oppenheim, *Ancient Mesopotamia: Portrait of a Dead Civilization* (Chicago: University of Chicago Press, 1964).

32. Stephanie Dalley, "Occasions and Opportunities 1: To the Persian Conquest," in *The Legacy of Mesopotamia* (ed. Stephanie Dalley; Oxford: Oxford University Press, 1998), 9–33.

33. Ibid., 18.

34. Ibid., 20.

potamian cultural advances that were disseminated throughout the ancient world.

For example, copies of cuneiform texts found throughout the ancient Near East document Mesopotamian advances in mathematics, such as the use of an approximation of π, the division of the circle into 360 degrees, and what later came to be known as "Pythagoras's theorem."[35] Cuneiform texts, likewise, testify to the Mesopotamian study of grammar and syntax (including the existence of bilingual and trilingual lexicons), which predates by one and a half thousand years the first Sanskrit grammar in India (which at one time was thought to be the earliest such study).[36]

Cuneiform texts that turn up outside Mesopotamia in the early and middle second millennium B.C.E. include a wide variety of genres, such as literary works like the *Sumerian King List* or the *Gilgamesh Epic* as well as business, legal, mathematical, lexical, astronomical, and divination texts. The result was a shared literature in Akkadian cuneiform and a shared tradition of "business, law, and administration" throughout the ancient Near East due to Mesopotamian influence.[37] Indeed, among the Elamites, Urartians, and Hittites, the influence of Mesopotamia was so powerful that Oppenheim goes so far as to call these cultures "satellite civilizations" of Mesopotamia, since they adopted, besides the Akkadian language, a substantial amount of Mesopotamian literary and cultural traditions.[38] In general, the "cultural authority" of Mesopotamia was such, explains Dalley, that even in periods of Egyptian or Hittite dominance in the ancient Near East, when Babylonia and Assyria were eclipsed politically, Mesopotamian cuneiform (and not Egyptian or Hittite) was still the scribal language of choice throughout the region.[39]

But it was not just that Mesopotamian civilization had a high degree of cultural development or that its cultural influence in the ancient Near East was immense. Peter Machinist demonstrates that there was an articulated consciousness of Mesopotamian cultural distinctiveness and superiority both in the north (Assyria) and in the south (Babylonia) and also a degree of what he terms "pan-Mesopotamian" self-consciousness.[40] While there were some differences in the way this consciousness of Mesopotamian superiority was articulated in the north and the south,

---

35. Ibid., 19.
36. Ibid., 18.
37. Ibid., 19.
38. Oppenheim, *Ancient Mesopotamia*, 67–69.
39. Dalley, "Occasions and Opportunities," 20.
40. Peter Machinist, "On Self-Consciousness in Mesopotamia," in *The Origins and Diversity of Axial Age Civilizations* (ed. Shmuel N. Eisenstadt; SUNY Series in Ancient Near Eastern Studies; Albany: SUNY, 1986), 183–202.

the common factor was a focus on the achievements of organized urban culture, typically associated with the institution of the monarchy. It was the city (sometimes with its rural environs), explains Machinist, that was thought to be "the only viable setting for the cultivation of human behavior and achievement—exactly our Latin-derived 'civilization.'"[41] As Bernard Batto puts it, "The ideal human condition was [understood to have been] achieved only in (Sumero-Akkadian) civilization, with its advanced knowledge or irrigation agriculture, urban comforts, and justly famous literary tradition in both Sumerian and Akkadian, all organized under the leadership of a divinely appointed king."[42]

Whereas ideological self-consciousness in northern Mesopotamia developed from the beginning as a relatively unified tradition that understood Assyria as a cultural and political unity, the south initially developed a series of relatively independent, competing traditions, centered around different cities, and it was only after the "theological and ideological achievement" of *Enuma Elish* that the centrality of Babylon as the epitome of Mesopotamian culture became the dominant consciousness of the region.[43] The other main difference between the north and the south was that while Assyria often adopted and adapted southern traditions and while Assyrian ruling elites in various eras sought to "identify with and incorporate Babylonian culture into their own,"[44] the south never reciprocated. Indeed, the "cultic and cultural primacy"[45] of Babylon was such that even when it was defeated militarily by Assyria, the cultural influence was still in a single direction. So prominent was this Babylonian primacy, explains Jacob Finkelstein, that from the beginning of the first millennium B.C.E. until the present day the name *Babylon* has come to stand for "the total intellectual and spiritual achievement of the various peoples who shared the three millennia of ancient Mesopotamia."[46]

Despite this prominence of the south, however, a fundamentally similar sense of Mesopotamian cultural superiority comes to expression in both northern and southern texts from widely different periods.

41. Ibid., 187–88.

42. Bernard F. Batto, "Creation Theology in Genesis," in *Creation in the Biblical Traditions* (ed. Richard J. Clifford and John J. Collins; Catholic Biblical Quarterly Monograph Series 24; Washington, DC: Catholic Biblical Association of America, 1992), 22.

43. Jacob J. Finkelstein, "Early Mesopotamia, 2500–1000 B.C.," in *Propaganda and Communication in World History*, vol. 1: *The Symbolic Instrument in Early Times* (ed. Harold D. Lasswell, Daniel Lerner, and Hans Speier; Honolulu: East-West Center of the University Press of Hawaii, 1979), 95.

44. Machinist, "On Self-Consciousness in Mesopotamia," 186.

45. Finkelstein, "Early Mesopotamia," 110 n. 127.

46. Ibid., 96.

In these texts we find the urban, civilized population of Mesopotamia (understood as a "definable, organized, sedentary community") polemically distinguished from the "strange" nomadic dwellers of inaccessible regions (deserts, forests, or mountains), who live in unstable dwellings, have unfamiliar customs, and speak confusing tongues (much like the later Greek notion of "barbarians"). Amazingly similar stereotypical descriptions of uncivilized peoples are found in Mesopotamian texts as widely separated in time as the late-third/early-second millennium and the Neo-Assyrian period.[47]

This ideological distinction between civilized Mesopotamians and others (that is, between insiders and outsiders) was not, however, meant to exclude permanently all other cultures from the attainment of civilization. While the categories were immutable, Machinist explains, individuals and groups could be transformed or converted and thus shift from the outside to the inside, as long as they adopted the accoutrements of Mesopotamian civilization (much as Enkidu the wild man became civilized by accepting the favors of the urban courtesan in the *Gilgamesh Epic*). The stereotypical descriptions of insider and outsider were thus ideological instruments of cultural co-option.[48] Indeed, the Neo-Assyrians especially saw it as their mission to Assyrianize other peoples—to "put into order" the peoples they encountered who were living "in confusion" and "teach them correct behavior, to fear god and king."[49]

But even before this specific Neo-Assyrian practice, the Late Bronze Age (1500–1200 B.C.E.) saw great mobility of populations between Mesopotamia and other lands, including the use of foreign mercenaries in Babylonian and Assyrian wars and the deportation of captives taken in such wars from their own lands to Mesopotamia. Such practices contributed to the dissemination of Mesopotamian culture in that such foreigners might return home due to retirement or ransom, "taking with them reports of the marvels they had seen and learnt abroad."[50]

Thus, we find that even after the development of alphabetic cuneiform scripts for other languages, such as Ugaritic or Hurrian, the cultural influence of Mesopotamia was so great that the Akkadian language continued to function in the ancient Near East as the lingua franca of administration and international communication, as is evident from Middle Bronze Age texts recovered from sites in Syria (Ugarit) and Egypt (el-Amarna).[51] And when other languages began to displace Akkadian cuneiform, Dalley explains, the Mesopotamian policy of massive

47. Machinist, "On Self-Consciousness in Mesopotamia," 188–90.
48. Ibid., 190–91.
49. Ibid., 189–90.
50. Dalley, "Occasions and Opportunities," 22.
51. Ibid., 23.

deportations, which continued into the Early Iron Age (first millennium B.C.E.), "was instrumental for ensuring that a common cultural background continued through many centuries."[52]

Since both the Assyrian and Babylonian empires practiced their deportation policy on the nations of Israel and Judah, whom they conquered in the seventh and sixth centuries B.C.E., respectively, it becomes clear that beyond the military and political devastation of these events, we have to take into consideration the possibility that these events functioned as instruments of Mesopotamian cultural and religious influence. In the case of the Assyrian deportation of Israelites, explains Dalley, "the royal family in exile resided at the Assyrian court and was introduced to its life-style," while elite "charioteers from Samaria were soon serving in the exclusive royal regiment alongside native Assyrian officers," and artisans often continued to practice their trades in exile.[53] Privileged deportees could thus have been subject to significant cultural influence.

The case of Manasseh, the Judean king, is most interesting in this regard, since 2 Chronicles 33:11–13 indicates that he was deported to Mesopotamia[54] by Esarhaddon and later allowed (probably under Ashurbanipal) to return home, "having absorbed Assyrian influence at the centre of power."[55] The Deuteronomic History portrays Manasseh as a paradigm example of an evil king, whose deeds were such that they outweighed all the good the other kings of Judah did (2 Kings 23:26). Among the list of Manasseh's idolatrous practices described in 2 Kings 21:3–6 are some that scholars think were due precisely to Assyrian or Babylonian influence.[56]

Of course, it is the later, Babylonian exile of the sixth century B.C.E. that is typically thought to have posed a significant threat to the faith of the deported Judeans, and many scholars have explored how diverse literature in the Hebrew Bible (such as Lamentations, the exilic psalms, Jeremiah, Isaiah 40–66, Ezekiel, the Deuteronomic History, 1–2 Chronicles, and the Priestly writing) might constitute theological responses to the crisis of exile.[57] Indeed, if the primeval history (Genesis

---

52. Ibid.

53. Dalley, *Legacy of Mesopotamia*, 62–63.

54. Whereas 2 Chronicles 33 suggests that Manasseh was taken to Babylon, historians think it was more likely to have been Nineveh.

55. Dalley, *Legacy of Mesopotamia*, 63.

56. See George E. Mendenhall, *Ancient Israel's Faith and History: An Introduction to the Bible in Context* (ed. Gary A. Herion; Louisville: Westminster John Knox, 2001), 162–65.

57. Ralph W. Klein examines these different blocks of literature for their distinctive theological contributions in the various chapters of his profound *Israel in Exile: A Theological Interpretation* (Overtures to Biblical Theology; Philadelphia: Fortress, 1979).

1–11) were read in the context of Babylonian exile (or if portions of the text were composed in response to the exilic experience), the critical stance of the text toward Mesopotamian cultural ideals would take on an even sharper edge.

But long before the Assyrian or Babylonian deportations of the seventh and sixth centuries, Israel would have come into contact with Mesopotamian cultural ideals, and it is not exceptional to think that preexilic Israelite writers attempted to address the challenge these ideals posed to Israelite faith. Beyond the obvious religious challenge posed by a worldview and social order organized around the supremacy of foreign gods (whether Ashur, Marduk, Enlil, etc.), the unique challenge posed by Mesopotamian civilization to Israel was the temptation to "buy into" Mesopotamian cultural ideals, believing the ideology of greatness propagated by this truly impressive civilization. Although this might initially seem innocuous enough, this would constitute the beginning of acceptance of the Mesopotamian worldview, with its affirmation of royal urban culture as normative and its demotion of ordinary human beings to the status of lowly servants of the gods, thus legitimating a fundamentally unjust social order as the divine will. In this worldview, humanity (and especially "backward" nations like Israel) would represent the forces of barbarism, restrained only by the redemptive and civilizing order of Mesopotamia, the source and epitome of human culture.

Besides experiencing a sense of their own cultural (and religious?) inferiority in the face of the grand achievements of this ancient and prestigious civilization, Israelite acceptance of Mesopotamian ideology may well have meant the end of Israel as a distinctive people with a historical mission that started with the call of Abraham's descendants to be a blessing to all the families of the earth. Even if Israel did not actually go so far as to worship Mesopotamian gods, the results of embracing Mesopotamian cultural values could be catastrophic, negating the distinctive covenantal shape of Israel's communal life before YHWH. If we take seriously the biblical construal of Israel's destiny, beginning with the departure of Abram's family from Mesopotamia, Israel's embrace of Mesopotamian values might well signal the forfeiture of Israel's historical vocation and thus the failure of God's redemptive purposes in history on behalf of the human race.

In what follows, I will read Genesis 1–11 (whenever it was composed) as an intentional response to Mesopotamian cultural ideals. When read against the backdrop of Mesopotamian traditions, it becomes clear that the primeval history functions both to recontextualize Israel's core theological and ethical traditions in terms of universal human history and that the categories for this recontextualization are taken precisely from these Mesopotamian traditions.

I do not intend to speculate on what set of historical factors prompted this recontextualization. But perhaps an analogy from my own experience will help to understand the need for this recontextualization. Growing up as I did a Christian in the Third World (Kingston, Jamaica), my sense of identity was decisively shaped by the cultural, geographical, and political shadow of North America, which I experienced as the prime exemplar of modern, Western culture. I found that it was not enough simply to nurture my own faith tradition or cultural identity in isolation from this large neighbor to the north. There came a time when I found it imperative to clarify the relationship of my own Christian beliefs and Jamaican culture to the culture and worldview of modernity, particularly as embodied in North America. Especially because of its powerful cultural and political influence on the Caribbean basin, I was forced to grapple with, and come to some sort of evaluation of, the practices and underlying ideology of North American culture in general and of the geopolitical force of the United States in particular. Clarifying the intersecting areas of influence and tension was especially important for developing a mature sense of self-identity.

It is significant that, although I later immigrated to Canada and subsequently moved to the United States—events that precipitated profound culture shock and intensified the need to grapple even more deeply with questions of identity—my need for worldview clarification preceded these moves.[58] Indeed, I have found that grappling with Western cultural values and influence (and especially their North American incarnation) has been an important part of identity formation for many people I have met from diverse parts of the globe. Such grappling seems to be intrinsic to the developmental task of immigrants and minorities, whether they live within or on the periphery of a dominant culture.

By analogy, then, even before Judean exiles were forcibly transported into Babylonia during the sixth century B.C.E. and confronted firsthand the massive cultural and political hegemony of the empire, it was important for Israel to grapple with the relationship of its own exodus and covenant traditions to the dominant culture and worldview of Mesopotamia. Also relevant to the analogy is that Mesopotamian civilization, although embodied in Sumero-Akkadian cultures and immensely influential over

58. Thus, a book that I coauthored with Brian Walsh after I moved to Canada that critically engaged Western culture and its worldview was actually begun while I was still living in Jamaica (the core of one chapter was written fully seven years earlier as part of my own process of worldview clarification); see Brian J. Walsh and J. Richard Middleton, *The Transforming Vision: Shaping a Christian World View* (Downers Grove, IL: InterVarsity, 1984). Thus any attempt to explain my own critical engagement with Western culture (as found in that book) solely by reference to my later immersion in North American culture would be sorely mistaken.

much of the ancient Near East, was associated above all with Babylon, much as America functions as the epitome of the widely disseminated "global" Western culture and worldview in our time.[59]

In what follows, I will examine the primeval history vis-à-vis Mesopotamian motifs and texts, focusing on how Genesis 1–11 presents a radical alternative to the Mesopotamian vision of humanity. Beginning with the affirmation of human dignity and agency associated with the *imago Dei* in Genesis 1, I will then examine aspects of Genesis 1–11 that are consistent with—and further develop—this alternative view of human agency, including the negative portrayal of the misuse of human agency (as violence) in the primeval history, concluding with a reading of the tower of Babel episode as ideology critique.

Throughout this exposition my purpose will not be to read Genesis 1–11 for its sources (typically thought of as J or P), but rather to place the text as a composite unity against the background of Mesopotamian ideology to see what sort of focus this particular placement might provide. I fully realize that my reading of the primeval history is often at variance with the interpretations of many reputable Old Testament scholars who appeal to the reconstructed theology of the putative sources of the text. It is good to heed John Rogerson's warnings about fixating on source analysis of the primeval history. Not only are attempts to date various strands of the text "at best plausible rather than probable, and involve circular arguments," but source analysis can "make us read the text superficially, as though we knew all that it has to say once we have assigned a date and setting." The important question, he continues, is "how do the narratives function within the whole, and what interest do we, the readers, bring with us to the interpretation of Genesis 1–11?"[60] It is clear that here, as everywhere else, meaning is a function of context, and the context I am interested in is Mesopotamian ideology.

I am emboldened, however, by my not being entirely alone in my reading of the primeval history, since biblical scholars interested in the

---

59. If we might press the analogy a bit, we might note the cultural similarity of the two neighboring nations of North America (the United States and Canada) and the two competing empires of Mesopotamia (Babylonian and Assyria). In both cases a largely shared culture coexists between two nations, with the cultural dominance of one over the other. It is further interesting that in both cases the cultural influence is from the south to the north. If we want to push the analogy even further, the European heritage of the United States and Canada is roughly parallel to that of the Sumerian heritage for Babylonia and Assyria (the difference being that whereas Sumer earlier occupied roughly the same geographical area that Babylonia later did, Europe is both contemporary with and geographically separate from North America).

60. John Rogerson, *Genesis 1–11* (Old Testament Guides; Sheffield: Sheffield Academic Press, 1991), 77.

Mesopotamian background of the text often come to interpretations similar to my own. Nevertheless, my reading of the primeval history should not be judged on the basis of support it finds in the work of others, as if a textual reading needs an authorized scholarly imprimatur. Rather, the adequacy of my reading of the text in what follows must stand or fall by the actual argument I make on its behalf. The primary question I am concerned with here is: What depth dimensions of the meaning of Genesis 1–11 are highlighted when the text is read against the background of Mesopotamian motifs and ideals?

The Affirmation of Human Agency in Genesis 1

The starting point for a reading of the primeval history as critique of Mesopotamian ideology is the claim in Genesis 1 that God granted a royal-priestly identity as *imago Dei* to all humanity at creation. This democratization of Mesopotamian royal ideology serves to elevate and dignify the human race with a noble status in the world, analogous to that of royalty in the ancient Near East.

Yet the *imago Dei* is not simply an affirmation of static status or privilege. Essential to the meaning of the image in Genesis 1 is the dynamic power or agency that God grants humans at creation (signified in the terms *rule* and *subdue*). Although it is not explicitly stated in Genesis 1, it is reasonable to think that this power is to be exercised responsibly, with God's own exercise of power in creation perhaps as the model (discussed further in part 3, below). With privilege comes responsibility. There is a call inherent in every gift. The *imago Dei* is thus inextricably linked to the gift and responsibility (delegated to humanity at creation) of exercising stewardship over the earth.

But whereas power in the Babylonian and Assyrian empires was concentrated in the hands of a few, power in Genesis 1 is diffused or shared. No longer is the image of God or its associated royal language ("rule" or "subdue") applied to only some privileged elite. Rather, all human beings, male and female, are created as God's royal stewards in the world, entrusted with the privileged task of ruling on God's behalf (1:26–28). The democratization of the *imago Dei* in Genesis 1 thus constitutes an implicit delegitimation of the entire ruling and priestly structure of Mesopotamian society (and especially the absolute power of the king). In the Genesis vision, it is ordinary humans (and not some elite class) who are understood to be significant historical actors in the arena of earthly life.

It is significant, in this connection, that while humans are granted rule over the earth and the animals, there is no mandate in Genesis 1 for humans to rule each other.[61] The democratization of the image in this text thus suggests an egalitarian conception of the exercise of power. Human beings are called to a fundamental mutuality in a shared task, "a cooperative sharing in dominion," as H. D. Preuss puts it.[62] Whatever interhuman hierarchies of power may have developed in human history, these are relativized by Genesis 1, which suggests that such hierarchies are not grounded in God's creational intent.

But is this egalitarian reading of the *imago Dei* legitimate? Although there is certainly a strong antimonarchical strand in both the Former Prophets and the Latter Prophets (which might well be echoed here), some might object that the text is part of the P tradition and so could not possibly be calling into question the priestly hierarchy instituted at Sinai. As I indicated at the end of chapter 3, I am not convinced that Genesis 1 indeed derives from the same Priestly tradition that is responsible for the levitical laws. Here I am in agreement with Phyllis Trible: "Whether we can continue to regard Gen. 1:1–2:4a as a priestly document is a moot point."[63] And if that is a genuinely open question, we are allowed to countenance the possibility of a significant tension between Genesis 1 and any notion of priestly hierarchy.[64]

But beyond the issue whether Genesis 1 could be in tension with priestly hierarchy is a more fundamental question: Is it conceivable that an ancient text, from a largely patriarchal society, should envision a fundamental equality between men and women (in any sense)? It is certainly possible that the language of Genesis 1, which attributes image and rule to all humanity, might constitute an example of what feminists call "false universalism,"[65] in that this seemingly universal language may have been understood (either by the author or early readers) as applying either exclusively or paradigmatically to men. Phyllis Bird, indeed, makes this suggestion, which she bases on a number of factors.[66] Besides

61. Noted by many scholars. See, for example, Mendenhall, *Tenth Generation*, 211; and Millard Lind, *Yahweh Is a Warrior: The Theology of Warfare in Ancient Israel* (Scottdale, PA/Kitchener, ON: Herald, 1980), 124.

62. H. D. Preuss, "דָּמָה *dāmāh*; דְּמוּת *dᵉmûth*," in *Theological Dictionary of the Old Testament* (ed. G. Johannes Botterweck and Helmer Ringgren; trans. John T. Willis, Geoffrey Bromiley, and David E. Green; Grand Rapids: Eerdmans, 1978), 3.259.

63. Phyllis Trible, *God and the Rhetoric of Sexuality* (Philadelphia: Fortress, 1978), 29 n. 63.

64. It is amazing how the assumptions that one brings to the text determine what one is allowed to see.

65. Marilyn J. Legge, "Colourful Differences: 'Otherness' and the Image of God for Canadian Feminist Theologies," *Studies in Religion/Sciences religieuses* 21 (1992): 68.

66. Phyllis Bird, "Sexual Differentiation and Divine Image in the Genesis Creation Texts," in *The Image of God: Gender Models in Judaeo-Christian Tradition* (ed. Kari Elisabeth Børresen; Minneapolis: Fortress, 1995), 12–13.

the overwhelmingly patriarchal character of ancient Israel, Bird notes the patently male experience and social models from which the forceful language of subduing and ruling are derived and highlights especially the androcentric character of the priestly tradition that Genesis 1 is typically reckoned as being part of (with its exclusion of women from priestly functions in Leviticus and the exclusively male focus of the P genealogies in Genesis). It is especially problematic that right after Genesis 5:1–2 reiterates the claim of 1:26–27 that both male and female are made in God's image (in the context of utilizing the term *ʾādām* for the human race) the very next verse (5:3) begins the genealogy of Adam and seems to limit the propagation of the image to the male line (in the context of utilizing *ʾādām* as a proper noun).

While it is possible that Bird is right about how Genesis 1 was actually read in some circles in ancient Israel,[67] it is unclear how a text that attributes the *imago Dei* explicitly to "male and female" (1:27) could be originally intended, or *legitimately* taken, as referring only to men. It is indisputable that the notion of humanity as *imago Dei* in Genesis 1 was articulated in the context of a patriarchal society and uses language taken from typically male social roles. What is disputable, however, is whether the *imago Dei* simply reflects the patriarchy of its social background or actively resists this background in order to present an alternative vision. It is clear, at any rate, that in the history of interpretation Genesis 1 came to be understood by scriptural readers as genuinely universal in intent and thus functioned as a basis for human equality, including equality between the sexes. Interestingly, Bird admits that this is a legitimate reading of the text, both permitted and encouraged by the lack of specified gender roles in its discourse, although (in her opinion) it likely goes beyond the intent of the priestly author.[68]

Whether attributed to authorial intent or rhetorical effect, then, the use of *imago Dei* language in Genesis 1 (derived from the ancient Near East) functions to delegitimate any intrinsically hierarchal social structure and to affirm the dignity and agency of all humanity. "If it is correct to see the terminology about the image of God as derived from royal theology," comments Jürgen Moltmann, "then this derivation itself contains revolutionary political potential: it is not a prince who is the image, representative, deputy and reflection of God; it is the human being—men and women in like degree, all human beings and every human being."[69]

67. Could Genesis 5:1–3 be an example of such reading?
68. Bird, "Sexual Differentiation and Divine Image in the Genesis Creation Texts," 24 n. 22.
69. Jürgen Moltmann, *God in Creation: A New Theology of Creation and the Spirit of God* (New York: Harper & Row, 1985), 219. Moltmann, however, suggests Egyptian,

Correlative with this mutuality of power and agency is the implicit claim of the *imago Dei* that all persons have equal access to God simply by being human. Given the convergence of royal and priestly functions in the ancient Near East (concerning mediation of the divine), the democratization of the image suggests that human beings do not need institutional mediation of God's presence by either kings or priests. Rather, just as the *imago Dei* in Genesis 1 democratizes royal ideology, the text suggests that human beings as the image of God are *themselves* priests of the creator of heaven and earth. The later Christian doctrine of the "priesthood of the believer" may thus be understood as legitimately grounded in the *imago Dei*. This doctrine articulates what we might call the redemptive restoration of the fundamental priesthood of humanity as *imago Dei*, after its distortion or diminution by sin.[70]

Going even further, we may take the claim that humanity is created in God's image as constituting an (implicit) critique of the mediation of the divine through cult images, as practiced, for example, in Mesopotamia. This certainly fits the rhetorical portrayal of creation in Genesis 1 as a cosmic sanctuary (explored in chapter 2), where humanity as *imago Dei* functions as a parallel to the role of the cult image in the temples of the ancient Near East.[71] Human beings as *imago Dei* are thus not only priests of the Most High, they are (if we may dare to say it) God's living cult statues on earth. Indeed, humans are the only *legitimate* or *authorized* earthly representations of God. As Walter Brueggemann puts it, "There is one way in which God is imaged in the world and only one: humanness!"[72]

I am not, of course, claiming that the prohibition of images in the Old Testament is derived historically from the notion of humanity as *imago Dei*, as this prohibition certainly predates Genesis 1. Nevertheless, if we interpret Genesis 1 against, on the one hand, the Old Testament's pervasive idol critique and, on the other, the prominent role of cult images in Mesopotamia, the claim that humanity is created as *imago Dei* suggests a rationale for the prohibition of images beyond anything we find explicitly stated elsewhere in the Old Testament.

---

rather than Mesopotamian, royal theology as the background of the image, something that I disputed in chapter 3.

70. For a profound meditation on the priesthood of humanity, see L. William Countryman, *Living on the Border of the Holy: Renewing the Priesthood of All* (Harrisburg, PA: Morehouse, 1999), 3–31.

71. See Rikki E. Watts, "On the Edge of the Millennium: Making Sense of Genesis 1," in *Living in the LambLight: Christianity and Contemporary Challenges to the Gospel* (ed. Hans Boersma; Vancouver, BC: Regent College Publishing, 2001), 148.

72. Walter Brueggemann, *Genesis* (Interpretation; Atlanta: John Knox, 1982), 32.

Certainly, one important underlying rationale for the prohibition of images is the guarding of God's transcendence by disallowing cultic manipulation, as many Old Testament scholars suggest.[73] The paradox of idolatry is that the very attempt to control divine presence (through images) results in the forfeiture of divine presence. Nevertheless, perhaps there is, along with this theological rationale for the prohibition of images, an anthropological rationale as well, concerning the protection of human dignity and agency. If the *imago Dei* indeed connects royal-priestly mediation of divine presence with cultural-historical agency, perhaps the practice of idolatry goes hand in hand with the forfeiture or diminution of the fundamental human calling to exercise significant power and agency in shaping human culture and civilization.

In this connection, it is interesting that no idolatry is mentioned in the primeval history, yet the text contains (as we shall soon see) accounts of impressive cultural innovation on the part of ordinary (non-elite) people and also of the violent misuse of human agency and power. Whether the delay of any mention of idols until the ancestor stories (in connection with the flight of Jacob and Rachel from Laban in Genesis 31:19–54) is intentional on the part of the author or editor of Genesis is perhaps impossible to say. However, it is certainly suggestive for a reading of Genesis in its final, canonical form. Perhaps we are allowed to connect the systemic practice of idolatry with the disempowerment of worshipers who, in effect, give over their fundamental human calling to mediate God's power on earth in significant cultural innovation by projecting this calling onto blocks of wood and stone—something that has not yet happened in the primeval history.[74]

We may arrive at a similar conclusion concerning the implications of humanity as God's image for Israel's idol critique by reflecting on the

73. See, for example, J. J. M. Roberts, "Divine Freedom and Cultic Manipulation in Israel and Mesopotamia," in *Unity and Diversity: Essays in the History, Literature, and Religion of the Ancient Near East* (ed. Hans Goedicke and J. J. M. Roberts; Baltimore: Johns Hopkins University Press, 1975), 181–90; and Robert P. Carroll, "The Aniconic God and the Cult of Images," *Studia Theologia* 31 (1977): 51–64.

74. Would it then be possible, in a wild imaginative leap, to speculate that the primeval history correlates with what anthropologists designate the "Neolithic revolution," when most of the basic technologies and arts of civilization were developed, which continued with only incremental changes, relatively speaking (represented by the various Bronze Age and Iron Age designations), until the scientific and industrial revolutions of the modern period (with roots in the Renaissance reappropriation of the *imago Dei* and the "dominion" mandate of Genesis)? Is it, further, possible that the Neolithic revolution, with its flourishing of technical/cultural innovation, historically predates the origin or widespread practice of idolatry as part of an organized hierarchical social system, which functioned to inhibit human agency? Although obviously highly speculative, such correlations may well be worthy of further reflection and investigation.

sociopolitical dimension of idolatry. Since construction of images and their consequent cultic functioning was supervised and controlled in the ancient Near East by priests (who were sometimes regarded as *imago Dei*), cult images may be understood as constituting a systematic attempt to regulate and control access to deity. As a pervasive social institution in the ancient Near East, idolatry is thus part of a larger ideological pattern that links false worship with an inequitable social order, perpetuating the privilege of those who oversee the cult and guaranteeing the subservience of the masses.[75] In this case, an anthropological rationale for the prohibition of images would be that idolatry is part and parcel of a larger priest-controlled social system that disempowers ordinary people by robbing them of both access to God and significant agency in the world.

Thus, beyond safeguarding the divine transcendence, the iconoclasm of the Scriptures may be interpreted also as protecting the integrity of the human worshiper. The pervasive prohibition and critique of idolatry in the Old Testament may be read as part and parcel of the Bible's distinctive emphasis on human flourishing and as integrally connected to the high status and calling of humanity that is articulated by the *imago Dei* in Genesis 1.

In connection with the priestly, cultic dimension of the *imago Dei*, it is further noteworthy that language of human service is entirely absent from Genesis 1. This is actually quite remarkable. Certainly, a canonical reading of Scripture (both Old and New Testaments) makes it clear that humans have a fundamental duty to serve and worship their creator, a duty that was encapsulated historically by the *Westminster Shorter Catechism* in the famous confession that the "chief end" of humanity is "to glorify God and enjoy him forever." Yet nothing analogous to this notion is explicitly stated in the Genesis 1 creation story (or in Genesis 2, for that matter). This should give us pause. While it is understandable that the idea of a degraded human nature is absent from Genesis 1 (the royal dignity and calling of humanity is incompatible with the Mesopotamian idea that we are created from the blood of God's primordial enemy), why is the notion of human service or worship of God missing? Would it not be possible to explain the royal function of humanity as the particular way in which we are destined to serve our creator? This is, of course, how biblical interpreters typically explain it. Thus Ralph Klein comments that "human beings are servants in the biblical perspective too, but theirs is a kingly, royal service that brings with it

75. A fascinating exposé of priestly privilege in the cult of Marduk is found in the Greek version of Daniel 14 (part of the tale of Bel and the Dragon), where Daniel proves to the king that the priests and their families actually eat the evening sacrificial meal set before Marduk's cult image.

much status."[76] In one sense Klein is right, since there is no intrinsic incompatibility between the high dignity and status of the human race and our duty to serve God. Yet we need to account for the conspicuous absence of service language from Genesis 1.

The avoidance of such language may suggest that the ideological context in which Genesis 1 was written was too fraught with the possibility for misinterpretation on that score. Minimally, we would be correct to see here a critical response to Mesopotamian ideology, in which humans are created to serve the gods by relieving them of their burdens.

But could this avoidance of service language derive more directly from the trauma of Babylonian exile? If this were the case, the rhetorical situation of Genesis 1 would thus be analogous to the contemporary predicament of women who have experienced sexual abuse by their fathers and who consequently find it impossible—at least for a time—to use "father" language to refer to God. The shock of abuse is simply too near, too close at hand. This analogy, applied to Babylonian exile, might help us understand why language of human service is absent from Genesis 1.

The problem with this interpretation, however, is that we would have to account for the centrality of the concept of the "servant of YHWH" in the theology of Second Isaiah (Isaiah 40–55), the prophet of the exile par excellence. It is, of course, possible that what we have in Genesis 1 and Isaiah 40–55 are two significantly *different* responses to the trauma of exile (human responses are, after all, not deterministically preprogrammed). But, beyond that, it is possible that Genesis 1 was not written specifically in response to the exile at all (and we really cannot be sure one way or another). Thus, rather than tie Genesis 1 to the Babylonian exile, it is perhaps safer to conclude simply that the manner in which the biblical vision of humanity is articulated in the text clearly distinguishes it from Mesopotamian ideology. The rhetoric of the text, both by what it explicitly says and by its omissions, highlights the radical distinction between oppressive Mesopotamian notions of human purpose (bond servants to the gods) and a liberating alternative vision of humanity as the royal-priestly image of God.

The place of fertility and nourishment is also distinctive in Genesis 1. Contrary to the *Atrahasis Epic* 3.7, for example, where the gods are threatened by human overpopulation and thus devise various means of thinning out the human race (including infertility, stillbirth, and spontaneous abortion), the creator in Genesis 1 freely grants fertility to both human and nonhuman as a permanent gift or blessing. That both vegetation and animals are able to reproduce themselves "after their kind" (Gen-

76. Klein, *Israel in Exile*, 128. Indeed, Walsh and I give a similar explanation of humanity as "servant" and "lord" in *The Transforming Vision*, 59.

esis 1:11–12, 21–22, 24–25) and that humans are blessed and gifted with fertility and commissioned to multiply and fill the earth (1:28) suggests that God is not threatened by the self-perpetuating nature of creatures. On the contrary, Genesis 1 understands fertility as an intrinsic part of organic creaturely life that does not need to be achieved or guaranteed by cultic means. Since the primary cultic means of securing divine blessing and fertility in ancient Mesopotamia would have been the sacrificial system—the provision of food and drink for the gods, as part of the imposed servitude of humanity—it is significant that in Genesis 1 it is God who graciously provides food for both humans and animals (1:29–30). Again, the text stands the Mesopotamian worldview on its head.

Thus every element of the account of human creation on the sixth day (image and rule, fertility and food) articulates a vision of the human role in the cosmos that is diametrically opposed to that of ancient Mesopotamia. In contrast to an ideology that claims that humans are created for a relationship of dependency, to meet divine need, God in Genesis 1 creates for the benefit of the creature, without explicitly asking for a direct return of any kind. And humans, in God's image, I suggest, are expected to imitate this primal generosity in their own shared rule of the earth.

But beyond the account of human creation on the sixth day, the portrayal of the heavenly bodies on the fourth day of creation may also be read as contributing to the affirmation of human dignity and agency. Since astral religion, in connection with the science of omens and portents (which later gave rise to astrology proper), played a central role in ancient Mesopotamia (the word *zodiac* is derived from an Akkadian word), the relatively minor place given to the heavenly bodies in Genesis 1 speaks volumes.[77] First of all, whereas sun, moon, and stars were divinities in ancient Mesopotamia, in Genesis 1 they are clearly creatures, explicitly said to be made by God. Second, the sun and moon are not even named in Genesis 1, further preventing the possibility that the sun (Hebrew *šemeš*) might be unintentionally identified with the Babylonian/Assyrian sun-god (Akkadian *šamaš*).[78] Instead, sun and moon are designated by their luminary function as the "great" and "small" lights.[79] While this is portrayed as a royal-

77. See the discussion of the luminaries in Gerhard F. Hasel, "The Significance of the Cosmology in Genesis 1 in Relation to Ancient Near Eastern Parallels," *Andrews University Seminary Studies* 10 (1972): 13–14; and idem, "The Polemic Nature of the Genesis Cosmology," *Evangelical Quarterly* 46 (1974): 88–89.

78. Whereas the word for "sun" is cognate in Hebrew and Akkadian, the word for "moon" is not: Hebrew *yārēaḥ* and Akkadian *sin*. The Hebrew word for "moon" is, however, cognate to Ugaritic *yariḥ*.

79. See Luis I. J. Stadelmann, *The Hebrew Conception of the World* (Rome: Pontifical Biblical Institute Press, 1970), 57–58.

governing role in Genesis 1, it does not determine human destiny or impinge on human agency in any way. Rather, the luminaries serve humanity by giving light and providing a temporal framework of days and seasons. Perhaps even more significant is the portrayal of the stars, given their pride of place in the Mesopotamian pantheon. In a reversal of the typical Mesopotamian order of importance (and the order of *Enuma Elish*), the creation of the stars is mentioned *after* the sun and moon in Genesis 1:16.[80] And their creation is relegated to a parenthetical statement ("almost as an afterthought"),[81] consisting of only two words: "and the-stars" (*wĕ'ēt hakkôkābîm*). By its understated rhetoric, therefore, the text subverts the notion that human behavior is fated by astral forces, thus contributing to the exalted picture of human agency and purpose associated with creation as *imago Dei*.

This affirmation of human agency in Genesis 1 gives new significance to the notion of divine rest in 2:1–3. Thus, when the creator ceases work on the seventh day, it is not the abdication of a petty deity from a burdensome task, as in some Mesopotamian creation accounts. Rather, God's rest in Genesis 2 represents the delegation to humanity of the royal task of administering the world on his behalf. Humans are entrusted with nothing less than *God's own proper work*, as the creator's authorized representatives on earth. Whatever other meanings God's rest has elsewhere in the Old Testament (for example, justification for the Sabbath, as in Exodus 20:11), in the context of the Genesis 1 creation story it appropriately symbolizes the beginning of the rule of the human race, their coming into their true power as makers of history, as representatives and emissaries of God, called to shape the world in imitation of the creator's own primordial activity on the first six days of creation.[82] In this interpretation, I fully realize that I am going against a venerable tradition in Old Testament scholarship that rather unreflectively claims that Genesis 2:1–3, as part of the P document, constitutes the institution of the Sabbath. While I do not contest that this is, indeed, how the text came to be read, I find no justification within the rhetoric of the text itself for this reading.[83]

80. Alexander Heidel, *The Babylonian Genesis: The Story of Creation* (2nd ed.; Chicago: University of Chicago Press, 1951; repr. 1963), 116–17.

81. Klein, *Israel in Exile*, 128.

82. I will explore the paradigmatic/ethical significance of God's rest on the seventh day in chapter 7.

83. Deuteronomy 5:15 grounds the Sabbath not in creation, but in the exodus from Egypt. This suggests that the institution of the Sabbath is not *intrinsically* linked to God's rest on the seventh day in Genesis 2:1–3 and may well predate this specific text.

The Affirmation of Human Agency in the Primeval History

Corroboration for the distinctiveness of the Genesis 1 vision of human historical agency—which also serves to confirm a royal reading of the *imago Dei*—may be found by comparing various aspects of the primeval history (Genesis 1–11) with ancient Mesopotamian notions that are well known from extant mythic texts. The primeval history is an extremely important context for interpreting the *imago Dei* since all three Old Testament references to the image (1:26–27; 5:1; 9:6) are embedded in this narrative-genealogical complex, which recounts the unfolding of universal human history prior to the call of Abram.

Let us begin with the references to humanity as *imago Dei* in Genesis 5:1 and 9:6. These references, and especially their placement or location in the primeval history, are particularly striking when compared with certain features of the *Sumerian King List*, an ancient text from the end of the third or beginning of the second millennium B.C.E., known from various editions, which traces the origins of the monarchy in Mesopotamia to a gift from the gods in primordial time, "when kingship was lowered from heaven" (line 1).[84] Not only does the human race in the genealogy of Genesis 5 take the place that the line of ancient kings occupies in the preflood section of the *Sumerian King List*, but Adam as the first person created in God's image (5:1) is clearly equivalent to A-lulim, the first king. Whereas the *Sumerian King List* goes on to list a dynastic genealogy of the various ancient kings and how long they reigned, 5:1–3 explains that Adam had a son in *his* image and likeness, by implication passing on the *imago Dei* to the entire human race. J. Maxwell Miller further points out that the next biblical reference to the *imago Dei*, the postflood assertion that humans are created in God's image in 9:6, finds a striking parallel in the statement in the king list that kingship was *again* "lowered from heaven" after the flood (line 41).[85] Whereas this second lowering was presumably necessary since the line of kings had been disrupted by the deluge, Genesis 9:6 asserts, by contrast, the unbroken continuation of the *imago Dei* among Noah's descendants, since all people are made in God's royal image.[86] A comparison of the placement of these

84. See "The Sumerian King List," in *ANET* 265–66 (trans. A. Leo Oppenheim).

85. See J. Maxwell Miller, "In the 'Image' and 'Likeness' of God," *Journal of Biblical Literature* 91 (1972): 295 n. 20.

86. Another way of relating the *Sumerian King List* to Genesis 5 is proposed by John Walton, which though interesting is highly speculative. Walton notes numerical parallels between the total for the ages listed in the two texts by converting the decimal system of the Genesis genealogy into a Sumerian sexagesimal system, while making a couple of other changes as well (such as treating the ages in the biblical list as consecutive and

imago Dei references with the *Sumerian King List* thus supports the notion that the *imago Dei* in Genesis constitutes a democratization of Mesopotamian royal ideology.

The divine origin of the Mesopotamian monarchy—represented by the idea that kingship was "lowered from heaven"—is found well beyond the *Sumerian King List*. Not only is it assumed in the long tradition venerating the king as the divinely chosen mediator of the gods (as we saw in chapter 3) and in the Neo-Babylonian Akitu Festival, which connects the rule of the human and divine kings (as we saw in chapter 4), it is explicitly expressed in the prologue to Hammurapi's law code. There the king who inaugurated the Old Babylonian Empire traces the legitimacy of his rule back to the primordial time when Marduk's cosmic kingship was established. At that time, Hammurapi explains—that is, in the beginning, at creation—the gods instituted his (Hammurapi's) kingship and ordained him from the beginning to rule Babylon, their chosen city:

> *When* lofty Anum, king of the Anunnaki,
> (and) Enlil, lord of heaven and earth,
> the determiner of the destinies of the land,
> determined for Marduk, the first-born of Enki,
> the Enlil functions over all mankind,
> made him great among the Igigi,
> called Babylon by its exalted name,
> made it supreme in the world,
> established for him in its midst an enduring kingship,
> whose foundations are as firm as heaven and earth—
> *at that time* Anum and Enlil named me
> to promote the welfare of the people,
> me, Hammurabi, the devout, god-fearing prince,
> to cause justice to prevail in the land,
> to destroy the wicked and the evil,
> that the strong might not oppress the weak,
> to rise like the sun over the black-headed (people),
> and to light up the land. (prologue 1.1–41)[87]

---

omitting Adam and Noah from the list). Once the conversion is done, the total of the ages of the kings in the *Sumerian King List* is within five years of the total of the ages of the patriarchs in Genesis 5, which leads Walton to posit their dependence on a common tradition. See John Walton, "The Antediluvian Section of the Sumerian King List and Genesis 5," *Biblical Archeologist* 44 (1981): 207–8.

87. Translation from Theophile J. Meek, "The Code of Hammurabi," in *ANET* 164 (emphasis added).

Hammurapi's rule is thus portrayed as grounded in creation order itself, and on this basis the king promulgates the law code so that justice might be done in the land.

Whereas Hammurapi grounds his own kingship in the primordial beginning, a later, Neo-Babylonian text known as VAT 17019 (which might be appropriately called *The Creation of Humanity and the King*) attributes the origin of kingship as an institution to the action of the gods at the time of creation. Using language and phraseology similar to that of the *Atrahasis Epic* and *Enuma Elish*, the first twenty-nine lines of the text tell of the creation of humanity to relieve the burdens of the gods, while lines thirty onward contain an account of the creation of the king, whose creation follows that of humanity, presumably to organize humanity in their service to the gods. The king is here described in glowing terms that stress his royal splendor and regalia, his divine origin, and his power in battle.[88] According to Richard Clifford, "the function of the text was to ground reverence for the king in creation."[89]

This notion that the monarchy is of divine origin, going back to creation, is correlated in Mesopotamian thought with the idea that the gods also founded the first cities, over which they ruled through the kings as their surrogates. The divine gift of royal urban culture, epitomized by the Mesopotamian city-state, was thought to have raised humans up from their original "primitive" or "savage" condition (the Akkadian word is *lulû*) by civilizing them.[90] Thus *Enuma Elish* (even more explicitly than the prologue to Hammurapi's law code) claims that the gods themselves built Babylon as their capital and cult center prior to the creation of humanity. And not only the *Sumerian King List*, but also myths like the *Eridu Genesis* (also known as the *Sumerian Flood Story*) and the *Theology of Dunnu* portray the divine founding of cities and the appointment of kings to rule them as stretching back to the origin of the world (although these myths disagree whether Babylon, Eridu, or Dunnu was the first center of civilization).[91]

---

88. VAT 17019 (from *Vorderasiatische Abteilung Tontafel*, published by the Vorderasiatisches Museum, Berlin) is discussed in Richard J. Clifford, *Creation Accounts in the Ancient Near East and in the Bible* (Catholic Biblical Quarterly Monograph Series 26; Washington, DC: Catholic Biblical Association of America, 1994), 69–71. See also M. Stol, *Birth in Babylonia and the Bible: Its Mediterranean Setting* (Cuneiform Monographs 14; Groningen: Styx, 2000), 148.

89. Clifford, *Creation Accounts*, 69.

90. W. G. Lambert and A. R. Millard, *Atra-ḫasīs: The Babylonian Story of the Flood* (Oxford: Clarendon, 1969), 18.

91. Patrick D. Miller Jr., "Eridu, Dunnu, and Babel: A Study in Comparative Mythology," in *"I Studied Inscriptions from before the Flood": Ancient Near Eastern, Literary, and Linguistic Approaches to Genesis 1–11* (ed. Richard S. Hess and David Toshio Tsumura;

Beyond the institution of kingship and the founding of cities, all significant human culture was attributed in some fashion to the gods in Mesopotamian thought. Thus we find the ancient Mesopotamian tradition of the seven primeval sages (known as the *apkallu*), sent by the god Ea before the flood, who are understood to be quasidivine beings (often represented as holy carp) who come from the primeval waters and are said to "administer the patterns" of heaven and earth, an expression that refers to the institution of technology and the civilizing arts.[92] Similar ideas of the divine origin of culture and the gods' establishing or instituting their essential nature (which humans simply follow) could easily be multiplied from a variety of Mesopotamian texts.

Thus, many Sumerian and Akkadian texts regard humanity as created first in a primitive and uncivilized condition and only later elevated by the gods who give them the gift of culture or civilization. This is the basic idea behind the cosmological section of *Ewe and Wheat* (discussed in chapter 4). Not only was humanity created to serve the gods by providing them with food and drink, but this text narrates how the gods had to give humanity the gift of agriculture and animal husbandry (symbolized by two goddesses), without which the human race would still be animal-like.

Similar ideas of a two-stage creation of the human race are found in a variety of other Mesopotamian texts. For example, *How Grain Came to Sumer* explains that humans were raised above their original primitive state by the gift of agriculture, when cereals, barley, and flax "descended from heaven," and the *Rulers of Lagash* (or the *Lagash King List*) understands the civilizing of humanity to have occurred through the gods' establishment of "kingship, the crown of the city" along with the concomitant divine gifts of spade, hoe, basket, and plow.[93] Likewise, the cosmological section of the disputation text known as *Palm and Tamarisk*, in one variant (the Emar text), tells of the gods' gift of cities,

---

Sources for Biblical and Theological Study; Winona Lake, IN: Eisenbrauns, 1994), 143–68. This essay, first published in the *Hebrew Annual Review* in 1985, compares the understanding of civilization and cities in the primeval history (especially the story of Babel in Genesis 11) with that of ancient Mesopotamian myths, particularly those texts usually called the *Sumerian Flood Story* and the *Harab Myth*, but renamed by Thorkild Jacobsen the *Eridu Genesis* and the *Theology of Dunnu*, respectively (thus highlighting the centrality of particular cities in the myths).

92. See Tikva Frymer-Kensky, *In the Wake of the Goddesses: Women, Culture, and the Biblical Transformation of Pagan Myth* (New York: Free Press, 1992), 111; Batto, "Creation Theology in Genesis," 21–22; Dalley, "Occasions and Opportunities," 16.

93. See Clifford, *Creation Accounts*, 47–48.

canal irrigation, and kingship to the previously primitive human race in order to uplift it.[94]

This attribution of human cultural achievements to the initiative of the gods (or semidivine primeval sages) strengthens my claim made earlier in this chapter that Israel's distinctiveness vis-à-vis the ancient Near East could be expressed in terms of whether ordinary humans are allowed to act in history. According to the worldview of Sumero-Akkadian myths, the gods act in history and change the course of human affairs. So do kings, as representatives of the gods on earth. However, the vast majority of the human race was understood to live relatively predetermined lives of mimetic repetition, beholden to their divine and human overlords, reduced to puppets in a social order in which they had no significant agency or freedom.

It is thus of immense significance that the primeval history recounts the founding of the first city not by God but by a human being (Genesis 4:17) and lists three brothers (Jabal, Jubal, and Tubal-Cain) as the inventors of metallurgy, music, and nomadic livestock herding (4:20–22). It is even possible that the text intends to suggest a historical origin for the cult, in its mention of a time when people first began to call upon YHWH (4:26) or in its prior reference to the offerings that Cain and Abel brought to God (4:3–4).[95] Later on, Noah is depicted as planting the first vineyard (9:20), and Nimrod is said to be the first warrior (10:8). This emphasis on the human role in sociocultural innovation is an important feature of the primeval history, which portrays humans in the process of exercising their fundamental vocation of transforming the world by the historical agency granted them at creation.

This interpretation of the primeval history is particularly emphasized by Tikva Frymer-Kensky in her superb study of the transformation of Mesopotamian (especially Sumerian) myth by the Bible. In the ancient myths, she explains, "the gods provide humanity with all the essentials of human civilization. By contrast, in the Bible, early humans develop their own culture. The human being, a creature created by God, is the

---

94. Ibid., 66–67. One other text sometimes cited in support of this understanding of humanity is the *Myth of the Pickax* or *Praise of the Pickax*. Whereas Samuel Noah Kramer understands the text to mean that the pickax was given to the human race in order to equip them for (cultural/technological) service of the gods, Thorkild Jacobsen disputes this interpretation, suggesting that the pickax was simply the tool that Enlil used to create humanity, by opening up the earth to allow humanity to emerge. It is possible, however, that both are correct, in that the tool of human creation is then given to humanity to uplift them culturally. See Clifford, *Creation Accounts*, 30–32, who bases his discussion on the recent analyses of various Sumerian scholars.

95. This is, of course, distinct from the typical source-critical claim that the P document understands the cult to have begun with the Sinai revelation.

initiator and creator of its own culture."[96] W. G. Lambert, likewise, contrasts the Mesopotamian penchant to trace human cultural achievements back to the beginning and to understand them as in some sense predetermined with the biblical tendency to recognize human cultural innovation.[97] Although Scripture portrays God as having regulated day and night, the seasons and the limits of the sea, Lambert explains, and certainly as interested in human conduct, "there is no parallel divine will manifested in the precise forms of human social life and the arts of civilization."[98]

Perhaps most significantly for purposes of comparison with Mesopotamia, the primeval history portrays a world without the institution of monarchy. While this would be literally unthinkable in Mesopotamian civilization (or indeed in any of the high cultures of the ancient Near East), on this point Israel's historical narrative is clear: Israel's own monarchy originated by human, not divine, decision in the tenth century B.C.E. and was initially opposed by YHWH.[99] Thus David Jobling writes: "The Deuteronomic History refuses this notion [of monarchy grounded in creation order]. It insists that monarchy in Israel *had a beginning*, and we should not underestimate how radical an affirmation this is."[100] Although the biblical text first interprets the desire for a king as a rejection of YHWH's kingship, the monarchy is nevertheless allowed as a divine concession to Israel, and the people are explicitly warned about the distorted "justice" (*mišpāṭ*) that will inevitably accompany the reign of human kings (1 Samuel 8).[101] Finally, after centuries of prophetic critique, the Israelite monarchy ends as a failed experiment in the sixth century, as the last king is taken captive into Babylonian exile.

96. Frymer-Kensky, *In the Wake of the Goddesses*, 108, esp. chaps. 9–10 for her fuller exploration of this contrast. Her conclusion to chap. 10 is worth quoting: "In Israel's philosophy of culture, humans have a greater role in the development and maintenance of the array of powers, functions, occupations and inventions that constitute civilized life than they ever did in ancient Near Eastern myth" (116).

97. Lambert, "Destiny and Divine Intervention," 69–72.

98. Ibid., 70.

99. This is in contrast to how some of Israel's poetry portrays matters. Thus royal psalms like Psalms 2, 45, 89, and 110 reflect many of the mythic themes that legitimated the monarchy in the ancient Near East. I will address this issue in chapter 6.

100. David Jobling, *1 Samuel* (Berit Olam; Collegeville, MN: Liturgical Press, 1998), 302 (emphasis original).

101. Although *mišpāṭ* in 1 Samuel 8 is usually translated "practice" or "custom" of the king (since these are well-attested meanings of the word), the text might be making an ironic comment about the sort of "justice" the people can expect from the monarchy. A contemporary version of such irony is found in Bruce Cockburn's song "Justice" (from the album *Inner City Front*, ©1981 by Golden Mountain Music Corp.), where the chorus states: "Everybody loves to see justice done / on somebody else." "Justice," in both this song and the biblical text, should be understood in quotation marks.

Scripture is also clear that the Torah is not promulgated by the Israelite king (contrast this with the Babylonian Hammurapi). Biblical law (whether in Exodus, Leviticus, or Deuteronomy) is consistently attributed to the mediation of Moses, whereas it is the king's primary duty to study the Torah and not exalt himself above other Israelites by inordinately increasing his power or wealth (Deuteronomy 17:14–20).[102] This notion of a limited monarchy—limited in historical origin and in duration, limited by the law of YHWH and by prophetic criticism—is radically unique, not just in Mesopotamia, but in the entire ancient Near East.[103] The distinctive application of the notion of *imago Dei* to the entire human race is thus in profound harmony with the antimonarchical tendency of the prophetic tradition in Israel.

The Misuse of Power in the Primeval History

Besides its emphasis on what we would regard as positive human historical innovation, it is significant that the primeval history also recounts the "invention" of murder and names Cain, the first murderer, as the founder of the first city (Genesis 4:17). Likewise, the three sibling innovators of various cultural achievements are all sons of Lamech, who is portrayed in the narrative as a violent man, engaged in the revenge killing of a youth who wronged him (4:23–24). He is also portrayed as the first polygamist (4:19), thereby "inventing" a form of systemic violence against women. Even Noah's achievement of planting the first vineyard is intertwined with his subsequent drunkenness and what seems to be the first case of incest (9:21–22).[104] And it is unclear if we are to regard the note about Nimrod as the first warrior (10:8) in a purely positive light. What becomes clear from the primeval history, then, is that the

102. Gunther H. Wittenberg emphasizes that the Israelite king is not the mediator of Torah; see "Old Testament Theology, for Whom?" *Semeia* 73 (1996): 235, where he disputes the claim made in Robert B. Coote and Mary P. Coote in *Power, Politics, and the Making of the Bible: An Introduction* (Minneapolis: Fortress, 1990) that the Old Testament was written from the perspective of the powerful ruling elites of Israel, who used the text to legitimate their own power.

103. Gabriel Sivan, in *The Bible and Civilization* (New York Times Library of Jewish Knowledge; New York: Quadrangle/New York Times Books, 1973), comments: "Monarchy, in contrast to the prevailing ancient view, was an earthly institution, neither permanent nor God-given" (149); "for the Hebrews, monarchy was not essential to the world scheme, but a later historical development" (148). The section in Sivan's book entitled "The Legal and Political Spheres" is an illuminating study of how biblical ideals of justice and equity have shaped Western political history.

104. The language applied to Ham, who "saw his father's nakedness," is used for incest in Leviticus 18:7.

cultural achievements of the human race testify not only to a God-given human power and agency, but also to the possibility of using that power/agency to accomplish evil. Specifically, the culture that humans develop is profoundly intertwined with violence.[105]

Indeed, so massive does the violence of humanity become that Genesis 6:11 describes the earth as "filled" with it. This description functions as an ironic allusion to the original human calling to "increase *and fill* the earth" (with progeny) in order to rule over it (1:28). Likewise, whereas humanity is portrayed in 6:1 as literally fulfilling the injunction of 1:28 to "increase" or "be great" (the verb *rābâ*) on the earth, 6:5 suggests an ironic fulfillment in its statement that human *evil* "increased" or was "great" (*rāb*) on the earth.[106] Such ironic references to the primal human mandate testify to the realism of the biblical narrative, which does not portray the exercise of human agency and power in idealized terms, but in terms of the actual ambiguities of history. That is, humans as *imago Dei* exercise their God-given power, but not in the manner that God intended.

The violence of the human race is described not only as filling the earth, but also as corrupting or polluting it (Genesis 6:11–12), and is said to be so deeply rooted in the human heart that God is grieved about the creation of humanity (6:5–6). God thus brings the flood to cleanse the earth of its pollution and to give humanity a new start in the person of Noah, who functions, in effect, as a new Adam (6:7–8). In the *Atrahasis Epic*, by contrast, the flood is neither restorative nor a response to human violence. Rather, it is one of a series of interventions by the gods, who are threatened by the proliferation of human beings upon the earth, since their incessant noisy activity (a reference, perhaps, to the development of human culture) is disturbing the gods' rest. Genesis, however, does not portray the creator as threatened in any way by human overpopulation or cultural activity, but rather as grieved by human violence. The flood is thus a restorative measure, in accordance with God's own deepest purposes for a world of shalom, and is initiated when humans do violence to each other and pollute the earthly environment that is

105. It is much too simplistic to claim that the primeval history (or the Yahwist) is simply negative about human cultural achievements. The matter is much more complex. The text understands sin (if we may use that term) primarily as violence, that is, as the distortion of the positive human capacity to exercise power. It is rooted, in other words, in the *imago Dei*.

106. On this point, see Edwin M. Good, *Irony in the Old Testament* (Philadelphia: Westminster, 1965), 86–87. The irony is even more extreme, however, since the language of Genesis 6:5 alludes to the repeated evaluation reports in Genesis 1 ("and God *saw that* it was *good*"). A literal translation of 6:5 is, "And YHWH *saw that* great was the *evil* of humanity on the earth."

their home. The difference between the flood accounts in Genesis and the *Atrahasis Epic* thus reflects a fundamental divergence in worldview. That violence and not overpopulation (or the noise that accompanies human proliferation or cultural activity) is the issue in Genesis becomes clear when we compare the ending of the *Atrahasis Epic* with Genesis 9. Whereas the *Atrahasis Epic* concludes with the gods decreeing various population-control measures for the human race, Genesis 9 contains a prohibition against murder, the first explicit articulation of law in the canonical narrative. Not only is this prohibition explicitly connected with the *imago Dei* in 9:6, but its function is precisely to limit or constrain human violence.[107] Thus, the flood story serves further to confirm the interpretation of humanity gifted with real historical power and agency, which is tragically being exercised against other human beings instead of used cooperatively in stewardship of the earth.

The Tower of Babel as Ideology Critique

The clash between Mesopotamian ideology and the worldview of the primeval history is nowhere more evident than in the tower of Babel narrative in Genesis 11:1–9.[108] This short narrative both deconstructs the pretensions of Babylonian ideology and, in the process, lends support to the interpretation of the *imago Dei* as the affirmation of human agency. The story portrays humanity, which had previously been expelled east of Eden (3:23–24), now attempting to return to Eden (*miqqedem* in 11:2, indicating the direction of their travel, most likely means "from the east," not "eastward" as some translations render it).[109] This attempt to recover a lost paradise, which may be understood as representing the mimetic impulse of ancient Near Eastern religion, is portrayed in terms of a human decision to settle in one place (contrary to the mandate given in 1:28 to fill the earth) and to build a city with a tower that reaches heaven. That the narrative alludes to the broad Mesopotamian ideal of

107. See the profound analysis in Tikva Frymer-Kensky, "The Atrahasis Epic and Its Significance for Our Understanding of Genesis 1–9," *Biblical Archeologist* 40 (1977): 147–55, esp. 151.

108. The analysis that follows is based on J. Richard Middleton, "The Deceptive Simplicity of Babel: A Socio-Literary Reading of Genesis 11:1–9," a paper presented to the annual meeting of the Canadian Society of Biblical Studies, May 28, 1998, at the University of Ottawa.

109. The issue of translation is debated, since the use of *miqqedem* in Genesis 13:11 seems to mean "eastward." Yet the preposition *min* (which is here attached to *qedem*, east) usually means "from," and this is indeed how the ancient versions render it. The matter comes down to a contextual decision of where the interpreter thinks the city builders came from.

urbanization/civilization is suggested by several factors: the reference
to the plain of Shinar (which some think is linguistically equivalent to
Sumer[110] and is clearly located in southern Mesopotamia according to
10:10), the historically accurate reference to Mesopotamian building
materials in 11:3 (baked brick was standard, in the absence of naturally
occurring stone), and the name of the city they build (bābel is simply
the usual Hebrew word for Babylon).

While we, with our well-developed historical consciousness, might
want to distinguish between the ancient Sumerians and the later Babylonian Empire that was the inheritor of Sumerian cultural ideals, the
reference in Genesis 11:31 to the city that Abram leaves as "Ur of the
Chaldeans" combines an important early Sumerian city with a later ethnic group in Babylonia. This anachronism, which comes after the tower
of Babel episode, blurs the lines between different historical periods in
southern Mesopotamia. This might suggest that the text constitutes a
critique of the entire project of Sumero-Babylonian civilization under
the rubric "Babel." Indeed, given the possible allusion to Assyrian imperial practice (as we shall soon see), the text may be addressing the entire
stretch of Sumero-Akkadian history (north and south), epitomized in its
paradigmatic Babylonian embodiment (much as America now stands
for Western culture in the eyes of much of the world).

What stands out about the tower of Babel story is (paradoxically)
its lack of critique of (indeed, lack of any reference to) Babylonian
religion. Whereas Mesopotamian ideology claimed that the first cities
were founded by the gods and Enuma Elish attributed the construction
of Babylon explicitly to Marduk's decision (with the Esagila temple as
his chosen dwelling), the Genesis 11 narrative portrays a purely human
building project. Twice it is humans who say, "Come, let us make" (11:3),
"Come, let us build" (11:4). This imitation of God's own address to the
heavenly court in 1:26 at the creation of humanity ("let us make") suggests that Genesis 11 is a portrayal of the human race exercising their
power of imago Dei in developing their own civilization.

It is common to find claims in Old Testament scholarship on Genesis
11 that the tower refers to a Babylonian ziggurat (that is, a high-rising
temple or cult site that provided a symbolic point of connection between
the city and the gods). Whereas earlier scholarship often connected
the tower to the Ezida ziggurat in Borsippa, recent scholarship usually
thinks that it represents the three-hundred-foot Etemenanki ziggurat
beside the Marduk temple in Babylon (the temple's name, Esagila, means

110. For a discussion of various interpretations of Shinar, see Victor P. Hamilton, *The
Book of Genesis: Chapters 1–17* (New International Commentary on the Old Testament;
Grand Rapids: Eerdmans, 1990), 351–52 n. 9.

"tower with its head in the clouds").[111] Indeed, the Etemenanki ziggurat lay in ruins for a long time and was completed by Nabopolassar, the founder of the Neo-Babylonian Empire. Furthermore, an inscription of Nabopolassar describes Marduk's commission to make the summit of Etemenanki "like the heavens."[112] Thus it would seem, at first glance, that the tower of Babel text describes (and critiques) a particular cultic structure.

Yet there is nothing even remotely cultic about the narrative portrayal of this tower in Genesis 11. Indeed, although the "city with a tower" (which could be a hendiadys, meaning a "towering city") is mentioned twice in Genesis 11:4-5, explicit reference to the tower disappears in the account of God's judgment on the city. Apart from the important fact that the word for "tower" (*migdāl*) in Genesis 11 is often used in the Old Testament with the sense of a fortress or an acropolis (Judges 8:9, 17; 9:46-52; Psalm 48:12-13 [MT 48:13-14]; Isaiah 2:15; Ezekiel 26:9; 2 Chronicles 14:7 [MT 14:6]), and cities may be said to have fortified walls reaching "up to the heavens" (Deuteronomy 1:28; 9:1), it is noteworthy that prophetic oracles against Babylon, especially in Jeremiah 51 and Isaiah 14:3-23, do *not* single out cultic practices, but rather imperial hubris, military fortifications, and oppressive power, portraying this in terms of Babylon's aspiration to reach up to the heavens (see especially Jeremiah 51:53; Isaiah 14:12-20).

Just as significant is the builders' statement, "Come, let us make/build . . . lest [*pen*] we be scattered" (Genesis 11:3-4), which finds a powerful echo in pharaoh's words, "Come, let us deal shrewdly with them lest [*pen*] they increase . . . and rise up against us" at the beginning of the exodus story (Exodus 1:10). It is noteworthy both that these words of pharaoh occur in the context of a monumental building project (storage cities, at least one of which is named in honor of a king) and that it is a project explicitly built on the backs of the oppressed.

This intertextual association of various elements of the Babel story with oppressive military/imperial power coheres well with the suggestion of David Smith that the story does not portray an idyllic world unified with a single primal language, but reflects the Neo-Assyrian imperial practice of imposing the single language of the conqueror on subjugated peoples.[113] Whereas Cyrus Gordon suggests that the

111. For an account of this debate, see Claus Westermann, *Genesis: A Commentary* (trans. John J. Scullion; Minneapolis: Augsburg, 1984), 1.541.

112. See André Parrot, *The Tower of Babel* (trans. Edwin Hudson; Studies in Biblical Archaeology; New York: Philosophical Library, 1955), 18.

113. David Smith, "What Hope After Babel? Diversity and Community in Gen 11:1-9; Exod 1:1-14; Zeph 3:1-13; and Acts 2:1-3," *Horizons in Biblical Theology* 18 (1996): 169-91. Although the Babel story is often connected by scholars to the Sumerian myth known

single language of the Babel story referred to the use of Akkadian as "an international lingua franca that made communication possible so that great projects like the Tower of Babel could be constructed,"[114] Smith's suggestion has the merit of taking into account the evidence of the forcible imposition of Akkadian as a means of imperial propaganda by the Assyrians. Thus we find that an extant Assyrian royal inscription declares that Ashurbanipal II "made the totality of all peoples speak one speech" and that "his sovereign approach made the unruly and ruthless kings speak one speech from the rising of the sun to its setting."[115] Likewise, a cylinder inscription of Sargon II boasts: "Populations of the four world quarters with strange tongues and incompatible speech . . . whom I had taken as booty at the command of Ashur my lord by the might of my sceptre, I caused to accept a single voice," which Stephanie Dalley interprets as part of the Neo-Assyrian policy of indoctrinating foreigners into their supposedly superior language and culture.[116]

The suggestion that the imperial imposition of a single language is part of the background of Genesis 11 has the further merit of taking seriously the fact that the Babel story *follows* the table of the nations in Genesis 10, which had already recounted (as natural) the development of multiple cultural, political, and linguistic groups (10:5, 20, 31). Whatever original meaning the Babel story might have had if it circulated as an independent work, in the final form of the text of Genesis as it now stands, multiple languages are portrayed as normal before Babel.[117] God's response of confusing the language of the builders cannot therefore be understood by canonical readers in any

---

as *Enmerkar and the Lord of Aratta*, which recounts the shift from an idyllic single language to multiple languages, this does not seem to be the emphasis of the Babel story. Furthermore, the central emphasis on city/tower-building in the Babel story is unparalleled in the Sumerian myth.

114. Cyrus H. Gordon, "Ebla as Background for the Old Testament," in *Congress Volume: Jerusalem, 1986* (ed. John A. Emerton; Vetus Testamentum Supplement 40; Leiden: Brill, 1988), 295, quoted in Hamilton, *Genesis*, 1.350–51 n. 7.

115. Smith, "What Hope After Babel?" 173. We may understand the renaming of Daniel and the three Hebrews in Babylon (Daniel 1:6–7) as an aspect of this cultural-linguistic imperialism. Colonial peoples are intimately familiar with this practice.

116. Dalley, "Occasions and Opportunities," 27.

117. Another possible way to read the juxtaposition of Genesis 10 and 11 is to view Genesis 10 as a general statement of human differentiation (in response to the commission in 1:28 to fill the earth), with Genesis 11 constituting a particular case of this differentiation (the case of Babel, which is portrayed as resisting such differentiation). This does not significantly change my interpretation of the thrust of the story. Thus Terence E. Fretheim explains that "11:1–9 serves as an *illustration* of the typical developments in 10:1–32"; "The Book of Genesis: Introduction, Commentary, and Reflections," in *The New Interpreter's Bible* (ed. Leander E. Keck et al.; Nashville: Abingdon, 1994), 1.413 (emphasis original).

unproblematic way as simple punishment. While confusion is certainly the initial result of multiplying the languages of Babel, in the context of the primeval history this is fundamentally a restorative move, reversing an unhealthy, monolithic movement toward imposed homogeneity.[118] Indeed, in the account of the day of Pentecost in Acts 2 (typically understood by Christians as the reversal of Babel) linguistic confusion is overcome, although not by the imposition of a single language. Multiple languages (and cultures) remain, but the presence of the Spirit overcomes the comprehension barrier. People hear/understand each other once again.

God's other response to Babel, the scattering of its population (Genesis 11:8), must likewise be interpreted as redemptive, in that it redresses the attempt of Babel to resist the original charge to the human race to multiply and fill the earth (1:28). Again, contextually, the table of the nations specifically mentioned the spreading of the nations as a normal part of human differentiation (10:5, 18, 32) and on one occasion (10:18) even used the same verb found in the Babel story (*nāpas*).[119] The implication is therefore not, as is often suggested, that Genesis 11 protests a human incursion into the divine realm (heaven). *God* is not the one threatened by this Promethean act of human assertion. Rather, a careful reading of Genesis 11 in the context of the primeval history suggests that Babel represents imperial civilization par excellence and that its imposed, artificial unity is a danger to *the human race*. God's remedy, therefore, not only enables humanity to obey the commission of 1:28 to fill the earth, but contributes to the diffusion of human power for the sake of humanity.[120] The Babel story thus coheres with the anthropological concern of the primeval history.

What we have in Genesis 11, then, is a critique of Mesopotamian civilization (including ancient Sumerian cultural ideals and Assyro-Babylonian imperial practice), perhaps even a critique of the mimetic ideal that this civilization embodies as it reenacts the primordial divine

118. I am well aware that the priority of Genesis 10 over Genesis 11 has historically been used by proponents of apartheid to justify the ideology of "separate but equal." It should be clear that such an ideology cannot be derived legitimately from the text. Not only does the cultural diversity of Genesis 10 not entail (racial) separation, but the critique of the monolithic, homogenous character of Babel in Genesis 11 serves the interests of justice—something that cannot be said of apartheid.

119. The verb used in 10:5 and 10:32 is *pārad*.

120. Other scholars note that the scattering is not punishment, but rather God's means of accomplishing the original calling to fill the earth in Genesis 1:28. See, for example, Turner, *Announcements of Plot in Genesis*, 31–32; and Fretheim, "Book of Genesis," 414.

order. The critique, however, is oblique. Just when we would expect a frontal attack on Mesopotamian ideology, exposing the idolatrous commitments of Mesopotamian religion, we find instead a very secular, even humanistic account of the origin of this imperial civilization. Instead of denouncing false religion, the Genesis 11 ideology/critique unmasks the human impulses that masquerade as religious legitimacy. Genesis 11 thus strips off the religious veneer of imperial Babylon (as the paradigm of Mesopotamian cultural achievement) to expose the underlying human impulse to exercise power over others—that is, the impulse to violence.

If this is, indeed, the thrust of the Babel story, it functions in profound harmony with the remainder of the primeval history that (as we have seen) typically portrays human sin in terms of violence (the misuse of power). No explicit violence is, however, mentioned in the Babel narrative. This is quite significant, rhetorically. In contrast to the escalation of violence that preceded the flood, the building project of Babel seems tame by comparison. It could actually be read as a model of nonviolent order and social cohesion—which is precisely how historical Babylon mythically portrayed its own society.

The narrative question then arises as to the rhetorical function of the Babel story as the climax and conclusion of the primeval history. What point, in its canonical context, does the narrative make? Would a reader be justified in thinking that the building of Babel functions as the appropriate narrative resolution to the story of violence told in Genesis 1–11? This is certainly a possible surface reading of the Babel story, at least at the beginning of Genesis 11. Like many today who are dazzled by the military might and the cultural and technological achievements of America (including American citizens claiming that it is the "greatest nation on earth" and others who look longingly toward this "land of opportunity"), it would have been a preeminent temptation for Israel in the context of the sober geopolitical realities of the ancient Near East to believe the allure of the mythic ideal of Mesopotamia (embodied most significantly in Babylonian civilization). A closer look at both Mesopotamian society and the context of the Babel story in Genesis 1–11 might suggest, however, a more critical reading. Could the order and unity of Babylon have been purchased at the expense of the subjugated masses who built and maintained the empire, serving its royal and priestly elites? This is certainly suggested by an intertextual reading of the Babel story with Exodus 1, and it would be a particularly appropriate application of Israel's formative exodus experience to the ideological challenge posed by Mesopotamian civilization.

It is my contention that the narrative of Genesis 11:1-9, even if it first suggests a superficial, surface reading that positively affirms Babylonian/Mesopotamian civilization, ends up subverting that reading. A canonical interpretation of the text suggests that it ultimately protests the hidden, systemic violence beneath Babylonian/Mesopotamian civilization by stripping away its putative divine legitimation. Babel is thus disclosed as nothing more than a human construction, and a violent one at that, in which those with power suppress the perceived social forces of chaos in the name of divine order. Thus, contrary to the mythic tradition that the name Babel means the "gate of god(s),"[121] Genesis 11 ironically claims that the true significance of Babel is "confusion."[122] The civilization that claimed to represent the epitome of order is unmasked as simply another form of chaos.

The Babel narrative of Genesis 11:1-9 thus functions as an appropriate conclusion to the primeval history. Having begun with God's creation of humanity as *imago Dei*, gifted with real power and agency in the world, Genesis 1-11 testifies to the increasing abuse of the power of *imago Dei*, culminating in the impasse of the Babel story, where that violence is substantially more organized (and hidden). This impasse will require a genuinely new departure in the canonical story, namely, the call of Abram (in Genesis 12), to bring blessing to all the families of the earth.[123]

When read against the background of Mesopotamian ideology, Genesis 1-11 discloses a worldview in which humanity is created in God's image and gifted by God with significant agency—able to make history, to affect the outcome of events in the real world, for good or ill. This latter point is important, since the worldview of Genesis 1-11 goes beyond a positive statement of God-granted human historical agency to stress that it is the misuse of precisely this agency that led to human violence in the world. In the end, this misuse leads even to the rise of powerful civilizations like the Assyrian and Babylonian empires, whose own humanly constructed ideology claims that such agency is reserved for its divinely legitimated rulers, while the majority of the human race is disenfranchised of such agency. It is thus a brilliant ironic move that the primeval history, which grounds its critique of Mesopotamian civilization in the creation of humanity as *imago Dei*

---

121. Hamilton, *Genesis*, 1.357.

122. Playing on the assonance of Babel (*bābel*) with the Hebrew word *bālal*.

123. Brian Walsh and I address the significance of this new departure in relation to the *imago Dei* in *Truth Is Stranger Than It Used to Be: Biblical Faith in a Postmodern Age* (Downers Grove, IL: InterVarsity/London: SPCK, 1995), 127-29.

in Genesis 1, actually utilizes a transformed (democratized) version of Mesopotamian ideology in order to subvert this very ideology.[124]

The Contribution of an Exilic Social Context

It is even possible, despite the ambiguous evidence available to us (see chapter 3), that this alternative biblical vision received its most decisive formulation (specifically, the use of *imago Dei* terminology) in the sixth century B.C.E., when Israel was directly confronted with the social embodiment of Mesopotamian ideology in the form of the Neo-Babylonian Empire. Although there is admittedly no clear proof for an exilic social context for Genesis 1, I do not believe that such a context can be definitively ruled out.

Even though Mesopotamian ideology undoubtedly presented an important challenge to Israel's faith prior to the exile, the challenge would have been significantly intensified by the direct confrontation with the institutions and social landscape of Babylonia that exile represented. It was one thing to have negotiated with Mesopotamian definitions of reality at a distance, at the periphery of the empire. It was quite another to be displaced from Judah and resettled at the empire's heart, daily confronted with an alien, imperial culture, with its own social order, institutions and symbolic univese. The exiles would have been subjected to the constant pressure of socialization and inculturation into the Mesopotamian worldview, which was embodied in the very fabric of the society in which they now found themselves.

Compounding this more direct confrontation with Mesopotamian ideology than Israel would have previously experienced was the trauma of profound, multilayered loss represented by exile. In the most basic sense, exile meant the loss of the land promised by God to Abraham and his descendants, a land that Israel had occupied for over six hundred years.[125] Exile also meant the ending of the two treasured and defining institutions of Israel, namely, the Davidic monarchy (sealed by God's promissory oath to David, according to 2 Samuel 7, some four hundred years earlier) and the Jerusalem temple (built and dedicated by David's son, Solomon). These twin institutions functioned as symbols of God's abiding presence in and blessing on Israel. Taken

124. A point made by Phyllis Bird, "Sexual Differentiation and Divine Image in the Genesis Creation Texts," 22 n.12.

125. Although loss of land for the exiles took the form of deportation or physical alienation, for those left in the land the alienation was sociopolitical, in that Judah was reduced to the status of a subservient Babylonian province.

together, these losses of institutions and land constituted the end of Israel as a nation.

But the loss signaled by exile was more than geographical and institutional. It was more, even, than psychological, the gut-wrenching experience of being uprooted from all that was familiar and being forced to resettle in an alien land and culture, a thousand miles from home.[126] Layered upon these losses—and deeply intertwined with them—was the loss of Israel's symbolic world. The physical facticity and psychological trauma of exile were accompanied, in other words, by a crisis of meaning.

Whereas the book of Lamentations is the classic statement of loss from the perspective of those left in the land, Psalm 137 is a communal lament of the exiles:

> By the rivers of Babylon—
>   there we sat down and there we wept
>   when we remembered Zion.
> On the willows there
>   we hung up our harps.
> For there our captors
>   asked us for songs,
> and our tormentors asked for mirth, saying,
>   "Sing us one of the songs of Zion!"
> How could we sing the LORD's song
>   in a foreign land? (Psalm 137:1–4 NRSV)

The point is not that the exiles were literally tortured or brutalized on an ongoing basis (we simply do not have enough information to reconstruct an accurate picture of the actual social situation of the exiles). Nevertheless, Psalm 137 realistically portrays the quandary of an Israelite exile unable to sing anymore a song of Zion (like Psalm 46 with its confidence in YHWH's protection of Jerusalem) now that the city had been destroyed.

Indeed, what now was Israel to make of God's ancient promises to Abraham, promises not only of a land but also of a special destiny for his descendants? What of God's eternal oath to preserve the Davidic dynasty, in light of its evident demise? What of God's presence among the people if the temple (and its sacrificial apparatus) no longer existed? How could Israel's narrative of historical destiny, a story of redemption and liberation (focused on the exodus from bondage in Egypt and incorporating the Davidic monarchy and the Jerusalem temple) turn

---

126. Babylon was about six hundred miles east of Jerusalem as the crow flies. The actual journey, which would have followed the northeastward curve of the Fertile Crescent, would have been closer to one thousand miles.

into a narrative of defeat and new bondage? Had YHWH the God of Israel failed? Had God been unable to protect Israel from its enemies? Was YHWH bested by Marduk, patron-deity of Babylon? Could Israel's God be trusted anymore? Was this God worthy of Israel's allegiance any longer?[127]

But beyond the specifically theological crisis (concerning God's power and trustworthiness)[128] was an accompanying crisis of *identity*. As Brian Walsh and I have argued, a people's sense of *identity* ("who are we?"), which includes their sense of calling and purpose, is deeply implicated in their sense of the *world*—the place or context, in the broadest sense—to which they belong ("where are we?").[129] Thus, a faith crisis generated by the loss of Israel's symbolic world inevitably led to a crisis of Israelite identity. What, indeed, would it mean to be a member of the chosen people of God in sixth-century exile, when one's familiar world of meaning had been brutally stripped away? Not only would the exiles have been daily confronted with a pervasive understanding of the superiority of Mesopotamian royal urban culture, but the vacuum of their own identity crisis would have made them supremely vulnerable to the Mesopotamian understanding of human identity and purpose.

One of the fundamental questions that the Israelite exiles would have faced, therefore, was whether they were going to acquiesce in the debilitating identity foisted on them by Babylon. According to this identity, the exiles were defined, along with the mass of the Babylonian populace, as powerless and insignificant servants of the gods. But they were, further-

127. Klein discusses questions such as these in *Israel in Exile*, 3–6.

128. While Klein calls the exile a *theological* challenge (ibid., 3), Bruce C. Birch describes it as a *spiritual* crisis in *Let Justice Roll Down: The Old Testament, Ethics, and the Christian Life* (Louisville: Westminster/John Knox, 1991), 282.

129. See the analysis of the intertwining of identity and world in connection with postmodernity in Middleton and Walsh, *Truth Is Stranger Than It Used to Be*, esp. 56. Walsh and I postulated in our earlier *Transforming Vision*, chaps. 1–2, that all worldviews answer four fundamental worldview questions: "Where are we?" (world), "Who are we?" (identity), "What's wrong?" (evil), and "What's the remedy?" (redemption). When N. T. Wright used our worldview questions in his analysis of first-century Judaism and the early Jesus movement in *The New Testament and the People of God* (Minneapolis: Fortress; London: SPCK, 1992), chap. 5, he insightfully suggested that the answers given to the questions of evil and redemption could be better understood as constituting a people's communal narrative, a suggestion that Walsh and I gladly embraced (see *Truth Is Stranger Than It Used to Be*, 63–64, 212 n. 5). Interestingly, James A. Sanders proposes that Israelite identity in the Babylonian exile was bound up with the shaping of Israel's communal narrative of redemption; "Adaptable for Life: The Nature and Function of Canon," in *Magnalia Dei, the Mighty Acts of God: Essays on the Bible and Archaeology in Memory of G. Ernest Wright* (ed. Frank Moore Cross, Werner E. Lemke, and Patrick D. Miller Jr.; Garden City, NY: Doubleday, 1976), 531–60, repr. in Sanders's *From Sacred Story to Sacred Text: Canon as Paradigm* (Philadelphia: Fortress, 1987), chap. 1.

more, the remnants of a conquered and subjugated nation, patently inferior to their civilized conquerors. Acceptance of this identity would have robbed the exiles of a sense of significant human agency and reduced them to perpetual victim status, at the mercy of the gods, the temple system, the king, and the social order of Babylon. But acceptance of this identity would have had repercussions well beyond the disempowerment of the exiles. Acceptance of this definition of identity would have nullified Israel's distinctive communal identity, which had been shaped by a sense of divine election and covenant, rooted in a narrative of redemption from bondage, issuing in a historical mission and destiny among the nations.

The crisis of Babylonian exile can thus be imagined as a traumatic loss of meaning and identity compounded by the confrontation with a vision of human identity alien to the deepest roots of Yahwistic faith. It constituted nothing less than a frontal challenge to Israel's distinctive identity as a "royal priesthood" and "holy nation" (as articulated in Exodus 19:3–6). One can further imagine that this challenge was met, head on, by the affirmation of human agency represented by the *imago Dei* in Genesis 1. If Genesis 1 were written—or heard—in the historical context of Babylonian exile, the *imago Dei* would have come as a clarion call to the people of God to stand tall again with dignity and to take seriously their royal-priestly vocation as God's authorized agents and representatives in the world.

But whenever the notion of humanity as the image of God was first articulated, it constitutes a remarkable theological achievement. In essential continuity with the ethical, religious, and social ideals of earlier Scripture, including the pervasive critique of idolatry and of absolute kingship in Israel, the author of Genesis 1 daringly seized on the bold symbol of the *imago Dei* to restate for a new context Israel's unique insight about being human. In what must be acknowledged as one of the most daring acts of theological imagination within Scripture, this unknown author chose to crystallize the central Israelite insight about being human in a term typically applied only to idols, kings, and priests—*ṣelem ʾĕlōhîm*—and thereby profoundly affected the worldview and theological imagination of generations of biblical readers.

PART 3

The Ethics of the Image

6

Created
in the Image
of a Violent God?

I
t has been my argument in part 2 that comparative analysis of the
ancient Near Eastern—especially the Mesopotamian—background
to the *imago Dei* confirms and deepens exegetical study of the meaning of this concept in Genesis 1. The cumulative evidence suggests that
the biblical *imago Dei* refers to the status or office of the human race
as God's authorized stewards, charged with the royal-priestly vocation
of representing God's rule on earth by their exercise of cultural power.
Further, I suggested that this interpretation of the image, wherein humanity is granted a share in God's rule (and thus may be said to be *like*
the divine ruler), underlies the coherent vision of humans as significant
historical agents in the primeval history (Genesis 1–11) and may be fruitfully understood as a form of ideological resistance to Mesopotamian
traditions that devalued the status and role of humanity.

But this royal-functional interpretation of the image, while exegetically
warranted and corroborated by comparative studies, remains a purely
formal statement and is thus inadequate as it stands. It is not enough
to claim an analogy or likeness between human power and God's own
power, even one that affirms an exalted human dignity and agency.

While this is an important step in the interpretation of the *imago Dei*, what is urgently needed at this point is an investigation into the *content or substance* of the sort of power that humans are expected to exercise in the divine image. If the *imago Dei* refers to human rule of the earth, what sort of rule is envisioned?

The question of how humans appropriately image or represent God is important to explore since we live in a world pervaded by the violent abuse of human power, often explicitly legitimated by appeal to God's will. Even when there is no explicit appeal to God, humans are religious creatures and tend—consciously or subconsciously—to reproduce in their actions something of the character of whatever they take as their ultimate point of orientation and value (their god/God). How we, therefore, conceive of the God in whose image we are created has significant ethical implications.

The trouble is that among the biblical portrayals of God as creator, we find—beyond the familiar accounts in Genesis 1–2—the quasimythic notion of God founding the cosmos through an act of primordial violence, which some biblical scholars claim is fundamental to the biblical portrayal of God as creator.[1] Such a conception of God, however, seems to enshrine violence as the quintessential divine action. The presence of the *Chaoskampf* or combat myth in Scripture (and especially its connection with creation) is thus highly problematic for those (ancient or contemporary) who believe that the canonical portrayal of the creator ought to be paradigmatic for the human exercise of power. This chapter will, therefore, examine the presence of the combat myth in the Old Testament and face squarely the ethical problems for human imaging that arise when the conquest of chaos is linked to God's creation of the world.

But, even more problematically, some scholars detect traces of the combat myth in Genesis 1 itself, thus leading to the suggestion that the biblical *imago Dei*, even when read in its own primary literary context, may serve to ground human violence. This requires us to explore the question whether Genesis 1 (the primary literary context for the *imago Dei*) participates in the combat myth or, on the contrary, articulates a distinctive (even a critical) alternative to this myth. In either case, the understanding of the God-creation relationship in the opening canonical creation account has significant ethical implications for the human exercise of power in the world.

1. The most famous recent proponent of this view is Jon D. Levenson, *Creation and the Persistence of Evil: The Jewish Drama of Divine Omnipotence* (San Francisco: Harper & Row, 1988; rev. ed. Princeton: Princeton University Press, 1994), esp. preface and chap. 1.

The Presence of the Combat Myth in the Old Testament

Biblical scholars have long recognized the presence in the Bible of the motif of God's conquest of primordial forces of chaos, where these forces are pictured mythically as the ocean or sea or as a dragon or monster associated with water. In these texts God's rebellious opponent is vanquished, either by being utterly annihilated or by being captured and bound and thus rendered impotent. The cosmos (the realm of order) is thereby established (or reestablished) in the face of threatening chaos or disorder.

Hermann Gunkel, in his groundbreaking 1895 work *Schöpfung und Chaos in Urzeit und Endzeit*, first traced the combat myth back to the Babylonian creation epic *Enuma Elish* (then only recently discovered in 1873), where Marduk vanquishes Tiamat and constructs the cosmos out of her corpse. Gunkel then proceeded to note a wide variety of biblical poetic texts in which the *Chaoskampf* could be found, stretching from the Psalms through Job to the prophets and right up to the book of Revelation (especially Revelation 12).[2] Ever since Gunkel the presence of the combat myth in the Bible (particularly the Old Testament) has been evident to biblical scholars.

While the Babylonian *Enuma Elish* is undoubtedly an important source for understanding the combat myth (and may even lie behind Genesis 1), it is unlikely that it is the most immediate source for most instances of the combat myth in the Old Testament. Most scholars today hold to a probable Canaanite (rather than a Babylonian) origin for the biblical combat myth. This is due to the cuneiform texts from Ras Shamra (ancient Ugarit) in Syria that came to light in 1928. Not only is Ugaritic a closer language to Hebrew than is Akkadian (the language of Babylon and Assyria), but the biblical YHWH is said in a variety of texts to have conquered (or that he will conquer) many of the same enemies mentioned in the Ugaritic literature.[3]

Thus, for example, in Ugaritic mythology Baal vanquishes a primordial enemy known variously as Prince Yam (Sea) and Judge Nahar (River), with the result that the order of the world is either founded or

2. Hermann Gunkel, *Schöpfung und Chaos in Urzeit und Endzeit: Eine religionsgeschichtliche Untersuchung über Gen 1 und Ap Joh 12* (Göttingen: Vandenhoeck & Ruprecht, 1895). A portion of this work was translated into English by Charles A. Muenchow and published as "The Influence of Babylonian Mythology upon the Biblical Creation Story," in *Creation in the Old Testament* (ed. Bernhard W. Anderson; Issues in Religion and Theology 6; Philadelphia: Fortress, 1984), 25–52.

3. For an English translation of the so-called Baal cycle of myths, see Michael David Coogan (ed./trans.), *Stories from Ancient Canaan* (Philadelphia: Westminster, 1978), 75–115.

restored.[4] Following this battle, Baal comes to dwell in the temple/palace that is built for him in celebration of his victory over the chaotic forces (much as Marduk has the Esagila temple in Babylon built for him after his defeat of Tiamat and the slaughter of Qingu).[5] In the Old Testament, not only do Sea and River (or Sea and Jordan) occur as parallel terms in the context of the combat myth in texts such as Psalm 89:25 (MT 89:26); 114:3, 5; and Nahum 1:4, but the Song of the Sea in Exodus 15 combines the victory at the Red Sea (15:1–12) with God coming to rest in his sanctuary in the promised land (15:13–19).[6]

This motif of the conquest of watery enemies is rarely, however, used in Scripture to denote God's creation of the world. More usually, the mythological waters allude either to historical enemies whom God has vanquished or will vanquish (as in Psalm 18:15–17 [MT 18:16–18]; 65:7 [MT 65:8]; 144:7; Isaiah 17:12–13) or to the Red Sea through which the Israelites passed at the exodus (as in Psalm 77:16–20 [MT 77:17–21]; 106:9; 114:3, 5; Isaiah 51:10; Habakkuk 3:8). Indeed, the Song of the Sea (Exodus 15) contains an interesting twist on this motif, in that God does not battle the waters at all, but uses them as his instrument against a historical opponent, the Egyptian army led by pharaoh.[7]

Besides battling the sea/waters in some texts, God is also depicted in the Old Testament as engaged in conflict with various beasts or monsters, usually associated with water, some with specific names such as Levia-

4. There is considerable disagreement about whether the conquest of chaos in the Baal myths is genuinely cosmogonic (referring to the founding of the world) or merely pertains to the preservation and renewal of the annual cycle of nature, in particular, the return of the fruitful seasons (fall and spring) after a time of chaos (summer drought or winter flooding). For various sides of this debate, see Avrid S. Kapelrud, "Creation in the Ras Shamra Texts," *Studia Theologica* 34 (1980): 1–11; Loren R. Fisher, "Creation at Ugarit and in the Old Testament," *Vetus Testamentum* 15 (1965): 313–24; Baruch Margalit, "The Ugaritic Creation Myth: Fact or Fiction," *Ugaritische Forschungen* 13 (1981): 137–45; Ronald A. Simkins, *Creator and Creation: Nature in the Worldview of Ancient Israel* (Peabody, MA: Hendrickson, 1994), 71–75; and idem, *Yahweh's Activity in History and Nature in the Book of Joel* (Ancient Near Eastern Texts and Studies 10; Lewiston: Mellen, 1991), 47–52.

5. On the theme of creation followed by temple building and divine rest, see Bernard F. Batto, "The Covenant of Peace: A Neglected Ancient Near Eastern Motif," *Catholic Biblical Quarterly* 49 (1987): 197–201.

6. For an excellent account of the Ugaritic background of the biblical combat myth, see John Day, *God's Conflict with the Dragon and the Sea: Echoes of a Canaanite Myth in the Old Testament* (University of Cambridge Oriental Publications 35; Cambridge: Cambridge University Press, 1985), 4–7 and passim. Day, however, goes overboard by claiming—incorrectly, in my opinion—that the background for Genesis 1 is Ugaritic, not Babylonian (50–52).

7. A point made by Frank Moore Cross, *Canaanite Myth and Hebrew Epic: Essays in the History of the Religion of Israel* (Cambridge: Harvard University Press, 1973), 131–32.

than or Rahab. Thus we find Isaiah 27:1 describing Leviathan (Hebrew *liwyātān*) as a serpent that God will one day vanquish. This beast is mentioned (not always in the context of a combat myth) also in Psalm 74:14; 104:26; Job 3:8; 41:1–34 (MT 40:25–41:26) and is usually understood by biblical scholars as the Hebrew version of the seven-headed water serpent known from the Baal myths as *ltn* (usually vocalized as *lôtān*).[8] Beyond the philological similarity of the names, Leviathan in Isaiah 27:1 and *lôtān* in the Baal myth are each described as a "fleeing" and "twisting" (or "crooked") serpent (the Ugaritic and Hebrew words used are precise cognates).[9] And Leviathan's "heads" are even mentioned in Psalm 74:14 (though their number is not specified).

Unlike Leviathan, however, no known parallel has so far turned up in ancient Near Eastern literature for Rahab. Although the term sometimes designates Egypt, as in Isaiah 30:7 and Psalm 87:4, Rahab is clearly a serpent in Job 26:12 and is mentioned in the context of the combat myth also in Job 9:13; Isaiah 51:9; and Psalm 89:10 (MT 89:11), with the term occurring in the plural in Psalm 40:4 (MT 40:5), usually translated "proud or arrogant ones." In some texts, YHWH's mythological adversary or enemy is not named, but is designated by the more general term *tannîn* (often translated "dragon"), as in Job 7:12; Isaiah 27:1; 51:9; Ezekiel 29:3; 32:2, with the plural *tannînîm* (dragons) occurring in Psalm 74:13.[10]

As with God's battle with the mythological waters, most of the references to God's defeat of these various monsters are not associated with creation, but rather describe God's historical judgment on foreign military or political powers. Among the clearest such references are the oracles against the nations in Ezekiel and Jeremiah. Thus Ezekiel 29:2–7 and 32:2–4 portray the Egyptian pharaoh as a great water monster (*tannîn*) whom God will pull out of the Nile with hooks or haul up with a net. Likewise, Jeremiah 51:34 pictures King Nebuchadnezzar of Babylon as a sea serpent swallowing Israel, and 51:44 goes on to

8. This vocalization was proposed by William F. Albright, "New Light on Early Canaanite Language and Literature," *Bulletin of the American Schools of Oriental Research* 46 (1932): 19, and is widely accepted today. It is disputed by J. A. Emerton in "Leviathan and *ltn*: The Vocalization of the Ugaritic Word for Dragon," *Vetus Testamentum* 32 (1982): 327–31.

9. This description of *lôtān* is found in M. Dietrich, O. Loretz, and J. Sanmartín, *Die keilalphabetischen Texte aus Ugarit* (Alter Orient und Altes Testament 24.1; Neukirchen-Vluyn: Neukirchener Verlag, 1976), #1.5.1.1–3. In the Ugaritic myth, this beast is defeated by Baal and the goddess Anat in a what seems to be a different battle from Baal's conquest of Sea/River.

10. The term *tannîm* in Psalm 44:19 (MT 44:20) may be a variant of either the singular or the plural, although it is also very close to the Hebrew for "jackals" (and is so rendered in many translations).

describe Bel (Marduk) as forced to disgorge what he has swallowed (a usage that hints at the near functional identity of the king and the god in Babylon).

The Misidentification of the Creation-by-Combat Motif

While I do not wish to deny that creation-by-combat occurs in the Old Testament, it is important to note that this motif is not nearly as common as many biblical scholars claim. It is certainly not as common as either John Day or Jon Levenson seem to think in their important studies of the combat myth.[11]

While Day does not suggest that all uses of the combat myth describe cosmogonic conflict or that all biblical cosmogonies manifest the *Chaoskampf* (he correctly lists many texts, including Genesis 1, that utilize the motif of God's nonconflictual division or containment of the waters),[12] he can boldly claim at the outset of his study that "the number of passages associating the conflict with chaos with the creation is sufficiently large to justify our seeing it as one of the major uses of *Chaoskampf* imagery in the Old Testament."[13] Levenson, however, goes well beyond Day both in assuming that most examples of the historicized combat myth represent cosmogonic conflict and in treating all biblical cosmogonies, except for Genesis 1 and Psalm 104, as examples of creation-by-combat.[14] Paradoxically, however, Day discerns the combat myth even in Psalm 104, a text that, in his opinion, "unambiguously makes it clear that the Old Testament can depict the creation as having been associated with a primordial conflict with chaos."[15]

Bernard Batto, however, is rare among contemporary biblical scholars in claiming to discern the presence of the *Chaoskampf* even in Genesis 1.

11. Day, *God's Conflict with the Dragon and the Sea*; Levenson, *Creation and the Persistence of Evil*. Levenson's exploration of the combat myth is limited to part 1 of his book, even though his preface to the 1994 edition affirms that the book's "central thesis" (xv) is about the combat myth.

12. Other creation texts that Day groups with Genesis 1, in that they are characterized by God's nonconflictual containment of the waters, include Psalm 33:7–8; Proverbs 8:24, 27–29; Jeremiah 5:22; 31:35; *God's Conflict with the Dragon and the Sea*, 56–57.

13. Ibid., 4.

14. Although Levenson at first suggests that the sport or play of God with Leviathan in Psalm 104:26 may not be quite so harmless and may in fact represent (as in Job 41:1–2 [MT 40:25–26]) "catching the great sea beast with a hook and line" (*Creation and the Persistence of Evil*, 17), in his more extensive analysis of Psalm 104 (in chap. 5), he refers to Leviathan as God's "toy" and is careful to distinguish this portrayal from creation-by-combat.

15. Day, *God's Conflict with the Dragon and the Sea*, 30.

Batto's interpretation, articulated in two recent works,[16] is summarized in the bold claim that the priestly writer (P)—under the influence of *Enuma Elish* during the Babylonian exile—transposed the entire Yahwistic (J) version of the primeval history (a story moving from creation to the flood), which he inherited, into "a scene in the divine sovereign's battle to overcome the chaos dragon."[17] While Batto grants that the sea monsters (*tannînîm*) have been demythologized in Genesis 1:21, and hence do not represent the forces of chaos, he does not think this applies to the deep in 1:2. Any claim that the primeval waters have been demythologized, he explains, "fails to reckon with 'the Abyss' (*těhôm*) itself as Ps primary symbol for the primordial archfoe of the Creator in Genesis 1."[18] Batto thus regards the deep (or "Abyss") in 1:2 as equivalent to "the personification of evil" and "the divine sovereign's archenemy."[19] While it may not be as personified as Tiamat, he explains, "it is nonetheless a force which must be subdued in order for the Creator's design to come into being."[20]

There will, undoubtedly, always be ambiguous texts about which biblical scholars legitimately disagree. Nevertheless, in my judgment the majority of putative creation-by-combat texts turn out, on close inspection, to refer either to some intrahistorical (or eschatological) conflict described in mythological language or to the nonconflictual containment of the primordial waters at creation. The tendency of biblical scholars to see creation-by-combat in texts where it is obviously not present is likely due to the legacy of Gunkel's form criticism—both to his influential comparison of *Chaoskampf* texts in the Bible and the ancient Near East and to the very assumptions of form criticism as a comparative discipline, which Gunkel inaugurated.

In his classic study of the *Chaoskampf*, Gunkel did not limit himself to Old Testament poetic texts that manifested the combat myth, but devoted a significant section of his analysis to comparing Genesis 1 with *Enuma Elish*. Among many similarities between the two texts, Gunkel noted the etymological relationship between *těhôm* (the Hebrew word in 1:2 for the "deep," the primordial ocean over which God's Spirit moves) and *tiʾāmat* (an Akkadian word meaning "ocean" or "sea," which func-

---

16. Bernard F. Batto, "Creation Theology in Genesis," in *Creation in the Biblical Traditions* (ed. Richard J. Clifford and John J. Collins; Catholic Biblical Quarterly Monograph Series 24; Washington, DC: Catholic Biblical Association of America, 1992), 16–38; and idem, *Slaying the Dragon: Mythmaking in the Biblical Tradition* (Louisville: Westminster/John Knox, 1992) 73–101.

17. Batto, "Creation Theology in Genesis," 32.

18. Batto, *Slaying the Dragon*, 213 n. 19.

19. Batto, "Creation Theology in Genesis," 36, 35.

20. Ibid., 33.

tions as the name of the divinized primordial ocean, also portrayed as a sea monster, in *Enuma Elish*).[21] Beyond the etymological connection of both words, Gunkel pointed out the remarkable thematic similarity of Marduk's mode of creating in *Enuma Elish* with that of the biblical God in Genesis 1. Whereas Marduk conquers Tiamat and splits her dead carcass in half in order to construct heaven and earth, two of God's creative acts in Genesis 1 involve separating or dividing the waters (on both the second and third days of creation).

The presence, thus, of a primordial watery soup or ocean separated and bounded to produce the differentiation of a complex world (along with other parallels) suggested to many biblical scholars over the years that Genesis 1 was influenced in some way by the ideas of *Enuma Elish* (if not by the text itself). Although Gunkel's own understanding of the relationship between the two texts was quite nuanced, his terminology was sometimes infelicitous. Gunkel, for example, described Genesis 1 and *Enuma Elish* as "one and the same myth which is preserved in two different but related versions,"[22] repeatedly referring to them as "recensions" of the same myth.[23] He even, on occasion, spoke of a hybrid "Marduk-Yahweh myth."[24] Such unguarded language on Gunkel's part may well have encouraged reductionistic understandings of Genesis 1 as merely a reflex of *Enuma Elish*.

The heritage of Gunkel's influential analysis may be seen even in passing comments made by biblical scholars about Genesis 1. Thus James Crenshaw observes that "water is the antagonistic element in the first creation story,"[25] and Bruce Birch comments that "in picturing creation as the overcoming of chaos the priestly creation tradition appropriates the battle with chaos tradition known elsewhere in the ancient Near East."[26] While these are not much more than summary statements made in passing that are meant to allude to a traditional scholarly judgment, the same cannot be said for Batto's sustained interpretation of the presence of the *Chaoskampf* in Genesis 1.

---

21. Whereas Gunkel claimed that *tĕhôm* was derived from *ti'āmat*, most Old Testament scholars follow Alexander Heidel's argument that this is morphologically impossible and that both words probably have a common Semitic root; *The Babylonian Genesis: The Story of Creation* (2nd ed.; Chicago: University of Chicago Press, 1951; repr. 1963), 100.
22. Gunkel, "Influence of Babylonian Mythology," 44.
23. Ibid., 46–49.
24. Ibid., 43.
25. James L. Crenshaw, *Story and Faith: A Guide to the Old Testament* (New York: Macmillan/London: Collier Macmillan, 1986), 39.
26. Bruce C. Birch, *Let Justice Roll Down: The Old Testament, Ethics, and Christian Life* (Louisville: Westminster/John Knox, 1991), 200.

But beyond Gunkel's explicit comparison of Genesis 1 and *Enuma Elish*, we have to reckon with the very assumptions of form criticism as a comparative discipline. Whereas form criticism is predicated on the similarity and constancy of leitmotifs found in quite different texts (even from different cultures), no two texts simply replicate the same motif in exactly the same manner, as Gunkel himself well recognized.[27] To assume that they do is to fall into a trap analogous to what James Barr calls the fallacy of "illegitimate totality transfer."[28] It is simply a methodological fallacy to assume that the mere presence of the combat myth in a biblical text means that it should be read as creation-by-combat or that any creation text that draws on the theme of God dividing or separating primordial waters must refer to a primordial battle. Yet this is precisely what Batto does with Genesis 1. The basis on which Batto judges that the deep is God's primordial archenemy in Genesis 1:2 is revealing. "The fact that the P account begins not with a dry wasteland," he explains, "but with the watery Abyss (*tĕhôm*), is the first indication that we are operating within the context of the Combat Myth."[29] But this simply does not follow—unless, of course, one first *assumes* that every cosmogony involving a watery beginning must involve conflict.[30]

While we should certainly not ignore the embeddedness of individual texts in larger patterns of meaning[31] (including shared motifs such as the combat myth), it is nevertheless important that we read each text for its own specificity and particularity—its "actuality," as James Muilenburg puts it.[32] Without such attentiveness to how individual texts

27. Many later practitioners of form criticism are not, however, as careful as Gunkel.

28. James Barr, *The Semantics of Biblical Language* (London: Oxford University Press, 1961), 218. Although Barr is here addressing illegitimate inferences from biblical word studies, his basic critique is relevant to the issue at hand.

29. Batto, "Creation Theology in Genesis," 32.

30. My point here is similar to John J. Collins's methodological caution about interpreting mythological motifs in apocalyptic literature, such as the possible Ugaritic background of the "son of man" in Daniel. Collins points out that even if "the 'one like a son of man' who comes on the clouds in Daniel 7 alludes to the Canaanite figure of Baal, this is not to say that he is identified as Baal, or that the full story of Baal is implied. It merely suggests that there is some analogy between this figure and the traditional conception of Baal"; *The Apocalyptic Imagination: An Introduction to the Jewish Matrix of Christianity* (New York: Crossroad, 1987), 16. Exactly what the relevant analogy is will have to be discerned from a careful reading of the text in its own particularity.

31. I attempted in chapter 2 to read Genesis 1 in terms of the symbolic world it shares with many other biblical (especially, creation) texts. In chapters 6–7 my focus is on the distinctive features of Genesis 1.

32. James Muilenburg, "Form Criticism and Beyond," *Journal of Biblical Literature* 88 (1969): 18.

utilize combat imagery, we are in danger of engaging in hermeneutical violence, a sort of "textual" racial profiling.[33]

Creation-by-Combat in the Old Testament

Although the vast majority of biblical texts that utilize the combat myth do not, in my opinion, designate creation, but rather God's struggle with and judgment on various political empires, either in the historical past or in the eschatological future, the Old Testament contains three rather clear creation-by-combat texts: Job 26:7–14; Psalm 74:12–17; 89:5–14 (MT 89:6–15). These poetic texts each portray God's creation of the world and the founding of cosmic order as issuing from the divine conquest of a primordial opponent or enemy, which is variously identified using the parallelism characteristic of Hebrew poetry. In Job 26 the opponent is the sea/Rahab/the twisting serpent, in Psalm 74 it is the sea/Leviathan/*tannînîm*, and in Psalm 89 it is the sea/Rahab/your enemies.

The Joban text, which comes in the context of the cycles of Job's speeches with his friends, seems to constitute an attempt, on either Job's or Bildad's part, to evoke the awesome ways of God, which are beyond comprehension.[34] First of all, creation is clearly depicted in Job 26:7–10:

> He stretches out Zaphon over the void,
>   and hangs the earth upon nothing.

33. The treatment that Isaiah 51:9–11 often receives from biblical scholars constitutes a rather egregious example of this phenomenon. This text is typically taken as representing creation-by-combat because the combat myth is used in 51:9b–10a. First, God's defeat of Rahab/the dragon is mentioned (51:9b), followed by God's drying up of the sea (51:10a). Yet 51:10b mentions, not creation, but the parting of the sea for the redeemed to pass through (a clear reference to the exodus), and 51:11 announces a second exodus for the exiles in Babylon. A contextual reading thus suggests that the defeat of Rahab/the dragon in 51:9b probably designates God's victory over the Egyptian army at the Red Sea. The text is not a cosmogony at all, yet it is frequently misread as a prime example of creation-by-combat.

34. Although Job 26:5–14 is not introduced as Bildad's speech, it is taken to be so by many commentators because Job's speech begins with 26:1, yet Job 27 begins by stating that "Job again took up his discourse and said" (NRSV), which suggests that his speech was interrupted. Indeed, the tone and content of 26:5–14 fit well with Bildad's previous speech in Job 25. On the other hand, 26:5–14 could well be Job's own articulation of creation-by-combat (compare 3:8 and 7:11–14), an articulation that is challenged by God's second speech from the whirlwind, which presents Leviathan not as an enemy of God, but as an untamed creature (like Job) in whom God delights. I defend this positive reading of Leviathan in God's second speech to Job in "Has God Come to Praise Job or to Bury Him? The Function of YHWH's Second Speech from the Whirlwind (Job 40:6–41:34 [Heb 41:26])," a paper presented at the annual meeting of the Canadian Society of Biblical Studies, at the University of Manitoba, Winnipeg, May 31, 2004.

He binds up the waters in his thick clouds,
and the cloud is not torn open by them.
He covers the face of the full moon,
and spreads over it his cloud.
He has described a circle on the face of the waters,
at the boundary between light and darkness. (NRSV)

Then God's conquest of mythical opponents is then portrayed in 26:11–13, with a conclusion in 26:14:

The pillars of heaven tremble,
and are astounded at his rebuke.
By his power he stilled the Sea;
by his understanding he struck down Rahab.
By his wind the heavens were made fair;
his hand pierced the fleeing serpent.
These are indeed but the outskirts of his ways;
and how small a whisper do we hear of him!
But the thunder of his power who can understand? (NRSV)

Although I take this text as articulating creation-by-combat, it is important to acknowledge that there is no explicit syntactical link between 26:7–10 and 26:11–14. Indeed, as in most Hebrew poetry, there are hardly any explicit syntactical connections between the various bicola or tricola of the text. It is well known that Hebrew prose narrative is typically characterized by parataxis (constituting a series of coordinate clauses, often connected by nothing more than the multiduty conjunction *wāw*), rather than the hypotaxis found in more structured languages like Greek or Latin (which are full of subordinate clauses). But Hebrew poetry is further characterized by asyndeton, evident in the almost complete lack of syntactical connections between lines. It is thus somewhat unclear whether the reference to creation in one section of the Joban text is meant to be interpreted by reference to the conquest of chaos in the next section or if a sequence of distinct events is being listed—first creation, then the conquest of historicized chaos. The thematic link between these two sequential sections, however, is the continued allusion to creation language in the second section (especially in 26:13), which suggests that the text indeed propounds creation-by-combat.[35]

35. It is simple honesty to admit that the interpreter must supply the necessary connections in the act of reading. This means that the gestalts with which we read Hebrew poetry are crucial for our interpretation of particular texts. While I do not assume that all references to the combat myth must refer to creation, I do not exclude this possibility a priori.

In contrast to Job 26, which cites the combat myth to evoke awe concerning the mystery of God, Psalms 74 and 89 clearly illustrate sociopolitical functions of the combat myth that are well known from the ancient Near East. That is, they link creation-by-combat in the divine realm with human institutions (and human power) on earth and are thus directly relevant to our topic. Whereas Psalm 74 appeals to the combat myth in connection with the Jerusalem temple (which has been destroyed), Psalm 89 connects the myth to the Davidic monarchy (which is in crisis). Both psalms are laments and may come from the very beginning of the exile, when the temple and the monarchy (both institutional signs of Israel's election) came to an end.

Psalm 74 calls on God to "remember Mount Zion, where you came to dwell" (74:2 NRSV) and describes the appalling destruction of the Jerusalem temple and the continued scoffing of Israel's enemies. In contrast to the present situation of crisis, the psalmist proceeds to draw on the ancient tradition of the *Chaoskampf*, portraying a time when God was clearly the victor over his foes (74:12–14) and following this by a description of creation (74:15–17). Since it is unlikely that the psalm intends to recount any mighty act of God *prior* to creation, the use of the combat myth in 74:12–14 should be interpreted as a reference to the primordial battle through which God founded the world.[36] Creation is the result of this battle (74:12–17):

Yet God my King is from of old,
  working salvation in the earth.
You divided the sea by your might;
  you broke the heads of the dragons in the waters.
You crushed the heads of Leviathan;
  you gave him as food for the creatures of the wilderness.
You cut openings for springs and torrents;
  you dried up ever-flowing streams.
Yours is the day, yours also the night;
  you established the luminaries and the sun.
You have fixed all the bounds of the earth;
  you made summer and winter. (NRSV)

The description of creation-by-combat in this psalm thus functions as a paradigm of "salvation" in times "of old" (74:12), when God asserted

36. A persistent minority interpretive tradition (usually called the "gap" or "restitution" theory) actually claims that the primordial battle took place *after* God's origination of the cosmos and that references to creation in the Bible thus refer to re-creation (after a demonic rebellion). For one of the better argued versions of this interpretation, see Gregory A. Boyd, *God at War: The Bible and Spiritual Conflict* (Downers Grove, IL: InterVarsity, 1992), 93–113.

his kingship over primordial opponents, and is meant to call God to act salvifically once again by defeating Israel's enemies in the present. Cosmic conquest of a primordial foe thus sets a precedent for the historical conquest of political and military enemies.

Particularly interesting, although only implicit in the psalm, is the connection between the combat myth and temple-building. Just as the conclusion of Baal's battles with his opponents (in the Ugaritic myth) results in the construction of his temple/palace, presumably if YHWH once more defeated the forces of chaos, thus enacting the primordial battle in history, the culmination of the victory would be God's coming to rest in his royal sanctuary in Zion. The implied outcome of the new battle would be a new temple. Israel's sacred historical cosmos would once again be secure.

Psalm 89 is even more instructive about the sociopolitical function of the combat myth in ancient Israel. Like Psalm 74, this psalm links God's primordial victory in the beginning with the possibility of a new victory in history against Israel's enemies (implied in 89:46–51 [MT 89:47–52]). In Psalm 89, however, the cosmic battle is connected not with the temple, but with the monarchy. Here God's primordial combat against the forces of chaos serves to legitimate the power and validity of the Davidic king (who, in effect, functions as God's image on earth).

The psalm begins by extolling YHWH's steadfast love and faithfulness, which are grounded in the primordial victory over chaos (89:1–18 [MT 89:2–19]). The psalm then recounts YHWH's (supposedly) unbreakable, eternal covenant with David (89:19–37 [MT 89:20–38]), contrasting this with the crisis of the Davidic monarchy, which testifies that the covenant is in fact broken (89:38–51 [MT 89:39–52]).

What is most illuminating here is the parallel between how God is described in the combat myth section of the psalm and the description of the Davidic king that follows this section. In 89:5–8 (MT 89:6–9) YHWH is praised as incomparable among the gods or heavenly beings:

Let the heavens praise your wonders, O Lord,
 your faithfulness in the assembly of the holy ones.
For who in the skies can be compared to the Lord?
 Who among the heavenly beings is like the Lord,
a God feared in the council of the holy ones,
 great and awesome above all that are around him?
O Lord God of hosts,
 who is as mighty as you, O Lord?
Your faithfulness surrounds you. (NRSV)

This incomparability is then interpreted in terms of God's victory over the primordial forces of chaos, by which the cosmos is founded (89:9–14 [MT 89:10–15]):

> You rule the raging of the sea;
>> when its waves rise, you still them.
> You crushed Rahab like a carcass;
>> you scattered your enemies with your mighty arm.
> The heavens are yours, the earth also is yours;
>> the world and all that is in it—you have founded them.
> The north and the south—you created them;
>> Tabor and Hermon joyously praise your name.
> You have a mighty arm;
>> strong is your hand, high your right hand.
> Righteousness and justice are the foundation of your throne;
>> steadfast love and faithfulness go before you. (NRSV)

After the description of creation-by-combat comes a brief stanza (89:15–18 [MT 89:16–19]) extolling the blessedness of Israel for having this warrior as their God. The next line (89:19 [MT 89:20]) begins by stating: "Then [ʾāz] you spoke in a vision to your faithful one" (NRSV), and it continues with what amounts to an expansion of the narrative account of the Davidic covenant found in 2 Samuel 7 (the text upon which this psalm obviously depends).[37] Quite unlike the narrative account of the origin of the Israelite monarchy in 1 Samuel 8 (where the monarchy is a late institution, historically speaking, and Saul, not David, is the first king), the mythical telescoping of events in Psalm 89 portrays the election of David as the next event immediately after the creation battle. This certainly warrants Richard Clifford's comment that "the psalm regards the founding of the house of David as part of the foundation of the world just as several Mesopotamian cosmogonies list the king and the temple as things created at the beginning."[38]

When God's relationship with David (and the line of Davidic kings) is then elaborated, the description goes considerably beyond the account of the Davidic covenant found in 2 Samuel 7. The "steadfast love" and

37. The text actually has "faithful ones" (plural) here, which leads some scholars to think that the psalm was later edited to effect a democratization of the Davidic covenant.

38. Richard J. Clifford, "Creation in the Psalms," in *Creation in the Biblical Traditions* (ed. Richard J. Clifford and John J. Collins; Catholic Biblical Quarterly Monograph Series 24; Washington, DC: Catholic Biblical Association of America, 1992), 63. A slightly different version of this essay was reprinted in Clifford's *Creation Accounts in the Ancient Near East and in the Bible* (Catholic Biblical Quarterly Monograph Series 26; Washington, DC: Catholic Biblical Association of America, 1994), chap. 7.

the "secure" kingdom that God promised David in the Samuel narrative (7:15–16), reflected in the recurring use of "steadfast love" and
"faithfulness" throughout the psalm, are here explained specifically in
terms of the *Chaoskampf*.[39] Not only will God defeat the king's foes,
who represent the forces of chaos (Psalm 89:20–24 [MT 89:21–25]),
but the king himself is described, in terms reminiscent of ancient Near
Eastern royal ideology, as the chosen representative of the divine on
earth. While 89:6 (MT 89:7) had claimed that none of the *heavenly* beings
could be compared to YHWH, who surpassed them all by virtue of his
conquest of primordial chaos, 89:25–27 (MT 89:26–28) suggests there
is one *on earth* who is indeed God's image (since, like God, he controls
the mythological waters). Thus YHWH says of David:

> I will set his hand on the sea
>   and his right hand on the rivers.
> He shall cry to me, "You are my Father,
>   my God, and the Rock of my salvation!"
> I will make him the firstborn,
>   the highest of the kings of the earth. (NRSV)

The king is both elevated to the status of God's chosen son and replicates in his own person the primordial victory over chaos. As Levenson
explains: "It is now the Davidic throne that guarantees cosmic stability,
the continuation of the order established through primeval combat.
In Psalm 89, as in the *Enuma elish*, the bond between the exaltation
of the deity and the imperial politics of his earthly seat of power is
patent. David is YHWH's vicar on earth."[40] Psalm 89 thus illustrates
very well the function of the creation-by-combat theme to legitimate
the monarchy, via a motif remarkably like the *imago Dei*. Indeed, the
term *highest* (*ᶜelyôn*), used of the Davidic king in 89:27 (MT 89:28),
may also indicate the ancient Near Eastern notion of the king's affin-
ity/likeness to the divine, since *ᶜelyôn* is used of God "Most High" in
Genesis 14:18, 19, 22 in connection with Melchizedek, the Canaanite
priest-king of Salem.

Likewise relevant to this theme are Psalms 2 and 110, the latter even
drawing on the Melchizedek tradition. Both are royal psalms that mention YHWH's oath or decree elevating the king to elite status. Whereas
2:7 describes the king's election or adoption as God's son ("I will tell of
the decree of the LORD: / He said to me, 'You are my son; / today I have

---

39. Whereas "steadfast love" in 2 Samuel 7:15 appears in both the singular (*ḥesed*) and
the plural (*ḥăsādîm*) in Psalm 89, "faithfulness" in Psalm 89 translates *ᵊmet*, the noun
that is cognate to "secure" (*neᵊmān*) in 2 Samuel 7:16.
40. Levenson, *Creation and the Persistence of Evil*, 22–23.

begotten you'"; NRSV), 110:4 characterizes the elect king as the high
priest of the Jerusalem cult ("the LORD has sworn and will not change his
mind, / 'You are a priest forever according to the order of Melchizedek'";
NRSV). Both psalms, furthermore, employ the combat myth (though not
explicitly in connection with creation) in order to legitimate the monarchy. They portray YHWH together with the Davidic king (as divine
father and earthly son) ruling from Zion and subduing Israel's enemies
in a joint-conquest motif.

These two royal psalms, in connection with Psalms 74 and 89, suggest
that the well-known complex of ancient Near Eastern ideas discussed
in chapter 4, concerning the mythic legitimation of human cultural
institutions (temple and monarchy) on earth, was known in ancient Israel. Even in the Bible, the combat myth—particularly when connected
to creation—could serve to ground Israel's historical exercise of cultic
and political/military power (by which the human world is ordered) in
God's primordial (violent) ordering of the cosmos.

The Ethics of Creation-by-Combat

Whereas my previous analysis of the function of the combat myth
in the ancient Near East (in chapter 4) suggests that cosmogonic conflict is ethically problematic, not all would agree with this judgment.
Levenson, for example, understands the creation-by-combat motif as
theologically and existentially profound. While his reasons are not
explicitly articulated, we may distill many interconnected points that
Levenson makes on behalf of the combat myth in *Creation and the
Persistence of Evil*.

First of all, creation-by-combat gives substance to the Bible's claim
of God's "mastery" or sovereignty by conceiving of this sovereignty in
relational terms, as the overcoming of a "worthy opponent."[41] Without
a powerful adversary, Levenson explains, God's sovereignty would be
purely formal and static. Indeed, God *needs* a formidable foe to conquer
in order to demonstrate his power.[42] Hence the phrase *Drama of Omnipotence* in the subtitle of Levenson's book precisely articulates the sense
of God's *achieved* mastery over primordial powers of evil and disorder
that Levenson thinks is crucial to the biblical concept of God.

Second, Levenson notes that the sense of the fragility of created goodness and order that accompanies the creation-by-combat motif is true

41. Ibid., xxv.
42. Ibid., 27. Note Levenson's strange attraction to Hegel's master-slave dialectic as a
way of articulating this claim (160 n. 1).

to human experience.[43] The created world is not stable, but is constantly under threat by the powers of evil, from which it must be protected. Hence biblical texts like Psalms 74 and 89 articulate the "yawning gap" between God's primordial victory over the forces of chaos and their recrudescence in the present.[44] That cosmic goodness or world order is always a provisional achievement on God's part, with evil/chaos just waiting to break through once more, testifies, in Levenson's opinion, to the realism of this ancient motif.

Putting aside, for the time being, the question whether the creation-by-combat motif best articulates either the biblical concept of a relational, sovereign God or the fragility of goodness in the created world, I will focus here on a further reason that Levenson gives for viewing the biblical creation-by-combat motif in a positive light. According to Levenson, humans are, ultimately, the prime beneficiary of the primordial exercise of divine power, in the sense that God's primordial conquest of chaos results in the elimination of threats to the historical human community. Creation-by-combat, he explains, involves "the establishment of a benevolent and life-sustaining order, founded upon the demonstrated authority of the God who is triumphant over all rivals."[45]

But this raises the question: *Whose* life is sustained by this order? Clifford points out that when the combat myth is combined (in the ancient Near East or in the Bible) with a cosmogony, the resulting cosmos is often (in his terminology) "ethnocentric."[46] Whereas a prominent feature of such cosmogonies (whether in *Enuma Elish* or the Psalms) is that they are concerned with the origin and founding of human society (a "life-sustaining order," as Levenson puts it), Clifford explains that "the society in question is not the human race as such but a particular people or nation, e.g., Babylon, Israel."[47] The world that is founded by primordial combat is thus the world of some particular group, with their own limited interests—a clear case of the "false universalism" discussed in chapter 5.[48]

43. Ibid., 49–50. The fragility of cosmic order/goodness is also encapsulated in the title of part 1 of Levenson's book ("The Mastery of God and the Vulnerability of Order") and in the subtitle to chapter 4 ("The Vitality of Evil and the Fragility of Goodness").

44. Ibid., 19.

45. Ibid., 47.

46. Clifford, "Creation in the Psalms," 59.

47. Ibid.

48. Gerhard von Rad certainly understands the ethnocentric logic of creation-by-combat when he comments that "presumptuous as it may sound, Creation is part of the aetiology of Israel!"; *Old Testament Theology*, vol. 1: *The Theology of Israel's Historical Traditions* (trans. D. M. G. Stalker; New York: Harper & Row, 1962), 138. Von Rad here draws out the theological implications of combining his assumption that creation in the Bible is fundamentally salvific (that is, involving the defeat of chaos) with his decision to read the Hexateuch (a story

Although such ethnocentrism might be relatively innocent if the group in question never encountered anyone who was different, the reality of other nations and ethnic groups with whom one must relate, and even compete, leads to the pressing question of how these groups will be understood in their relationship to each other. The consequence of defining one's own people or nation as the normative and true humanity, whose origin is traceable back to and grounded in creation itself, is that everyone else is relegated to the status of other—other than truly human, other than legitimate, other than normative—and thus regarded as inferior in status if not downright evil. Particularly when a people's national/ethnic identity is both grounded in creation and understood to be established by the conquest of chaos, then threats to this identity must be vanquished by enacting the chaos battle against one's historical competitors, who are understood as enemies of righteousness.

This means that power in the combat myth is conceived of as a zero-sum game and thus can never be shared. Since power—like cosmos or order—is treated as a finite quantity or scarce commodity, victory is always at someone else's expense. The success of one group or person thus *requires* the defeat of others. The creation-by-combat theme thus legitimates a fundamental us/them distinction, with only a win/lose alternative. Given this analysis, I suggest that Clifford's description of ancient cosmogonies founded by combat as "ethnocentric," although undoubtedly correct, is too tame. Such cosmogonies are not simply ethnocentric; they are inherently competitive, even violent and militaristic.

The Babylonian version of the combat myth (*Enuma Elish*) clearly illustrates this point, especially when its popularity in the sixth century B.C.E. is linked with the rise of the Neo-Babylonian Empire. As we have seen (in chapter 4) from Paul Ricoeur's analysis, the primordial cosmogonic violence in *Enuma Elish* functioned as the mythic legitimation of Neo-Babylonian imperial aspirations, with the king, representing the god Marduk, establishing the Babylonian Empire by vanquishing Babylon's enemies, who were regarded as the historical embodiments of primordial chaos. Through what

---

stretching from creation to land possession), rather than the Torah/Pentateuch (a story beginning with creation and ending without a settled land), as the basic canonical unit recounting Israel's founding story. If the account of creation in Genesis 1 (with which the biblical canon starts) were, indeed, an instance of the *Chaoskampf*, such that Israel's land possession constituted a mimetic, microcosmic enactment of this primordial macrocosmic victory, von Rad's summary of the function of creation might well be justified. But as we shall soon see, Genesis 1 cannot be legitimately read as an example of primordial combat. Indeed, it is possible that the exclusion of (violent) land possession (Joshua) from the first canonical unit of the Hebrew Scriptures (Torah/Pentateuch) was a necessary implication of the Genesis 1 creation account, which, as the beginning of the primeval history, functions as the etiology not just of Israel, but of *all* nations (see Genesis 10).

amounts to a theology of holy war, Babylon's defeat of its enemies was understood as reestablishing sociopolitical order in history, in imitation of Marduk's establishment of the cosmos in mythical time.[49]

Texts like Psalms 2 and 110, however, do not explicitly link the combat motif with creation, yet seem to provide divine legitimation for nationalistic (perhaps even imperial) military aspirations in ancient Israel. Such texts raise the question whether it makes any significant difference whether the combat myth is used in connection with creation or with history.[50] Does not either use suggest that violence is God's characteristic action, thus legitimating human violence in the world? Indeed, Levenson suggests that "too much can be made of the distinction between the myth *with* creation and the myth *without* creation."[51]

On the contrary, however, I think that much needs to be made of this distinction, on two counts. First of all, whereas creation-by-combat typically assumes a fundamental us/them distinction and functions to legitimate ethnocentric or even imperial aspirations, this is not a necessary feature of the myth when it is disassociated from creation.

Thus, in prophetic oracles against the nations (Egypt and Babylon, for example), the *Chaoskampf* is used to portray YHWH's judgment on these nations *without the mediation of Israel*. Perhaps more importantly, this judgment on the nations (couched in combat-myth language) follows upon YHWH's use of these very nations *to judge Israel*. This certainly suggests that the combat motif, when decoupled from a cosmology (as is typical in the Old Testament), is not always motivated by a nationalistic sensibility that exalts Israel at all costs. Indeed, Millard Lind, who examines the biblical traditions of Israel's military or political defeat at YHWH's own hand, comments that "while ancient Near Eastern nations occasionally saw their gods as fighting against their own city or nation, Israel expressed this as a continuing theological principle that ruled both her historical writing and her prophetic thought."[52] It is possible that this continuing theological principle is intrinsically connected to the relatively peripheral status of creation-by-combat in the Old Testament. Perhaps the typical decoupling of the combat myth from creation in Scripture is part and parcel of an alternative vision.[53]

49. Paul Ricoeur, *The Symbolism of Evil* (trans. Emerson Buchanan; Boston: Beacon, 1969), esp. 194–98.

50. I suggest that Psalms 2 and 110 utilize cosmogonic conflict as a background assumption, even though this is not explicitly articulated in the text of either psalm.

51. Levenson, *Creation and the Persistence of Evil*, 12 (emphasis original).

52. Millard C. Lind, *Yahweh Is a Warrior: The Theology of Warfare in Ancient Israel* (Scottdale, PA/Kitchner, ON: Herald Press, 1980), 112.

53. Bernhard W. Anderson suggests that one possible reason why the theme of creation is significantly underemphasized in the Old Testament, in contrast to its prominent place

But there is a second, and perhaps more important, reason to distinguish between the combat myth with and without creation. The use of a historicized combat myth (that is, without creation) to describe in vivid poetic language a particular historical event (like the exodus or God's judgment on various nations) makes no particular assumptions about the primordial or normative character of violence or evil. Rather, evil is treated as an intrahistorical reality, without assigning it ontological or originary status.

Creation-by-combat, by contrast, ontologizes evil, understanding it to be at least equiprimordial with God and goodness and perhaps even more primordial, as in the *Enuma Elish*, where the olden gods are the locus of chaos and where order (represented by the younger gods) is later. But not only is evil (in the form of chaos) given primordial status, the conquest of this evil/chaos to found the ordered world enshrines violence as the divinely chosen method for establishing goodness. Ricoeur's explanation is particularly illuminating:

> It will be seen what human violence is thus justified by the primordial violence. Creation is a victory over an Enemy older than the creator; that Enemy, immanent in the divine, will be represented in history by all the enemies whom the king in his turn, as servant of the god, will have as his mission to destroy. Thus Violence is inscribed in the origin of things, in the principle that establishes while it destroys.[54]

Whereas in the ancient Near East the king is authorized to enact the primordial combat in the historical present against the forces of chaos, the combat myth does not strictly require a monarchy. In the contemporary world, where human agency is more widely diffused, a democratized *imago Dei* combined with the us/them framework of the chaos-cosmos scheme may harbor significant potential for the legitimation of human violence at numerous levels.

The Function of the Combat Myth in the Contemporary World

An important exploration of the sociopolitical implications of the creation-by-combat motif in contemporary society may be found in

---

in the ancient Near Eastern worldview, is precisely that Israel needed to be weaned off of a pagan view of creation (that is, grounded in mimetic violence). By contrast, Israel's exodus faith, focusing on historical liberation from injustice, dominates the Old Testament. See *Creation versus Chaos: The Reinterpretation of Mythical Symbolism in the Bible* (1967; repr. Philadelphia: Fortress, 1987), 49–55.

54. Ricoeur, *Symbolism of Evil*, 182–83.

Pedro Trigo's profound study of creation theology from a Latin American liberation perspective.[55] In a particularly insightful section entitled "From Chaos and Cosmos to Faith in Creation,"[56] Trigo persuasively demonstrates that the same basic chaos-cosmos polarization that functioned in ancient Babylon undergirds various geopolitical and ideological splits in the contemporary world, both within and between nations and groups of nations, especially between the wealthy and the poor of the world.[57] Trigo has in mind such ideological polarizations as North-South, West-East, Capitalist-Communist, Industrialized World–Developing World, where the split replicates the chaos-cosmos scheme.[58] The key issue here is not whether there is an explicit myth of primordial combat (this is not likely in the contemporary world), but rather whether the security and well-being of one member of the polarization (cosmos) is thought to be of primary importance and is understood as fundamentally threatened in some way by the other member (chaos). The result, over time, is a sense of the fixity and inevitability of this polarization, such that identity becomes defined in terms of opposition to one's enemies.

What all contemporary versions of this chaos-cosmos polarization thus have in common with the Babylonian combat myth is that they accept the validity of the chaos-cosmos polarization as inevitable. Ultimately, this is based on a fundamentally ambivalent judgment about the nature of reality. Goodness is not understood to be primordial. "Violence is original, primordial," explains Trigo. "Chaos comes before cosmos, and abides at its heart still; therefore, it cannot be transposed."[59] The result of taking the chaos-cosmos setting as constitutive of reality is that cosmos, or righteousness, is understood to exist only in eternal struggle against chaos. "In a chaos-cosmos setting, the only salvation is a precarious one, never definitive, always under threat—and hence militant, sectarian, and self-repressive."[60]

This suggests that creation-by-combat does not constitute quite as salutary an account of the fragility of created goodness as Levenson might think. Whereas the realism of the combat myth may certainly ground impassioned prayer (supplication and even complaint, as in

55. Pedro Trigo, *Creation and History* (trans. Robert R. Barr; Theology and Liberation Series; Maryknoll, NY: Orbis, 1991).

56. Ibid., 69–110.

57. Ibid., esp. 73–79.

58. Trigo was writing before the fall of the Berlin Wall and the breakup of the Soviet Union. Today he might add polarizations such as Christian-Muslim or America (and its allies) versus those nations designated the "axis of evil" by United States President George W. Bush.

59. Ibid., 80.

60. Ibid.

Psalm 74 or 89), it leads ultimately not to gratitude for God's sustaining generosity but to profound anxiety and a sense of constant threat. The tragic result of this anxiety and sense of threat is interhuman and intrahuman violence, whether overt or systemic. Thus Trigo explains that life lived according to the chaos-cosmos scheme tends to consist in ideological and political warfare against those regarded as one's enemies, who are demonized and stripped of their humanity.[61] This is his assessment of the oppressive function of the Western, North Atlantic worldview from the perspective of the marginalized (those identified with chaos) in Latin America.

Walter Wink, in an important study of the social power of evil, likewise elaborates on the function of the combat myth—which he terms "the myth of redemptive violence"—to legitimate both the national security state and a "spirituality of militarism," not only in ancient Babylon, but also in the contemporary world, where nations seek to subdue or exterminate their competitors.[62] Wink insightfully illustrates the presence of this myth throughout American popular culture, characterizing it as "the original religion of the status quo, the first articulation of 'might makes right.'"[63]

Catherine Keller even links the combat myth with the oppression of women.[64] In a stimulating section of her insightful *From a Broken Web*, she exposes what she takes to be an ontology of violence implicit in the traditional conception of the God-creation relationship found throughout Western history, from Aristotle through the Bible to contemporary Judaism and Christianity.[65] Keller understands the typical conception of the God-creation relationship as encoding the "separable," active, heroic male ego as the divine, normative element (God) in a religious worldview, in contradistinction to the nondivine element that is characteristically understood as female, passive, and inferior or evil (creation).

Here it is significant that Keller understands the (typically male) active ego to require a "monstrous" opposite (typically identified as female) that must be subjugated,[66] much as Levenson claims that God needs a worthy opponent to subdue in order to demonstrate his mastery.[67]

61. Ibid., 80–84.

62. Walter Wink, "The Myth of the Domination System," in his *Engaging the Powers: Discernment and Resistance in a World of Domination* (Minneapolis: Fortress, 1992), 13–31.

63. Ibid., 16.

64. Catherine Keller, *From a Broken Web: Separation, Sexism, and Self* (Boston: Beacon, 1986).

65. This is the burden of Keller's argument; ibid., 47–92.

66. Ibid., 78, 79, and passim.

67. Levenson, *Creation and the Persistence of Evil*, xxv, 27, 140, 160 n. 1.

Noting that women are often associated with nature and matter in Western history (hence the well-known double entendre of "matrix"),[68] Keller claims that the traditional model of God's transcendent, sovereign relationship of *power over* the world typically serves to legitimate the heroic-matricidal impulse, that is, (divine) male domination of (monstrous) female/nature.

Keller explicitly links this *power over* relationship to the combat myth, drawing on Ricoeur's analysis of its problematic ethical implications, with one caveat. While utilizing Ricoeur's insight into the connection between a violent myth of origins (such as *Enuma Elish*) and continuing historical violence (as in Babylonian imperialism), Keller critiques Ricoeur for conveniently ignoring "that the primordial enemy [in *Enuma Elish*] is a woman and that the cosmos established by her destruction is not accidentally a patriarchy."[69] Keller then analyzes the oppressive patriarchal social structures of ancient Greece and Mesopotamia and locates their ideological roots in paradigmatic Greek and Mesopotamian myths of a heroic male god's primordial slaying and dismemberment of a female monster (whether Greek Medusa or Babylonian Tiamat, to give two of the most famous examples) in order to found the world: "Huge pieces of history begin to fall into place: it is the heroic-matricidal impulse that provides the common denominator of the misogyny of Greece and of the Near and Middle East."[70] While Keller wrongly (in my opinion) claims to discern this same impulse (that is, the combat myth) in the creation account of Genesis 1, she insightfully links the logic of creation-by-combat (in which chaos is violently suppressed) with the long history of the marginalization and suffering of women within the patriarchal religious traditions of Judaism and Christianity, a history that continues right up to the present.[71]

It would be a mistake, however, to limit the attraction of the combat myth to those who actually hold power, who want to protect their

68. On the relationship between the oppression of women and the environmental crisis, see Susan Griffin, *Woman and Nature: The Roaring inside Her* (New York: Harper & Row, 1978).

69. Keller, *From a Broken Web*, 77.

70. Ibid., 86.

71. Ibid., 73–92. Keller, who is not a biblical scholar, simply follows the traditional misreading of Gunkel by comparing *Enuma Elish* with Genesis 1 and claiming to see a submerged, more subtle *Chaoskampf* motif in Genesis 1 (in the course of her comparison, she makes much of *tĕhôm*, which is cognate with *tiʾāmat*, being feminine in Genesis 1:2). Significantly, Keller comes to read Genesis 1 quite differently in her more recent book, *The Face of the Deep: A Theology of Becoming* (London: Routledge, 2003), where she treats *tĕhôm* not as a primordial enemy to be suppressed, but as the plethora of possibilities that God will draw upon to create.

own privileged status from outside threats (a possible implication of the analysis so far). Susan Wendell is surely correct that the power differential between groups means that not everyone's exclusionary and oppressive practices have equal weight since "one group of people may have more power to call itself the paradigm of humanity and to make the world suit its own needs and validate its own experiences."[72] Nevertheless, we need to consider that the violent suppression of otherness can be rooted not only in an attempt to protect one's existing privilege but also in an attempt to exact recompense for being victimized and disenfranchised by those in power.

Thus Trigo explains that along with legitimating the violence of those in power, the combat myth is a pervasive temptation for marginalized groups seeking liberation from oppression. Trigo suggests that it is a particular temptation of some base communities and liberation theologians in Latin America "to 'buy' the chaos-versus-cosmos schema, and simply throw in our lot with the excluded, chaotic member."[73] In this left-wing version of the myth, the terms of the schema undergo what we might call a Nietzschean "transvaluation of values,"[74] resulting in the valorization of the chaotic marginalized and the demonization of those who stand for false order.[75] The tragic result of this reversal of the chaos-cosmos scheme is the legitimation of perpetual revolution and continued violence, indeed terror, in the name of the never-ending liberation struggle.

The most obvious examples of this commitment to perpetual violence in the world today can be found in radical Islamic movements (such as al-Qaeda, Hamas, or Islamic Jihad) that utilize terrorist methods—including suicide bombings—in a total war against perceived enemies. Whether such violence is a function of valorizing the pole of chaos or of putting oneself in the place of the enemy as the custodian of cosmos and the exemplar of true humanity (or some inconsistent combination of the two), it is clearly rooted in an oppositional definition of one's own identity (which demonizes the enemy) and is often connected to a deep and pervasive sense of victimization and disenfranchisement.

Even with the case of violence directed at perceived rivals by those who actually hold power, a sense of prior victimization is often a mo-

72. Susan Wendell, "Towards a Theory of Disability," *Hypatia* 4 (1989): 112.

73. Trigo, *Creation and History*, 79.

74. In *Beyond Good and Evil*, Friedrich Nietzsche referred to the transvaluation (or revaluation or inversion) of values effected in the past by Christianity (chap. 3, §46) and Judaism (chap. 5, §195) and of the future transvaluation of values he himself looked forward to (chap. 5, §203).

75. Trigo, *Creation and History*, 80, 86.

tivating factor. Prominent examples of this at the end of the twentieth century include so-called ethnic cleansing in the Balkans (perpetuated by the Bosnian government) and tribal warfare in various African nations (such as the violence against minority Tutsis by the Hutu-led government in Rwanda). In each case, some cultural or ethnic group, often barely distinguishable (by outsiders) from other similar groups, having nurtured a long-term and deeply rooted memory of oppression, attempts to use its newfound status or power to eradicate its perceived oppressors, while conveniently disenfranchising them of full humanity.

But beyond movements or groups that advocate explicit physical violence directed against enemies, increasing numbers of politically conservative Christians in the United States use triumphalistic language about Christian "conquest" of America in God's name. Although many American Christians combine such triumphalistic language (inconsistently) with an otherworldly eschatology of escape to heaven, a significant minority movement within conservative American Christianity known as Theonomy or Christian Reconstruction uses such language to advocate the "reconstruction" of America as an Old Testament theocracy, with full implementation of Mosaic laws and sanctions, in the service of a postmillennial eschatology of this-worldly progress.[76] Reconstructionist David Chilton actually combines triumphalistic language of conquest with a royal-functional interpretation of the *imago Dei* in Genesis 1. Thus he exhorts Christians in the dominant secular culture of America: "We must stop acting as if we are forever destined to be a sub-culture. *We are destined for dominion*; we should straighten up and start acting like it."[77] Chilton clearly connects this reference to dominion with the *imago Dei* when he goes on to write: "We are the shapers of world history. God has remade us in His image for world dominion . . . and commissioned us to take over the world."[78]

As if such conquest language were not troubling enough, some prominent members of the Reconstructionist movement actually advocate the Christian use of imprecatory psalms in public worship, for the explicit purpose of calling upon God to eliminate abortion doc-

76. On the Reconstructionist movement, see the helpful summary in Rodney Clapp, *The Reconstructionists* (2nd ed.; Downers Grove, IL: InterVarsity, 1990). The two most central texts for this movement are Rousas John Rushdoony's *Institutes of Biblical Law* (Nutley, NJ: Craig Press, 1973) and Greg L. Bahnsen's *Theonomy in Christian Ethics* (Nutley, NJ: Craig Press, 1977).
77. David Chilton, *Paradise Regained: A Biblical Theology of Dominion* (Tyler, TX: Reconstruction Press, 1985), 218 (emphasis original).
78. Ibid., 219. It is indeed ironic that these comments come in a chapter entitled "The Great Commission."

tors, gay-rights activists, and liberal politicians and judges, often by name, since as enemies of righteousness they do not deserve to live. Thus Chilton explains that "church officers must pronounce sentence against oppressors, and Christians must follow this up by faithful prayers that the oppressors will either repent or be destroyed."[79] The dehumanization of the other that characterizes such a practice, as well as the aggressive language about taking back America found among many conservative Christians, is rooted in the oppositional sense of identity that derives from the chaos-cosmos scheme and is fueled by the perception of being a righteous remnant under attack by the forces of evil.[80]

The Problem of Genuine Ideology Critique in Genesis 1

It is thus troubling that Batto draws upon precisely this oppositional sense of identity in his proposal that Genesis 1 (in which he claims to discern the combat myth) was intended to address Israel's sense of injustice and disenfranchisement during the Babylonian exile. Assuming a sixth-century date for the text, Batto suggests that "within an exilic Israelite community, still in shock over their world being turned topsy-turvy by the superior, infidel Babylonian Empire,"[81] the use of the combat myth by Genesis 1 was "intended to offer hope to discouraged Israelites that Israel's god is the divine sovereign who slays the chaos dragon whenever and wherever it reappears: what he did to Pharaoh and his Egyptian hosts, he will do again to their infidel Babylonian masters."[82]

If Genesis 1 did, indeed, contain a version of the combat myth, it must be admitted that this reading of the existential function of the text would be historically plausible. Whether or not we assume an exilic context for Genesis 1, creation-by-combat could have provided a ready vehicle for Israel's ideology critique. Instead of simply accepting the claims of Mesopotamian ideology, in which Israel would have been identified with the pole of chaos in the chaos-cosmos schema, Israel could accept the basic schema while reversing its poles, thus identifying

79. Ibid., 216. Similar comments, in the context of a particular conflict between church members and the American government, may be found in the sermon by Ray Sutton entitled "Imprecatory Praying (Psalm 83)," available on an audiotape distributed by Still Waters Revival Books, Edmonton, AB, Canada.

80. However, as Ernest Becker insightfully warns, with even the best of intentions, we may "cause evil by heroically wanting to triumph over it"; *Escape from Evil* (New York: Free Press, 1975), 51.

81. Batto, "Creation Theology in Genesis," 32.

82. Ibid., 34.

themselves with cosmos, order, or righteousness (grounded in creation) and understanding Babylon as aligned with the forces of chaos. Just as Babylonian ideology understood Marduk, represented by the Babylonian king, as subduing the enemies of Babylon (which, during the exile, came to include Israel), an Israelite version of the chaos-cosmos scheme might replace Marduk with YHWH, who subdues the forces of chaos embodied in the evil Babylonian Empire. That this historical possibility is not at all farfetched is suggested by the god Ashur replacing Marduk in his role as conqueror of Tiamat and king of the gods (reflecting the era of Neo-Assyrian ascendancy in the ancient Near East) in some extant Assyrian versions of *Enuma Elish*. Could Israel, in attempting to resist or polemicize against Babylonian ideology, have adopted the Babylonian creation-by-combat motif, simply replacing Marduk with the biblical God?

The very plausibility of Batto's reading of Genesis 1 suggests that the ethical questions I have raised concerning creation-by-combat cannot be reduced to a function of contemporary sensibilities (though they certainly are that). These questions are also rooted in critical reflection on the historical options open to ancient Israel. Whereas I argued in chapter 5 that the biblical *imago Dei* affirms human dignity and agency in the face of a dehumanizing Mesopotamian ideology, the temptation to passive acquiescence in a subservient, victim identity would not have been the only challenge to Israel's self-understanding presented by Mesopotamia. A second, and equally significant, challenge arising from the confrontation with Mesopotamian ideology would be the temptation to assert a heroic, violent identity *in opposition to* the subservient status of humanity in Mesopotamia.

Another way to put the historical issue is to note that Mesopotamian ideology presented Israel with the alternatives of assimilation or resistance. In opting for resistance, however, the relevant question is what form this resistance would take. The trouble with using the combat myth—especially in combination with the *imago Dei*—to resist or polemicize against Mesopotamian ideology is that it would turn Israel into a mirror image of its enemy, with the very real danger of reduplicating Babylonian or Assyrian violence. Not only would the *imago Dei* in Genesis 1 constitute a prime example of false universalism (since the text does not mention Israel specifically, but rather speaks of *humanity* as the image of God), but the biblical *imago Dei* could well function to legitimate an oppressive wielding of power on the part of Israel, parallel to the tyrannical power and privilege granted the Mesopotamian king by virtue of his kinship with the gods. Especially when the *imago Dei* is grounded in the combat myth, the one in the divine image (the king or Israel) simply replicates or embodies the primordial violence of the myth on the plane of history against those regarded as enemies.

The implication of the above analysis is that although Israel's use of creation-by-combat to resist Mesopotamian ideology might initially seem attractive to a minority people in the face of a powerful empire, this resistance would turn out to be quite superficial. In their very attempt to resist and critique Mesopotamian ideology, the biblical writers would, paradoxically, have appropriated this ideology as their own.[83] Thus, if Genesis 1 indeed harbored a *Chaoskampf* motif, the text would simply replace one form of ideology (in the pejorative sense) with another. Rather than providing a genuine alternative worldview, this resistance by appropriation would actually reinforce the depth of the victory of Mesopotamian definitions of reality. The point is that violent resistance to a myth of violence is not true resistance. It is, on the contrary, capitulation to that very myth. Thus if Genesis 1 did utilize some version of the chaos-cosmos scheme to articulate God's creation of the world, this would seal the ideological triumph of Mesopotamia.[84]

Since both passive acquiescence in victimhood and violent resistance are forms of assimilation to Babylon, we need a *tertium quid*, a third option that goes beyond these false alternatives. This means that providing an alternative to the Mesopotamian answer to the "who are we?" worldview question is only a half-step for Genesis 1. Of crucial importance is that the text's answer to the question of human identity (*imago Dei*) be accompanied by a radically distinctive answer to the "where are we?" question as well (the question of the world in which

---

83. I argue that this is exactly what happened in the case of Rastafarian reggae artist Peter Tosh. Not only do Tosh's songs critique "Babylon" (symbolizing the power of postcolonial racism, oppression, and injustice in the world) by recourse to a version of the chaos-cosmos scheme, in which Tosh is aligned with God as creator and his victory over Babylon is rooted in creation, but Tosh as a person became increasingly prone to paranoia and suspicion of others, seeing enemies and opponents everywhere, right up until the time of his tragic murder in 1987. See J. Richard Middleton, "Identity and Subversion in Babylon: Strategies for 'Resisting against the System' in the Music of Bob Marley and the Wailers," in *Religion, Culture, and Tradition in the Caribbean* (ed. Hemchand Gossai and Nathaniel Samuel Murrell; New York: St. Martin's, 2000), 194–96.

84. Alice Ogden Bellis makes a similar point in a review of Martin Kessler's *Battle of the Gods: The God of Israel versus Marduk of Babylon: A Literary/Theological Interpretation of Jeremiah 50–51* (Studia semitica neerlandica 42; Assen: Van Gorcum, 2003). Commenting on what she considers the author's overblown (and unsubstantiated) contrast of YHWH and Marduk, especially his dismissive imputation of hubris to Marduk, Bellis notes that "it seems inequitable to condemn the pride of Babylon's gods while engaging in proud contempt for the Babylonian god Marduk. . . . Such hubris is more in line with what is condemned in Jer 50–51"; *Review of Biblical Literature* (2004), http://www.bookreviews.org; accessed July 3, 2004.

we live).[85] In the face of a dehumanizing and violent Mesopotamian ideology, what Genesis 1 especially needs to articulate for ancient Israel (and for us as contemporary readers) is a conception of the God-creation relationship distinct from creation-by-combat that can ground normative, nonviolent human agency.

The Reframing of the Chaos-Cosmos Scheme in Genesis 1

It is significant that Trigo, who has seen firsthand the oppressive effects of the combat myth in Latin America, posits what he calls an "atheism with respect to the divinity of the chaos-cosmos setting."[86] As a matter of principle, he declares, "I cannot assign the name reality to what my faith tells me is a distortion of reality."[87] Acknowledging that reality is, indeed, often *experienced* in terms of chaos-cosmos polarizations, Trigo is, nevertheless, unwilling to grant this experience primordial or sacred status, explaining that "we cannot accept that this polarized setting should express the original constitution of reality. Consequently, neither can we place ourselves at either term of any of these polarizations."[88]

Instead, the entire chaos-cosmos framework must be challenged. The only adequate answer to this false ideological polarization, says Trigo, is faith in God as creator, particularly as articulated in Genesis 1. The opening canonical creation story, explains Trigo, provides a normative vision of the world that can "break the spell" of the chaos-cosmos scheme.[89]

It has long been recognized by biblical scholars that the creation account in Genesis 1 draws on ancient Near Eastern—especially Mesopotamian—creation motifs, many of which are found in *Enuma Elish*. It is crucial to note, however, that the text draws on these motifs in such a manner as to articulate a radically distinctive vision of reality. In this vision, God's relationship to the world is understood as predating the origin of violence (which is portrayed as beginning with human disobedience in Genesis 3). Although not all biblical scholars believe that Genesis 1 is intentionally polemical (against either *Enuma Elish* or the combat myth), I believe that my prior reading of the primeval history

85. See my previous discussion of these questions at the end of chapter 5.
86. Trigo, *Creation and History*, 84.
87. Ibid., xviii.
88. Ibid., 81. Contrast this with Levenson's claim that the continuing experience of violence and oppression throughout history *appropriately* fuels the power of the combat myth; *Creation and the Persistence of Evil*, 49–50.
89. Trigo, *Creation and History*, 84.

as a critique of Mesopotamian ideology renders it eminently plausible that the text proposes a critical alternative to creation-by-combat, which was part and parcel of this ideology. Indeed, a close reading of Genesis 1 discloses three crucial dimensions of this creation account that directly contradict the *Chaoskampf* theme.

The first dimension of the account that contradicts the *Chaoskampf* is the role given to the traditional chaotic elements from the ancient Near Eastern combat myths. The primordial ocean (*tĕhôm*) in Genesis 1:2 and the waters on the second and third days of creation are not portrayed as God's mythological enemies. Indeed, it is somewhat reductionistic to refer to the primordial waters in Genesis 1 as chaos, since this term has become so freighted with the notion of that which resists God's will. In Genesis 1, the deep is no threat, and so God does not need to fight it, though God does separate or divide the waters for various cosmic structures to emerge.[90]

But not only are the waters thoroughly demythologized in Genesis 1, so are the sea monsters or dragons (*tannînîm*) in 1:21. Although *tannîn* (in the singular or plural) is often paired with Leviathan or Rahab in biblical poetic texts and treated as YHWH's mythological adversary, this is certainly not the meaning of the term in Genesis 1. On the contrary, the *tannînîm* are explicitly said to be created (*bārā'*) by God, which directly contradicts the typical role of the primordial forces of chaos in the combat myth. This vision of the dragons as part of God's peaceable kingdom has affinities to Psalm 104, which says that YHWH formed (*yāṣar*) Leviathan to sport or play with (104:26).[91] To use Gunkel's words, the sea monsters in Genesis 1 are "transformed into a remarkable sort of fish, which is to be included among the other created beings."[92]

The second dimension of the Genesis text that clearly distinguishes it from creation-by-combat is the decided ease with which God creates, in contrast to Marduk's bloody struggle against a primordial enemy. This ease is suggested by the immediate and unproblematic response of creatures to God's commanding fiats. The typical pattern of divine command (for example, "let there be light" or "let the waters be separated") followed by an execution report ("and there was light," or "and it was so") pictures God as encountering no resistance in creating the world. God commands, and creation obeys God's every word. To put it

90. In Keller's words, the deep is simply "a matrix of possibilities," the raw materials from which God elicits the created order; *Face of the Deep*, 169.

91. As Levenson puts it (citing one of his students), the feared primordial sea monster of ancient Near Eastern mythology is pictured in Psalm 104 as the biblical God's "rubber ducky"; *Creation and the Persistence of Evil*, 17.

92. Gunkel, "Influence of Babylonian Mythology," 49.

differently, God rules willing subjects, who do not have to be coerced or subdued to his will.

Indeed, this is a ruler who does not command so much as *invite* creatures to respond to his will. This invitational character of God's creative fiats is indicated by their not being imperatives at all, but Hebrew jussives (which have no exact counterpart in English).[93] As Eugene Roop explains, the force of the Hebrew jussive can range "from the very strong (almost a command) to the very soft (almost a wish)" and "always possesses a voluntary element."[94] Whether we read the rhetorical intent of these jussives more traditionally as God's commands, on analogy with the sovereign decrees of a king (to which there is no resistance but the willing submission of creatures), or, following Walter Brueggemann, as God's gracious "summons" or "permission" for creatures to exist,[95] we are certainly very far removed from the *Chaoskampf* motif. In Roop's words: "Creation comes by divine direction, not by a dictator's demand."[96] The ease of creation—indicated both by the jussives and by the immediate compliance of creatures—is a prominent rhetorical feature of Genesis 1, reflected even in the gentle, repetitive cadences of the text, which progressively builds to a climax, but unlike a genuine narrative contains not a trace of plot tension or resolution (that is, there is no evil to be resisted or overcome).[97]

The third rhetorical indicator that differentiates Genesis 1 from the combat myth is God's evaluation of each stage of the creative process as "good" (*ṭôb*) and in 1:31 of the entire finished product as "very good"

93. Whereas the Hebrew imperfect is typically used for permanent decrees or standing orders (such as "you shall do x" or "you shall not do x," as found in the Decalogue), the imperative is typically used for a specific injunction addressed to a particular person at a given point in time. Morphologically, the jussive is usually a contracted or short form of the imperfect, but its function is similar to the imperative in that it does not usually articulate a permanent order, but an encouragement to act on a particular occasion.

94. Eugene F. Roop, *Genesis* (Believers Bible Commentary; Scottdale, PA/Kitchner, ON: Herald, 1987), 27.

95. Walter Brueggemann, *Genesis* (Interpretation; Atlanta: John Knox, 1982), 30.

96. Roop, *Genesis*, 27.

97. The jussives fit with Keller's suggestion that creation in Genesis 1 does not portray God mastering chaos, but rather as soliciting its virtual forms. "Such solicitation," she comments, "when expressed as divine speech, may sound less like command than a seduction" (*Face of the Deep*, 115). "Might the imperatives [that is, jussives] metabolize into such suggestive theograms as John Macquarie's divine 'letting be,' John Cobb's 'lure' to creative transformation, Rita Nakashima Brock's 'divine Eros'?" (116). Keller's characterization of the creative process in Genesis 1 is far removed from her earlier claim to "see a subtle belligerence at work behind the serene transcendence of the priestly scenario" (*From a Broken Web*, 86) or her charge that the text reflects *Enuma Elish* to such an extent that "the brutal cosmocrat Marduk bequeaths his patrimony to the Hebrew creator" (87).

(*ṭôb měʾōd*). The word *ṭôb* has in this context at least a twofold connotation, esthetic and ethical. The cosmos is good in two senses: it is
both pleasing to God, as a beautiful, well-constructed world, and it is
evaluated positively since it enacts God's will (and is not recalcitrant
or rebellious).[98]

Thus Day explains that, in contrast to a primordial battle, creation in
Genesis 1 is simply "a job of work."[99] God is pictured here not as warrior,
but as craftsman or artisan. Or, in Levenson's terms, this is "creation
without opposition."[100] On this point, nothing could be further removed
from *Enuma Elish*, which is filled with bloody battles between the gods
(culminating in Marduk's dismembering of Tiamat). The prominence
of the creation-by-combat theme in *Enuma Elish* represents primal
evil as a constitutive dimension of the cosmos, which has always to be
violently repressed that it might not overwhelm the fragile cosmic order
imposed by the gods.

Genesis 1 as a Normative Framework

Beyond providing an alternative to the devaluation of human status
as found in Mesopotamian ideology, then, Genesis 1 articulates an alternative to the violent cosmogony of the chaos-cosmos scheme. Whereas
the text's anthropological alternative of humanity as the image of God
functions as a distinctive answer to the question of human identity ("who
are we?"), the text's theological or cosmological vision, which portrays
an originally good creation, functions as a distinctive answer to the
broader question of world or context ("where are we?") Both levels of
the alternative vision of Genesis 1 are necessary to provide a genuine
alternative to Mesopotamian ideology. Indeed, the vision of human
identity proposed in Genesis 1 is inadequate (even dangerous) without
being framed by the nonviolent vision of the God-creation relationship
articulated in the text. The full-fledged ideology critique of Genesis 1, in
other words, consists not simply in an exalted vision of human identity
and agency, but one grounded in a larger vision of the world as God's
good creation. Together, this two-pronged ideology critique calls for all
humanity (including Israel) to exercise power differently from anything
implied by cosmogonic conflict.

98. These dimensions of *ṭôb* correspond to the two primary images of God as artisan
and ruler (see chapter 2).

99. Day, *God's Conflict with the Dragon and the Sea*, 1, 49, 52, 61.

100. This is the title of Levenson's chapter on Psalm 104 (*Creation and the Persistence
of Evil*, 53–65), a phrase that he also uses to characterize the Genesis 1 creation account
(127).

If a theology of holy war (with disastrous implications for human oppression) grows naturally out of the worldview articulated by creation-by-combat (that is, evil is primordial chaos, while goodness, represented by cosmic order, is later, founded by the vanquishing of chaos), it becomes evident that a creation that is originally "very good" would sustain an entirely different sort of historical action.

The sort of historical action implicated in the vision of Genesis 1 is well illustrated by contrasting comments made by Trigo and Levenson about how evil is to be treated. Commenting on the implications of the combat myth, Levenson claims that it is a mistake to regard goodness as basic to all that exists. Rather, he explains, "Some things exist that ought not to, and these deserve to be blasted from the world."[101] Levenson is, admittedly, writing before the terrorist attacks of September 11, 2001, and his comment is about God's (not our) eradication of evil. Nevertheless, despite his best intentions, Levenson's comment is alarming because it could easily be used by religious fundamentalists, whether Christian or Islamic, as a warrant for violence, or even terrorism. It is certainly rooted, as he himself recognizes, in the logic of the chaos-cosmos scheme, which requires that all threats to the fragility of cosmic order be suppressed or eliminated.[102]

While Trigo does not deny the reality of the struggle against historical evil, he nevertheless claims that the goodness of the "almighty-God-with-us" (his phrase) is more primordial than either evil or the struggle against evil.[103] And to illustrate that the *us* in the above phrase must not be understood in a narrow, partisan, or ethnocentric manner (but in some sense must include even our historical opponents), Trigo makes what is a remarkable claim for a liberation theologian writing in the 1980s. He explains that Ronald Reagan (then president of the United States), although justly denounced for the violence he perpetrated in various Latin American countries, is nevertheless "a person for whom one ought to pray"—he is even "a candidate for salvation."[104]

Trigo can make this claim because he distinguishes radically between, on the one hand, creation as the conquest of chaos (a salvific event), which demonizes and absolutizes two sides of a historical struggle, and, on the other, normative biblical creation faith, which

101. Ibid., xxiv.
102. My comments here are not meant as a repudiation of Jon Levenson, a biblical scholar for whom I have the utmost respect and whose work has been very valuable to me (otherwise I myself would be guilty of utilizing the combat myth for polemical purposes). But I do think it is legitimate to point out possible undesirable consequences of a theological position, esp. in a chapter on ethics.
103. Trigo, *Creation and History*, 84.
104. Ibid., 86–87.

relativizes both sides of this struggle vis-à-vis the sovereign and transcendent creator. It becomes evident, then, that the contrasting ways in which the struggle against evil is articulated in Levenson and Trigo stem from the divergent models of creation that they take to be normative. These models not only appeal to different biblical portrayals of God's power, but have significantly different ethical implications for humanity made in God's image. It is the divergent ethical implications of these models that lead Brueggemann, who is typically highly suspicious of Old Testament creation theology,[105] to nuance his suspicion by acknowledging the "important distinction between 'creation-chaos' and creation as a transcendent reference that destabilizes all ideological claims."[106]

Yet, granted that Genesis 1 constitutes a distinctive creation account without cosmogonic conflict, what are we to make of the undeniable fact of creation-by-combat texts in the biblical canon? Do not such texts (even the few I have admitted) constitute a compromised vision of reality—one that is in tension with the cosmogony of Genesis 1?

In addressing this question, canonical readers of Scripture ought to face squarely the presence of cosmogonic conflict in those texts where it genuinely occurs. Indeed, we need to confront the overwhelming violence that pervades the Bible—from the widespread patriarchal social structure and assumptions that underlie the biblical text (which certainly constitutes a form of systemic violence against women) through the holy wars of Israel against the Canaanites (at God's command), to the plethora of violent incidents attributed to God's people in the historical books or to God directly (including eschatological violence). It simply does no one any good to ignore texts and themes in the Bible that one may experience as difficult, even repugnant. The avoidance of reality is not a biblical value. On the contrary, the very existence of troubling texts in the biblical canon is testimony to its realism.

The question for us as contemporary readers, however, is what we are to make of such violence. I propose that as we enter the ongoing canonical dialogue between biblical texts that seem to be in tension and grapple with much that is ethically problematic in the pages of Scripture (including cosmogonic conflict), we take seriously the placement of Genesis 1 as the prologue or preface to the biblical canon. Gerhard von Rad's famous comment that the canonical placement of Genesis 1 is a

105. For my analysis and critique of this suspicion, see J. Richard Middleton, "Is Creation Theology Inherently Conservative? A Dialogue with Walter Brueggemann," *Harvard Theological Review* 87 (1994): 257–77.
106. Walter Brueggemann, "Response to J. Richard Middleton," *Harvard Theological Review* 87 (1994): 284.

mere "circumstance" with no theological significance must be rejected.[107] Even Levenson, who initially claims that we should not "overstress" the significance of Genesis 1,[108] since he thinks that the *Chaoskampf* is the standard biblical way of depicting God's sovereignty, is constrained to admit that the opening biblical creation account (which does not contain cosmogonic conflict) "now serves as the overture to the entire Bible, dramatically relativizing the other cosmogonies."[109]

But Genesis 1 does not just relativize the creation-by-combat motif. Rather, by its alternative depiction of God's nonviolent creative power at the start of the biblical canon, the text signals the creator's original intent for shalom and blessing at the outset of human history, prior to the rise of human (or divine) violence. As the opening canonical disclosure of God for readers of Scripture, Genesis 1 constitutes a normative framework by which we may judge all the violence that pervades the rest of the Bible (including, but not limited to, texts of cosmogonic conflict). It also provides a framework for judging human violence in the contemporary world (including violence perpetuated in the name of religion) since such violence stands in direct contradiction to the disclosure of God's power in Genesis 1. How this disclosure constitutes a positive paradigm or model for the exercise of human historical power in a world filled with violence is the topic of the next chapter.

107. Gerhard von Rad, "The Theological Problem of the Old Testament Doctrine of Creation" (trans. E. W. T. Dicken), in *Creation in the Old Testament* (ed. Bernhard W. Anderson; Issues in Religion and Theology 6; Philadelphia: Fortress, 1984), 54.
108. Levenson, *Creation and the Persistence of Evil*, 5–6.
109. Ibid., 100.

7

Imaging God's Primal Generosity

This study began by exploring the meaning of the *imago Dei* in its immediate literary context and wider symbolic world (part 1) and then investigated Mesopotamian ideology as a plausible social context of the image to see what further light this context would shed on its meaning (part 2). The last chapter (the beginning of part 3) addressed the ethical question of whether the *imago Dei* might be implicated in the legitimation of violence, including whether Genesis 1 contains an implicit combat myth. Although it might seem appropriate now simply to restate my conclusions and bring the discussion to an end, I am going to take the risk of pressing toward a further ethical question that is yet unanswered, but that is directly relevant to this project.

Granted that God is portrayed in Genesis 1 as both artisan and ruler (as we saw in chapter 2), bringing into being a wisely crafted world through the exercise of royal power, and granted, further, that Genesis 1 does not harbor a version of the combat myth, but instead portrays God's relationship to the created order in fundamentally nonviolent terms, we still need an ethical analysis of the *positive* characterization of God's rule in Genesis 1. If for no other reason than that the human

vocation is modeled on the creator rhetorically portrayed in Genesis 1,
it is imperative for us to explore more fully the sort of creative power
the text depicts God as exercising. As Walter Brueggemann insightfully
puts it, "We are indeed made in the image of some God. And perhaps
we have no more important theological investigation than to discern
in whose image we have been made."[1] Indeed, says Brueggemann,
"our discernment of God has remarkable sociological [read, ethical]
implications."[2]

Creation as the Unilateral Imposition of Transcendent Will

But this exploration of how God is rhetorically depicted in Genesis 1
is important also because significant ethical objections have been raised
against the model of God's relationship to the created order typically
associated with the opening biblical creation story—even when this is
distinguished from the combat myth. Central among these objections
is the widespread contemporary notion that Genesis 1 is at the root of
the environmental crisis.

The popularity of this claim stems primarily from the famous 1967
article by Christian historian Lynn White Jr. entitled "The Historical
Roots of Our Ecologic Crisis."[3] Similar critiques have, however, been
widely proposed, most notably by historian Arnold Toynbee, Buddhist
philosopher Daisetz T. Suzuki, cultural critic Theodore Roszak, and
scientists Ian MacHarg and David Suzuki (among many others).[4] It
has now become popular wisdom to make the historical claim that the
modern environmental crisis, which is the direct result of the exploitative
stance toward nature characteristic of modern, Western science, can
be traced back to the culture of Western Christianity in which modern

1. Walter Brueggemann, *The Prophetic Imagination* (2nd ed.; Minneapolis: Fortress,
2001), 8.
2. Ibid.
3. Lynn White Jr., "The Historical Roots of Our Ecologic Crisis," *Science* 155 (March
10, 1967): 1203–7, repr. in Wesley Granberg-Michaelson, *Ecology and Life: Accepting Our
Environmental Responsibility* (Waco: Word, 1988), 125–37.
4. Arnold Toynbee, in *The Toynbee-Ikeda Dialogue* (Tokyo: Kodansha, 1976); Daisetz
T. Suzuki, "The Role of Nature in Zen Buddhism, *Eranos-Jahrbuch* 22 (1953): 292; Theodore
Roszak, *Where the Wasteland Ends* (Garden City, NY: Doubleday, 1972); Ian MacHarg,
"The Plight," in *The Environmental Crisis: Man's Struggle to Live with Himself* (ed. Harold
Helfrich; New Haven: Yale University Press, 1970); and David Suzuki, *Subdue the Earth*,
the third video in *A Planet for the Taking*, an eight-part series produced by the Canadian
Broadcasting Corporation (1986). For a wide survey of this critique in recent literature,
see Cameron Wybrow's excellent study, *The Bible, Baconianism, and Mastery over Nature:
The Old Testament and Its Modern Misreading* (New York: Peter Lang, 1991), esp. 3–35.

science arose. This culture, notes White, was informed paradigmatically by the creation story in Genesis 1.

Two dimensions of this overall critique are especially relevant for our consideration. First, White and company claim that nature (the nonhuman creation) is devalued and desacralized as an inert object, related to God only extrinsically in the Bible (and especially in Genesis 1), which thus makes it available for human manipulation and exploitation. According to White, the biblical worldview not only understood God as absolutely transcendent, but effectively exorcized all spiritual or divine powers from the natural realm, with the result that "the old inhibitions to the exploitation of nature crumbled."[5] Thus Ronald Reagan, then governor of California, is cited by White as a latter-day inheritor of this worldview, when he reduces nature to mere physical facticity in his famous comment: "When you've seen one redwood tree, you've seen them all."[6]

Second, White claims that this reductive "denaturing" of creation is compounded by the creation of humans in the image and likeness of God, granted a mandate of limitless dominion over the nonhuman creatures, charged to subdue the earth in God's name. Thus humans "share, in great measure, God's transcendence of nature," says White, and the biblical creation account teaches that "no item in the physical creation had any purpose save to serve man's purposes."[7] Together, this picture of a desacralized cosmos, a transcendent God, and an elevated human status reveals a hierarchical dualism of God and humans on the one side and nature on the other, thus legitimating human coercive domination of nature, in imitation of God's primordial coercive relation to the natural world.[8] What is perhaps most crucial for our discussion is that God's extrinsic, over-against relationship to the world (a relationship characterized by the unilateral exercise of absolute power over, on God's part) gives humans (in the divine image) license to appropriate and exploit the world as the "masters and possessors of nature" (to use René Descartes's famous phrase).[9]

5. White, "Historical Roots of Our Ecologic Crisis," 133.

6. Ibid., 135.

7. Ibid., 132.

8. Both dimensions of the charge are lucidly addressed by Wybrow in *Bible, Baconianism, and Mastery over Nature.* His careful examination of the understanding of nature and dominion in pagan antiquity (chaps. 1–2), in the Bible (chaps. 3–4), and at the start of the modern scientific era (chap. 5) serves as perhaps the most comprehensive rebuttal of the ecological objections in the literature. Wybrow, however, unwisely follows the idiosyncratic opinion of biblical scholar James Barr in disassociating the *imago Dei* from the mandate to dominion in Genesis 1.

9. René Descartes, *Discourse on the Method of Rightly Conducting One's Reason and Seeking Truth in the Sciences* (trans. Donald A. Cress; Indianapolis: Hackett, 1980), 33.

This ecological critique is combined with feminist concerns about the traditional picture of God in the writings of Sallie McFague. In her widely read book *Models of God: Theology for an Ecological, Nuclear Age*, McFague utilizes a nuanced version of the ecological critique to call into question the model of God's sovereign relationship to the world presupposed in the Genesis text.[10] Admitting (perhaps with an eye to White) that it is "simplistic to blame the Judeo-Christian tradition for the ecological crisis, as some have done, on the grounds that Genesis instructs human beings to have 'dominion' over nature,"[11] McFague nevertheless indicts what she describes as "royalist, triumphalist images for God—God as king, lord, ruler, patriarch"—that is, the classical Jewish and Christian "monarchical" model of divine transcendence and sovereignty over the cosmos.[12]

McFague indicts such images because she understands this model of God to have functioned historically as an exemplar or paradigm for human violence (as humans, particularly men, have imitated their divine monarch). But beyond this violence, McFague intimates a different (disempowering) function of the monarchical model, which is perhaps more characteristic of women's experience. According to McFague, the monarchical model of God fosters, at worst, "militarism and destruction" (if humans—typically men—*imitate* God's sovereignty) and, at best, "attitudes of passivity and escape from responsibility" (if humans—usually women—understand themselves in *contrast* to God, who has all power).[13] McFague thus proposes alternative, nonviolent, and empowering models of God for an "ecological, nuclear age," namely, God's embodiment in the world, God as mother who births the universe, or God as lover and friend of the earth.[14]

Unfortunately, the model of divine creative power represented in the objections of White and McFague finds unwitting support both in the standard theological account of creation in the Christian tradition and in the comments of many biblical scholars concerning Genesis 1. It is intriguing that many—if not most—Christian theologians un-

---

10. See Sallie McFague, *Models of God: Theology for an Ecological, Nuclear Age* (Philadelphia: Fortress, 1987), esp. 63–78, on the monarchical model of God. A similar argument is articulated in idem, "Models of God for an Ecological, Evolutionary Era: God as Mother of the Universe," in *Physics, Philosophy, and Theology: A Common Quest for Understanding* (ed. Robert J. Russell et al.; Vatican City: Vatican City Observatory/Notre Dame: University of Notre Dame Press, 1988), 249–71.

11. McFague, *Models of God*, 68.

12. Ibid., 61.

13. Ibid., 69. McFague herself does not distinguish these as typically male and female experiences of God. But this distinction would be consistent with her argument.

14. Ibid., 69–87. For God as a mother giving birth to the universe, see McFague, "Models of God for an Ecological, Evolutionary Era," esp. 255–62.

problematically assume the very model of divine power that White and McFague decry as the basis for their understanding of God as creator and the world as creation. Michael Welker describes this theological model as a generalized hierarchical picture of production, causation, and dependence.[15] Citing many prominent definitions of creation in the theological literature, Welker uncovers the widespread consensus in the Christian tradition that creation (whether as act/process or as product) consists in a simple "pattern of power."[16] As act or process, creation is typically thought of as being *unilaterally caused or produced* by a transcendent reality, while as product, it involves *absolute dependence* on this transcendent reality. Not only is this a remarkably thin and abstract notion of creation (as will become clear), but as Welker points out, it is wrongly (though widely) assumed that such a notion of the God-creature relationship adequately characterizes the biblical creation accounts in Genesis.

But not only theologians assume this model of creation. Biblical scholars typically read Genesis 1 as exemplifying a similar understanding of the God-creation relationship. This comes especially to the fore in comparisons between the creation accounts in Genesis 1 and Genesis 2. The obvious (and undeniable) differences in content, sequence, style, and emphasis of the two accounts are typically portrayed in the literature in terms of two central contrasts, namely, between God's transcendence and immanence, on the one hand, and between the orderliness and unpredictability of creation, on the other.

As an example of the first contrast, James Crenshaw distinguishes the portrayals of God in the two creation accounts: "In the first account the Deity is transcendent, removed from any contact [with the world] except verbal, whereas the second story emphasizes divine nearness in very concrete ways."[17] Tamara Cohen Eskenazi likewise explains that the creation accounts portray "God as both magisterially remote (Genesis 1) and intimately engaged with creation (Genesis 2)."[18]

The second contrast is illustrated by Robert Alter's depiction of creation in Genesis 1 as essentially a harmonious "balancing of opposites" in contrast to the concern evident in Genesis 2 with "the complicated and

15. Michael Welker, "What Is Creation? Rereading Genesis 1 and 2," *Theology Today* 48 (April 1991): 56–71.

16. Ibid., 59.

17. James L. Crenshaw, *Story and Faith: A Guide to the Old Testament* (New York: Macmillan/London: Collier Macmillan, 1986), 39.

18. Tamara Cohen Eskenazi, "Torah as Narrative and Narrative as Torah," in *Old Testament Interpretation: Past, Present, and Future: Essays in Honor of Gene M. Tucker* (ed. James Luther Mays, David L. Petersen, and Kent Harold Richards; Nashville: Abingdon, 1995), 17.

difficult facts of human life in civilization."[19] And Crenshaw, in a similar manner, states that whereas "within the Priestly creation account there is complete symmetry,"[20] Genesis 2 portrays reality as "unpredictable."[21]

Both sets of contrasts are brought together in an important rhetorical study of Genesis 1–2 by Dale Patrick and Allen Scult entitled "Genesis and Power."[22] Like Crenshaw, Alter, and Eskenazi, these authors attempt not to sever, but to creatively juxtapose (as complementary) the portrayals of God in the two creation accounts. For Patrick and Scult, Genesis 1 and 2 portray two necessary, but fundamentally different, types of power, which they name divine authorship (Genesis 1) and divine authority (Genesis 2). Whereas "authorship" refers to "a circumscribing force" extrinsic to that over which power is exercised and that is able unilaterally to "determine the outcome" (much as an author transcends and is able to control what she writes), "authority" refers to a form of power that is more relational and engaged, indeed is "embroiled in the indeterminacy of conflict."[23]

Whatever the good intentions of Patrick and Scult (and others) who desire to keep both portrayals of divine power in creative tension, if Genesis 1 does indeed portray God as an extrinsic, transcendent force or will unilaterally imposing order upon creation as an inert object, then I would agree in principle with White and McFague. Given the

19. Robert Alter, *The Art of Biblical Narrative* (New York: Basic Books, 1985), 143, 145.

20. Crenshaw, *Story and Faith*, 61.

21. Ibid., 60. I do not mean to single out Crenshaw, Alter, or Eskenazi for special critique. Their comments are simply typical of a widespread and persistent assumption among biblical scholars concerning the portrayal of God and creation in Genesis 1. The persistence and widespread character of this portrayal may well be connected with the idea of the combat myth, which involves the imposition of order on recalcitrant chaos. But beyond that, the perception of the priestly creation story as one of invariant order par excellence may go back to a peculiarity of the history of critical biblical scholarship. In this scholarship, the literary style of the so-called priestly document (of which Genesis 1 is thought to be a part) has historically been contrasted with that of the so-called Yahwist document (which includes the Genesis 2 creation story). Sean McEvenue's survey of scholarly evaluations of the narrative style of the Priestly writer notes the frequency with which terms like *pedantic*, *stereotyped*, and *monotonous* arise in the works of prominent scholars like Julius Wellhausen, S. R. Driver, Gerhard von Rad, and Claus Westermann; see Sean E. McEvenue, *The Narrative Style of the Priestly Writer* (Rome: Pontifical Biblical Institute Press, 1971), 5–8. Although McEvenue does not deal explicitly with Genesis 1, it is a short step from the assumption of a pedantic, monotonous, and artificial literary style for the priestly writing in general to the claim that the priestly creation story is characterized by repetitive order and imposed symmetry. But this is, of course, merely a supposition on my part.

22. Dale Patrick and Allen Scult, *Rhetoric and Biblical Interpretation* (Sheffield: JSOT Press, 1987/Almond Press, 1990), 103–25.

23. Ibid., 117.

notion of humanity as *imago Dei*, this picture of divine creative power (upon which humans are to model their actions) could very well serve to legitimate aggressive control and limitless exploitation of the natural world or possibly passivity and disempowerment in some cases (as McFague intimates).

It is important to grasp the force of the ethical problem here, especially the connection between the *Chaoskampf* and the exercise of unilateral sovereign power on God's part. Admittedly, there seems to be a huge gap between the overt violence of the combat myth and the peaceful submission of creatures to God's creative will as portrayed in Genesis 1. But when we consider that violence is precisely what happens when unilateral power meets resistance, the *Chaoskampf* may well be waiting just out of sight. Whereas the portrayal of God as divine warrior in Genesis 1 would constitute the text's endorsement of explicit violence from the beginning of the world, White's and McFague's critical (and even Patrick and Scult's more sanguine) discernments of an extrinsic divine transcendence deterministically ordering creation (a form of a primordial coercion) might constitute the endorsement of a *potential* or *implicit* violence at the human level.

These critical reflections on the sort of divine power portrayed in Genesis 1 render the paradigmatic or normative character of this text immensely problematic, especially for those, like me, who are interested in what sort of ethics the text might authorize. But they also make the text worthy of further study. These objections thus require us, minimally, to investigate whether a responsible reading of Genesis 1 discloses an oppressive ideology of power or whether this ideology is more a function of the text's later effective history, that is, how it has been received by successive communities of interpretation throughout the ages.

While this chapter does not claim to be any sort of definitive answer to these important ethical objections, it does constitute an attempt to explore further what sort of creative power Genesis 1 rhetorically depicts God as exercising, specifically with the above objections in mind. Whereas in chapter 2 I read the creation story in terms of its shared symbolic world with other biblical texts, here I intend to reread it more closely for its peculiarities, highlighting unusual or unique aspects of the text that are little noted by scholars. I intend to mine to the fullest Gerhard von Rad's famous statement about the literary details of Genesis 1: "Nothing is here by chance; everything must be considered carefully, deliberately, and precisely."[24] One of my questions here is whether Genesis 1 depicts God's creative power in such a way as to allow for genuine

24. Gerhard von Rad, *Genesis: A Commentary* (trans. John H. Marks et al.; rev. ed.; Philadelphia: Westminster, 1972), 47. William P. Brown likewise comments that Genesis

creaturely freedom (which includes the possibility of resistance).[25] My own close reading of Genesis 1 suggests much more than that, namely, that the text depicts God's founding exercise of creative power in such a way that we might appropriately describe it as an act of generosity, even of love. This depiction arises from a number of rhetorical features of the text.

Variations in the Literary Pattern of Genesis 1

The first feature is the curious occurrence of nonpredictable variations in the literary patterning of Genesis 1. These variations fly in the face of the well-worn characterization of the rhetorical world of Genesis 1, by numerous commentators, as a world par excellence of ordered regularity and balance, where everything is tightly pinned down.

First, there are variations in what I have called the pattern of panels in the text, that is, the division of God's creative acts into two symmetrical triads or corresponding panels of three days each. As discussed in chapter 2, the first panel (days 1–3) has to do with God's acts of *division* or *separation*, by which the various regions or realms of the created order are brought into being, while the second panel (days 4–6) has to do with God *filling* these separated regions with living or mobile beings (see fig. 6).

On days 1–3, God separates light from darkness (day 1), then separates the waters above from the waters below by an expanse or dome (day 2), and then separates the waters below from dry ground (day 3). Corresponding to days 1–3, we have days 4–6, on which God fills precisely the static spaces just created with the mobile creatures that appropriately inhabit them. Thus, corresponding to the separation of light and darkness on day 1, God sets the luminaries in the sky (day 4); corresponding to the separation of sky and waters on day 2, God fills the waters with fish and the sky with birds (day 5); and corresponding to the separation of dry land from the waters on day 3, God fills this land with land animals of all sorts, including humans (day 6). And run-

---

1:1–2:3 is "the most densely structured text of the biblical corpus"; *The Ethos of the Cosmos: The Genesis of Moral Imagination in the Bible* (Grand Rapids: Eerdmans, 1999), 36.

25. Here, to a much greater extent than in chapter 6, I am putting "present-day theological questions" to the biblical text; Rolf Rendtorff, *Canon and Theology: Overtures to an Old Testament Theology* (trans. and ed. Margaret Kohl; Overtures to Biblical Theology; Minneapolis: Fortress, 1993), 40. Or, to phrase it differently, here "the message of a text with its own particularities is used to clarify one's present life"; Henk Vroom, "Religious Hermeneutics, Culture, and Narratives," *Studies in Interreligious Dialogue* 4 (1994): 203.

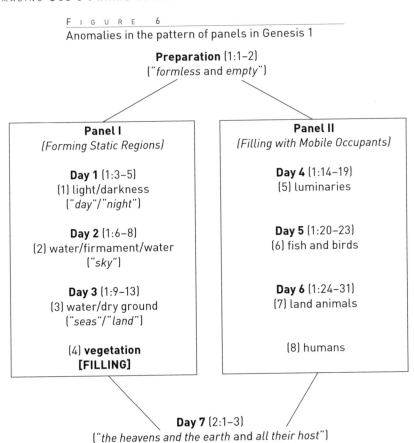

FIGURE 6

Anomalies in the pattern of panels in Genesis 1

Preparation (1:1-2)

("*formless* and *empty*")

Panel I	**Panel II**
(Forming Static Regions)	*(Filling with Mobile Occupants)*
Day 1 (1:3-5)	**Day 4** (1:14-19)
(1) light/darkness	(5) luminaries
("*day*"/"*night*")	
Day 2 (1:6-8)	**Day 5** (1:20-23)
(2) water/firmament/water	(6) fish and birds
("*sky*")	
Day 3 (1:9-13)	**Day 6** (1:24-31)
(3) water/dry ground	(7) land animals
("*seas*"/"*land*")	
(4) **vegetation**	(8) humans
[FILLING]	

Day 7 (2:1-3)

("*the heavens and the earth* and *all their host*")

ning through the correspondences, there is an observable progression, repeated in each panel, from heaven/sky (days 1 and 4) to waters (days 2 and 5) to earth (days 3 and 6).

The pattern of the corresponding panels certainly constitutes beautiful symmetry, and it seems—at first blush—to corroborate the judgment of many biblical scholars concerning the prominence of balance and order in the text. Yet two anomalies are found in this pattern.

First of all, God's fourth creative act (on day 3), the creation of vegetation (plants and trees) on the land, is technically an act of *filling* (not separating), which seems out of place in terms of the literary structure of Genesis 1. Yet it could be said that plants and trees are not mobile creatures (in the same sense that fish, birds, animals, humans, and the heavenly bodies are) and so there is also a sense in which they fit in the first panel, which describes the creation of static realms. Indeed, they both fit and do not fit. They seem to be borderline creatures that overlap the panels.

The second anomaly in the literary pattern of the panels is God's fifth creative act (the heavenly bodies) on day 4. Although this is certainly an act of filling (which fits days 4–6), it might appropriately have been placed in the first panel (days 1–3) since the stated purpose of the sun and moon is to *separate* day from night or light from dark (this is, however, temporal, not spatial separation).

Thus both the last creative act on the first panel (days 1–3) and the first creative act on the second panel (days 4–6) overlap the panels in a symmetrical asymmetry. So we have the interesting phenomenon of two sets of borderline creatures (vegetation and the heavenly bodies) that blur the boundaries between the panels as commonly understood. Would it be appropriate to say that, although Genesis 1 is clearly concerned with ordered categories of creation, this order is not rigid? Indeed, we could say the categories have fuzzy boundaries.[26]

But we could even go further and note that the correspondences between days 3 and 6 are not quite precise. At first glance, these two days seem balanced with each other in that (unlike the other days of creation) each contains two creative acts (the separation of dry land from water and the sprouting of vegetation on day 3; the creation of land animals and humans on day 6). Nevertheless, even here there are asymmetries. Thus, day 6 contains not just two creative acts (land animals and humans), but also God's assignment of food to these (and other) creatures (birds are also mentioned). The result is that the two creative acts on day 6 do not exactly correspond to the two acts on day 3. Rather, they correspond only to the first creative act on day 3 (the separation of dry land from water), while the second of the two acts on day 3 (the sprouting of vegetation) corresponds to the assignment of vegetation for food on day 6.[27]

26. Another case of literary variation that involves overlap of boundaries is the threefold occurrence of blessing in the text—twice within and once outside the panels of six creative days. Twice God blesses living creatures with fertility—the flying creatures and water dwellers on day 5 and humanity on day 6. But there is surprisingly no blessing mentioned for land animals. Instead, we find that the seventh day is blessed, though this is blessing for sanctification, not for fertility (and only here God's blessing is not accompanied by direct speech). Not only is the blessing of the seventh day an unexpected variation, but it serves rhetorically to connect the seventh day with the prior six days of God's creative activity, even though it stands structurally outside the two panels of six creative days.

27. Even here, however, there are variations between the terms used for vegetation on days 3 and 6. Thus day 3 (1:11–12) refers to two categories of vegetation (*dešeʾ*), specified as plants (*ʿēśeb*) and fruit trees (*ʿēṣ pĕrî*) that bear fruit (an expression that is, admittedly, redundant). While day 6 specifies plants (*ʿēśeb*) and trees (*ʿēṣ*) with fruit (a somewhat

Beyond the pattern of the panels, there are important literary variations in what I have called the fiat pattern of the text, which suggest a
highly complex notion of order. In chapter 2 we noted the recurring
pattern of (1) God's fiat ("let there be") followed by (2) an execution
report ("and it was so") and (3) an evaluation report ("God saw that it
was good"). This basic pattern is repeated for each of God's eight creative acts over six days of creation.

FIGURE 7
Variations in the fiat patterns of Genesis 1

Creative Acts		Sequence of Elements		
act 1	God's fiat	summary execution report	evaluation report	extended execution report
act 2	God's fiat	extended execution report	summary execution report	(no evaluation report)
act 3	God's fiat	summary execution report	evaluation report	(no extended execution report)
act 4	God's fiat	summary execution report	extended execution report (earth as actor)	evaluation report
act 5	God's fiat	summary execution report	extended execution report (doubled)	evaluation report
act 6	God's fiat	extended execution report	evaluation report	(no summary execution report)
act 7	God's fiat	summary execution report	extended execution report	evaluation report
act 8	God's fiat	extended execution report	summary execution report (displaced)	evaluation report (displaced)

Yet this pattern is inexplicably broken at several points (see figure 7).
For example, the execution report ("and it was so") is missing from God's
sixth creative act (fish and birds) on day 5 and from God's eighth creative act (humanity) on day 6. Likewise, the evaluation report ("God saw
that it was good") is missing from God's second creative act (separation
of the waters) on day 2 and from God's eighth creative act (humanity)
on day 6.[28] Actually, it is not quite accurate to say that the execution

different linguistic construction) as food for humans (1:29), the food for animals (1:30)
is called "green plants" (yereq ʿēśeb), a somewhat ambiguous term that is taken by
interpreters to be either simply a variant of plants (ʿēśeb) or, more generally, "greenery,"
that is, as equivalent to the more inclusive category, vegetation (dešeʾ) on day 3. This is
all highly confusing. One would think that in the interests of symmetry it would not be
very difficult for the author of Genesis 1 to be more consistent in his terminology.

28. One could simply account for certain missing elements by noting that the text
provides seven instances of the execution and evaluation reports in a scheme of eight

report or the evaluation report is missing from God's eighth creative act (humanity). That would be too simple. Technically, they are not missing, but *displaced*, the execution report to 1:30, where it serves to conclude God's assignment of food to both humans and animals, and the evaluation report to 1:31, where it functions to summarize God's evaluation of the entire creative process ("God saw all that he had made, and behold it was very good).[29]

To make things even more complicated, however, the text contains two quite different sets of execution reports. Whereas the first type reports in summary fashion that "it was so" (or, in the first case, that "there was light," which is itself an internal variation), the second type is more extended and reports some specific action of God (making, creating, or separating). The second type either occurs in lieu of the first type (in one instance, on day 5) or (more typically) supplements the first type, though in one case (God's third creative act, the separation of land from water) it is simply absent.[30]

Furthermore, the order of the elements in the fiat pattern is not always the same for each of the eight creative acts.[31] Even the fourth, fifth, and seventh creative acts, which on the surface seem to follow an identical pattern, harbor a further variation in the form that the extended execution report takes. In the fourth act, the extended execution report does not report God's action at all, but that of the earth or land, while

---

creative acts, so there is bound to be one of each item missing. This still does not account for which element is missing in each particular case. And that in some cases the particular element is present but displaced suggests that matters are somewhat more complicated.

29. While some Christian commentators (going back to Ambrose) persistently continue to interpret the evaluation report in 1:31 as applying to humanity, thus resulting in the idea that things were not *very good* before humanity appeared on the scene, Jewish interpretation typically notes that the evaluation report is missing in the case of humanity either because humanity is incomplete (and thus *not yet* good) or that God knows that human rebellion will soon follow.

30. A further variation in the fiat pattern is that some creative acts are accompanied by God naming creatures. But this naming occurs only on the first three days of creation (the significance of this limitation will be addressed later in this chapter). There is, however, further variation *within* this variation. Thus, on days 1 and 3, God names the *realms or categories* that have been separated (light and darkness are named "day" and "night" in 1:5; the dry land and the waters are named "earth" and "sea" in 1:10). On day 2, however, God does not name that which has been separated, but *the separator itself* (the expanse or dome that divides the waters is named "sky" in 1:8). A further variation is that the naming itself occurs at different places within the fiat pattern (twice after and once before the evaluation report). This is simply further evidence that the text's order is highly complex and flexible.

31. Although this variety is characteristic of the Hebrew text (MT) of Genesis 1, it is not always evident in the Septuagint. Indeed, the Septuagint here often harmonizes and systematizes the variations of the MT, sometimes supplying missing items or arranging them in a more consistent pattern.

in the fifth act the report is doubled, reporting first that God made the great lights and then that God placed them in the dome of the heavens. Furthermore, this execution report is so expanded that it has become an extended purpose statement for the creation of the heavenly bodies. That is, even when the extended execution report appears in the same relative position in the fiat pattern, there are internal variations in the nature and function of the item.

A further, equally nonpredictable variation in the fiat pattern is that half of the fiats (creative acts 1, 2, 3, and 5) simply call a particular creature to exist (or to be separated, as in act 3), without specifying how that will come to be (for example, "let there be light" or "let the waters be gathered"), while the other half (acts 4, 6, 7, and 8) name a creature that God has previously created and invite that creature to actively participate in the creative process (for example, "let the earth produce vegetation").[32] All of this suggests that although there is, indeed, a discernable pattern to each of God's eight creative acts, this pattern is by no means simple, obvious, or predictable. It is, on the contrary, highly complex. Although not referring to this particular point, Gabriel Josipovici's comment is certainly apropos, namely that there is a notable "balance of symmetry and dissymmetry" or a "pattern of repetition and innovation" throughout the Genesis 1 creation story.[33]

Beyond these, other nonpredictable variations in the text are relevant for our consideration. Whereas the text predictably uses a cardinal number in the "evening and morning" formula concluding the first day of creation ("day one") and ordinals for the rest ("second day," "third day," etc.), we find the unexpected presence of the Hebrew definite article in the formula for day 6 ("and there was evening and morning, *the* sixth day") and in the references to day 7 ("*the* seventh day"), in contrast to the lack of the article in the first five occurrences of the formula.[34]

---

32. We could say that the first type of fiat names only the object and not the subject of the action (as the second does). This would, however, be a comment about the force of the text's *meaning* and not technically a comment on the *grammar* of the Hebrew text. Grammatically, the difference is that the first type has the creature in question as the subject of the verb *to be* (and in one case as the subject of a passive verb *be gathered*), whereas the second type has the creature as subject of some other (active) verb, which implies that creature's participation in creative activity.

33. *The Book of God: A Response to the Bible* (New Haven: Yale University Press, 1988), 64–65. This balancing of repetition and innovation is typical of Hebrew literary style in the Old Testament.

34. This literary variation probably serves rhetorically to emphasize the special, climactic character of days 6 and 7, highlighting (respectively) the creation of humanity in God's image and the completion of God's creative work.

We might further cite the distribution of God's acts of "creating" (*bārā'*) versus "making" or "doing" (*'āśâ*) throughout the text (*bārā'* in 1:1, 21, 27 [three times]; 2:3; and *'āśâ* in 1:7, 16, 25, 26, 31; 2:2 [twice], 3). While the words do have differing semantic ranges, there is no un-equivocally clear rationale for their distribution in 1:1–2:3.

While none of these literary variations is strictly predictable, some of them do make sense in terms of the architectonic scheme of the text, perhaps highlighting rhetorically some important point. Many of the variations, however, seem on the face of it random (and it is not an easy task to determine which are which).[35]

But more than that, the sheer number of variations in the pattern-ing of the text can be multiplied almost indefinitely (I have barely scratched the surface). There are even nuanced subvariations within the variations. Although I have already indicated some of these, there are others. Thus we find the intriguing fact that of the four times that a creature in invited to participate in the creative process, only once is it actually reported that a creature acted on the invitation (the land brought forth vegetation); in the other cases, the creature is called to act, but *God's* action is reported.[36] And there is the further varia-tion that while the first seven of God's fiats are jussives (in the third-person singular), the eighth is a (first-person plural) cohortative ("let us make"), where the subject of the action is God together with the (implied) heavenly court.[37]

This complexity reminds me of nothing so much as fractal geometry in contemporary chaos theory, the phenomenon whereby complex, non-Euclidian shapes (like a coastline or the edge of a leaf) remain equally complex no matter what level of magnification is used to observe them. No matter how deep you go with a fractal shape (like the classic Man-

35. This is because so many conflicting (ad hoc) explanations for particular variations are suggested by commentators. It is thus hard to know whether the explanations really explain the variations or exist primarily in the mind of the commentators. At any rate, whatever the explanation in particular cases (for example, that the missing evaluation report for the second creative act might result from a residual suspicion of water as representing chaos in the combat myth), I am here interested in the *rhetorical effect* of the variation in the patterns.

36. Presumably primary and secondary agency are compatible. There are, however, other explanations; for example, that the creature in question was unable to act, since it did not possess the requisite generative powers, an interpretation that goes back to rabbinic sources; see Wybrow, *Bible, Baconianism, and Mastery over Nature*, 122.

37. Without intending to bore the reader (since the variations could be multiplied indefinitely), we could note further that in three of the four cases where God's fiat does *not* invite a creature to actively participate in creation the verb *to be* is used (God invites various creatures to exist), whereas in one case (God's third creative act) a different verb is used (God calls the waters to *be gathered* to one place).

delbrot set; see fig. 8), you never reach a straight line; there is always more complexity to be found.[38] The literary variations of Genesis 1:1–2:3 are, I submit, analogous to fractals in this respect.

F I G U R E   8
Mandelbrot set

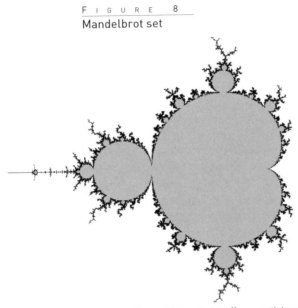

Gallery of Images, Department of Mathematics, Harvard University http://www.math.harvard.edu/~ctm/gallery/julia/Mfull.gif.

But many of these literary variations are like fractals also in being fundamentally unpredictable. That is, whereas the world rhetorically depicted in Genesis 1 is certainly ordered, patterned, and purposive (a point often noted by commentators), this world is not mechanistically determined, as if it were governed by ineluctable, ironclad Newtonian laws. If we take the text's rhetorical form as reflecting in some way its substantive message, the literary variations suggest that creation is neither random (stochastic) nor strictly predictable (deterministic). There is a certain (if I might dare to say it) incipient subjectivity or freedom granted to the cosmos by God, by which it is allowed, in response to the creator's call, to find its own pattern (this is especially evident in

38. Fractal geometry tries to model naturally occurring complexity in the world by generating figures, like the Mandelbrot set, that show an equal level of complexity no matter how great the magnification. You can experiment with magnifying a Mandelbrot set on Drexel University's math website by going to http://mathforum.org/alejandre/applet.mandlebrot.html (note that *Mandelbrot* is misspelled in the website address).

FIGURE 9
The Lorenz Strange Attractor

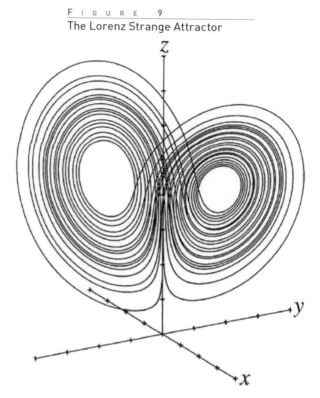

From "Wanderers in Space," the astronomy website for Tufts University
http://ase.tufts.edu/astroweb/view_pic.asp?id=175.

the variations in the fiat pattern).[39] The God who is artisan and maker, reflected rhetorically in the complex literary artistry of the text, does not overdetermine the order of the cosmos.

There is a helpful analogy here to what chaos theorists call a "strange attractor." The notion of a strange attractor is an attempt to describe the stabilizing factor in systems of turbulence (such as a waterfall, the stock market, or the human brain). As such, it is an alternative to the two main types of attractors previously known in physics, namely, fixed points (in steady-state systems) and limit cycles (in continuously

39. Many biblical passages describe the subjectivity or responsiveness of creation to God. For a discussion of these passages, see Brian J. Walsh, Marianne B. Karsh, and Nik Ansell, "Trees, Forestry, and the Responsiveness of Creation," *Cross Currents* 44 (1994): 149–62; Wybrow, *Bible, Baconianism, and Mastery over Nature*, 109–34; Terence E. Fretheim, "Nature's Praise of God in the Psalms," *Ex auditu* 3 (1987): 16–30; and J. Richard Middleton and Brian J. Walsh, *Truth Is Stranger Than It Used to Be: Biblical Faith in a Postmodern Age* (Downers Grove, IL: InterVarsity, 1995), 147–52.

repetitive dynamic systems).[40] Although the path of motion around a strange attractor looks, on the surface, random, it is actually fractal, paradoxically exhibiting infinity and unpredictability within a closed, finite system (like the Lorenz attractor; see fig. 9).[41] This is very like the literary pattern of Genesis 1, which combines a repetitive order with unpredictable variations to form a meaningful, though complex, pattern. Thus, if we take the rhetoric of the text seriously as embodying something of its worldview, and if we follow up on the analogy from chaos mathematics, not only does Genesis 1 depict a fractal universe, but it depicts a creator less like a Newtonian lawgiver and more like a strange attractor.

God Shares Power with Nonhuman Creatures

While this noncoercive freedom that God grants to creation is not exactly synonymous with generosity or love (on most understandings of these terms), it is a move in that direction. A much clearer move, however, is the text's depiction of the process of creation as God sharing power with creatures, inviting them to participate (as they are able) in the creative process itself.[42] Thus, among the many purpose statements given for the

40. The term *strange attractor* was coined by David Ruelle and Floris Takens, "On the Nature of Turbulence," *Communications in Mathematical Physics* 20 (1971): 167–92. Good introductions to chaos theory include James Gleick, *Chaos: Making a New Science* (New York: Viking, 1987); and Ian Stewart, *Does God Play Dice? The Mathematics of Chaos* (Oxford: Blackwell, 1989). George Lakoff's marvelous book *Women, Fire, and Dangerous Things: What Categories Reveal about the Mind* (Chicago: University of California Press, 1987) goes well beyond mathematics and chaos theory to show connections between the findings of a large number of disciplines on what he calls "motivated" patterning (96), distinct from the traditional false alternatives of either random/stochastic or predictable/deterministic patterns. By articulating examples of such motivated patterning in the world studied by biology (chap. 11), Lakoff implicitly reopens the old question, long laid to rest by deterministic science, of intelligent design in nature (see esp. chaps. 4–8 in part 1).

41. The Lorenz attractor is a butterfly-shaped system that contains an infinite number of trajectories that never intersect one another within a bounded space. By plotting the trajectories over time in three-dimensional space, the strange attractor, which governs the chaotic system, can be discerned.

42. Walter Brueggemann and Terence E. Fretheim are among the few Old Testament scholars who foreground the risk-taking, power-sharing character of God rhetorically represented in Genesis 1, thus challenging traditional readings of the text. See Walter Brueggemann, *Genesis* (Interpretation; Atlanta: John Knox, 1982); Terence E. Fretheim, "The Book of Genesis: Introduction, Commentary, and Reflections," in *The New Interpreter's Bible*, vol. 1 (ed. Leander E. Keck et al.; Nashville: Abingdon, 1994); and idem, "Creator, Creature, and Co-Creation in Genesis 1–2," in *All Things New: Essays in Honor of Roy A. Harrisville* (ed. Arland J. Hultgren, Donald H. Juel, and Jack D. Kingbury; Word and World Supplement Series; St. Paul: Word & World, 1992), 11–20. Fretheim has been particularly

creation of the greater and lesser lights (sun and moon) is the statement that they are to *govern* the day and the night (1:16, 18). If we think about it, this correlates perfectly with their purpose (also stated) to *separate* day from night (1:14, 18). Both governing (or ruling) and separating are paradigmatically divine acts not only in the ancient Near East (especially in Sumerian and Akkadian creation accounts), but also in Genesis 1, where God's sovereign creative activity on days 1–3 consists precisely in three acts of separation by which the major spaces or realms of the created order are demarcated. Likewise, the "expanse" or "firmament" (*rāqîaᶜ*) that God created (on day 2) is granted the godlike function of separating the waters above from the waters below (1:6), in imitation of God's own separation of light from darkness on day 1. Rhetorically, this implies that sun, moon, and firmament, like humans in God's image, participate in (or imitate) God's own creative actions, even though the term *image* is never specifically used of them. God grants these royal tasks to creatures willingly, allowing them a share of his power and rule.[43]

But these are by no means the only divine or godlike actions that creatures participate in. On days 3, 5, and 6 (in 1:11–12, 20, 24), God invites the earth (twice) and the waters (once) to participate in creation by bringing forth living creatures. Whereas the earth is invited to produce first vegetation (1:11) and later land animals (1:24), the waters are invited to teem with water creatures (1:20).[44] They are invited, in other words, to exercise their God-given fertility and thus to imitate God's own creative actions in filling

---

important for my own understanding of God's relationship with the created order. Although the rhetorical reading of Genesis 1 presented in this chapter was developed before I read either of his works cited above, I was already fundamentally indebted to his classic study *The Suffering of God: An Old Testament Perspective* (Overtures to Biblical Theology; Philadelphia: Fortress, 1984) for his insightful elucidation of the biblical portrayal of God as passionately involved with creation.

43. As Fretheim puts it, "God's relationship with the world is such that God from the beginning chooses not to be the only one who has or exercises creative power"; "Creator, Creature, and Co-Creation," 15.

44. The first two of these three commands/invitations are rhetorically distinguished by a cognate accusative construction in the Hebrew, involving assonance between the verb and its object in each case (thus 1:11 literally says, "let the earth green with greenery" or "let the earth vegetate vegetation"). William P. Brown ("Divine Act and the Art of Persuasion in Genesis 1," in *History and Interpretation: Essays in Honour of John H. Hayes* [ed. M. Patrick Graham, William P. Brown, and Jeffrey K. Kuan; Sheffield: JSOT Press, 1993], 24, 27) calls this feature *figura etymologica* and detects it at two other places in Genesis 1—in 1:15 ("let them be *for lights* in the expanse of the sky *to give light*") and in 1:20 (based on his reconstruction of a lost consonant from the Hebrew *Vorlage*, suggested by the Septuagint), which would make two occurrences in this verse ("let the waters *cause swarms of living creatures to swarm* and *cause flyers to fly about* in the expanse of the sky"). Brown defends his reconstruction of the *Vorlage* of Genesis 1 at greater length in *Structure, Role, Ideology in the Hebrew and Greek Texts of Genesis 1:1–2:3* (Atlanta: Scholars Press, 1993), 139–40 n. 29.

the world with living things. Actually, God takes quite a risk in calling for the earth to produce vegetation since up to that point in the story God has not yet engaged in the act of filling (it is not until days 4–6 that God fills with mobile beings the regions or spaces demarcated on days 1–3). So, on day 3, the earth literally has no model or exemplar to follow. Indeed, on the next day, it is *God* who imitates the *earth's* prior creative action by filling the sky with heavenly bodies, which in the literary structure of Genesis 1 is a derivative action.[45] God is, rhetorically speaking, preempted by the earth and does not seem to be threatened by this.[46]

But beyond the invitation to the earth and the waters, both plants and animals are created after their "kind," with the ability to reproduce. Whereas God calls the plants to sprout (on day 3) with the seeds necessary for self-propagation, God "blesses" the fish and the birds on day 5 and humans on day 6 with fertility and commands them to multiply and *fill* the waters and the earth (again) in imitation of God's own creative acts of filling.[47]

While these dimensions of the Genesis 1 creation story are not often noticed, attention to these rhetorical features points us to a God who does not hoard divine creative power, with some desperate need to control, but rather to a God who is generous with power, sharing it with creatures, that they might make their own contribution to the harmony and beauty of the world.[48]

The Human Contribution as *Imago Dei*

But the contribution of creatures, which God not only allows but indeed encourages, is clearest and most decisive in the case of humanity, to whom God explicitly grants the status and role of *ṣelem ʾĕlōhîm* (the image of God) and the commission to extend God's royal administration of the world as authorized representatives on earth.

45. Indeed, all God's acts of filling (the sky and sea with birds and fish on day 5 and the land with animals and humans on day 6) are derivative in this sense, coming as they do after the earth's creative activity.

46. I am not claiming that the text assigns any autonomy (ontological or otherwise) to creatures, since all the "divine" or "godlike" functions of creatures that I enumerated are themselves God-given and delegated. Yet I want to take the rhetoric of the text seriously in its portrayal of genuine creaturely power.

47. "Both human and nonhuman creatures are called to participate in the creative activity initiated by God"; Fretheim, "Creator, Creature, and Co-Creation," 14.

48. This reading certainly contravenes any interpretation of Genesis 1 that claims that humans are absolutely unique among creatures in imaging God. The picture given in the text is considerably more nuanced than that.

What is paradoxical is that precisely at this point my reading of the text is in significant tension with the rhetorical study of Genesis 1 by Patrick and Scult previously cited.[49] Patrick and Scult claim that God is depicted in Genesis 1 with such absolute power that humans are rendered powerless objects of divine will (a depiction, at least implicitly, of God as tyrant and certainly in conflict with my claim regarding generosity and love). God's power, according to Patrick and Scult, is literally "authorial," indicated by (among other things) creation by the word. It is the power of an author over a composition or an inert piece of work. Humans, by contrast, they correctly note, are the subjects of no actions in the text. Humans quite literally do nothing in Genesis 1.[50] This portrayal of God vis-à-vis humans in Genesis 1 is "balanced," they argue, by the more "parental" image of God in Genesis 2, where humans are depicted as agents in their own right, conversing with, even resisting, their creator/parent.[51]

There is some truth to this reading. While humanity is the (implicit) grammatical subject of *rādâ* (to rule) and *kābaš* (to subdue) in Genesis 1:26 and 1:28, this language occurs in God's commissioning of the human creature and not in any reported action performed by humans in Genesis 1. The trouble is that Patrick and Scult draw what I believe is an unwarranted conclusion from this important point. Not only do they ignore the text's clear and explicit assertion that humans are created *like* this "authorial" God, commissioned to rule the animals and subdue the earth (which they would be hard put to explain),[52] but their reading does not take into account the structural relationship between 1:1–2:3 and what follows. Whereas God grants humans the power of agency on the sixth day of creation, setting the stage, so to speak, for the drama of human history-making, the actual exercise of human agency does not begin until the paradise/fall story of Genesis 2–3.

There are two important literary clues for understanding Genesis 1 not as an alternative creation story to Genesis 2 (which it either

49. Patrick and Scult, "Genesis and Power."

50. Patrick and Scult actually claim that there are no creaturely actors at all (human or otherwise) in the Genesis 1 creation account, whereas the text itself clearly represents the earth/land as an active participant in creation (1:12).

51. To illustrate the range of interpretations possible on this point, Francis Watson (*Text, Church, and World: Biblical Interpretation in Theological Perspective* [Edinburgh: Clark/Grand Rapids: Eerdmans, 1994], 150) argues for a fundamental *congruence* (rather than contrast) between Genesis 2 (the quest for a human dialogue partner for *ʾādām*) and Genesis 1 (God's quest for a human dialogue partner). My understanding of the relationship between these two chapters is more complex than either of these options.

52. Indeed, this would constitute an oxymoron, on their reading.

IMAGING GOD'S PRIMAL GENEROSITY

contradicts or balances), but as a prelude to the rest of the Genesis narrative, setting up the normative conditions for what follows.[53] The first clue is the highly significant absence of the concluding "evening and morning" formula on the seventh day, an absence that Augustine noted sixteen centuries ago.[54] Each day of creation is concluded by the line "and there was evening and there was morning," day one, second day, third day, and so on, until the sixth day. But when creation is complete and we would expect a final formula, "There was evening and there was morning, the seventh day," there is none, which leaves the attentive reader hanging and suggests that the seventh day is open-ended or unfinished.[55]

In the literary structure of the book of Genesis, the seventh day has no conclusion since God *continues* to rest from creating, having entrusted care of the earth to human beings.[56] Thus the paradise/fall story of Genesis 2–3 takes place (as do all the events narrated in the book of Genesis and, by extension, in the rest of the Bible) on the seventh day, when God rests, having delegated postcreation rule of the earth to humanity. God's rest does not here mean cessation of all divine action, only that the initial conditions of a meaningful world are completed. Indeed, God continues to act, upholding the universe by divine power and effecting deliverance from bondage and sin.[57] As Henri Blocher comments: "God's sabbath, which marks the end of creation, but does not tie God's hands, is therefore coextensive with history."[58]

Here it is important to note that the seventh day specifically represents *God's* rest, not yet the *human* Sabbath. "Of that [human Sabbath]," notes Gerhard von Rad, "nothing at all is said here."[59] While the text certainly "provides the unspoken foundation for the future institution of the Sab-

---

53. I am indebted for this interpretation to A. M. Wolters, "The Foundational Command: 'Subdue the Earth!'" in *Year of Jubilee; Cultural Mandate; Worldview* (Study Pamphlet 382; Potchefstrom: Institute for Reformational Studies, 1999), 27–32.

54. Augustine, *Confessions* 13.36. This absence is noted by many biblical scholars (for example, von Rad, *Genesis*, 63), though few draw the requisite conclusions from it.

55. That the final formula is missing, comments von Rad, is, "like everything else in this chapter, . . . intentional"; ibid.

56. Contra Watson (*Text, Church, and World*, 143, 313 n. 3), who claims that God's rest is necessitated by the labor implicated in the metaphor of God as artisan constructing the cosmos. I argue that God's rest follows naturally on the heels of God's (royal-parental) delegation of responsible stewardship to humanity.

57. Thus in the New Testament, Jesus defends healing on the Sabbath because the Father also works (salvifically) on the Sabbath (John 5:17).

58. Henri Blocher, *In the Beginning: The Opening Chapters of Genesis* (trans. David G. Peterson; Downers Grove, IL: InterVarsity, 1984), 57.

59. Von Rad, *Genesis*, 62. Likewise, Eric E. Elnes emphasizes that "it is only God who ceases activity on the seventh day"; "Creation and Tabernacle: The Priestly Writer's 'Environmentalism,'" *Horizons in Biblical Theology* 16 (1994): 146.

bath," explains Nahum Sarna, the institution of the Sabbath would be jarring in the opening biblical creation story for many reasons.[60] Not only does the sequential, ascending numbering of the days of creation require a genuine climax (the seventh day), rather than a fixed, cyclical institution (the Sabbath), but "the Sabbath is a distinctively Israelite ordinance" that would be "out of place before the arrival of Israel on the scene of history."[61]

Connected to this latter point is a further reason why reference to the Sabbath would not make sense in the present context. Since the opening biblical creation story applies royal-priestly functions (originally derived from only one elite segment of the human population) to the entire human race, it would be strange if this same text limited God's blessing and sanctification of time to only one segment of the human temporal continuum. If the text universalizes or democratizes the *imago Dei* (and especially if it treats the entire created order as a cosmic sanctuary, as we saw in chapter 2), it would stand to reason that the seventh day is not likely to refer to the exaltation of one particular day of the human week, but rather to God's sanctification of the entirety of human history. This would simply be in keeping with the universalistic thrust of the text.

This means that the paradise/fall story of Genesis 2–3 is not technically an expansion of the sixth day of creation from Genesis 1, such that we are now living in the sixth day.[62] Sometimes in an attempt to connect our present experience with the text, theologians (and others) refer to the era of human history (typically characterized by freedom or creativity) as the *eighth* day of creation.[63] But this interpretive move is strictly unnecessary in the context of the Genesis narrative, which knows no conclusion to the seventh day. Indeed, the last word of Genesis 2:3

60. Nahum M. Sarna, *Genesis* (JPS Torah Commentary; Philadelphia: Jewish Publication Society, 1989), 14.

61. Ibid.

62. As H. Paul Santmire suggests; "The Genesis Creation Narratives Revisited: Themes for a Global Age," *Interpretation* 45 (1991): 372–73.

63. While Orthodox Christian theologian Nicolai A. Berdyaev is most usually associated with this idea (see Miroslav Volf, "The Eighth Day of Creation," *Books and Culture* 10.1 [Jan.–Feb. 2004]: 24), the concept of a post-Genesis 2:3 eighth day of creation has also been used to describe the development of Jewish civilization and technological innovation (Samuel Kurinsky, *The Eighth Day: The Hidden History of the Jewish Contribution to Civilization* [Northvale, NJ: Aronson, 1994]) and the history of innovation in molecular biology (Horace Freeland Judson, *The Eighth Day of Creation: Makers of the Revolution in Biology* [rev. ed.; Cold Spring Harbor, NY: CSHL Press, 1996]). A web search also yields the *eighth day* as the name of various justice organizations and ecological groups, as well as a writing workshop, an alternative press, a food co-op, an experimental music group, and various poems, books, and films—all focusing on some aspect of human freedom, creativity, or participation in the historical process.

is an infinitive (la'ăśôt), which conveys a sense of open-endedness by rhetorically evoking action that is unfinished.[64] This leads to the other literary clue for the relationship of Genesis 1:1–2:3 with what follows, namely, the tôlĕdôt formula in Genesis 2:4a, which introduces the "generations" of the heavens and the earth, in the sense of what developed out of them. Although it is traditional for biblical scholars to treat these tôlĕdôt statements as conclusions (and one still finds such treatment today), a careful reading shows that not all of them can plausibly function as conclusions, whereas they all function very well as headings or superscriptions.[65] Throughout the book of Genesis the phrase these are the tôlĕdôt of X (Terah, Noah's sons, Ishmael, etc.) introduces either a list of progeny descended from the one named (their genealogy) or an ensuing narrative involving prominent members of the named person's progeny.[66] But in 2:4a the formula is distinct in that it serves to introduce both the first episode of human history (Genesis 2–4) and the entirety of human history in the book of Genesis (and perhaps all human history) as what developed out of "the heavens and the earth" that God has just finished creating.[67] That 1:1–2:3 as a literary unit falls outside the tôlĕdôt structure of Genesis suggests that it functions as a prologue to the rest of the book, constituting a description of the initial conditions that (ought to) hold for the rest of the story.[68] One could, then, using philosophical

64. Genesis 2:3 is often translated: "God blessed the seventh day and sanctified it because on it he rested from all the work of creating that he had done." Yet this simplifies the ambiguity at the conclusion of the verse, which literally states that God "rested from all his work that God created to do/make." Indeed, it is somewhat unclear who is the subject of the final infinitive. While it is often taken to be God (and that is not impossible), Ibn Ezra proposed that the verse means that "God ceased from all his work that God created [for man] to [continue to] do [thenceforth]" (cited by Sarna, Genesis, 15). On this reading, even the concluding infinitive opens up a new, unfinished human future.

65. While Gerhard von Rad thinks that tôlĕdôt is typically a title or heading in Genesis, he denies it is such in Genesis 2:4a on the basis that it derives from priestly tradition and so must be associated with the P creation story; Genesis, 63. I do not find this a particularly persuasive argument.

66. The headings divide the book of Genesis into eleven sections, six of which occur in the primeval history (1:1–2:3 [prior to any heading]; 2:4–4:26; 5:1–6:8; 6:9–9:28; 10:1–11:9; 11:10–26), with the remaining five sections constituting the ancestral history (11:27–25:11; 25:12–18; 25:19–35:29; 36:1–43; 37:1–50:26). Whereas most of the sections in the primeval history contain a mixture of narrative and genealogy, the sections in the ancestral history alternate between narrative and genealogy.

67. According to George W. Coats, Genesis 2:4a functions as the introduction, not just to the paradise/fall story, but to "everything"; Genesis: With an Introduction to Narrative Literature (Forms of Old Testament Literature 1; Grand Rapids: Eerdmans, 1983), 43.

68. As Brueggemann puts it, Genesis 1 "is the presupposition for everything that follows in the Bible"; Genesis, 22. Note also Watson's claim that the Genesis 1 creation story "must

language (derived from Immanuel Kant), refer to 1:1–2:3 as standing in something like a *transcendental* relationship to what follows. It is because the text sets up the normative conditions for creation—and not because it portrays God as having all power—that no human activity is reported in the Genesis 1 creation story.

This interpretation is corroborated by a notable asymmetry within Genesis 1 between God's acts of separation (acts 1–3, on days 1–3) and filling (acts 4–8, on days 3–6), which further contributes to the text's portrayal of God's primal generosity. The asymmetry consists in the intriguing detail that while God names the various realms or spaces that have been separated, God does not name any of the inhabitants of those realms. Why does God refrain from naming these creatures? Perhaps because the creator does not want to hoard this prerogative, but, on the contrary, wishes to give space for humanity to complete this privileged task. However, humans do not name anything in Genesis 1. We have to wait for Genesis 2, where the first human indeed names the animals, as an expression of human rule as the image of God.[69]

Genesis 1:1–2:3 thus portrays God as taking the risk first of blessing human beings with fertility and entrusting them with power over the earth and the animals and then of stepping back, withdrawing, to allow humans to exercise this newly granted power, to see what develops.[70] Contrary to Patrick and Scult's analysis, Genesis 1 depicts what is precisely a loving, parental exercise of power on God's part.[71] Indeed, God in Genesis 1 is like no one as much as a mother, who gives life to her children, blesses them, enhances their power and agency, and then

---

determine the theme and scope of the story that follows. The 'beginning' referred to at the outset is *also* the beginning of a book, and engenders in the reader's mind the expectation . . . of a coherent plot"; *Text, Church, and World*, 153.

69. Here I follow Phyllis Trible regarding the significance of naming in Genesis 2–3 as an expression of human rule or power; *God and the Rhetoric of Sexuality* (Philadelphia: Fortress, 1980), esp. 133–34. My one disagreement with Trible is that I do not think the power involved in naming inevitably involves subjugation in any negative sense. It does, however, involve a power differential between the one naming and the one named. Thus, parents name children, but adults do not typically have the right to (re)name other adults.

70. My account here has significant resonances with the emerging theological/ philosophical model of God's power known as "freewill theism" or the "openness of God." When I first developed this interpretation of God's power in Genesis 1 I had not yet heard of this model and was only introduced to it when Clark Pinnock, one of its foremost theological proponents, engaged me in dialogue on the subject after I had given a paper on Genesis 1 at the annual meeting of the Canadian Evangelical Theological Association, at Brock University, St. Catharines, ON, May 1996.

71. This is not simply my own suggestion. Numerous students have suggested this model during classroom exegesis of Genesis 1.

takes the parental risk of allowing her progeny to take their first steps, to attempt to use their power, to develop toward maturity.[72] That this maturity is radically different from the unlimited exploitation of the world that White and others are so worried about is indicated by the central fact staring us in the face: the text itself states that God's action and rule are paradigmatic for human action. This is indicated both by the notion of humanity created in God's image and likeness and by the text's canonical placement at the beginning of Scripture. Given the portrayal or rendering of God's power disclosed by a careful reading of Genesis 1, I suggest that the sort of power or rule that humans are to exercise is generous, loving power.[73] It is power used to nurture, enhance, and empower others, noncoercively, for *their* benefit, not for the self-aggrandizement of the one exercising power.[74] In its canonical place in the book of Genesis, the creation story in 1:1–2:3 thus serves as a normative limit and judgment on the violence that pervades the primeval history, indeed the rest of the Bible and human history generally.[75]

In pointed contrast to this violence, especially as portrayed in Genesis 3–6 (the account of human development from the garden to the flood), a beautiful example of the loving exercise of power is found in the actions of Noah in the context of the flood story. In Genesis 3, the primeval human pair rebel against God, and then the man begins to rule the woman (a rule that is not reciprocated) and names her Eve (thus treating her as he did the animals).[76] In Genesis 4, Cain impulsively

72. Even the nuances of *tôlĕdôt* contribute to this picture. A plural noun formed from the verb *yālad* (to bear, beget), *tôlĕdôt* is a developmental, birthing word, and its placement in Genesis 2:4a suggests by its connotations a parental, nurturing picture of God.

73. As Helen A. Kenik puts it, the "central tenet" of biblical creation theology is that *"God wills that life be for others"*; "Toward a Biblical Basis for Creation Theology," in *Western Spirituality: Historical Roots, Ecumenical Routes* (ed. Matthew Fox; Notre Dame, IN: Fides/Claretian, 1979), 69 (emphasis original). Although Kenik's exploration of this theme is based more on the creation account in Genesis 2, it is applicable also to Genesis 1. Indeed, it is rooted in the *imago Dei*.

74. A theological analysis of divine power quite congenial to my own is found in Kyle A. Pasewark, *A Theology of Power: Being beyond Domination* (Minneapolis: Fortress, 1993), esp. 186–235. It is interesting that Pasewark traces the notion of power as the "communication of efficacy" (a non-zero-sum notion) back to Martin Luther's description of God's creative power in Genesis 1.

75. For a discussion of the normative character of Genesis 1 in relation to the violence that pervades Scripture, see Middleton and Walsh, *Truth Is Stranger Than It Used to Be*, esp. 127–40.

76. Again, I follow Trible, *God and the Rhetoric of Sexuality*. George W. Ramsey disputes Trible's interpretation of this verse (and her claims concerning the significance of naming) in "Is Name-Giving an Act of Domination in Genesis 2:23 and Elsewhere?" *Catholic Biblical Quarterly* 50 (1988): 24–35. While Ramsey is certainly correct that naming does not necessarily imply domination or control in the Bible (as Trible seems to say), this does not address a nuanced variant of Trible's point (which I would like to advance), namely,

murders his brother Abel out of resentment, while he-man Lamech boasts to his two wives (the first reference to polygamy in the Bible) that he has in vengeance killed a youth for daring to injure him. And this violent propensity spirals out of control until in Genesis 6 humans fill the earth with their violence or bloodshed (*ḥāmās*), and the earth, which God created good, becomes corrupt and God is "grieved" (*ʿāṣ ab*) that he ever raised such an ungrateful brood of children (6:5–6). And then comes the flood. But while humans in the primeval history typically use their power autonomously and thus violently, Noah is a righteous man (6:9) and so exercises power in a different manner. It is significant, I believe, that the one righteous person in the antediluvian period exercises rule over the animals by taking them on the ark and thus preserving their life in a time of threat.[77] Noah in the flood story is an example of someone imitating the paradigmatic life-enhancing use of power that God is depicted as exercising in Genesis 1.

The Liberating Image

Like every reading of any text, this one is contestable, subject to dispute at various points and (admittedly) dependent on the preunderstanding and commitments of the interpreter. Nevertheless, in view of what is ethically at stake here, I have taken the risk of offering a reading of Genesis 1:1–2:3 that foregrounds the question of God's power. Although I largely share the ethical concerns of White and McFague, I believe these concerns are simply misguided in the case of Genesis 1. While it is undeniable that the text has historically been read through the lens of the Western aspiration of the scientific conquest of nature, with resulting violence against women and the environment, Genesis 1 is by no means locked into this economy of meaning. On the contrary, a close reading of the text reveals that God is depicted neither as a warrior creating by primordial violence (as we saw in chapter 6) nor as an extrinsic transcendence unilaterally imposing order on the world.

Rather, Genesis 1 artfully shatters both ancient and contemporary rhetorical expectations and, instead, depicts God as a generous creator, sharing power with a variety of creatures (especially humanity), inviting

---

that naming is typically an act involving asymmetrical power (that is, one with superior power usually does the naming). Whether that power will be used for domination is a separate issue. Genesis 1 certainly suggests that it need not be so used.

77. This point is also noted in Richard J. Clifford, "Creation in the Hebrew Bible," in *Physics, Philosophy, and Theology: A Common Quest for Understanding* (ed. Robert J. Russell et al.; Vatican City: Vatican City Observatory/Notre Dame, IN: University of Notre Dame Press, 1988), 165.

them (and trusting them—at some risk) to participate in the creative (and historical) process.[78] In Brueggemann's summary, the picture of God in Genesis 1 and of humanity as *imago Dei* foregrounds "the creative use of power which invites, evokes, and permits. There is nothing here of coercive or tyrannical power, either for God or for humankind."[79] Drawing both on the text's rhetoric of God's "gracious self-giving" as the model for human action and its protest against ancient Near Eastern views of human servitude, Brueggemann concludes: "The text is revolutionary."[80]

I, of course, harbor no illusions that this alternative reading of the *imago Dei* in Genesis 1 can change by fiat an ingrained mindset or habitual praxis concerning the use of power. Nevertheless, given the long history of misreading both divine and human power in Genesis 1 (which constitutes an act of violence against the text), perhaps it is time to begin a pattern of reading differently, respecting the alterity of the text, listening for its word to us, attending to its disclosure of God and the human calling. Perhaps, then, our practice of reading (which we might call a hermeneutic of love) would be in harmony with the new ethic of interhuman relationships and ecological practice that we are aiming for and that is rooted in the *imago Dei*, an ethic characterized fundamentally by power *with* rather than power over.[81]

In the end, the liberating character of the *imago Dei* is grounded in the nature of God, who calls the world into being as an act of generosity. This means that we cannot artificially separate our vision of God's redemptive love from an understanding of God's creative power. A careful reading of Genesis 1:1–2:3 thus converges on John 3:16. In both creation and redemption, "God so loved the world that he gave . . ."

---

78. The interpretive process at its best may be understood as an act of loving power, an attempt to image God, characterized also by risk.

79. Brueggemann, *Genesis*, 32.

80. Ibid., 33.

81. See James H. Olthuis, "Otherwise Than Violence: Towards a Hermeneutics of Connection," in *The Arts, Community, and Critical Democracy* (ed. Lambert Zuidevaart and Henry Luttikuizen; Cross-Currents in Religion and Culture; London: Macmillan, 2000), 137–64.

Index

Abdi-milkutti, 120
Abel, 296
Abyss, 241, 243
action theory, 27n39
Adad, 106–7
Adad-shumu-usur, 114–16, 117, 120
Adam, 20, 45, 46, 47
Adam, A. K. M., 65
agriculture, 52, 60, 89, 159–60
Ahmose, 109
Akhenaten, 103
Akitu Festival, 181–83, 214
Akkad, 119
Akkadian, 96–98, 166, 196–98, 199, 224
Albertz, Rainer, 131n142
Albrektson, Berktil, 107, 119, 121, 173, 188, 189
allusion, 62
al-Qaeda, 258
Alt, Albrecht, 187n5
Alter, Robert, 15n1, 49, 275–76
Ambrose, 282n29
Amon, 109
Amon-Re, 27, 109
An, 158
analogy, 88
ancient Near East
  parallels, 10, 26–27, 36, 66, 93–94, 107–8, 121–22, 186
  suzerainty treaties, 69
  worldview, 81–83
Anderson, Bernhard W., 76n90, 253n53
angelic beings, 56–59
Ani, 103
aniconism, 188–89
animal kingdom, 52
animals, 19
Annegarra, 159
Anshar, 162
ante-Nicene fathers, 28
Antiochine school, 28
Anu, 97, 152, 154, 161, 162
Anunna, 158
Anzu, 179
Apartheid, 225n118
apocalyptic literature, 243n30
Apsu, 162
Aquinas, 19, 20n17

Aristotle, 256
ark of the covenant, 189
Aruru, 95, 97
asceticism, 24
Asharedu the Older, 113
Ashnan, 156–57
Ashur, 120, 161, 261
Ashurbanipal, 200
Ashurbanipal II, 224
Ashurnasirpal, 105n41, 121
Asselin, David Tobin, 53n22, 167, 174
Assyria, 123–24, 137–38, 170, 172, 196, 197, 200, 224
Assyrian kings, 119
astral religion, 211–12
Asushunamir, 97
Ater, 276
Atrahasis, 151–54
Atrahasis Epic, 131–33, 137, 149–54, 155, 156, 158, 166, 174–76, 210, 215, 220–21
Atum, 109
Augustine, 19–20, 24, 291
authority, spheres of, 72
autonomy, 289

Baal, 81, 84, 237–38, 243n30
Babel und Bibel school, 186–87
Babylon, 126, 165, 170, 172, 178, 198, 226
Babylonia, 123–24, 135, 137–38, 196, 197, 222
Babylonian empire, 200, 252–53
Babylonian exile, 186, 200–201, 202, 210, 218, 228–31, 260
Babylonian imperialism, 257
Babylonian kings, 119
Babylonian Theodicy, 132
Bakhtin, Mikhail, 62n51
Balkans, 259
Barr, James, 29, 44, 243
Barth, Christoph, 29n46
Barth, Karl, 21–24, 27n39, 29, 49, 55, 187
Barth, Markus, 187n5
Batto, Bernard, 172, 175n80, 198, 240–41, 243, 260–61

Becker, Ernest, 260n80
Bel, 130, 137
Bellis, Alice Ogden, 262n84
Berdyaev, Nicolai A., 292n63
Berkhof, Hendrikus, 18, 21
Berkouwer, G. C., 17, 21n21
Bernstein, Richard, 37
Bezalel, 85, 87–88
Bible
  canonical approaches, 64
  and extrabiblical material, 94
  iconoclasm, 207–9
Biblical Theology Movement, 186–87, 193, 195
Birch, Bruce, 242
Bird, Phyllis, 118, 205–6, 228n124
Black, J. A., 182–83
Blenkinsopp, Joseph, 84n103
blessing, 50, 85n108, 280n26, 292
Blocher, Henri, 74n86, 291
body, 24–25
Bonhoeffer, Dietrich, 22
Borsippa, 182
Boyarin, Daniel, 63, 64
Breasted, J. H., 103n33
breath, 85–86
Brettler, Marc, 71, 72n81
Brock, Rita Nakashima, 265n97
Bronze Age, 208n74
Brown, William P., 86n113, 122, 288n44
Brueggemann, Walter, 105, 188n7, 192–93, 207, 265, 268, 272, 287n42, 293n68, 297
Brunner, Emil, 22
brutality, 10, 34
Buber, Martin, 22, 27n39, 72n81
building metaphor, 77–81
burnt offering, 169n57
Bush, George W., 255n58

Cain, 134, 295
Cairns, David, 19
Calvinism, 31, 34–35, 37
Calvin, John, 21
canals, 152–54, 155–56

299